SELF-PORTRAITS

SELF-PORTRAITS

THE GIDE/VALERY LETTERS

1890–1942

Edited by
ROBERT MALLET
Abridged and Translated by
JUNE GUICHARNAUD

The University of Chicago Press / Chicago & London

An unabridged version of this book was originally published in 1955 by Librairie Gallimard, Paris, under the title *Correspondence, 1890–1942, André Gide–Paul Valéry*. Copyright by Librairie Gallimard, 1955.

The authorized English translations of the works of Paul Valéry published in the United States vest exclusively in the Bollingen Foundation. Their permission to publish June Guicharnaud's translation of the Valéry letters is gratefully acknowledged. Authorized English translations of the works of André Gide published in the United States vest exclusively in Alfred A. Knopf, Inc. We acknowledge their permission to publish Mrs. Guicharnaud's translation of the Gide letters.

Library of Congress Catalog Card Number: 65-25125
THE UNIVERSITY OF CHICAGO PRESS, CHICAGO & LONDON
The University of Toronto Press, Toronto 5, Canada
English translation © 1966 by The University of Chicago
Published 1966
Printed in the United States of America

CONTENTS

INTRODUCTION

In 1950 André Gide said to me: "I feel inclined to read the letters Valéry sent me." He had me look for the large box containing more than two hundred letters and the photographs of Valéry on his deathbed. He gazed at the photographs for a long time and commented upon them with quiet gravity. He spoke to me of that "handsome face" which still exuded "intelligence walled up in the silence it had so often provoked." Then he recalled the exemplary death of his friend, that serene and courteous death followed by a grandiose state funeral, "which he surely would not have refused but at which he would have smiled." André Gide then gave me to understand that, like Valéry, he had not wanted to make provisions for his burial in advance. One year later he died, and his own death could not have been more reasonable. In 1950 he often told me that he felt he was nearing the end, and could but congratulate himself on it, for dying well appeared easier to him than aging well. On the day on which he felt inclined to reread Valéry's letters, his vivacity and his alert mind made him seem like a surprisingly young old man. He sat down near me, straightened his thick horn-rimmed glasses, and began to skim through the first letters he had received from Valéry, those of 1890 and 1891. He interrupted his reading with exclamations: "What style!" "What precociousness!" "What intelligence!" At the end of two hours he said: "I think these letters should definitely be published."

"At the same time as yours?"

"Yes. But that is not what delights me. I no longer remember my letters, but I'm certain that I'll prove to be very dull, very colorless, compared to him. I'm also certain that I was less prolific."

"You have always written shorter letters than your correspondents."

"I was bound to. I made a business of friendship. It is a very tiring business, one that requires constant attention. It wore me out. I never wrote much to any one person, but I wrote to many."

"Do you think that one makes up for the other?"

"No indeed, since each friend feels wronged. And the first person I wronged was myself. In the case of Valéry, the difference in the length of the letters is far less embarrassing than the difference in tone. Valéry was a remarkable letter writer. Perhaps I could have answered him suitably. But the fact is that my answers lacked brilliance. However, I must resign myself to including my letters. If I decide to publish our correspondence, it is for him and not for me. It is important that he be known as he showed himself to me when he was twenty. Many opinions will have to be revised."

André Gide entrusted me with bringing out the letters, and for several weeks I came to his apartment and proceeded to collate and decipher the texts. Very often he sat down beside me and helped me date a letter or make out a word, and took pleasure in reading aloud certain passages he particularly liked.

"Do you know any prose that is as instinctively well-wrought? Valéry, who always preached about polishing one's writing, proved that he could do without it. His words were polished the minute he wrote them; in fact I might say: the minute he found them."

My work was interrupted by André Gide's illness. When I returned to the rue Vaneau, it was to bow before a face that still bore the mask of intelligence, but one that was already joining Valéry's in the petrification of silence.

Valéry's letters had been put back in their box. A few days later a seal was affixed. It was necessary to wait several weeks for the formality of the breaking of seals to take place. The day I returned to André Gide's study to continue my work, I was overwhelmed by the feeling of being left to myself, deprived of all help, at grips with an all-too-secret master. I had to replace the most reliable of commentators, and the best way to succeed was to call on my memory, evoking in turn the two men I had had the good fortune to know. Corresponding to the image of an aged Gide, amicably disposed to confide in me, was that of a fifty-year-old Valéry, who treated me with the paternal solicitude reserved for the playmate of one of his sons.

I remembered a smiling gentleman of whom I dared not ask the smallest question but who liked to question me about my tastes. For me Paul Valéry was still the mysterious great man who took interest in a child and provoked in that child those unrestrained remarks which parents generally try to stifle. Twenty years later I was able to situate the expression of that great man between the lines of his letters and thus set up a balance with André Gide's presence. When the letters were finally put at my disposal by Mme. Valéry, a good many gaps were filled in, a good many shadows lifted. The words of the two correspondents began to live again, as if all the seals of their mutual silence had been broken suddenly.

Paul Valéry was performing his military service when, in May, 1890, at a celebration of the University of Montpellier's 600th anniversary, he met twenty-year-old Pierre Louÿs for the first time, at Palavas. The young provincial was immediately charmed by the ease of manner and literary culture of the Parisian, one year his elder. A letter that Pierre Louÿs addressed to his friend André Gide, who had remained in Paris, shows that the good impression was reciprocal: "And now the deep friendships, concerning which I can do no more than give you names, and which today take precedence over all the others: Bérard and Barbier, two *belle-lettriens* from Geneva; Paul Valéry, a young man from Montpellier who spoke to me of *La Tentation* and of Huysmans, of Verlaine and of Mallarmé in such terms! . . . You know, I really commend this one to you." A few days later he added: "It is Valéry who interests me the most"; [1] then, back in Paris, he intentionally baited the troubled Gide by pushing his virulent coquetry to the point of reproaching Gide with having sent him a letter that was too friendly: "I am angry with you for having written me such a good letter, because that spoils all my plans. I was just beginning a voluminous and abundant correspondence with Valéry and preparing to send you a very laconic card to tell you that I had no time to study two friends at once, and that for the time being you were put aside." [2] Gide was used to such useless provocations. It was not until much later that they were to cause a breach. At that time, Pierre Louÿs, his former classmate at the Ecole Alsacienne and a brilliant *licencié ès lettres et ès sciences,* liked to take advantage of the prestige he had with Gide. He could not resist the pleasure of telling him about some exceptional friend he had just discovered, thus appearing to diminish the value he attached to his friendship for Gide, but not without also giving him proof of his confidence. In the matter of complexity, Louÿs could match Gide any day. Although he divulged his new friendship somewhat perfidiously and ostentatiously, and not without an ulterior motive, he must be given credit for having been the first to discover the grandeur of an adolescent mind and for telling Gide about it. He gave proof of his confused feelings in a letter he addressed to Valéry in December, 1890, announcing Gide's impending trip to Montpellier to visit his paternal uncle Charles Gide, a professor of the faculty of law: "Don't believe a word of what he will tell you about me: you know me far better than he does, and his competence when it comes to me is well known. Don't show him . . . any of my letters. I like separate friendships. But I'm very happy that you should see him and I hope he will be as dear to you as he is to me." [3] Louÿs' reserve is evident, but so is his desire to act as an intermediary between two friends whom he might have left in the dark about one another. His role here is of capital importance, for without

[1] Letter dated June 4, 1890. Fragment published by Henri Mondor in *Les Premiers Temps d'une amitié: André Gide et Paul Valéry,* Monaco, Rocher, 1947.
[2] *Ibid.*
[3] *Ibid.*

his introduction Gide would doubtless have stopped in Montpellier without even suspecting Valéry's presence.

In the month of December, 1890, it would seem that André Gide decided to go to Montpellier for reasons of a family nature, but one can imagine how the prospect of meeting Valéry aroused his curiosity, thus hastening his departure and prolonging his stay in a city ordinarily wanting in youthful contacts. Some days before leaving Paris, he noted in his *Journal:* "ETHIC: Never mind about *appearing. Being,* alone, is important." He was twenty-one. He was writing *Les Cahiers d'André Walter,* and sought his guiding principle in the confused issue of what people wanted him to be and what he wanted to be. He was troubled, feverish, and gloomy with small provocation. During that period, Valéry, just released from military service, a student of law without a vocation, a skilful poet and one already wary of his gifts, was also in the midst of a crisis: he was hesitating between the appearance of literature and the realities of the mind. Optimism was not his strong point. On December 9 he wrote to Pierre Louÿs: "It is time that Gide came to speak to us of hope and rebirth; the winter hours are slow and bleak." [4]

What were the first conversations between Gide and Valéry? We have no idea, since neither one bothered to note them down. But we do know that Valéry was conquered by Gide straightway, and said to Pierre Louÿs, with an impetuosity that must not have been especially agreeable to the latter: "My dear fellow, I am in ecstacy and in raptures over your friend Gide. What an exquisite and rare mind, what enthusiasm for beautiful rhymes and pure ideas. . . . I envy you such friendships. I feel that if I lived at your side, sustained by those ardent talks, constantly warmed at those magic inner fires which you are, O poets, I would work with vigor and saintliness." [5] And a few days later, after having noted the following, very Gidian, reflection on the relationship of Louÿs and Gide: "Your friendship seems to bear out the opinion which situates the cause of affections in a certain dissimilarity . . . ," he was to say of Gide:

He is the most amiable, the most given to dreaming, the most secretly musical, the most loving of young men. . . . We spend many short hours together; my silly romantic and medieval manias have often caused him to wander around that old cathedral whose sad mysterious stones have so deeply weighed upon my soul. . . . He will repeat to you what we said, he will tell you about the unspeakable and disorderly hole in which I smoke so many cigarettes on the pretext of working, he will be able to evoke for you the peaceful rue Urbain-V, provincial and musty, with its weeds along the walls and the

[4] *Ibid.*
[5] *Ibid.*

evenings filled with neighboring angelus bells. . . . I hear them with melancholy as I finish this letter at the end of the day.[6]

For his part, Gide, in *Les Nourritures terrestres,* in enumerating the most poetic places he had ever known, was to mention:

In Montpellier the Botanical Gardens. . . . I remember how with Ambroise, one evening, as in the gardens of Academus, we sat on an ancient tomb, completely surrounded by cypress trees; and we chatted slowly, chewing rose petals. One night, from Le Peyrou, we saw the distant sea, silvered by the moon; near us stretched the cascades of the city water tower; black swans fringed with white swam on the peaceful garden pool.

The "ancient tomb" of which he speaks is that which a local legend attributes to Narcissa, daughter of the English poet Edward Young, who died in France in 1736. The tomb bears the inscription: *Narcissae placandis manibus,* "to appease the shades of Narcissa," the phrase Valéry was to use as the epigraph for his *Narcisse.*

The descriptions that both men gave of their walks together express a romantic sentimentality of a similar order. The quality of emotion was not merely a surface tremor. Despite a fleeting tone of melancholy in fashion with the young "decadents" of the period, influenced by the evanescent dilettantism of Des Esseintes, an emotivity of that kind stirred the depths of both temperaments, activated by a common desire not to accept the world through the vision of others. Pierre Louÿs' romanticism was not of the same nature: it remained that of a young aesthete who was more troubled by the appearance of things than by their mechanism, more attracted by artistic expression than by its significance, and less a thinker than a dreamer.

In Valéry, Gide found a partner who was equal to him. Both felt they were of the same stature, and thus their eyes were able to meet. A friendship sprang up at first sight between the two young men. Beyond literary preoccupations, they both felt the seriousness of their spiritual pursuits. But even then, Gide proved to be less sure of himself with Valéry than Valéry was with him. Sixty years after that stay in Montpellier, he was to evoke the inscription that hung on the wall of the little room, cluttered with books, in which his new friend received him: "BE CONSTANTLY ON YOUR GUARD." Before amusing him, the display of such advice troubled him. He understood the need for being on one's guard, but only after having forced himself to reflect on it. His natural bent led him to revise the rules and regulations that people wanted to impose on him, by the decision to accept everything that was offered him. He was

---

[6] Sunday, December 21, 1890. In *Letters à quelques-uns,* Paris, Gallimard, 1952.

to create his world by *adding* more than by *subtracting*. Valéry, on the contrary, was to create his thought and his life by refusing and denying. One was to open his arms, the other to press them more closely together. The Gidian embrace was the result of a confidence which, far from denying doubt, accompanied it and motivated it. What Valéry's joined hands were finally to contain was a dense crystallization of thought due to distrust.[7]

Back in Paris, Gide admitted to Valéry how apprehensive he was about writing to him: "Faced with this new affection, I felt so fearful and so clumsy that this is the fourth exordium of the long letter I am trying to write, for you. . . . I have childish fears of going against your will and risking something or other that might displease you."[8] And ten days later he repeated: "I am unceasingly afraid of making some blunder in my letter."[9] He was also fearful of Valéry's judgment of *Les Cahiers d'André Walter,* and waited several weeks before deciding to send him a copy. This provoked the following comment from Valéry, in which the psychologist puts his finger on Gide's sensitive spot: "Sad because of you! put that well in your mind! but sad also because of me! Sad . . . not to have been able to give you real confidence."[10]

The letters between the two friends succeeded each other at a rapid pace. They are full of literary considerations, in a style that is wilfully emphatic or precious, and with constructions which, in one as in the other, show the influence of Mallarmé. Gide soon proved to be demanding. He had to have "a suprasensible and nearly mystical communion . . . that sweetness of knowing the other's soul to the very depths."[11]

Out of a need for communion in truth, he thus demanded the complete effusion of his correspondent's soul, which was, he felt, "religious."[12] Valéry's soul was religious, but in a way that eluded Gide's perspicacity, which at this point erred by diagnosing too precipitously, ascribing his own feelings to others. He was doubtless unaware of certain passages of a letter-manifesto which Valéry had addressed to Pierre Louÿs a few months before: "Paul-Ambroise Valéry adores that religion which makes beauty one of its dogmas and Art the most magnificent of its apostles. Above all, he adores his own Catholicism, somewhat Spanish, very Wagnerian and Gothic."[13] André Gide's religiosity was that of a Protestant who was

[7] On November 7, 1899, Valéry was to write: "Of all the possible feelings, the strongest in me is that . . . of infinite distrust. I can have no confidence in what comes and goes. I don't trust it. That is why I have sought more constant things."

[8] January 16, 1891.

[9] January 26, 1891.

[10] March 6, 1891.

[11] March 21, 1891.

[12] *Ibid.*

[13] *Lettres à quelques-uns,* p. 20. This passage is preceded by the word "I."

horrified by Catholic pomp, by everything ceremonial, by precisely that magnificence coupled with a medieval spirit—which he, a man of the Reformed Church, judged obscurantist—and by the Spanish coloring, which to his mind was as excessive as the Germanic hallelujah.

During the Easter holidays, Valéry described the Mass he attended on Palm Sunday, and showed that, above all, he was touched aesthetically, but without speaking of aesthetics and allowing a doubt to hang over his belief. Gide's *Journal* of 1891 gives proof of his own constant preoccupation with religion and of the fact that he had not yet rid himself of Protestant teachings, being unable to distinguish religion from ethics, which Valéry managed to accomplish instinctively. Actually, Gide was by far the more religious: to the tendencies of his nature were added the effects of his upbringing. One could not imagine him being areligious even in a family of atheists, whereas had Valéry been brought up by parents other than his own, he might well have had no interest in religion whatever or only been interested in it as a social and political fact. Although Gide was no metaphysician, he was more nearly so than Valéry: he had the sense of what was sacred, whereas Valéry perceived the existence of that sense in others but heard no echo of it in himself. On the religious level Gide and Valéry were thus somewhat dissimilar from the very beginning, since the Protestant was still trying to make a religion to his own measure, while the Catholic had already refused religious garb and had no further interest in being fitted for it. In his autobiographical text of 1890 Valéry clearly explains his point of view:

As for pure belief! This is what he thinks (wanting above all to be frank, and above all frank with himself): The crudest of hypotheses is to believe that God exists objectively. . . . Yes! he exists and so does the Devil, but within us! The Worship that we owe him is the respect that we owe to ourselves, and that means: the seeking of something Better through our own strength in the direction of our aptitudes. In two words: God is our *personal ideal,* Satan all that tends to turn us away from it.[14]

It was not for many years of fluctuating and maneuvering that Gide came round to precisely Valéry's conception of divinity. The words of the twenty-year-old Valéry could be taken for those of the eighty-year-old Gide, the Gide of *Ainsi soit-il ou les Jeux sont faits.*

For Valéry the chips were very nearly down in 1891, in matters of religion as in matters of literature. He had found his lines of force and kept them all his life. If he then published texts in avant-garde reviews, he did so without any great conviction. The only true literary joy he experienced he owed to Mallarmé, to whom—on the advice of Pierre Louÿs, in October, 1890—he sent some of his poems, and who answered him with astonishing

[14] *Ibid.*

and generous clairvoyance. What he liked in Mallarmé was the effort he made toward an ultimate austerity, the tension of language that provoked a vibration at the edge of silence, the passion for perfection that bordered on renunciation. As early as April 15, 1891, after having brought out his *Narcisse,* he wrote to Gide: "I am one of those for whom a book is holy. A man writes *One,* and that one is the good one and the only one of his being, and he disappears. . . . Have no fear of my poems: they shall be silent and their buzzing of useless flies shall not trouble our slow walks." In August, 1891: "Nothing exists: the beyond no more than intelligence and style." And in September, 1891: "In passive as in active art, I have found nothing but reasons for anger and disgust!" Gide, on the contrary, then held literature in great esteem and took the writing profession very seriously. When he stopped writing, it was "to learn," he said, and he reproached himself for having temporarily given up "producing." The word "production," which recurs several times in his writings of 1891 and 1892, horrified Valéry. The differences in their temperaments on that point came to a head in March, 1892. To Valéry, who declared: "I am very aware—too aware perhaps! . . . You know perfectly well that there is no point in writing in order to be silent, and merely to repeat one myth—or another," [15] Gide replied: "One should do nothing in life but write books; how everything else annoys me!" [16]

The year 1892 was decisive for Valéry. Having been troubled in 1891 by a first sentimental affair which he directly transformed into a test case, being gifted with that clairvoyance in regard to one's self and others which unmasks the traps of passion without preventing them from functioning, and already convinced of the vanity of the fortunes and misfortunes of this world, the young man was to experience that well-known *nuit de Gênes,* which has been given far too much importance, to the point of being compared to the night of Pascal's revelation. The comparison is risky, for although Pascal and Valéry were both struck by an Evidence, the former drew from it the strength of his adherence, and the latter that of his refusal. The night experienced by Valéry was to take on a symbolic significance which he himself did not recognize until far later, in raking up his past. He did not even allude to it in his letters to Gide. The fact remains that in Genoa, during the fall of 1892, in the crash and dazzle of a thunderstorm, he found himself enlightened by the convictions he had held up to that point but had never put into practice. It was the blossoming forth of everything that had been developing in him, everything he had been secretly nurturing and which could come to light only by breaking down the walls, just as every flash of lightning cracked the shell of the oval sky,

[15] March 18, 1892.
[16] March 21, 1892.

and liberated the light as well as the peril. That night Valéry, in a state of shock brought about by the evidence of the vanity of writing and the emptiness of the creative act, gave up the idea of a literary career. In giving it up, he accepted the dangers of withdrawal, dangers multiplied by skepticism.

If fate had willed that he die at thirty, he would have given us a replica of Rimbaud's adventure; and in fact his letters as an adolescent show much of the same violence and rebellious cynicism. He would have left us a few poems, two shattering texts: *Introduction à la méthode de Léonard de Vinci* and *La Soirée avec Monsieur Teste,* several notebooks of private observations, and letters of the quality of those printed here. If Rimbaud had lived longer, would he have kept his silence? The decision to be silent has no better support than death. But Valéry's renouncement of his renouncement was in no way a disavowal. It was a way of confirming his renouncement, since all the works written after his resurgence, twenty-five years later, were to be expressions of an uncompromising lucidity, an objectivity without illusion, and an unequivocal skepticism. They were to imply no change in attitude, but were rather to reveal an inner venture and to disclose an occult monologue.[17]

Valéry has sometimes been reproached with having illustrated a paradox, and it was precisely the ties that bound him to Gide which made the spectacle more impertinent: to have put such vigor and subtlety into repudiating literature, and then finally behaving like a typical littérateur, subjected to the rules of publishing, the whims of journalism, and the charms of *salons,* academies, and honors, whereas Gide, who never made it a secret that he was carving out a career for himself as a writer, did a far better job than he of keeping away from all the sham of "literary glory."

Clearly, had Valéry never re-entered the literary lists (he would have said: circus), the main elements of his thought would have reached us posthumously [18] and the work of the exegetes would have been that much more difficult. But the concessions that he made at the end of his life did not diminish his principles; they simply humanized them by adding a precept to so many demonstrations: gratuitous thought is conceivable only in a cell with watertight compartments; as soon as that cell becomes part of a beehive, sooner or later communication is inevitable. To begin with, Valéry was solicited by other members of the community—by Gide, the very first—who begged him to let the public benefit from his findings and

[17] Valéry himself asked the question (July 21, 1912): "Does not publishing what I wrote mean sanctioning the renouncement and the catastrophe of why I had renounced what I wrote?"

[18] On April 18, 1899, Valéry himself planned a "posthumous" edition of his poems, to be published during his lifetime. "I am seriously thinking of collating my verses. There begin the difficulties. I want to present them with their posthumous character."

spoils. Some would say that he easily allowed himself to be forced into it. He would have readily agreed with them. His repugnance at publishing was counterbalanced by his desire to *prove,* not to *be approved* (he, in contrast to Gide, never sought approbation). Other considerations much less intellectual intervened and prompted him to try his luck as a writer. Valéry had family responsibilities. The disdain for a literary career is far more understandable in a bachelor like Paul Léautaud than in a married man and father of three children. Gide's indifference to literary honors would probably not have been so great had he been forced to work for a living. This does not mean that had Valéry remained a bachelor he would not have ended by giving in to the temptation of becoming an influential master. He held the highest trumps; his accumulated meditations had acted like a spring ready to be released. And perhaps he thought, like Baudelaire, that "the taste for productive concentration in a mature man should replace the taste for dwindling away." [19] Thanks to that power of irony with which he could strike down others—and which, out of goodness, he used but rarely—he was to find it attractive and instructive that literary success came to one who had professed to scorn it, and came because he had done so more spectacularly than others, that is—a new anomaly—by his silence. Once he had chosen to express himself like his fellow writers, it was only normal that he no longer seek to evade the rules of the game and even that he throw himself into it with all the resources of his temperament. This explains the almost immediate transition from his being incognito to his being well known, from the most secret withdrawal to the most official kind of life. Valéry knew how to play. He played earnestly out of courtesy for others, as well as for his own pleasure. The main thing was that he never forgot it was a game. He always played without being taken in, but zealously enough not to take in those whose ideal was not satisfied by a game. He was thus able to safeguard the honor of his mission and to act as a professor of poetics at the Collège de France, he who believed so little in the professoriate and still less in the teaching of poetry.

Be that as it may, Valéry's renouncement of literature in 1892 corresponded to the most sincere of exigencies. He shaped the features of his destiny on his own person. If in 1895 and 1896 he published *Introduction à la méthode de Léonard de Vinci* and *La Soirée avec Monsieur Teste,* it was then no longer to be in contact with others; it was in order to deal intellectually with himself: he was taking stock of his thinking, as if it were for the last time. At that moment Gide was, on the contrary, going through a crisis of literary growth and was devoting himself to what he

[19] *Journal intime,* quoted by Gide in his preface to *Les Fleurs du Mal,* reprinted in *Incidences.*

hoped would be persuasive works: *Paludes, Le Voyage d'Urien, Les Nourritures terrestres*. He was looking for an audience. To this difference in intellectual orientation, which is evident in the correspondence from the very beginning, was added the divergence of two sentimentalities, one as tormented as the other, but for very different reasons. Gide's friendship was subject to such unmasculine languor that sometimes one thinks one is reading the letters of a woman in love: "I feel the same about friendship as I would about a mistress," he writes; [20] or again: "I could not sleep all night; such things pain me, as if they had been done by a mistress." [21] The tone is that of a man addressing a woman: "In my seraglio I have a deeply recessed and very special bedchamber for you—as if enclosed with panes of blue hothouse glass." Such overstated language would not seem to surprise Valéry, who answers with much tenderness but without the slightest ambiguity and without anything that could be considered sensuous. Valéry's tenderness is of a poetic nature; Gide's is already carnal, but unconsciously so. It is with honesty that he writes: "In affection I suffer from all that the other hides from me—from me who can hide nothing." [22] Until that day, he had nothing to hide from Valéry. The peculiarities of his nature had not yet been disclosed to him. He was then secretly engaged to his cousin Madeleine Rondeaux, whom he idealized as Emmanuèle in *Les Cahiers* and *Les Poésies d'André Walter*. We shall never know what was in the letters he wrote to her, because the woman who four years later was to become his wife threw hundreds of them into the fire on a day of great distress, when—generous as she was—she could not help but make that gesture, prompted less by revenge than by despair. We shall therefore never know in what tone he spoke to her and how he expressed a feeling that was made up entirely of love and which he was to call Love. But from what he has confided, one may suppose that he put into them the best of himself and that the formulas he used were no more sensual than those he addressed to his favorite friends.

How does Valéry, who also suffers from effective febrility, greet declarations such as "Excuse this long silence, I beseech you tenderly. . . . I still cling to the desire for your gentle tenderness. . . . I am almost afraid of seeing you again and of both of us feeling that at a distance our intellectual wedding was more easily mystical and spiritual." [23] He answers in the same pitch, but his tone is not nearly so solemn, despite an evocation that is meant to be poignant: "I await you, dear and noble friend, with an impatience to see you that no! you could not imagine. . . . Come then

[20] June 17, 1891.
[21] *Ibid.*
[22] March 21, 1891.
[23] May, 1891.

and awaken the ancient roses and drooping lilies, like an angel of old, a terrible and fragile angel of old, one breath of whom would have given rise to the pink awakening of the corollas in the gardens." [24] If Gide's mysticism creates a nearly androgynous angel, the angel imagined by Valéry is, as we can see, more literary than disturbing. The true angel of dogma, he is asexual. (It should be pointed out that at the time, Gide's unawareness of his homosexuality, together with his already well-defined temperament, led him—out of sexual conformity—to adorn the men he dreamed of with the charms of women. Later on, with women, he was to do the opposite.)

The two young men's adoption of the familiar *tu* in place of *vous* sheds light on their respective feelings. Gide was the first to use it, but not without the shyness—pretended?—of a woman, inadvertently going back to *vous,* skilfully mixing sentences that showed reserve through the use of *vous* with those that became almost provocative because of the *tu.* Valéry employed the *tu* without ambiguity and without embarrassment. The intimacy of the two correspondents became more pronounced. It was Valéry who was the first to approach the theme of love and confided to his friend: "Ah! do you know what a dress is—even as a thing apart— especially apart from any oversimple desire of the flesh? But only the dress and the eye." [25] And Gide, by such comments as: "Ah! pure spirits! And now your heart has sung of a new tenderness. Don't think that I blame you for it," reveals an involuntary feeling of regret. He also added, as if he feared being seen through: "As for me, I have never known anyone but Emmanuèle; but she has forever perfumed my heart, my mind, and my soul. Nothing should be scorned but lying." [26] Several times he alluded to carnal purity, however difficult it was for him to maintain. [27]

When his engagement to Emmanuèle became official, he proved that his feelings were not so simple as he would have liked people to believe or would have liked to believe himself: "One thing saddens and somewhat frightens me, a coincidence which, between two kinds of happiness, will force me to choose the rarest. I say this *very confidentially to You:* . . . I am very much afraid of having to choose between you two." [28] Valéry was not capable of such ambivalence, and answered straight out: "You must stay close to 'the rare and radiant' E." But Gide, a prey to his own inner workings, like the future *Jeune Parque,* could not help but continue to

[24] May 8, 1891.

[25] July 4, 1891.

[26] July 9, 1891.

[27] See his letter of July 14–15, 1891. In his *Journal* of March, 1893, he wrote: "Until the age of twenty-three, I lived completely virgin and totally depraved, so crazed that I sought everywhere some bit of flesh on which to press my lips."

[28] August 28, 1891.

parallel the two affections, and from La Roque, the very day his fiancée left, he wrote to Valéry, then sojourning in Paris, to ask him if they could meet, and called him "little altar boy." [29] It so happened that while in Paris, Valéry realized that Gide had confided very intimately in others, and he reproached him violently for it. Gide, at bottom, was delighted: "What are you angry with me for, Paul Ambroise? Because I prostituted myself with someone else? But you know well that my soul is constantly in heat; it must take its fill. . . . But this rage suits you. I'm pleased that you got into it." [30] The two friends made it up after a meeting in the Luxembourg Gardens, and Gide then carped on his need for friendship: "I wanted to *make friendship* as one 'makes love.' It's ridiculous. . . . I shall keep this, and break myself of the rest." [31] As a matter of fact, exactly two years later, during his first trip to North Africa, he "broke himself of the rest" in the company of a woman named Meriem, the beautiful Oulad Naïl courtesan, and was to discover at the same time that he was not made for that kind of love,* but without yet daring to satisfy his natural bent. All he needed was the example of Oscar Wilde at Blidah, in March, 1895, to take the plunge. And then, what new anxiety he felt, what remorse: he could no longer write, as he did in 1891 with regard to Emmanuèle: "Nothing should be scorned but lying," for now he had to lie, and not only to his fiancée—to Valéry as well. His anguish is more especially understandable given his coming marriage, when his life was to be *"decidedly"* at stake." And when he admits that he thought of his fiancée "with fatiguing steadiness," [32] one grasps—something Valéry could not then do—a foreboding of the drama hidden by those words.

As he was to build his affective life between an embraceless love and loveless embraces, and in that way was to find an oscillating balance, his letters to Valéry were to lose their juvenile sentimentality, their effeminate languor. He was no longer to call him "satanical priest," "angel of sweetness," or "little altar boy." At almost the same time that he freed himself physically, Valéry also put an end to his lack of experience. Their correspondence is no longer filled with touching adolescent emotions, a mixture of their carnal anxieties and the torments of their minds. Henceforth the tone is to change: each one, in a simplified style, expresses an *état d'âme* which has nothing in common with *vague à l'âme*. Gide, a young married man, continued to wander around North Africa, and found the material for his next books by experiencing it. Valéry gave up Montpellier

---

[29] Beginning of October, 1891.

[30] October 7, 1891.

[31] November 3, 1891.

* *Translator's note:* Jean Delay, in his *Youth of André Gide* (Chicago, University of Chicago Press, 1963), refutes this point of view on the basis of new evidence.

[32] Grignon, May, 1895.

and went to Paris in search of a job. In December, 1895, Gide said with satisfaction: "I am beginning to try to corrupt the young by preaching Nomadism"; and Valéry, with resentment: "I, who wished to expect nothing except from myself and who find nothing in myself but bafflement." As it developed, Gide made every effort day by day to come out of himself and go toward others, claiming to enrich himself by the greatest possible number of contacts; Valéry shut himself up within his consciousness in order to try to reach the obscurest, and hence the purest, part of what he was. Holding all literature in contempt, he desired to see himself seeing himself and being seen; he wanted to discover the mechanism of his perceptions and that of the eyes that perceived it. Gide, in order to *learn,* sought a spectacle; Valéry, in order to *understand,* attempted analysis. A spectacle implies surface, an analysis depth. Gide's concern with "being sincere" was echoed by Valéry's preoccupation with "being lucid." The satisfaction procured by sincerity can make one forget the lapses in perspicacity. But lucidity allows of no illusion as to frankness with respect to oneself. This explains why Valéry's maturity could not be achieved without despair, without a vertiginous contemplation of that which is relative and, soon, nothingness itself. And it is not surprising that Gide, in fulfilling himself, found in his temptations and then in his attempts— however much he doubted—the joy of spending himself in order to acquire, at any price, the experience that exalted him. Valéry assembled the pieces of his monster; Gide molded his. "Monsieur Teste" and "L'Immora- liste" were ready to make their way. They could not go hand in hand, for the Immoralist still believed in an ethic, even if only to destroy it, whereas Monsieur Teste was outside all ethics, or else, as Valéry phrased it, "in the ethic of death." [33]

Monsieur Teste's creator lived in a Paris boardinghouse in the rue Gay- Lussac. The dimensions and austerity of his room were those of a cell. On one wall hung a reproduction of Ligier Richier's skeleton; on another, a blackboard covered with figures, equations, geometrical formulas, and cryptic words. A perpetually open trunk was the library. A tiny table served as a desk. Valéry covered pages and pages of notebooks with his incisive handwriting, intriguing the friends who came to see him, but never giving away his secrets. He declared all idols outlawed save one, to which he sacrificed the others: the Intellect. And if he studied Leonardo da Vinci, it was to bring to light the method of a mind that was able to rid it- self of the affective apparatus to which the common run of mankind wrongly attributes virtues of fulfilment. He aspired to enter into the pri- vacy of the brain cells, into the abstract mechanism of connections, to which he wanted to give concrete form. The drawing of the skeleton he

[33] November 10, 1894.

hung next to his bed constantly reminded him of the truth of man's bone structure, the permanence of the solidity under the ephemeral elasticity of muscles.

Gide was concerned with nothing but the flesh and the forms of the flesh, and in order not to lose anything of the Protean sap, he embodied all the roles that were open to him. He made the mind itself into something carnal, whereas Valéry treated the body as a cluster of ideas.

From that point on, the two men were to pursue their respective ways, knowing well their differences and their similarities. Their friendship could no longer be called into question. It was part of their existence, like one of those familiar—and indispensable—realities which only death can snatch away. They kept up constant relations and were quick to write to one another when they were separated and their tête-à-têtes interrupted. When the events of 1940 kept them apart for long months, they contrived to correspond by interzonal cards. After a meeting in Marseilles in 1942, Gide left for North Africa and did not return for three years. On May 9, 1945, Valéry, learning that he was to see him again, noted: "Surprise. A shock too." [34] The shock was to have a salutary effect on an organism that had been deeply attacked by illness. The next day Valéry noticed that "Gide's return" had "somewhat changed his 'humors,' " and he made plans for their reunion which involved Jean Cocteau. [35] At the end of May, he took to his bed, never to arise again. Gide gave him all his attention, going to see him and offering constant proof of his affection, and on July 19, the day before Valéry's death, Gide was there, together with the family, hopelessly waiting, while Valéry, conscious and courageous, was already isolated from the world in his final meditation.

The letters exchanged by the two friends spread over more than half a century and number almost five hundred. The subjects touched upon are of the most varied: ethics, literature, political and family events. The struggles with their consciences, their psychological analyses, their impressions when traveling, their financial reports, Valéry's utter distress on Mallarmé's death, his hesitations about publishing his writings, Gide's encouragement and the emotion he felt on reading *La Jeune Parque,* the anxieties of both during the two wars, their mutual concern about health—which plays an important part—the anecdotes, the secrets, the flashes of wit, the traits of character, the enthusiasm and the disgust, the fits of anger and their abatement, repudiation and fresh plans, all are interwoven with the spontaneity of facts and temperaments, and are flawlessly bound together by the most exemplary fidelity.

[34] Unpublished notebook.
[35] On May 14 he noted: "Gide, Cocteau . . . after all, men of the *ancien régime* along with me."

There is, however, one subject that is never broached in their correspondence: homosexuality. Gide never makes the slightest allusion to it, and if Valéry speaks of it, he does so before discovering his friend's tendencies. Eight years after their first meeting, Gide has still not given away his secret, and Valéry, with a naïveté explained by his innate incapacity to imagine habits "outside the norm," is surprised by the tone of *Saül,* which is "made ambiguous by his violent pederastism." He adds: "I have still not really understood the king. He is perfectly clear in the play with relation to the action. He is not, with relation to me, to you, to us. I am trying to find some of Saül's ideas in me . . . What really bothers me in your play is its 'perverse' and 'disquieting' nature. I was surprised by it." [36] Gide might have seized the opportunity to tell his friend the truth. But he did no such thing. He neither dodged the subject nor approached it indirectly; he gave a straight answer—but it was a lie: "I have been reproached enough with my subjectivity in *Les Cahiers, Les Nourritures, Paludes,* etc., so that I may finally treat myself to the pride of apparently having created a type in which nothing of me can be found." [37] Valéry, like everyone else—but not much sooner than Claudel—was to end by discovering Gide's special tastes. That discovery was not to provoke any conflict or any uneasiness between the two friends, whereas it was to be the cause of Gide's breaking off with Claudel, who came to assume the attitude of a judge vis-à-vis a sinner.

Possibly later on, in the course of their innumerable conversations, Valéry and Gide *took the risk* of speaking of homosexuality, but how could the nature of such comments have been other than uncomfortable and risqué, since the two men could have done no more than state their dissimilarities, having no possible recourse to intelligence.

It might also seem surprising to find no allusion in their correspondence to subjects that were nevertheless of the utmost concern to Gide—for example, his dealings with Christianity and communism. To explain such lacunae by the conversations that took place between the two writers is not enough, for their letters touched on intimate questions which surely they had had the opportunity of discussing when together. The real explanation can be found in Gide's reserve, which had nothing to do with modesty and corresponds to an absence of the need or even the desire to confide in letters. Valéry was always the one who took the initiative when it came to confidences. Gide did no more than answer, and his letters are much shorter than those of his friend. On that point he was right: Valéry proved to be far superior to him as much in his tone as in his *élan.* He went deep within himself; he discovered himself completely. The Gide-Claudel correspondence had already shown the same inequality, due not to Gide's

[36] July, 1898.
[37] October 22, 1898.

want of aptitude but to his want of appetite. As he himself admitted, he kept up too many friendships to be able to give all of himself to each one. He was forced to cut himself into pieces. And why would he have revealed himself in his letters when he did so constantly in his books? For him writing was not an outlet. It allowed him to establish guide marks; it was a means of keeping his ties, not of justifying them. For Claudel, always in exile, letters served as much to provoke friendships as to maintain them, and because of his missionary temperament, they were filled with the warmest of words. Valéry—without ever seeking to persuade—put quite as much warmth into his letters: he gave all of himself in order to free himself. Everything he did not say in his works he confided to his correspondent, both out of a selfish need and out of friendship, for, contrary to Gide, he professed that he did not divide himself and that "each of my real friends has me COMPLETELY!" [38] We thus come to the apparently paradoxical conclusion that the writer who was the least reserved was full of secrets and that the one who was the most mistrustful unbosomed himself unreservedly.

Gide, conscious of his inferiority, was to ask Valéry not to judge him by his letters: "Yours are so full, so rich, so affectionate that in comparison I feel like a poor wretch." [39] If he felt like a poor wretch compared to Valéry, it was not only in the realm of letter writing. All his life he was to be impressed—and apparently troubled—by his friend's intelligence. It leads one to think that it made him size up his own more accurately and that he felt the comparison was not to his advantage. The correspondence is studded with remarks that prove his uneasiness—and his modesty: "One must be either stupid or conceited not to find one's self half-witted compared to you" (November, 1894); "We'll chat, but you will triumph because I'll stammer" (October, 1899). He often comes back to the charge, and more explicitly, in his *Journal*: "Visit from Paul Valéry. A charming visit but one that left me dead tired" (May, 1906); "Yesterday I spent almost three hours with him. Afterward, nothing at all was left standing in my mind" (February, 1907). On September 5, 1936, he compared Malraux to Valéry, explaining that in conversation the person either speaks to is "left behind": "That is why any conversation with those two friends is always, for me at least, somewhat mortifying, and I emerge more overcome than exalted." And on July 17, 1941: "Reading Valéry, one acquires the wisdom of feeling a bit more stupid than before." [40] The nature of the

[38] September, 1891: "You are, however, the only one to whom I say certain things," Valéry added.

[39] October 25, 1922.

[40] Gide confirmed these feelings after Valéry's death: "Most often, after my conversations with Paul Valéry, my mind and my heart were capsized. He shatters your mind with a word, wrote Mme. Teste of her husband. Yes, it was indeed what I felt also." (*L'Arche*, October, 1945.)

prostration felt by Gide after a conversation with Valéry is shown to have evolved. At the beginning the only feeling he had was that of being badly equipped to counter. He was annoyed at appearing inferior. He then ended by seeing his incompetency as no more than proof of everything that separated him from Valéry. The distance between them saddened him, because he was sometimes forced to avoid conversation in spite of himself, in order not to provoke useless arguments. He wrote: "Besides, I never argue with him; he quite simply strangles me and I struggle back"; [41] "The moment he broaches a question of literature or art, my only desire is to cut it short immediately"; [42] "Valéry, amazing as always, but in a cosmos in which I cannot breathe." [43]

How could a friendship spring up and develop if it is true that one of the partners found breathing so difficult in that atmosphere? This correspondence proves that Gide could find no abatement of his malaise in Valéry's approbation of his works. Valéry, past the age of indulging in mutual admiration, had no scruples about criticizing Gide—with regard to *Les Caves du Vatican* and *Si le Grain ne meurt,* for example—or keeping an expressive silence concerning other books. This distressed Gide and sometimes even mortified him: "I cannot keep from regretting, oh, very selfishly, that Valéry never made an effort to understand me better. And I could only suffer from it, without every harboring resentment for the fact that the ingenious structure of his mind had to exclude everything that I made my reason for being and my life." [44] Some years later he was to resign himself to it, and explained why: "I consider myself of very small account compared to him, but I am now able not to suffer from it any more. He bothers me no longer; I have created my works according to a design that is different from his, which I understand too well and admire too much not to allow that these works of mine could not figure in his system and have no value in his eyes. He is right, and my friendship even approves of his not 'considering' me." [45] That was a serene comment, the comment of a seventy-three-year-old man who is sure enough of his success no longer to fear being misunderstood by one of his best friends.

In 1927 Valéry was asked to participate in a collective *Hommage* to Gide. [46] He wrote a letter expressing his great "regret" at having "to renounce" describing for the public "the singular figure" of Gide, "who is

[41] *Journal,* February 9, 1907.

[42] *Ibid.,* February 19, 1912.

[43] *Ibid.,* May 28, 1921.

[44] *Ibid.,* March 8, 1931. In 1945 he was to write in *L'Arche:* "I suffered from his scorn, but recognized the right and reason of his scorn, a right acquired by sheer struggle."

[45] *Ibid.,* May 5, 1942.

[46] *André Gide,* Capitole, 1928.

the most original personage and one of the most important writers of current literature." [47] He gives no reason for his renouncement. It can be guessed: his perplexity at having to speak of a living friend, whose personality he prefers to his works. Nevertheless, in his letter of refusal he did explain how he envisaged the study that he was not going to write; and those in charge of the *Hommage,* only too happy to have a text from him, even an unofficial one, used it to head the volume. In it he describes the happy evolution of two characters who are contrary to one another and yet inseparable:

I have now known him intimately for some thirty-five years, years during which our differences developed admirably. Our feelings about almost everything are generally opposed, but the opposition is so natural that it amounts to a harmony and creates between us a truly rare freedom in the exchange of our thoughts. I should therefore have tried to paint a Gide using the method of our differences, for as a method it seems to me the most accurate, the most honest, and the one least contaminated by the absurd practice of judging.

On careful consideration of their correspondence, we realize that Valéry and Gide painted one another by "using the method of their differences," and that that improvised method is, at bottom, the most *rational* one, because it depends in great part on their *sensibilities,* a contradiction from which Valéry would have rightly drawn the most ironic of conclusions, but which nonetheless gives their exchange all its value of constructive spontaneity.

The largest group of letters, and the richest ones, those of the years 1890–99, bring out—as we have seen—the salient features of the two young men, and prove that, whatever the ups and downs of their destinies, their youths foreshadowed rigorously the lines of their maturity: a straight line for Valéry, a sinuous one for Gide, both of which were in the ascendant, and both of which stopped at the frontier of the transcendant as if by common consent, in order to take inventory of the territories conquered by force of arms from the human world, which was never human enough. It is in this sense that the two writers were "harnessed to the same beam," [48] with the possibility, at the end of their careers, of moving at the same pace, in order to drag behind them a mutual load of humanity. Before combining their efforts in the radiance of their old age, they did not deny themselves the privilege of choosing their duties and their pleasures as they saw fit, each in his own way and with his own assents and his own protests. They had no scruples about expressing, behind the scenes, opinions that could have been judged a condemnation of what the other thought. When Gide wrote: "Intelligence no longer seems to me the expensive pearl for

[47] Letter dated December 5, 1927.
[48] Valéry to Gide, October 17, 1900.

which one sells everything else. The vanity of understanding everything is as ridiculous as any other and more dangerous. After a short time, what one understands the least is one's self," [49] he was calling to account Valéry's "frenzy of lucidity." [50] And Valéry called to account Gide's sincerity about passion when he declared: "Intentional sincerity leads to the kind of reflection which leads to doubt, which leads to nothingness." [51]

As early as 1894, Valéry put his finger on the sore point: "I see, I feel, that we love each other, but each of us shows the other what terrifies him the most." [52] For André Gide, the danger lay in the cerebral games that led to nothing but their own virtuosity and, for want of something better, must be sufficient unto themselves, since they refuse to allow of the necessity of a balance between the senses and thought. He declared: "what is admirable on this earth is that one is forced to feel more than to think." [53] Two years before, Valéry had written him: "For me every specific subject comes down to a series of physical and mental operations expressed in mathematical terms. These terms are invariable, and they are as *thought out* as possible." [54] He was to see the experiment through, [55] and at the time it prompted him to say seriously to Gide: "I promise you the energetics theory of syntax," [56] causing Jules Renard to note ironically: "He would like to make up a table of logarithms for littérateurs." [57] He then ascertained that consciousness, brought to its culminating point, is no longer taken in by appearances and possesses itself with mastery. Thus consciousness in its pure state, isolated from its context in order to be maintained in that purity, no longer has an object. It is the only reality, a perfect entity, but useless by definition. In finding such a definition, Valéry also found nothingness. [58] An infallible presence of mind corresponds to an absence. Driven to the wall by his own success, he felt the vanity of it. And the despair of Narcissus or the Angel who looks at himself in the water without recognizing himself expresses his merciless lucidity regarding the

---

[49] *Journal, Feuillets,* 1901.

[50] Valéry, *Propos me concernant.*

[51] *Choses tues.* In his letter of October 16, 1899, Valéry said: "That aggressive kind of sincerity of which I tend to rid myself since it did not give me what I was looking for in adopting it . . ."

[52] November 10, 1894.

[53] *Journal, Feuillets,* 1901.

[54] October 16, 1899.

[55] "What struck me more than anything else was that no one ever saw anything through." (Letter to Gide, November 10, 1894.)

[56] April 9, 1902.

[57] *Journal,* 1896–99.

[58] "An enormous portion of my work . . . was to make myself definitions. To think by means of my own definitions was for me a kind of goal." (Letter to Gide, May, 1921.)

value of lucidity, as well as his famous line: "Soleil, Soleil, faute écla-
tante." [59] Having loyally proved that "pure Reason" annihilates itself like
fires that destroy themselves while triumphing, Valéry did not change his
direction. He was now better armed to continue on his course toward the
useful point at which consciousness retains its efficacy with the minimum
risk of error.[60] And he was gradually forced to incorporate sensibility into
his system. Monsieur Teste had already admitted that "suffering means
giving supreme attention to something, and I am a bit of an attentive
man." [61] Supreme attention, Paul Valéry's objective, is thus inseparable
from suffering. It explains such somber remarks as: "My being can hang
out the sign: 'Well known for its Great Poisons.' " [62]

He then tried to come to terms with sensibility in order to take apart its
mechanism,[63] and like Gide, he paid tribute to carnal energies.[64] At the
same time as he agreed to give the body its due, he stopped denying the
phenomenon of inspiration.[65] Of course, in his works we could easily find
contradictory remarks on the virtues of the body and inspiration, but we
are following the course of his general evolution which, despite some
acceleration and pulling up short, tends to discover the point at which the
body fuses with the mind, and at which magic fuses with the rational, at
the very moment that Gide was trying to do the same with other methods.
His formula "Sometimes I think and sometimes I am" [66] is a perfect
illustration of the distance covered and the objective sought—that is, a
harmony, in what one does, between what one feels and what one knows.

Valéry, who in the beginning must have smiled at Urien's pretentious
words: "We have had enough of thinking. We have switched to action," [67]
and who, always a prey to the demon of self-criticism, declared: "So many
things must be ignored in order to act" [68]—Valéry, in turn, launched out
into literary action and met up with Gide, whose political action was about

[59] *Charmes.*

[60] In *Mon Faust* he has Faust say: "They understood that the intellect alone can lead
only to error and that one must learn to subject it entirely to experience."

[61] *La Soirée avec Monsieur Teste.*

[62] July 6, 1921.

[63] In *Suite* he wrote: "Sensibility is fundamental. The greatest problem, the sole
problem, is that of sensibility." And in *Histoires brisées:* "The true gods are the forces
or powers of sensibility."

[64] In *Eupalinos ou l'Architecte:* "O my body, you who remind me at every moment
of the temperament of my tendencies, teach me secretly the exigencies of nature."
See also *Mon Faust.*

[65] "I must admit it, I give in. True artists are like drunkards; inspiration is all;
lucidity is its negation." (Letter to Gide, July 13, 1906.)

[66] *Choses tues.* Cf. *Moralités:* "Tired of being neither angel nor beast, he resolved to
be now one, now the other, now body and now spirit."

[67] *Le Voyage d'Urien.*

[68] *Choses tues.*

to begin. He had no illusions. In fact, that is what gave him the strength to play the part of a littérateur. Gide, on the contrary, was led into militant politics by illusions alone. Some years later, the two writers were to be on an equal footing in active life, one because he was to lose his illusions, the other because he was not to acquire any.

The respective positions of the two friends faced with the same political problems are a spectacular expression of their divergencies. Gide's adherence to communism makes their innate differences more perceptible and leads perhaps to oversimplification, the one appearing uniquely as a militant, the other as an aesthete. Gide did take a militant position, but without wanting to lose his free will; thus he was inevitably led to give up his militancy. Valéry considered politics a chronic, incurable disease, yet that did not stop him from seeking remedies for it by being one of the first to defend the idea of a European community. Gide was uncomfortably conscious of his bourgeois well-being. Valéry, who was little inclined to feel remorse for something he had not chosen, was more concerned about the fate of societies than that of certain classes. To be sure, he hoped for an improvement in the status of society, but not through violence, for to his mind the means used were more inhuman than the customs in need of reformation. His rationalism kept him from rising to the bait: under the worm he sensed the hook. Experience confirmed his inclination and therefore his refusal. Gide, on the contrary, saw nothing but the ideal result and allowed himself to be carried away by an *élan* that came from the heart. Valéry's lucidity gave rise to a "What's the good of it?" which, confined to the limits of an individual existence, does not lend itself to criticism and becomes almost aggressive in collective life. Gide's hopes rang with a generous sound, but he was to be more reproached for having overestimated them than Valéry was for never having had them. On his disenchanted return from the U.S.S.R. he was to be censured by those who had at first thought they should praise him, and was to draw sarcastic remarks from those who had censured him for deserving such praise. Valéry saw that political mishap as confirmation of the selfish advantages procured by the attitude which some years later was to be called a "refusal to commit one's self." But even when he was over his infatuation and well out of any militant activity, Gide remained a man who believed in progress and who wanted to contribute to it, a man who would not break with his fellow men and who hoped to be able to make himself heard until his very last breath. Thus, compared to Valéry, he seemed to be a proselytizer, just as Claudel did when compared to him, with one difference: he never tried to have the slightest influence on Valéry.

Gide's importance is apparent here in his role as a "hyphen." Between Paul Valéry and Paul Claudel—who have been jokingly called two opposite poles—no dialogue was possible. Claudel himself told me: "I have always had great esteem for the poet. As for the thinker, I find that he leads to a dead end. I have preferred never to enter into an argument with him. It would have served no purpose either for him or for myself. We would have worn ourselves out for nothing." Neither of the two writers, in effect, would have been harnessed by the other. Diametrically opposed, they confronted each other not as adversaries but as men who knew they were impregnable. Their situation was acknowledged as an accomplished fact, with no hope of change—a break, a gap. Gide worked his way into it as an intermediary. He was a friend of both. Between confidence and distrust, between the light one receives and the light one gives one's self, between eternal life and nothingness, on the borderline of vocation and the irrevocable, of mystical sensuality and the cerebral mystery, at the crossroads of searching questions and of consciousness, Gide took his stand, malleable enough to adapt to contrary forms, strong enough to resist them, and of a nature in which were mixed many other elements—a bit of Valéry and a bit of Claudel, along with much that was anti-Claudel and anti-Valéry.

Gide the mediator, the wire that transmitted the currents from one pole to the other, the relay station in which a sense of community persisted contrary to all hope—what finer compensation for that which has been called inconstancy or duplicity, what better justification for an oscillating life, turned in on itself, unfolding, ebbing, and flowing.

The way believers have of doing away with logic or making it their own worried Gide and gave him cause for reflection, but so did the blind confidence that rationalists have in their catechism. "The Cartesian does not accept the possibility of ever being surprised," he stated in his *Journal*, "in other words, he does not accept being taught." [69] He himself never stopped accepting the possibility of being surprised. He gave the impression that he liked to surprise himself, and that his ability to evolve can be explained by his desire to be taught by allowing himself to be surprised.

Valéry was not the Cartesian criticized by Gide. He knew that the unforeseeable is part of what a logician must foresee. He did not claim to be safe from surprises, but he sought to limit them. Surprise for him was not delight; it was merely a necessity to which he had to adapt. He thought that one learned more by eliminating the cause for surprises than by preparing for them. And he said to Gide: "I am *deletions*." [70] He learned, in effect, by deleting. He constantly rectified, and rectified himself. It was always the same sentence that he corrected, whereas Gide went from one

[69] *Journal*, April 8, 1930.
[70] September 20, 1932.

sentence to another without crossing out a word. Valéry's corrections could transform the terms of the sentence by reversing the meaning; he never added, he replaced. Gide refused overprinting, and juxtaposed. But finally, each one went back over what he did in order to learn, and both minds met on the level of their search.

"I am nothing but *seeking*. What is a man who does not seek? I am going so far in the direction of that involuntary will that I am unable to conceive of one's having found something and of one's becoming set." [71] That is how Valéry put it. And so, one might think, did Gide. As it was, he went one better: "Believe those who seek; question those who find." [72] Valéry could not have subscribed to that statement, for while he admitted that man was nothing but seeking, he was far from making the search an end in itself and considered it rather a tainted progression: "Man is absurd because of what he seeks, great because of what he finds." [73] His way of writing "because" (*par ce que*) is intentionally ambiguous. Is the absurdity in the seeking or simply in the object of the search? Is it not absurd to seek, assuming that it is impossible to find anything? And if no discovery is possible, why assert that man is great because of what he finds? It would seem that for Valéry only the object of the search was absurd, but the differentiation is so subtle that it becomes chimerical, for all seeking is an object in itself.

Valéry cannot escape from the contradiction which made him refuse to believe that one can find anything and yet made him speak of the greatness of one who does find something, unless we infer from these propositions that man is condemned to absurdity as he is to seeking, greatness for Valéry being no more than a dream. He realizes that the desire to find something torments humanity and is never satisfied, save in those, like Claudel, whose findings, he believes, are proof that one finds only what one bears within one's self—that is, one finds one's self, but without ever discovering anything on the outside, there where creation should coincide with the creature, and not the creature with the creature. Whence his anxiety, in seeking with no illusions, and the vertigo that overwhelms him at the end of his pursuits, overhanging their own fathomless depths.

But facing the future, "forever starting and re-starting," like the sea, Valéry could stop being Narcissus, thrown into despair by his own features. He was then the knowingly exalted author of a *Jeune Parque* turned toward the sun, and from the top of the *Cimetière marin* cried out his optimistic words: "we must try to live." It was not unintentionally that Gide, in 1939, ended his *Journal* with those words, which were not his own

---

[71] *Réponses.*
[72] *Ainsi soit-il ou les Jeux sont faits.*
[73] *Choses tues.*

but which might so well have been that a critic attributed them to him.[74] Trying to live implies being in search of both what is most reasonable and most carnal. And so we see the two writers participating in the same venture. What does it matter that one is prompted by "an involuntary will" and the other by a voluntary will, that Valéry makes his search into a mountain pass over which he advances with no hope other than that of testing his lung power, and that Gide, although seeing no way out, transforms his into a triumphal way: both men take the same direction. They walk as if inspired by common shadows in the light that each one makes for himself, and they are great not because of what they seek, but because they seek.

"I do not portray being, I portray transformation." Gide's attention was drawn to that formula of Montaignes's, and he commented on it. He saw it as the expression of "the nonstability of the human personality, which never *is* and gains awareness of itself only in an elusive becoming." [75] Here his thinking coincides perfectly with Valéry's.

Fifty years of correspondence gives proof of the continuity of an investigation conducted by two minds fascinated by the same question, the same enigma. Each has his own method of inquiry. Valéry often hides his sensibility—his "tenderness," said Gide—under witticisms. Out of modesty, he is ironic, playful, sometimes cynical. From one sentence to another, he goes from jesting to anguished confidences, from serenity to rebellion, and has no fear of appearing many-sided, as he shows himself to be what he is, apart from all literature. Gide, who is a curious combination of Huguenot puritanism and the shamelessness of a disciple of Rousseau's, is incapable of joking about anything that means much to him. He takes the chance of scandalizing, yet with a decorum that should not be mistaken for reserve. He knows how to behave even when he lets himself go. He uses his life in the creation of his *œuvre*. His letters are merely hors d'œuvre, but one finds the whole man in them, for his reticence and his silence are as eloquent as his effusions.

The dialogue between the two investigators is more a parallel than a debate. They compare their opinions more than they contrast them. They do not interrogate each other. They understood from the very first that they were made to esteem each other, not to influence each other. Even though they end by foregoing all stylistic effects in their letters, they have a mutual passion for literature. Gide was right when, as of 1891, he wrote to Valéry: "We have [literature] 'in our blood,' like the germ of a disease, and we shall never be without it." [76] That inevitable and necessary

---

[74] Cf. the letter of Feb. 5, 1940, in which Gide apologizes for that mistake, and that of Thursday (February, 1940), in which Valéry shows how amused he was at it.

[75] Preface to *Les Pages choisies de Montaigne*.

[76] May 12, 1891.

intoxication allowed them to make literature not an end but a means. Thus Valéry was able to remain a littérateur without publishing a line, or rather—and even better—was able not to become a littérateur while making writing a profession. Thus Gide's free and easy life as an adolescent was the best guarantee of his sincerity as a writer. "If I were kept from writing, I should kill myself," he said to Valéry in the gardens of Montpellier, to which Valéry replied: "And I should kill myself if I were forced to write." [77] In these exchanges, two natures, in disclosing themselves, have the good fortune to complete themselves, no longer as artists but as men who, preoccupied though they may be with aesthetic matters, yet make it clear that they place the value of established meaning beyond the value of symbols.

Friendship has given the meeting of these temperaments the scope of an event, an event provoked by literature but which cannot be explained by it alone. "Friends are these two men who *saved* from chance and accident an occurrence that was commonplace and that would very likely have fallen, such as it was, into the statistics of the molecular shocks of mankind." [78] In so defining friendship, Valéry defines the exceptional occurrence to which this correspondence bears witness.

ROBERT MALLET

LETTERS

NOTE

This American edition of the Gide-Valéry correspondence, based upon a volume edited by Robert Mallet, and first published in France in 1955, contains a majority of the letters exchanged between the two writers between 1890 and 1942. In this abridgment, which was meant to eliminate either a fair amount of repetition or insignificant detail, the proportion of letters from year to year corresponds almost exactly to the original. Moreover, all the letters here translated are complete, and the "ellipsis" dots (. . .) scattered throughout do not indicate cuts, but are merely the original punctuation reproduced from the French edition. A number of translator's notes have been added to explain breaks in continuity, any references that might be obscure to American readers, and an occasional play on words that is untranslatable.

JUNE GUICHARNAUD

LETTERS

— 1890 —

1. André Gide to Paul Valéry

Montpellier [December 21, 1890]. Sunday

Dear friend,

I am absolutely distressed to have to go back on my word, but I had not reckoned with our morning service, to which I am taken by my parents. I cannot get out of going with them: in fact, I have just enough time to make my apologies and to ask you for another appointment. Tomorrow is impossible: I shall be in Nîmes; but Tuesday, if you could come to the rue Castillon, I should impatiently await you at ten o'clock or at two; if you happen not to be free either in the morning or in the evening, please leave word for me here at the hotel, suggesting something else.

Your devoted,

A. Gide

[77] Quoted by André Maurois in *Introduction à la méthode de Paul Valéry,* Cahiers Libres, 1933.

[78] January 1, 1925.

2. Paul Valéry to André Gide

Sunday [December 21, 1890]

Don't be distressed, dear fellow, about having to go back on your word, but if you get to Nîmes, stroll around in the old cathedral, for me. I just wrote to the rue Vineuse,[1] then *worked* a bit, inspired by you, O laborious one. I have a bit more courage, but how far I feel from what it would really take. Men are so little aware of how painful it is for a *child* to ask for the moon and to stretch toward the impossible star his little hands, his vain hands!

Adieu until Tuesday, at two; I shall come and intrude upon you in the rue Castillon.   P.

3. André Gide to Paul Valéry

Montpellier, Wednesday [December 24, 1890]

It is just as I feared, dear friend, the morning service, the Christmas tree in the evening, and, in the hours between morning and evening, the falderal one hangs, the little candles one lights as ornaments for the branches.

I shall leave in a few days; I want us to see each other once again, but once only, for fear of clumsily encroaching upon the secrets of letters. It would be in the moonlight, wouldn't it, where, when one can no longer speak, silence is not so strange, where words are useless. It would be without a word—among the obscure flowers.[2]

Friday, if you like, I shall come and pick you up, as I did the first time, at the Association, at about quarter past eight.

Your companion in silence,

André Gide

P. S. My uncle C. Gide[3] has just this minute asked me to invite you to dinner on Friday. I am almost tempted to make my apologies for this, which will perhaps bore you. But I do hope that we shall be able to go out in the evening.   A. G.

---

[1] The address of Pierre Louÿs, whom Valéry met at Palavas in May, 1890, during a celebration of the University of Montpellier's six hundredth anniversary. Valéry has just completed his year of military service ("voluntariate") in the 122nd infantry regiment stationed in Montpellier. Cf. *Quinze Lettres de Valéry à Louÿs,* Paris, Monod, 1926.

[2] *Sans dire—parmi les fleurs obscures*—a line from one of Gide's poems which was to be part of *Les Poésies d'André Walter.*

[3] Charles Gide (1847–1932) was the younger brother of André Gide's father. He was then professor at the Montpellier Faculty of Law. He was later to be appointed full professor of comparative social economics at the Paris Faculty of Law. André Gide, in the company of his mother, paid him frequent visits.

4. *Paul Valéry to André Gide*

Wednesday, end of December, 1890

I am overwhelmed, my dear *Durval*,[4] by your uncle's kindness, and am very much afraid that he shall meet a very awkward fellow on Friday evening. Do please thank him for me, while awaiting the day after tomorrow.

I should have so much liked to meet you on Christmas day—for reasons . . . I shall long be angry with myself for not having shared, that day, alongside you, the magnificence of the antiphon and the thundering organs, for not having received in your company the blessing distributed from the monstrances and the great majestic movements traced in the haze of incense by the sacerdotal arms weighed down by maniples! . . . I spent this afternoon around the confessionals in *my* cathedral, where the kneeling forms of the penitent were awaiting the time of repentance. And that called up so many daydreams! Under the purplish glow of the stained-glass windows, at twilight, how much was expressed in the open eyes of those diverse figures! . . . Tomorrow, at the Low Mass, I shall go and catch the mysterious glitter of the ciborial gold under the candle, as the priest goes from believer to believer, carrying the host at the tips of his fingers! And I shall also go to High Mass! When, from the mouth of the mitered and splendid bishop, the Latin of Gospel-book prose will revive the waning fervor and rekindle for a moment the magical Sirius of the three fabulous kings! Until Friday.

P.-Ambroyse

— 1891 —

5. *Paul Valéry to André Gide*

[Beginning of January, 1891]

Would you, dear friend, have the goodness—the charity—to bring with you tomorrow, when you come to see me, the poetry notebook from which I could copy *Les Chercheuses de poux?*[1] Besides, there is no doubt that when I have you here, in my power, you will be forced to dictate to me

---

[4] Bernard Dural was, along with André Walter, one of André Gide's pseudonyms, which he was to use in *Les Cahiers d'André Walter* to conceal another aspect of himself.

[1] By Arthur Rimbaud.

those verses, modestly half-veiled, which you have *noted* for André Walter and which I love from afar, like those Mohammedan women whose eyes are all one can see under the covering.

Until tomorrow,
Paul Valéry

6. *André Gide to Paul Valéry*

Friday evening [P.* January 16, 1891]

I hope, dear friend, that you have imagined everything, as a reason for my silence, but negligence or forgetfulness, and you are surely right, for everything is true other than that. As a matter of fact, the reasons for the delay of this first letter are numerous: to begin with, I have been back in Paris only a little less than a week, and, as I had warned you, I could not really write to you until I got back, having, since our by this time distant parting, lived through days of life so full that no extraneous occupation could have a place in them. Days which, later, you may perhaps know, synthesizing in a few hours the entire past of a life, like those poems of Poe we spoke about, an entire poem in a supreme refrain. Then, once in Paris, I was so overwhelmed by tasks so numerous and absorbing that, full of anxiety, I saw as more and more remote the beloved moment in which I could tend to the budding intimacy of the sweet friend I found in you.

When the moment finally came, faced with this new affection, I felt so fearful and so clumsy that this is the fourth exordium of the long letter I am trying to write, for you, and last night [2] I turned in at about one in the morning, so weary and dissatisfied that I threw the first three into the fire, before getting to bed.

Truely, I still don't dare make this first letter very long (please forgive me) : I have childish fears of going against your will and risking something or other that might displease you.

I shall wait until you give me courage, until you tell me a little of this or that, encouraging me to write to you: the fact that I want to so much is what makes me completely awkward. I am afraid that this first letter will serve as a standard for those which follow and that out of clumsiness I shall set our future correspondence, all of it—on the wrong track. I am afraid that you will not be in harmony with its mode, and I would prefer to be led by you.

I should like (even if the only result of this correspondence is your fortunate arrival in Paris)—I should like it to have a certain unity, a

---

* *Translator's note:* P. = Postmarked, here and throughout.

[2] Here Gide used the word *harsoir*, Old French for *hier soir*. Paul Claudel, during the same period, used it in his play *La Ville*, Act I.

certain fixed tone, a certain stable originality, which will give it a very special flavor; finally, I should like to talk with you about things that I cannot talk about with others, and should like you to do the same. For example, as it seems to me you have suggested, each one of these letters would be some subtle landscape of the soul, full of quivering half-tones and delicate analogies awakening like echoes of the vibrations of harmonics;—some specious vision that would be followed, in a gentle flow, by the deductions of our dreams. And this kind of confiding would reveal us one to the other, strangely and delightfully, by showing one of us the association of such fragile images in the other. . . . Please tell me, and very quickly—is that what you want—is it? or if it's something else? At any rate, this kind of confiding might be merely one part of our letters and the rest might be filled with some amusing futility—some tale *ad libitum,* some critical daydream about something recently read—we might even, if you absolutely insist, speak of literature. . . . Still I should prefer to give up that sort of correspondence to our colleague Louis,[3] who is more suited than I am to lecturing and provoking (and I think it is a difficult subject, rich in disputes—is it not enough for us to know that we both live for that disappointing chimera?) at least if we spoke about it, it would be to criticize affably and gently, wouldn't it, to praise rather than to blame (for the best punishment one can inflict on bad things is not to speak of them;—criticism keeps one from forgetting them). Do please understand that I am not putting under the heading of "literature" our own productions and our plans and our dreams,—I mean that, on the contrary, in no matter what sort of letter, you would submit your new fancies to me, as (if you ask me to) I will speak to you of mine,—and that we will chat mutually about our reciprocal works, and that we will advise each other, criticize each other, appreciate each other, etc.

And now, I await your letter, which will be the *first* of *our* letters, for this one is merely a prelude: do write to me at length; you have, I know, all the time in which to do it; and I shall try to answer you likewise, however plagued I may be by daily tasks (I have still not finished the transcript of my book).[4]

[3] Pierre Louis (1870–1925), who was soon to sign Pierre Louÿs, had been a close friend of André Gide's since they had been classmates together, in 1888, at the Ecole Alsacienne.

[4] *Les Cahiers d'André Walter, oeuvre posthume* was published at the author's expense in 1891, by the academic house of Didier Perrin, with an introduction signed P. C. (Pierre Chrysis, pseudonym of Pierre Louÿs). This first edition, of about 70 copies, put up for sale on February 27, 1891, was to be almost entirely destroyed by order of André Gide. A second and corrected de luxe edition, of 190 copies, was published by Art Indépendant. It no longer contained the introduction signed P. C.

Au revoir—and don't make me wait too long; I am distrustful and jealous as the very devil. If I don't receive a letter from you in the coming week, I shall imagine the nastiest things—that you forgot me—that I bore you. . . . If this correspondence tires you, we can slow it down as much as you wish later on.

And now, I bid you goodnight. Your budding, and already devoted, affectionate, etc., friend . . . gifted with all the most exquisite qualities.

André Gide

(Alias Walter, alias Bernard Durval)

4, rue de Commaille, Paris

7. *Paul Valéry to André Gide*

Monday [in André Gide's handwriting]
January 19, 1891

. . . There were artisans, friends of Death, who polished tombstones, with some *eternal* resignation, at the pale close of a beautiful winter's day. The earth was maternal and made me think of ideal, deep, and solemn graves—graves of souls, at the pale close of a beautiful winter's day. . . . What did you say that was indifferent and *literary,* denied by your eyes, when I left you there, near the cemetery? . . . But what did the pines and the gentle languid cypresses say and what did your mind say, your mind always deeply moved and roving, always eager to know that from which it must part?

You have seen the sea since then, and the mountains and the turmoil of the *deplorable and cherished* city. You have forgotten; but I, I dream still, for my eyes are immobile. I have provoked within me the desire of feeling to the bone the magic of things; I have read great pages in Schopenhauer and have more clearly fathomed the beloved Baudelaire, my own, my intimate, the Baudelaire of certain pages on ecstacy. Then again and always the solitary Poe, and a little Mallarmé. All that is not literature; it is very far from Flaubert and it is very lofty.

And you?

. . . I pine away by the fire awaiting what will never come. Fortunately the days slip by.

Now and then, plans light up the obscurity of my boredom, like enchanted palaces. I hear my verses singing and shining, without being able to grasp them and keep them. . . . They fly off! the palaces tumble down, and again I pine away to death by the fire.

You are full of dawn. You are starting the rare review [5] that will be

---

[5] *La Conque.*

our *Parnasse contemporain.*[6] The first novel is constructed,[7] the others are being formulated. Secretly your known self is building up. Then one day, Paris knows of a name. It is yours. . . . Paris! no matter, but you, at least, you are conscious of *being!*

I have labored, I have acted—therefore, I am!

But when will *I* do something? I continue to see before my eyes the slim booklet that you know about, a half-dozen poems, *Narcisse, Tempus,* etc.[8] I am obsessed by that, and discouragement keeps prowling round me. Poetry is so difficult, the page of flesh that one tears out, without shrieking like Musset, but secret and unheard of, with smiles . . . opened onto sadness.

I am envious of muscles, of serene will power, of the dream that knows how to stop, of the rhyme that comes; yet there is a lack of real inner tears, and anyway, I don't know, really I don't know. . . .

Louis will show you, my dear fellow, the *paradoxical* and labored and miscarried sonnet which I childishly sent to Heredia. I shall have scruples about writing it out for you: it sincerely sickens me. Are you reading the strange poems I so strongly commended to you? What do you think of them? What of *your own* are you going to put in *La Conque?*

Adieu, dear fellow, I cannot make this letter any longer or any less oppressive. It is a quintessence of memories, and every line I have written has had painful correspondences for me . . .

I am vaguely working these days on a whimsical article on aesthetics which *Art et Critique* will probably not use . . . if I finish it![9] In any case, I might ask you in advance the favor of getting it back from the editors were it to be turned down.

Adieu. . . . When will I see you again?

P.-A. Valéry

8. *André Gide to Paul Valéry*

Monday, January 26, 1891

In my very first letter I fail to keep my promise: I'm going to speak to you of literature, and do forgive me. *Ars non stagnat:* ah! to be sure!

It is evolving frightfully within me. You see: I was, still at the time I

---

[6] *La Parnasse contemporain, receuil de vers nouveaux* was published in 1866; a second series, prepared in 1869, was published in 1871; and a third in 1879. Mallarmé contributed to the first and second volumes, but was excluded from the third for being too hermetic. Anatole France, one of the editors of the third volume, had been opposed to him.

[7] *Les Cahiers d'André Walter.*

[8] *Narcisse* was to appear in the first issue of *La Conque,* March 15, 1891.

[9] The article did not appear in *Art et Critique.*

had seen you, still after I had returned to the city, an unrelenting scoffer at what I might call "your school" and took the position that I myself was an apostle of new truths (meaning truths of art), truths opposed to yours. I knew I was infinitely a symbolist, but as Hegel understands it with regard to the Hindu aesthetic—but also like Schopenhauer and like Maeterlinck in *Les Aveugles*,[10] and I believed that those aestheticians of today were plunged in vague nimbi, almost unconscious, obscure out of delight in their beloved words for the words themselves, etc.

Since then, everything has changed. Mallarmé is the main reason for it. Loving him, I get the impression that I had not yet either loved or admired: it is an enraptured merging of me into him. He has written all the poetry I should have dreamed of writing.

—Then a rather vulgar article, in the issue of *La Plume* devoted to Jean Moréas,[11] but of utmost importance to me for it contains a history of the new school and an account of its dreams. I learn from it that Maeterlinck is a symbolist (I mean one of their school)—and all their theories a straight justification of my book, when my own sentences are not actually transferred from it directly. Well then, I am a symbolist, there is no doubt of it. They say that Moréas is the leader. Oh! no—but surely it is Mallarmé—a Parnassian perhaps with regard to form, but a symbolist in his soul.

Mallarmé, then, for poetry, Maeterlinck for drama—and although next to them I feel somewhat of a weakling, I add Myself for the novel. Then come the others, and may the new "genres" find new voices, who will be just as lofty as Mallarmé, as Maeterlinck . . . and as I myself if reality doesn't demolish my dream.

(As for Mallarmé, do please tell me what of his you know, so that I can initiate you into new passages, copying them out for you with pleasure.)

A second evolution within me which is as extraordinary for me as the first: I am writing poetry! Now do realize that I had not written any for more than two years (the poems in my book are retrospective), and that I believed strongly that never again would I write any.

In my entire life I had not written more than fifty lines. And now I have begun again: a little for *La Conque,* but that is no more than the occasional cause, the real reason is that they flowed out of somewhere on my lips. I shall send them to you as soon as the poem in which they

[10] A play by Maeterlinck published in 1891.

[11] The issue of January 1, 1891, was almost entirely devoted to Moréas. There were, as well, as extracts from the poet's works, articles by Anatole France ("La Poésie nouvelle: Jean Moréas"), Barrès ("Jean Moréas symboliste"), and a long unsigned article. That is, no doubt, the one Gide is criticizing.

are grouped is finished—and do tell me whether or not they are too childish. I wrote them with almost no difficulty, in fact with that serene intoxication brought by rhyme which has gently come about: but I somewhat mistrust that sort of spurious facility and I fear the awakening after the pleasures of Idumaea.[12]

Meanwhile, this new chimera has taken complete possession of me—and with all the numerous daily tasks, I cannot write you any further today. In spite of that, I do complain about the brevity of your letter. I loved it strangely. I am unceasingly afraid of making some blunder in my letter, and that it will displease you: show me that it's not true by answering quickly. In my seraglio I have a deeply recessed and very special bedchamber for you—as if enclosed with panes of blue hothouse glass.

Au revoir, my friend, I should like to find some gesture of discreet tenderness for my adieu.

How long until our next meeting? So long. Your friend

André Gide

P. S. Send me your most recent poetry.

9. *Paul Valéry to André Gide*

February 1, 1891 [in Gide's handwriting]
My dear caloyer[13] of the symbolic mount,

Two words in haste to congratulate you on that miraculous and divinely fatal conversion; for all burning and pure spirits always finally come to adore the very holy Icons of art, in the ultimate and delightful chapel of Symbolism.

I cannot spare the time, I shall explain why, or I would have devoted this letter, which is again literary, to describing the new art to you in my own terms. That will be the subject of some short treaties which I denominate in advance: *Preface to a Future Book.*

Know, O good neophyte whose breastplate and ephod are already being embroidered, that Louis, our magical Director (and for me a *spiritual director* as well), has just asked me for a certain initial *prelude* for the first issue of the resounding conch.[14]

---

[12] An allusion to Gide's poem *La Nuit d'Idumée* (supposedly inspired by the first line of Mallarmé's *Don du Poème*), which was published in issue No. 2 of *La Conque,* April 1, 1891, but was not to be included in *Les Poésies d'André Walter.* Gide was again to evoke "the mountains of Idumaea" in *Paludes.*

[13] An Eastern monk of the Order of St. Basil.

[14] *La Conque,* or *The Conch,* subtitled "Anthology of the Youngest Poets," was founded on March 15, 1891, by Pierre Louÿs. The first issue announced a series of twelve instalments, of one hundred numbered copies each, printed on de luxe paper, the last to be dated January 1, 1892. In the company of a brilliant team of

He does not even leave me the time to object and to point out his audacity in asking this Unworthy One for forty lines,—when he has in hand the superb and completed *Stigmate*,[15] of the desirable length.

I took up my pen, and here I am in the throes of anguish. For the only way my long-imagined *Narcisse*[16] should be written is scrupulously, in short periods of time. And I suffer from feeling it grow almost *easily,* and I am very moved for I see the Work ungratefully becoming separate from me and enticing the dream of myself as a solitary ephebus.

For mercy's sake, if I finish it, and if I send it to L., judge it, and without *the devil's advocate,* and damn it forever, for it could not be worth anything so hastily done. But you cannot imagine the heart-rending struggle!

I thank you for your offers as regards Mallarmé: a corner of heaven opens up. I know his *Après-Midi du* [*sic*] *Faune* which will be put on in Paris,[17] and a few other poems, *Fenêtres, Fleurs,* four sonnets, etc.[18]

---

collaborators, Leconte de Lisle, José-Maria de Heredia, Mallarmé, Henri de Régnier, and Maurice Maeterlinck, Valéry was to publish a poem in each of the ten issues, Gide in only three (No. 2: *Nuit d'Ildumée;* No. 10: *Poésies d'André Walter;* and No. 11: *La Promenade*).

[15] A poem by Louÿs, dedicated to Valéry and dated September, 1890, was included in Roberti as *Les Stigmates.*

[16] This poem, published as *Narcisse parle* (in *La Conque,* March 15, 1891, and then in *L'Album de vers anciens,* 1920), was to be the first of the three stages of *Narcisse.* Paul Valéry, on September 19, 1941, in the salon of Mlle Marguerite Fournier, in Marseilles, was to explain the origin of it, after having recalled the inscription on the tomb in the Montpellier Botanical Gardens: *Narcissae placandis manibus,* "to appease the shades of Narcissa." "This name Narcissa suggested to me that of Narcissus. Then developed the idea of the myth of the perfectly beautiful young man, or he who found himself so in his image. I was, at the time, writing a very first Narcissus, an irregular sonnet, the source of all these successive poems. Shortly after, I met Pierre Louÿs (then Pierre Louis), a meeting which came about quite by chance and which lasted only a few minutes on the outskirts of Montpellier, on the shores of the sea. This meeting had the greatest influence on my literary life. We at first exchanged letters regularly and very actively, and then poems. In short, the following year, he created *La Conque,* intended for no more than a few amateurs, and printed in a limited edition (of about a hundred copies). As it happened, that little improvised work had an unexpected success, of which I was almost unaware." (Cf. "Valéry vivant," in *Cahiers du Sud,* 1946.) André Gide, for his part, was to bring out, in 1891, a booklet entitled *Le Traité du Narcisse (Théorie du symbole),* published by Art Indépendant. It contained a drawing by Pierre Louÿs.

[17] The *Théâtre d'Art* was to devote the evening of February 27, 1891, to Mallarmé's *L'Après-Midi d'un faune* and to Pierre Quillard's mystery *La Fille aux mains coupées.*

[18] Mallarmé's *Fenêtres, Fleurs,* and *Sonnets* were published in *Le Parnasse contemporain* in 1866.

Of *Hérodiade* I know the fragment in *A Rebours* [19] and another, the one sent by Louis which begins:

> *Oui, c'est pour moi, pour moi,* etc.

and ends:

> *Hérodiade au clair regard de diamant!*

Above all, show me your young verses which I imagine to be as delicate, as exquisite, as deep and gentle as I knew you to be. . . . Adieu.

Paul Valéry

10. *André Gide to Paul Valéry*

Paris, Sunday [February, 1891]

I send you these lines [20] and I have no time for anything else. Louis is pressing me for his *Conque* and I am giving him what little is left over from my worries as a budding publicist. I have launched out, for that friendly review, into a sort of impossibly abstruse and outrageously symbolic poem: [21] as a first attempt, I think I have taken on a far too heavy load and will come out from under it pitifully depressed. They [*sic*] are not yet finished and besides would look pitiable next to the Mallarmean stanzas.

Do please be satisfied today with *Hérodiade:* it is indeed worth my letter and the best of them.

My tender regards.

Your sweet friend,
André Gide

[19] In J.-K. Huysmans' *A Rebours* (Paris, 1884), the main character, Des Esseintes, in precious and delicate language, gives praise to Mallarmé's poetry, especially to the poem *Hérodiade,* which was published in *Le Parnasse contemporain,* and quotes about ten lines from it. Paul Valéry discovered *A Rebours* in 1889. Des Esseintes left a deep mark on his sensibility through the model of aesthetic and sensual strangeness he suggests. Valéry lost no time in reading the authors Des Esseintes admired, more particularly, Verlaine, Tristan Corbière, Edgar Allan Poe, Villiers de l'Isle-Adam, Baudelaire, and Mallarmé. That same year, 1889, Valéry dedicated a prose poem to Huysmans entitled *Les Vielles Ruelles,* as Henri Mondor first pointed out in "Paul Valéry et *A Rebours*" (*Revue de Paris,* March 1947).

[20] *Hérodiade.*

[21] *La Nuit d'Idumée,* the rough draft of which Gide was to send to Valéry in his letter of March 1, 1891.

11. Paul Valéry to André Gide

[February, 1891]

My dear friend,

I am hallucinated by Hérodiade, the glaucous Hérodiade in the sinister gold of the flames of her hair, dressed as for a sad and burning feast which sets the mirrors afire. And I suffer, I bleed with pity for having in that drawer so many indigent stanzas and that deplorable *Narcisse.* To have not written that poetry and to write poetry! And this supreme poem oppresses me like a twinge of remorse!

Thank you for all the trouble I give you and all the pleasure you have given me.

Nevertheless, I should have really liked to read your symbols, which I have guessed and am already fond of.

If you have read my hasty poem,[22] so far from the ideal work and which I hope to rewrite some evening or other (for without that hope I should suffer), tell me clearly, as a lucid and sober part of myself, what you infer from it. Louis remains mute, which distresses me but is quite natural, whether he is too busy or dares not tell a ferocious truth.

Yours, then, will be the decisive word, and I go along with it even now, reserving, though, the right to answer back.

And that novel which is already printed, when will it blazon forth in the shop windows or on the salmon-colored list of the review? This is a show of impatience, since you ruthlessly put me off reading it until its final full-bloom.

Were you, or *He* [*Lui*],[23] at the Symbolists' banquet? [24] Well, the *school* is rising—if that can be called rising. Mallarmé's name is coming into the sun—and I regret it almost!—as I deplore *Lohengrin* played in France.

I loved the reprobation and that glorious indifference which protected pure art and made me think of it as a kind of secret and favorite vice, a debauch that one hides . . .

We smile, we greet people, we shake hands affably, we pass exams, we are soldiers—but . . . that is merely make-believe and painted canvas, the incurable aesthetic diathesis pursues its inner course, eats away at conventional ideas, knocks down base desires and the *impure spirit,* swells unknown tumors, exacerbates certain parts, while the patient comes, goes, and lives. That's us!

Adieu to you, in whom a suave and mystical universe is housed; here

---

[22] *Narcisse parle,* which Valéry sent to Louÿs.

[23] Pierre Louÿs.

[24] The Moréas banquet, which André Gide mentions in his answer.

are a few lines that are not yet written and never will be. . . . It is a play
of vague words, plus a perfume, not yet music, less than nothing.

P.-A. V.

Sur Le Minuit Futur [25]

A minuit sur la montagne calme!
la mer comme un soufe dans des palmes
la mer comme une veuve, à mi-voix
pleure la morte Lune et les bois . . .

Les harpes légères du silence
sur le minuit s'écoutent languir.
Il n'y a plus d'heures ni d'espérances
les fleurs sont mortes sans un soupir.

Toi! le seul qui vis, ô Cœur solitaire,
et sur la montagne et sur la terre
tu dors! et la mer t'appelle en vain . . .

Peut-être sans êveil tu reposes . . .
tu rêves qu'il n'y a plus de demain
comme il n'y a plus de lune et de roses!

P. V.

12. *André Gide to Paul Valéry*

Wednesday [February, 1891, Paris]

Dear friend,

I no longer despair of my book not pleasing you, after a certain
acclaim I have received from on high, which has reinflated my pride
more than ever; especially after the note and conversation with Mallarmé, who just read it. Through what mysterious and predestined
harmony, through what anticipated relation ("very possibly mathematical"), did you write for me, without knowing me, that song of twilight,
dreamed of for me—and then dedicated—for this friend of Silence? [26]
And however did you have the foresight to divine, even before its
conception, the written praise of the Master: "The softest veil cast over
a phase of dead youth,* which your book almost left to be guessed; and
enveloping in *Silence* a face that is still recognizable as that of a rare

---

[25] This poem was unpublished until the Gide-Valéry *Correspondance* was published
in Paris, in 1955.

[26] An allusion to Valéry's *Le Bois amical.*

* *Translator's note:* "Le plus suave, voilà jeté sur une phrase de jeunesse morte,"
obviously a misprint or a misreading. I have used the phrase as quoted by Jean Delay,
in his *La Jeunesse d'André Gide:* "Le plus suave voile jeté sur une phase de jeunesse
morte."

Intellectual." Then, conversing with me last evening: "Your book," he said, "is a book of silences. You managed to do the most difficult of all things: to keep silent;—so that all the thoughts are in the spaces between the lines." [27]

Do you remember that, when we were together, I told you of my desire to suppress the emotions without mentioning them? I appreciate this praise from Mallarmé more than any other . . . up to now.

Yet that from Barrès was more unexpected . . . for there in the back rooms at Perrin's, waiting at the entrance of the publisher's office, near bundles of my book on the shelves, there he was, and distractedly skimming through, fell in love with it—announced to Perrin that the book is "astounding"—and complained of not knowing me. So that the next day I rushed over to visit the Free Man [28]—he kept me to lunch— and in the evening took me to the Moréas banquet.[29] You will think me frightfully unpleasant for shamelessly flaunting my proud joy. Do believe, though, that the strongest motive for such boasting is to provoke in you some desire for this book, after I had so much feared that it would displease you, and me along with it, as its author.

I shall keep Mallarmé's note, for, yes—it was indeed to be that: "A veil cast like a shroud to embalm dead youth."

---

[27] Gide had left a copy of his book at Mallarmé's, with the following note: "I hesitated, sir, to leave you this book, the sad child of a 'nuit d'Idumée.' I should have liked to have been with you to protect it by saying a few words, as an apology for offering you this prose at a time when your name alone was known to me. I have since read your poems (less than two months ago) and you taught me shame for my book and the boredom of poetry, for you have sung all the lines I should have dreamt of writing." (February 5, 1891. *Collection Henri Mondor.*) Mallarmé, who called Gide "the rare Intellectual," invited him to his home in the rue de Rome, "before anyone else, on Tuesday evening, a little before eight, so that we can speak better together." Also with regard to *Les Cahiers d'André Walter,* Maeterlinck wrote: "This sad and marvelous breviary for virgins" is, "at certain times, as eternal as the *Imitation.*" And Henri de Régnier, very interested by the work, invited Gide "to go with him to Monsieur de Heredia's."

[28] Barrès' novel *Un Homme libre,* or *A Free Man,* was published in 1889.

[29] This banquet, given in honor of Moréas, who himself initiated it on the occasion of the publication of his *Pélerin passionné,* took place on February 2, 1891, at the house of the Learned Societies, with Mallarmé presiding. Because of the 94 guests at dinner, a liveliness that came close to disorder, and many toasts, it caused a great stir. This, for example, was Mallarmé's toast:

"To Jean Moréas

"who is the first to make a meal the outcome of a book of poetry (a favorable omen), and has brought together to celebrate *Le Pélerin passioné,* all the auroral young men and some of their ancestors.

"This toast

"in the name of our dear absent Verlaine, the comrade Arts and several of the Press, in my own, with all my heart."

Thank you for your letter: my alacrity in answering it testifies to the pleasure it gave me. I love your poem not as the best but as the most "for me." I should imagine a piece—short—but *really* "of *silence,*" that would seem no more than a musical flow in which the initiated reader would group the sensitive notes according to his inner emotions—or like a useless lyre, silent and completely lifeless, in which breath would circulate, during the reading aloud, provoking in the relation of the strings the melodious outbreak of abstruse harmonies. That must be done. Your piece comes near to it but I still feel the *phrases* too much. I know nothing about your *Narcisse,* except what Louis has told me, that is, all the good in the world.

Would you be as kind as you have been up to now and copy it down for me—and I shall do the same for you for the Trouble I shall give you in rewriting your poems yet again. And one more favor: when you send them to me, please set them out on a separate sheet of paper. I like the idea of being able to assemble them afterward.

I should like to get into your personal life somewhat and to be led there by you yourself. All my efforts to please are meant only for that sentimental initiation. Tell me, for example, whether you believe that love is bearable—and how; or avoidable—and how; or if it is desirable. But speak to me: I assure you that a few pages of my book will give me away to you more than numerous letters would give you away to me. And I am sometimes terrified at thus prostituting my poor virgin soul in the shop windows at every crossroads.

> May grace be within you.
> A. Gide

13. *Paul Valéry to André Gide*

February 15, 1891 [in Gide's handwriting]

I am so pleased with your happiness, my friend; it is the feeling of strength and the radiance of inner light. Something joyous and readily bright rises in you like the stem of a lily climbing to the lips of the sun. But you are very wicked indeed to make me desire for so long the complete possession of your soul through your book. It almost saddens me to realize that it is known to others before I have known it. At all events, I can guess at the salutary effect of your pride at seeing it greeted with such eminent approval. Real life, that consisting of successful and abundant creation, and of chosen victories, is opening up before you, the pure road is flowering under your magnificent stride. How does it make you feel? Tell me about it at length. . . . I hear the sound of a piano near me, vaguely tormenting and troubling me with delights. Why?

Louis sent me his portrait. He is very handsome, like the priest of a fabulous religion whose prayers would be the most beautiful poems in the world. When will we have our effigy? . . .

Well, I am sending you, since you want it, this *Narcisse* who weeps in the blue woods . . . as far from the sad and beautiful young man I had dreamed of as one could imagine. I wrote this poem, to order, as you know, in two days or six hours' time, and I am sorry about it. It will start off *La Conque* in a miserable way, and I will blush with embarrassment . . . Tell me as frankly as you once spoke under the cypresses and terebinths of this moonlit part of the world which I, myself, have not forgotten—tell me what you think of it.

I am sending you the only copy I have, for I burned my rough draft so as not to see it again except in print.

Adieu, my friend.

Your uncle[30] had the goodness to invite me to an evening reception for students which he gave recently. The memory of you inevitably haunted me among so many strangers who interested me not at all. And again I saw on a table the horrible *Princesse Maleine*,[31] whose escaping terror in some measure seized me anew.

Once more adieu.

> ". . . Here is the twilight."
> P. Valéry

14. *Paul Valéry to André Gide*

[end of February, 1891]

Busy, no doubt, with the publication of the Book, you have kept silent, my dear friend, for twenty-five days . . .

It is fine to love silence and to express it in mysterious lines, but to love it that much, enough to stop writing . . .

> P.-A. Valéry

15. *André Gide to Paul Valéry*

Paris, Sunday morning, March 1 [1891]

Your quietly reproachful note arrived, dear friend, at just the right moment this Sunday, at a time when I can write to you: a heavy cold is keeping me in the house, at least until noon, and last evening, out of foresight, I got rid of some minor correspondence with tradesmen.

I am absolutely ashamed at having provoked your reproaches, for I find it bitter to think that you could have believed I had forgotten. I am sending you, to counter that unfortunate thought, the beginnings of a

---

[30] Charles Gide.
[31] A poetic drama, written in the purest symbolist spirit, which in 1889 made Maeterlinck famous.

letter which is already old and which each day I vainly tried to finish.[32]
I am starting afresh on another, for one cannot, says the Gospel, sew
new pieces of cloth on an old garment without tearing the materials—
then again, I am already completely changed! . . .

On the advice of Barrès, I had been to see a few people, and all
except one were so charming that in no way was I sorry for my visits:
yet one person was enough, one of the last, who perhaps never
suspected the resentment he caused in me—then also, the fatigue—and
the boredom—and heavens knows what else . . . in short, a deplorable disgust for the whole business came over me so strongly that I
dropped all the rest of it—then my pride, at feeling bigger than they,
was awakened, although by some Bohemian, and was excited yet again
by a word from Henri de Régnier: "Go to see Vanor? [33] but he would
talk about it all his life!" and as, still laughing, I was speaking to him of
what had begun to disgust me so strongly (those few visits to spread
the news of my book): "In literature, you understand, one must not be
polite: politeness leads to involvement."

Well now I have had enough; I am dropping the whole affair, and
that's that—but I am so weary of this ridiculous fluttering about that I
could cry and I want to harness myself to some new tasks.

And now let us speak of other things: I am rereading for the ?th time
your *Narcisse:* I must admit to you that I like it but not without
reservation as I do some of your other pieces, perhaps because that sort
of subject treated by you gave promise of slower delights and because
certain exquisite lines recalled that promise and made one regret their
isolation in this piece:

> J'entends les herbes d'or grandir dans l'ombre sainte
> . . . Si la fontaine claire est par la nuit éteinte—
> Mes lentes mains dans l'or adorable se lassent—

and many others—and particularly the quatrain:

> Adieu! reflet perdu sous l'onde calme et close.
> Narcisse, l'heure ultime est un tendre parfum
> Au cœur suave. Effeuille aux mânes du défunt
> Sur ce glauque tombeau la funérale rose.

That's perfect: it pleases me to write them out again, and their
perfection impels me to make some adjoining criticism:
"Ainsi, dans les roseaux harmonieux jeté" smacks a bit too much of

[32] For the text of this unfinished letter, see below, Letter 16.
[33] Georges Vanor, pseudonym of Georges Van Ormelingen, a regular visitor at
Mallarmé's Tuesdays, the author of a pamphlet on *L'Art symboliste,* with a preface
by Paul Adam, and of one lyrical work, *Les Paradis.*

Hérodiade at the mirror—let it be said in passing. In general the lines in this long piece seem to me to have in some measure been written one by one and not, as would be fitting, four by four: in my opinion, several of today's poets have somewhat the same failing of writing a succession of beautiful lines rather than a sequence of them: one replaces the other and often negates (harmonically speaking) the previous one. The ever-growing desire for a perfection of form and sound leads to carving out each line specially and doing damage to the entire period: it was by means of opposing failings and qualities that poets like Lamartine or Corneille in *L'Imitation* managed, with inane and fuzzy lines, to fill a stanza of four or six alexandrines with a sustained inspiration of perfectly even intensity and harmony. It meant nothing, and each line was separately unquotable, but as a whole it took on a superb swinging balance—sometimes.

Sunday evening

Do excuse this rigmarole which seems to be about you and in fact is but in connection with you. To come back to *Narcisse,* I might say also that I regret the overdiversity of impressions, or rather, of illuminations; it lacks somewhat a unity of lighting, and one is no longer certain, owing to an absence of shadows, whence comes the daylight, the nocturnal brightness: because of that somewhat too-even atmosphere (take that as symbolically as possible, or don't take it at all), it appears somewhat fragmentary; every vision seems brief and is modulated before being melodiously spread out; with that number of lines, I feel that you might have evoked slower images. I am afraid that you were rather in a hurry to write it, and if that's true, you must have the courage to rewrite it: the piece is worth it, and I know you well enough to hope for an exquisite poem as a result: you would take long hours to do it in, hours completely haunted and solitary in the enchantment of the one dream: that would be necessary for the reflective unity of Narcissus in his watery dream. (I am thinking of *lympha fugax,*[34] which I immediately find enchanting.)

To act like a *normalien* * right to the end, excuse me for finding altogether below your level:

> Que je déplore ton éclat fatal et pur—
> . . . . bras . . . . *dont les gestes sont purs.*

But do believe at least that I take the liberty of making such criticism only because in you, whom I feel can do exquisite things, all flaws seem worse.

[34] Horace, *Odes,* II, III, 12.
* *Translator's note:* A student at the Ecole Normale Supérieure.

And now, how will I dare send you my piece? [35] Well, my excuse is that—since the first twenty lines of two years ago—these are the first I have written. I shall send it to you, for it is not likely to come out in the first issue of *La Conque:* Leconte de Lisle takes up too much space.[36]

                              Monday morning

I live in expectation, as I did before writing *André Walter,* I live in the expectation of a new time of work. I have great fears of having lost that vigor for producing which I had when I was younger, and which was so violent it astounds me today—and what terrifies me about myself in that respect is that I admire others too much without the constant proud desire "to do better," which the artist should never renounce. I admire too much and almost lazily, and I admire *André Walter* in the same way, with the retrospective lassitude of having been the one who built a dream of that sort. Do you know that I then had admirable confidence, I was ready to believe in the future. Later on, I shall again talk about those days, for things seemed to me beautiful. And now I want to go after even more arduous victories, for I fear that while at rest, my powers will become sluggish. Besides, daily contact with brute realities (beautiful, too, and alas!) made me lose faith in the dream, the magic faith, the "proof" of things one does not see, as the apostle said. My poor soul, which at first thought it was alone, and was intoxicated by its solitude—and which peopled its solitude with visions that broke out of itself—now it quivers at outer delights, for they too are joyous, it quivers and vainly seeks refuge, in some Thebaid or other, from the ravishing assault of the outside world—which surrounds it, poor little thing!

Ah! if it were possible, I should like the clear faith of my childhood—again!

I should like there to be between us [a missing word, no doubt]—and I have told it to you already—above literature: and that is why—and out of delicate coquetry—I am not sending you my book, and also perhaps out of fear that within you the book will spoil the dream of the book—say out of pride, if you choose. And then also out of a desire for strangeness—and I don't love you any less for it—but I am still somewhat afraid that you would love me less for it once you have read it—this book. All the same, if you were to happen upon it—this book—I consent to your taking it, but as a book by someone else, by a stranger whom one is not likely to see, as a work from beyond the grave by a deceased André Walter. Then in Paris, when you come, I will write you a lovely dedication.

[35] *Nuit de prière.*

[36] Leconte de Lisle started off the first issue of *La Conque* with a long poem: *Soleils! Poussières d'or . . .*

Adieu, my sweet friend, write to me as I write to you—at length; and speak to me of you and me as I speak of you and me to you, or still more intimately, for you can be certain that I will outdo that intimacy in my answers.

And don't stay too angry with me, for I fret terribly at the thought of displeasing you.

Truly your friend,
André Gide

Excuse me for sending you the rough draft of my piece, I have no time to recopy it; in *La Conque* the entire beginning will be omitted. The piece begins with "L'azur s'est attristé, etc." *

16. *André Gide to Paul Valéry*

[Included with Gide's letter of March 1, 1891, was this unfinished letter written previously and never sent. We shall place it here despite its earlier date.]

Tuesday 24 [February, 1891]

Dear friend,

Oh how hateful a friend is a friend who promotes a book! Since my last letter, especially during the last week, I have had nothing but practical thoughts (or almost), and my beautiful soul has become so self-seeking and so low that from close to I think I would give you the impression of a deplorable scoundrel. Louis finds me depraved, I find myself worse than that, and in reaction I have never had a more violent desire to see once again your cerulean, poet's conscience. I assure you that the tasks I'm gambling with today come so unnaturally to me that I need a will more assertive and cruel than that which it took to write an entire book; but the fear of reproaching myself in the future for not having pushed my luck right to the end and for having backed away from the little bruises on my childish conscience saves me from flinching, and also the feeling, which grows stronger each day, that my weariness is so great, I need all my youthful enthusiasm, and all my naïveté about wicked men, to bow down to them in this way; and that I would never again be capable of such foul deeds, and that my poor bruised soul, another time, alas! would be too disgusted with them. And so, as much so as not to have to do it again as out of mad ambition, out of a concern for conquering—Jesuitical, as Barrès would have it— my eyes drop no lower than that fixed goal of dazzling glory which my boundless pride will have so desired! And its dazzle blinds me to this unpleasant promiscuity.

* *Translator's note:* Included with this letter was the poem *Nuit de prière,* which was to appear in *La Conque* with minor changes and the definitive title *Nuit d'Idumée.*

I will not lower myself twice to seek glory, and if I don't seize it today, then I shall wait until it comes.

. . . .

[André Gide]

17. *Paul Valéry to André Gide*

March 6, 1891

Yesterday, at midnight, I called you wicked and cruel, sir, for the person who knew you, this winter, is not yet dead in me. . . .

To believe in You, to make your existence into a serene habit of one's soul, to choose your thought intuitively as an abode perfumed with violets and silence in which to abide during the choice hours when one dreams; then to go to the home of an almost unknown person, and to find on the table *André Walter* gallantly dedicated, when you refuse it to me; and, owing to M. Redonnel's [37] kindness, to open it for a minute to a page which one feels has been written for one's self, yes, for one's self, one predestined night (you know, that sentence, in very musical infinitives, which speaks of a pensive stroll . . . ?). And must one not repeat: wicked!

Wicked creature, you are the one who is forgetting the night, and I am most offended.

. . . So I am not to smell the funerary and tender fragrance of that dead youth, and this first book which you have twice concealed from me will be unknown for how much longer! to me?

Your denial, André, came before the cock had scarcely crowed!

Or I imagine, rather, that you think I am unworthy. Better, no doubt, that your musical story of a soul in a shroud be told to the "others," to the little critics of *La Plume* and similar periodicals! . . .

Yesterday, at midnight, "upon a midnight dreary," prostrate in an armchair, and surrounded by a languid veil of smoke, the raven that haunts me returned because of you and I was sad because of you.

Sad because of you! put that well in your mind! but sad also because of me! Sad (and this baleful refrain is called for) not to have been able to give you real confidence, and not to have been able, perhaps, to raise myself in your thoughts a bit higher than a little *Bérénice*.[38] Sad also at having forgotten what courage is, and at seeing the work I somewhat desired already useless and come to ruin. The house is no longer visited by hope, and the arm drops in terror. Gone is even the former interest in coming to Paris! . . . Why? To be a new unknown on that sickly review? And for all the glory to be able to shake five hundred wary

[37] Paul Redonnel was editorial secretary of *La Plume*. He lived in Montpellier, where he edited *La Chimère*.

[38] An allusion to Maurice Barrès' novel *Le Jardin de Bérénice*, published in 1891.

hands in the cafés? I who have never dreamed of having the affection of more than about ten analogous hearts, scattered among men whom I would not know. I for whom poetry was to be the supreme priesthood of an exquisite religion and as strait as the arms of the Christus are strait! . . .

A while back I told Louis my dream:

On the shores of the very gentle and virginal sea, to haunt the old cloister of Mont-Saint-Michel and to grow salted roses in the low and tender gardens with artists touched by emotion and weary. To dream no longer of books—but of boundless hours, to sit in a pure cell with the sound of the Ocean, one's knees still bruised by prayer and one's brow still burning from the blessing in the chapel. There, one sole bell would ring out, and for eternity one would spend the last glimmerings of one's art in slowly finding the words for a psalm to the Virgin, so as to bequeath it, and so that one's survivors would sing it for a long time still, anonymous, suave, lost in the bundles of those left us by the mystical centuries. The terraces gently lend themselves to monastic dialogues, to the humble modesty of monastic dialogues!

Don't be vexed with me for this silent desire so often repeated in my monotonous letters. One is so alone that the same thoughts are always there!

Adieu. This letter is short, but how is one to write? Guess everything it hides. Adieu. You know what I hope for.   P.

18. *André Gide to Paul Valéry*

Paris [P. March 8, 1891]

Dear Valéry,

I like you tremendously. I am writing to you with India ink on Japanese vellum—and well, it can't be helped, I am sending you my book: by God, I just can't bear not to. I love your melancholy quarrels: the suavity of your reproaches consoles me for deserving them—do you think then that in a few months more, after some ten languid letters more, I will not be able to have any further secrets from your soul?

Before receiving your letter, I was sad and exalted, I am writing to you at once.

You are right, my friend, I no longer hope that you will come to Paris. Life here is not for real poets—now I have only selfish reasons for hoping that you will come, near me, far from all the din, even that of the coteries, solitary and contemplative, and we would leave those around us to their agitation.

I wanted to see this sad world a little, and I am already alarmingly nostalgic for my dream: I would have wept from boredom this evening without the music which for two hours has lulled that boredom with monotonous and wild lullabies. Never have I felt so strongly the imperious joy of the solitary dream, as at the piano, in the proud echo of the music, of the solitudes of others, remembered from long past, exalting the intoxication that I found in my own. Poe, Delacroix, Schumann, and all the great men, actually, even in the midst of crowds—and that is what creates the sobs in their works, more than the vain loves of women; and that is what makes them wrap themselves superbly in the irony of dandyism, seek sleep for their thoughts in the stupor of intoxication—and that is what gives Byron that grandeur, at least, of having made his way alone, throughout the entire world, bearing everywhere the gigantic boredom of his solitude.

What madness came over me, wanting to escape from it? I have seen but very little of this world, but I am already so sad about it I could cry. Those cafés you speak about, those chaps who hold out their wary hands—it's sickening, I assure you. And this afternoon at Heredia's! [39] I was really terrified by that ferocious scramble known as—"the literary world"? They furiously eat each other up. Ah! what selfish hate one feels in those souls. . . . Everything becomes a matter of journalism and the making of reputations—Heredia's salon is like an advertising agency—and that is why Louis and de Régnier took me there—but today I had quite enough—I'll wager you could not stand it either—and I really admire Louis, who leaves one gathering only to go to another, and at the end of the day counts up the number of hands he has shaken. When the world is not as one dreams it, one must dream it just as one wants it, that's what I have come back to, for it is from there that I took off. During that time, I had a few beautiful illusions—I believed that the young people of today were capable of great enthusiasm and that I was born to lead it [*sic*]—I saw my book as a repetition of *Hernani;* but since 1830, brains have cooled down terribly, one no longer gets carried away, one calculates—and I cannot get over that, for otherwise this symbolic renaissance, of all of them, would have been a joy to live through.

So I am again taking refuge in studious solitude, but a solitude which this time is lighted up by the reflection of close and endearing friendships—and by yours more than ever, sweet Ambroise—and the whole previous discourse was to tell you that.

Yet the chats with Mallarmé and Sully Prudhomme in particular are still dear to me—and with a few other friends, three perhaps, if I count

[39] José-Maria de Heredia had been living since 1885 on 11 *bis* rue Balzac, in a huge apartment where he received on Saturdays from three o'clock on. The gatherings, affable but noisy, differed greatly from those at Mallarmé's on Tuesdays. Among those who met there were Leconte de Lisle and Sully Prudhomme, Henry Bordeaux, Henri de Régnier, Louis Bertrand, Jean Psichari, Albert Samain, Pierre Louÿs, A.-Ferdinand Hérold, R. de Bonnières, Henri Mazel, and Dr. J.-C. Mardrus.

correctly—one in particular,[40] who fell in love with you upon hearing me read a few of your poems! (*Le Jeune Prêtre, Le Bois amical*) [41] and whom I will introduce you to if you come. And then, to go back in time, a few I love also because they were alone—and I really feel that without that sentimental anachronism we should have tasted together that friendship, that ineffable friendship, instead of my running after their remains, like Pollux after Castor's: Delacroix, Schumann, Flaubert, Fromentin, Michelet—that's all, I think. You will understand also, after you have read my book, that I have had close friendships so secret that after having lost them one is forever in mourning. Let us both at least take advantage of the fact that we are only separated by space— and I send you my book. I have great fears that my prose will not quite please you, and I like our friendship enough so that I shall be highly vexed at my book if it upsets it, however little.

At least, write to me *at great length* in answer, or else I shall believe all sorts of tiresome things.

Au revoir; I like you very much, but quarrel with me anyway: it shows me that you like me a little, and I need to know it.

André Gide

19. *Paul Valéry to André Gide*

Wednesday [March 11, 1891]

Do you remember that pale evening when, standing in the hotel room [42] that was glorified both by your books and by you, you read me some poems?

---

[40] Probably the young Camille Mauclair or André Walckenaër.

[41] *Le Jeune Prêtre* and *Le Bois amical* were to be published in the August 1, 1891, and January 1, 1892, issues of *La Conque,* respectively. Valéry, on the advice of Pierre Louÿs, included in his first letter to Mallarmé *Le Jeune Prêtre* and *La Suave Agonie* (which was published in the June 1, 1891, issue of *La Conque*). A few days before, Pierre Louÿs had given Mallarmé one of Valéry's poems, *Pour la Nuit,* and according to him (in a letter to Valéry of October 15, 1890), Mallarmé, upon reading it, exclaimed: "Ah! It is very good. . . . He is a poet, there is not the shadow of a doubt. . . . Great musical subtlety," and asked to see others. On Louÿs' suggestion, Valéry sent more of his poems to Mallarmé, with a letter that began: "Dear Master, a young man lost in the depths of the provinces, who by the chance discoveries of some rare fragments in reviews had the possibility of guessing the secret splendor of your works, dares introduce himself to you . . ." Mallarmé's answer was immediate: "My Dear Poet, the gift of subtle analogy, along with the adequate music, you surely have that, which is everything. I had said that to our friend M. Louis; and say it again, before your brief and rich poems. As for advice, nothing can give it but solitude and I envy yours, as I recall hours of youth in the provinces somewhere near where you are, hours I shall never find again." (Letters quoted by Henri Mondor in "Le Premier Entretien Mallarmé-Valéry," in "Valéry vivant," *Cahiers du Sud,* 1946.)

[42] André Gide's hotel room during his stay in Montpellier in December, 1890.

In your book, I have come upon the very same impression of obscure peace, yet of illumination and of the loftiest sadness.

I had never felt any poetry as I did that which you deigned to read to me—that evening in December.

Never did I so keenly feel my own inner existence and the painful youth of an intellectual—as in your *André Walter*.

O thank you for your beginnings in a minor mode, the unexpected beginnings of exquisite pages, they seem to be words that might already have begun behind the veil—then, a mysterious breeze rends it— . . . and you speak.

You were the first to think of establishing that thematic of dreams: there, a resounding sentence from Flaubert, a Baudelairian line that gleams out—then a few muted chords, and you develop the accompaniment and the arpeggios latent in your mind—often an accompaniment of tears, and arpeggios of a higher and seraphic and also nuptial tenderness.

The broken music, the broken wing, leaps and languishes, bottomless words open up like chasms, others are chapels. Then pages—at one go—that even now must be quoted completely because they are beautiful and new—how far you are, O happiness, from the sycophancy and artful skill of Barrès!

And all the casuistry of our powerless hearts (of mine), how you weigh it, how it is blasted by phrases. Art, love, faith, my poor *self* struggles among those great phantoms whose reality grows pale. And then out of your book soars: One must create, One must love, One must believe.

The symbolic garden opens at our step, blooming, fragrant. We leave it no more. But what to pick? To be André Walter in order to pick at once the three flowers, the lotus, the rose, and the lily! and to carry in our perishable being the three beings, Allain, Emmanuèle, Spinoza! [43] But then does he go mad? *He must not have gone mad.* Perhaps! . . .

Higher still. The icy peak. At its foot. Everything. The boundlessness of religions, the scope of philosophies, the Ocean of loving purely. Your hand drew me up there. Thank you again. And so: "All this is yours—if you wish to love me.— Yes, O lord."

And we shall love you in your book for those kingdoms you bestow upon us, and for those faintly perceived grandeurs.

Rain "on the summer dust": all ignorant flesh sheds and stirs. The emanations intoxicate it, everything within one stretches—but here is the solemn sunset, "it is the time when oxen come to drink." Everything

---

[43] Allusions to the three main characters of *Les Cahiers d'André Walter*.

rises. Boundless adoration of the evening. Nothing left but silent organs in the soul.

Night of white stars—all is purified. It is universal understanding, the conscious divinity which descends from the heavenly bodies onto the predestined human head, crowning it. Those are your landscapes.

Oh when, when (never perhaps?) will I retell you your work, on the banks of the Seine,—behind a high church?

This evening, go out. Look at the star Sirius burning with so much mystery and promise—yet somewhat fatal. I, too, shall look at it—this evening.

Adieu.

P.-A. Valéry

P. S. A thousand thanks for your last note, whose beginning terrified me the least bit. You are enchanting, I am a little annoyed at having dedicated *Le Paradoxe* to you, it is so commonplace.*

20. André Gide to Paul Valéry

[Paris], Thursday [P. March 21, 1891]

I looked for Sirius, the friendly star that you too were watching;—I looked for Sirius and did not find it: a bank of clouds was hiding its distant gleam.

"If you were to love me?"— . . . and you answer "Yes!"—it is an absolute that terrifies me. . . . What do you know of it yourself? and until when? and to foresake each other . . . afterward?

All affection troubles me, for I don't relax in friendship, but want it to be ever more enduring, more profound, and more trusting—in a word, vigilant, and in me, painfully jealous, which often changes it into passion or (such is ours, is it not?) into a suprasensible and nearly mystical communion.

Is it necessary then that the idea of moral election and religion intrude, so that one sole form of worship with sacred rites makes the gestures parallel? and that one sole glimmer bids us take similar roads? Necessary also is that sweetness of knowing the other's soul to the very depths. Do you want that?

You now know all of mine, at least in one of its phases—for like the beautiful moon, it has its phases, my soul, and like the moon it constantly gravitates round some mysterious pole. But of you, what do I

* *Translator's note:* In a letter of March 11, 1891, Gide told Valéry that he had been shown an issue of the review *L'Ermitage* (actually that of March, 1891), and in it had discovered a poem by Valéry dedicated to him. That poem was *Le Paradoxe,* dedicated to Claude Moreau (the pseudonym of Pierre Louÿs) and to Bernard Durval (in other words, André Gide).

know? I know that your soul is precious and religious, but do I know the poles which from afar have led it in its course through immaterial space? or by means of what mathematical relations the curve of their [44] parabolas overlapped for a moment?

What will you think of this metaphysical jargon? To repeat, without metaphors, what you have doubtless intuitively understood from the preceding lines: I cannot be satisfied with an imperfect communion, and your letter is too exquisite not to make me wish for a surrender of your most intimate thoughts: in affection I suffer from all that the other hides from me—from me who can hide nothing.

Have you realized, Paul-Ambroise, that I shall soon see you again—I am joyous at that hope when I dream of everything we shall be able to say, during those shorter evenings when we shall make our way under the stars, now that we have smoothed the paths on which our minds will make their way together.

I shall come to Montpellier in a month and a half I think,—for my family, certainly, but a good deal for you also: that will be worth many letters—although yours are often more subtle in essence than improvised comments. Your last was more precious to me than any other I have received about my book, and I really believe that I should have written it for you alone, then you would have been the only one to love it, so happy am I that it pleases you.

You make me see André Walter greater indeed than I created him, for faced with the vision you evoke in your lines, I feel as far as you can feel from that "icy peak" on which you are writing it. I didn't dare believe that you would like him, my wild hero, and now I should be pleased if a little of that affection for him spread to a few others as well. In fact, I think that were my pride to be inflated a bit more, I should not even be able to do without ambition, and the "others," but I should then need to feel the esteem of someone like you. How much we shall have to talk over together!

Au revoir. I cannot write you any further, and I could not write you any earlier, in spite of how very much I wanted to: I find no time for anything.

Your friend,
André Gide

I almost forgot, so sure was I that I had already done so, to tell you how very good I thought your "paradox." I was unable to obtain it, as *L'Ermitage* [45] is nowhere on sale; I found it in my reading room and

---

[44] No doubt the souls of Gide and Valéry.

[45] *L'Ermitage*, a monthly literary review edited by Henri Mazel, was published for the first time on April 1, 1890. Paul Valéry published a poem, *Blanc*, in the

regret not being able to tell you the very sentences and the details that particularly interested me—but I could not take out the article.

Its form is truly admirable, especially the beginning, and that dream of harmony crystallized in unreal architecture which ends it.

Its form even highly astonished me, for I did not expect from you (you can see that I'm frank) such power in the third section.[46] In any case, I want to reread it, slowly and at home. I now hope for all manner of beautiful things from you. You have given me a ridiculous but very great desire to write an article myself, after Louis' and yours, one that would be "the same" although without any idea of redoing yours—and I may very possibly write it so that those three interviews on architecture would bring us together yet again.

André Gide

21. Paul Valéry to André Gide

This evening [May 8, 1891, in Gide's handwriting]

I await you, dear and noble friend, with an impatience to see you that no! you could not imagine.

I do not want to tell you once again of the boredom of my days and the deathly fear of my long nights, but I am horrible these days. Imagine, I am seeing blood.[47]

. . . Those soldiers who fired on the crowd, I envied them, and oh to fire on all the World! I detest the masses, and even more, the Others! Imagine that in my weak mind I pressed dry, to the point of boredom, many books and beautiful things, I am exhausting an art form in a quick spasm, and am so panic-stricken that I am haunted by a panorama of slaughter, and blinded by ravaged lights.

I almost wish for a monstrous war in which to flee amid the shock of a crazed and red Europe, in which to lose the memories of, and the

---

December, 1890, issue, and then his prose work *Le Paradoxe sur l'Architecte* in March, 1891. A new poem, *Celle qui sort de l'onde,* was to be published in June, and then *Intermède* in 1892.

[46] The third section—separated from the text of *Le Paradoxe*—became *Orphée,* in *La Conque.* Reworked once again, the poem was published much later in *Poésies de La Conque* (R. Davis, 1926), and then in *Poésies* (Gallimard, 1929, *Album de vers anciens*).

[47] This letter was inspired by the serious events that had just taken place at Fourmies, in northern France. Total or partial strikes broke out in a great number of textile centers, because of demands for an eight-hour day and a raise in salaries. At Fourmies, on May 1, a crowd of 4,000 people gathered in front of a spinning mill. As the gendarmes were greeted by hooting, the local authorities called out the troops. There were a few arrests. In the afternoon the crowd tried to free the prisoners. The troops fired on the demonstrators, killing about ten people, whose funerals took place on May 4 before 30,000 spectators. A general strike was then feared. Political and social tension reached a climax.

respect for, all writing and all dreams in real visions, the funereal stamping of plashing clogs and the earsplitting sound of rifle fire, and never to come back from it!

I don't know what blood is speaking in me, or what wolf of olden times yawns in my boredom, but I feel it there. Hideous mechanical literature sickens me, and all life is not worth the trouble. Does this barbarian surprise you?

Come then and awaken the ancient roses and drooping lilies, like an angel of old, a terrible and fragile angel of old, one breath of whom would have given rise to the pink awakening of the corollas in the gardens, and who, with the motions of his hands, would have caused the pale fragrances and chaotic leaves to obey, in Eden?

A star alights on a calyx, and shines through the thin silk of the petals, and throbs. Ah! how much night there is! To grasp it! To brood it in the hollow of childish hands and to laugh at holding it captive,—a Star! It is difficult. Well then! blood!

P.-A. Valéry

22. *André Gide to Paul Valéry*

In the morning [P. May 12, 1891]

Sweet Ambroise,

Can this warrior be you? ah! young priest, you dream of the impact of shuddering weapons as well, and it is blood-colored that you see the setting sun, when it turns crimson! . . .

Your letter is beautiful, and I am ashamed to then come and write you mere phrases. Words are no more than literature: and literature does not make one drunker than anything else. We have loved it as the most beautiful thing—at least so we thought then—and well, it's just too bad, we shall take our leave of it, without looking behind. We did not love it with an indispensable love, did we?—because it was It, and because it was Myself,—but rather because we found nothing better to indulge in.

How I love your letter! (the beginning at least,—for I love to hear you cry out, and I prefer your sentence, when it tears itself asunder, to your murmur)—and how I love you! I want to talk to you: I have need of it—a furious need which frets and rankles at the impossibility of being directly satisfied.

Our meeting is again delayed: * I am not even at Uzès but at Lafoux,[48] where my beast is taking plenty of showers.

---

* *Translator's note:* In a letter of May, 1891, Gide had explained to Valéry that their meeting would be put off for at least two weeks, because his grandmother, whom he had planned to visit in Montpellier, had returned to Uzès, a little town in the Gard, in southern France. Gide's father's family had originally come from there.

[48] A hydropathic resort in the Gard.

Everything is patched up at once, body and intellect, by great blasts of cold water; I feel better; I am again becoming religious and philosophical. What a strange machine is mine! is ours! . . . —your hallucinations are frightful: they got me dizzy at first.

Do you know that *I was absolutely unaware* of what was happening at Fourmies. You made me "read newspapers," O poet! I was unaware of everything. In a cowardly age such as this, the slightest jolt seems excessive, we have become more deeply conscious of the drama in meditating on the Gospels; now, it is *individuals* who are killed, and in spite of ourselves, it is individuals that one's imagination sees in the crowds. What lassitude! and how much they thus hurt us, those who Christianly drew *each one* gradually out of the multitude where he had at first lived intermingled! How very tiring it is to be forever on stage, before one's self and before God, if not before the others: all of us! we are all in the foreground, and our soul is no longer resigned to playing the humble part of an extra, they have so convinced each one that his salvation means something. Do not keep looking at us! we are weary of posturing.

It is your eyes that have inflated our pride in appearing. The comedy will be played out just as well without us, and we, poor buffoons, are not the ones who will make you more clearly *understand*. . . . How tiresome it is always to be the center of the world and always to bear round one's self that gravitation! What misery! When we have some faith, some love, we ourselves gravitate round the thing adored, in it we forget ourselves—and repose is in self-forgetfulness. To forget one's self, to adore . . . it was for that, was it not, that we have loved all that literature! . . . and we shall come back to it always. . . .

How I understand you, my friend! how I love you! Yes, we shall come back to it, you understand, back to that literature, in spite of ourselves, we shall fall back into it always. We have it "in our blood," like the germ of a disease, and we shall never be without it—alas! And it, in fact, is what troubles you with such desires for battle; like those who, tired of loving, want to bruise some bit of white flesh,—it is sadism, my friend,—literary sadism.

Oh, isn't it true that we could really relax, in some completely physical enthusiasm; brutal and frantic. To end up like an animal, without thinking, since that is tiring, and completely numbed through intoxication, since otherwise we would be afraid of dying; to end up with *the others,* in a pile, without speaking, since we would not know one another. But what vinegar and what gall it would take, O Lord, at that supreme moment, to put our soul to sleep!

Poor souls! Poor souls! how sick are our wills! Would it not be still better to go and cry in a church?

O Lord, teach us words of love rather than words of hate.

O Lord, teach us forgetfulness, and deliver us from the burden of our ponderous souls . . . O Lord!

Deliver us, O Lord, from all that literature.

Adieu, Paul-Ambroise.

You know, don't you, that I am your friend?   A. G.

Write to me at *Uzès, Gard* (that's all you need for the address).

23. *Paul Valéry to André Gide*

[May 30, 1891]

My dear runaway,

I stop, dreaming of exiles, and I pluck the pale petals of memories, and I throw them into the wind behind you.

You passed through like a smileful of things, which subsides directly as solemnity closes in.

I am bored, the hours dance round me. At times "where am I?" Truly the minutes are like flies buzzing in the heat. I read nothing but my textbooks. And I am stagnating in the smoke of eternal cigarettes.— Ruysbroek [49] haunts me and would tire me, of course. A few others as well.

Louÿs, who wrote to me again, is triumphing and holds us in contempt, both of us, in the name of Mallarmé—who is against *Là-Bas!* [50] Being of no importance, I no longer dare say a thing.

Who am I? . . .

He of obscure gardens where water dreams alone. What should I do? Quiver at everything!—And cherish creatures of the future in the contemplation of a few now, in the present. I like flowers too much not to see them elsewhere. And my lamp itself is a singular eye that tells me what is necessary. And so my dreams settle and fall asleep in the ultimate dazzle of the crystal pendants.

Then, in memories, things take the form of evangelical parables, and speak. Do remember then how, one evening, we must have eaten roses and sat on an empty tomb.[51] That says it all. The supreme altar of that religion which remains to us, under the trees, pronouncing dead words.

[49] Jean Van Ruysbroek (1294–1381), nicknamed "the Admirable One," wrote a considerable number of works in Flemish which were then translated into Latin by Surius. Ernest Hello, in 1869, published in Paris a first French translation of Ruysbroek's *Selected Works*. In 1891 Maurice Maeterlinck published, in Brussels, *L'Ornement des Noces spirituels,* or *The Splendor of the Spiritual Espousals.*

[50] J.-K. Huysmans' novel, published in 1891.

[51] An allusion to the time when, during the Christmas holidays, in 1890, Gide and Valéry sat on a tombstone in the Montpellier Botanical Gardens and chewed rose petals. This moment is often recalled in their letters.

. . . Or else, distant and celebrated, the Sea! It was like a promise of light and accessible to the feet of the prophets. All the constellations lost themselves in it; but in our perhaps all-embracing minds it was just a small glimmer, the whole of it! Someone's name takes up more space in our brains than the world; and the ingenuous hope, whose reflection vaguely illumines us like a beginning of dawn, dims, with its gleam, a star even as it tumbles down on a sun. That is why we declare that we must give ourselves an impossible goal, beyond spiritual conceptions, one that burns us from afar, without our daring to perceive it.

"Burn," meditate on that word in the mystical order. It's terrifying.

Good night.

P.-A. Valéry

24. *André Gide to Paul Valéry*

Uzès [P. June 11, 1891]

Still more news: * a periodical dinner is being organized, called the Seven Sages: [52] Robert de Bonnières, André de Guerne, Pierre Quillard, Bernard Lazare, Henri de Régnier, Ferdinand Hérold, Pierre Louÿs. That, I think, makes the seven of them, those sages, who—in order to be able to solemnly peripateticize after the meal—will take themselves off to distant Versailles, where they can chat near the marble statues, and prowl the yew-lined walks after austere agapes.

I am sending seventy-three lines to *La Conque.*[53]

Why were you not with me on my recent promenade? I would have shown you that poem and you would have removed the uncertainty that is bothering me, of knowing whether it is charming or worse. Why were you not at Les Baux? First of all, we would have chatted—and

---

* *Translator's note:* In a letter of June, 1891, Valéry wrote Gide the news that he had received a letter from Louÿs, and "more news," that the painter Félicien Rops (1833–1898) was doing a frontispiece for *La Conque.*

[52] Robert de Wierre de Bonnières (1850–1905) contributed to *Le Figaro* from 1880 to 1890 under the pseudonym of Janus. He was the author of *Monach* and *Le Baiser de Maïna.*

André de Guerne (1853–1912) wrote his *Poèmes d'Histoire de Religion* in the manner of Leconte de Lisle's *Poèmes barbares.*

Pierre Quillard (1864–1912), a poet and Hellenist, was the author of *La Fille aux mains coupées, La Lyre héroïque et dolente,* and translations from the Greek.

André-Ferdinand Hérold (1865–1940), poet, critic, and playwright, was a great friend of Pierre Louÿs, who in 1895 was to devote a study to him in *Le Victorieux.*

Bernard Lazare, whose real name was Lazare Bernard (1865–1903), was the author of authoritative works on Semitism and anti-Semitism, and contributed to various literary reviews.

[53] The long poem *La Promenade,* published in the December, 1891, issue of *La Conque.*

about so many things! have you read Psichari's article on modern prosody?[54] I should have liked to know what you thought of it. I am beginning to form very clear ideas in the matter of versification and soon, after having doubtless buried some courageous first attempts, in *La Conque,* I believe I shall venture to write a book of songs in a form that is mine and with which I am becoming acquainted. Perhaps I'm wrong.

Les Baux, you know, is *admirable,* and you lost a great deal:* perhaps the society of others terrifies you; in that case, I absolve you and I sympathize. But Les Baux is admirable; we should have meditated together on truly rare beauties. And, you know, in the narrow valley, courts of love were once held round the ladies—and there the troubadours sang amorous lays and romances.

You know, in those rocks, Dante conceived his hell, and the road lost in a dark grove—the *diritta via smarita* (is that how it's spelled?)

Since I last saw you I've read Rosny's *Le Termite*[55]—it is *very good;* you really should know it. I want to know Rosny: he wrote me a very fine letter about *Walter,* and I want to go and see him. I assure you that, along with Huysmans, he is one of the best as far as prose is concerned.

The other day, the day before yesterday, I was overcome by a fit of spleen, just as I was last summer. At such times I suffer from a wayward and fierce ennui: my soul is full of excessive and painful tenderness and of such pride, to boot, that all the tenderness falls back on itself, unused and turbulent. As a matter of fact, it is an almost lyrical state.

What else? The life of Auguste Comte is ridiculous: I had to give it up. I am finding rare delights in Taine's *La Littérature anglaise.*[56] I have five books which I'm reading at the same time.

I return to Paris next Monday, do remember it so that none of your letters go astray. Perhaps I shall send you a few words to Louis to mail, if I am able to resist the desire of immediately going to see him. Each day we send each other a short note, or the news of the day; it's sometimes rather pleasant.

And of *course* we are satanical,** young priest.

[54] Jean Psichari, son-in-law of Ernest Renan and father of Ernest Psichari, a linguist and grammarian, and the author of many works on linguistics.

* *Translator's note:* In a letter postmarked May 16, 1891, Valéry regretfully refused Gide's invitation to join him at Les Baux at the end of May, as he had to prepare for an exam and had to cope with some difficulties at home.

[55] A novel about literary customs, published in 1890.

[56] Hippolyte Taine's *L'Histoire de la littérature anglaise* was published in 1864.

** *Translator's note:* In his letter of June, 1891, Valéry wrote: "[Louis] claims that I am satanical because I like Huysmans."

Please give the Aesthete Coste[57] some very amiable greeting from me, and take care that he does not forget me.

With love, O bad priest.[58]

Your

André Gide

25. Paul Valéry to André Gide

Montpellier [June 15, 1891]

I was so proud, my dear friend, when I read in Maeterlinck's interview that very true and very glorious line which linked your *Cahiers* to what the Flemish tragic poet considers lofty works.[59]

Surely that makes up for a few stupid articles and scratches hidden in some poor rags. How much will you bet that your sales will be "good." I say this maliciously. I regret not being with you, for I should have enjoyed your very noble pride. You know that I like what is rare, concentrated, precious, crystalline, and *total,* and you can calculate what I am losing by your living so far away. You see, you began to give me a little pride—now, I *doze.*

I'm weary, what with a facial neurasthenia that bestows continual insomnia, and an impending exam in which I am bogged down. I'm almost blissful, for I feel as empty as the space beyond the System could wish. In my sleep I wrote a line that will be for *La Conque*— probably by itself for . . .

Assise la fileuse au bleu de la croisée . . .[60]

As for the dinner of the sages, one member I don't like is B. L.,[61] Hebrew and parodist.

[57] Albert Coste, a friend from Montpellier, a doctor, and the author of a study of the occult sciences. A solitary thinker, interested in but few men, he was to regret his faithful friend Valéry's departure for Paris.

[58] An allusion to Valéry's poem, *Le Jeune Prêtre,* or *The Young Priest,* who "weary of exegesis and liturgical chants" dreams of "battle and shuddering weapons."

[59] In March, 1891, following the publication of Maurice Barrès' *Le Jardin de Bérénice* and Moréas' *Le Pèlerin passionné,* Jules Huret began an "Inquiry on Literary Evolution" in *L'Echo de Paris,* asking the most famous men of letters of the time their opinion of symbolism. Huret went all the way to Ghent to question Maeterlinck, who revealed to him his literary preferences (*L'Echo de Paris,* June 15, 1891) and mentioned—after Villiers de L'Isle-Adam, Mallarmé, Verlaine, Barrès— Henri de Régnier, Vielé-Griffin, and Moréas, and added that his "other preferences" in France were: "Puvis de Chavannes, Baudelaire, Laforgue, *Les Cahiers d'André Walter* . . ."

[60] The first line of the poem *La Fileuse,* which, in its earliest form, was published in the September 1, 1891, issue of *La Conque.*

[61] Bernard Lazare.

Psichari's article is an approximation of questionable value. He is not yet the one who will write that still unwritten Poetics. Prosody is a kind of algebra: that is, the science of the variations of a fixed rhythm according to certain values given to the signs that compose it. A line is the equation which is correctly laid out when its solution is an equality, that is, a symmetry. Rhythm is a question of submultiples. What is admirable about it is that it uses and aesthetically exaggerates the unconscious obedience of our being—*all of it*—to measure and balance. There are people who walk, who digest *out of tune!* Dissonance and the minor mode have a quality of rending the heavens, for, in effect, the heavens should appear to us as free, outside all rhythm, incommensurable! I shall set down my ideas about that on paper one of these next days.

That is why I have the deplorable originality of preferring to everything (in the art of color and line) adornment such as the Egyptians, the Gothics, the Persians conceived it natively, etc., etc.

I am radically boring you with my monomaniacal dissertations. Some other time I shall pour it all out to Louis, for really it's unfair to take such advantage of one person.

The Aesthete Coste thanks you and returns your greeting. We are occultizing a bit more, following a certain lecture that appalled Montpellier. Imagine, a stern professor, Sabatier,[62] affirmed the visitation from the height of his Rostrum. All our provincial brains were terrorized to see the white rays descend into their dark imaginations. It was known and explained such a long time ago by the occultists. Beware of the Elementaries and the Ternary; will official Science now reread *Marie la Juive*[63] and explain the *Sepher Jezirah*[64]. . . .

I have in mind a prose poem that makes me regret not having Mallarmé's alchemical writing tools. Anyway, I shall try a kind of maieutics, which will perhaps be a Caesarean operation.

Adieu, I go back to my books, quaking. But before I do, I congratulate you again for having got the purest, the least courted, and the most desirable praise from such a secret mind as Maeterlinck.

P.-A. Valéry

---

[62] Auguste Sabatier, professor of the history of religion, dean of the Paris School of Protestant Theology, and the author of many works on theology, the history of religion, and exegesis.

[63] Probably Mary (or Miriam), the sister of Moses and Aaron, who, after the crossing of the Red Sea, was prompted by the prophetic spirit and composed the hymn that bears her name. Paul Valéry, the previous year, had written a poem entitled *Myriam,* which he was not to give to any review, and which was discovered by Pierre-Olivier Walzer (*La Poésie de Valéry*, Geneva, Pierre Cailler, 1953).

[64] Chaldeo-Semitic poetry.

26. André Gide to Paul Valéry

[P. June 17, 1891]

Your letter has come back to me from Uzès, my friend; I had left there two days early—I shall soon tell you why.

Your letter pleases me; you know, you are my most faithful, my dearest, my best correspondent. Thank you for your congratulations on Maeterlinck's implicit praise; indeed, I think it is the most precious perhaps, because it's the most discreet, the simplest, and has already "taken place." As for sales, I am almost afraid that they will be good, and although I passed in front of Perrin and Bailly [65] last evening, I didn't dare to go in, for fear of smiling in front of them, in spite of myself, on hearing them "inform me of the good news."

"I radically bore you". . . your phrase is unbearable; you always tell me that after you have interested me.

"Rhythm is a question of submultiples"—perfect; I shall remember that.

You must also tell me whether you are for or against the mute *e* (I mean, for or against eliminating it). Yesterday we discussed the question for a long hour, de Régnier and myself, and *we decided* that the mute *e* was the special and most essential music of French poetry. Eliminating it means only one thing: an insensitive ear.

I lived all of yesterday afternoon with Henri de Régnier.[66] He—charming, in his room and smoking, I—stiff in my frock coat; my shyness disappeared enough so that I could really enjoy him, and his conversation is exquisite. We know your sonnet *Orphée* by heart. Naturally, we talked about you. What was the strange row Louis kicked up about one of your pieces that was put in *L'Ermitage?* We don't understand it at all. I thought (and I thought rightly, didn't I?) that his virtuous and furious indignation was altogether his own and that you were not so vain or so proud as to spoil your joy because of the place you occupied in some review or other. Isn't it true that our joys should not be earthly in any way? They should be altogether pious.

Louis hurt me cruelly yesterday. It was in order to deliver my piece to him on the 15th, as he wanted me to, that I came back from Uzès two days early, and without my mother. You know how my feelings are; they paroxize [*sic*] themselves immediately. The desire I had to

[65] Gide's publishers.

[66] André Gide met Henri de Régnier regularly at Mallarmé's Tuesdays and José-Maria de Hérédia's Saturdays. "Among the young poets, Henri de Régnier was certainly the most outstanding," he was to write in *Si le Grain ne meurt*. Their very friendly relations were to "cool off" considerably as the result of a disparaging article that Gide, urged by the impetuous Vielé-Griffin, was to write and publish with regard to Régnier's novel *La Double Maîtresse*, in 1900. It was, he himself admitted, "a rather serious mistake in itself and because of its consequences."

see him again really burned my heart; I feel the same about friendship as I would about a mistress—(we have told each other such things, you know)—and I had invited him to dinner that first evening, being absolutely incapable of keeping up that hoax I had planned: staying in Paris without him knowing about it.

Instead of finding Louis himself at the house when I got back at seven, I found a letter from him. He informed me that he was dining in town and added "besides, do not come and annoy me now, I am completely involved in taking my degree" etc.[67]

I could not sleep all night; such things pain me, as if they had been done by a mistress.

As soon as I got up yesterday morning, however, I went there. He received me with his fine smile, as a result of which I am always powerless and I forgive. He told me that I was absurd to interpret his letter in that way: "don't I know him better, must all that be taken seriously? etc." Finally, as I wanted nothing more than to smile, I smiled, but the wicked creature added: "Anyway, I can only give you a few minutes, for I have work to do at the Sorbonne." But as he managed to have me admire some new books he pulled out of his library, those "few" minutes were an hour and a half.

We left together and the time passed (Oh the sweetness of intimacies!) hearing him run down Huysmans to the advantage of Michelet's *La Sorcière*,[68] etc.

He told me about their dinner at Versailles—it's awfully good of you to exclude B. L.[69] alone. Régnier is the only one of them all, I find, who is a bit of a sage—a bit decent. In fact, he is the only one who found an excuse for not going. The six others strolled about in the paths of the great park—solitary and frosty.* And do you know how those gentle-

---

[67] The entire letter from Pierre Louÿs reads as follows: "June 16, 1891. My dear Friend, as my brother and I find it absolutely impossible to understand your card, it is hardly possible for us to agree on what it means. Is your piece arriving, or are you arriving, or is one arriving carrying the other? In the event that it should be you, I should regret it because I am dining in town. And the rest of my evening is taken until eight in the morning. Besides, do not come and annoy me at this time. I am completely involved in taking my degree [*license*] and no one sees me anywhere but at the Sorbonne. *Vale.* P. L." (Quoted by Paul Iseler, in *Les Débuts d'André Gide vus par Pierre Louÿs,* Sagittaire, 1937.) On the bottom of that letter, André Gide had written: "This is the answer to a letter I wrote to Pierre Louÿs informing him of my arrival after a month and a half away. I had invited him to dinner one of the first evenings and I had such a strong desire to see him again that I had hastened my departure, moved it up two days, for the sole pleasure of seeing him again earlier." This was but one of the episodes in the often stormy friendship between the two poets, until they finally broke off relations in 1895.

[68] Published in Paris in 1862.

[69] Bernard Lazare.

* *Translator's note:* "solitaire et glacé," from Verlaine's *Colloque sentimental.*

men, those littérateurs, spent their time? Using blunt pencils, they covered the beautiful white vases round the fountains with two hearts pierced with an arrow, under two names which they wrote out: Vincent d'Indy and Haraucourt[70] (this is true, it appears)—then in huge capital letters, the name of PSICHARI—under all the statues. It was Hérold and de Bonnières who conceived those aesthetic pleasures.

Then Louis spoke to me of you; he is vexed with you for not proclaiming Heredia and de Lisle and claims that you, too, see no more than one wall of the temple—the one offstage—and he finds you *"monotonous."*

Moreover, he is now carried away by young Camille Mauclair,[71] whom he recently *discovered*. (He's the one who devoted a charming article to me in *La Revue indépendante*.) Did he speak to you about him? I shouldn't think so, but it is obvious that we are on the wane. As for me, he gave me to understand that the spot reserved for the piece he asked me to write was taken by this so-called Mauclair and that I should have to be published in a future issue. But as my piece pleased him, there is some question of ousting the great Hollande[72] for me—I think—and I don't know if I want that very much. But if he does that for me, it is "on condition," he says, that I not open his last letter, which should come back to me from Uzès. It appears that it's the only one he has written me that is a bit confidential; he was sorry about it directly and begged me not to read it. I received it last night: I have it here next to me, I have not opened it, I don't even have a desire to open it. Besides, I have the sickening feeling that, in this mysterious letter, it would be the *same thing all over again*. Even in the envelope it seems esoteric only on the outside.

Despite all that, I love Louis as I could not help but love someone with whom I have shared all the first virginal dreams. I feel I still have that tenderness for him—a weakness, perhaps, and that I continue to be his friend, but he can no longer be mine; on his side, my heart is now but a painful wound. He has already spoken to me several times like a bad mistress, and the bruise of last evening fell there where the scar tissue had hardly formed.

I expect no further joy from him; I now have nothing but trouble from him.

I am writing you this fateful letter because my soul is filled with gall; only a few months ago I should have accused myself and laid all the

---

[70] The poet and playwright Edmond Haraucourt (1865–1941).

[71] The poet, novelist, critic, and art historian, whose real name was Camille Faust (1872–1945). Mauclair was to contribute to many literary reviews, and, with Lugné-Poe, was to found the Théâtre de l'Œuvre in May, 1893.

[72] Eugène Hollande, a contributor to various literary reviews, particularly *La Conque* and *La Nouvelle Revue*.

blame on myself, but some arrogant pride or other has now taken hold of me, because in spite of all that, I feel *faithful?* And I know that my heart is right, and that it is all love, and that it has no hate, but only that it suffers very much.

Through the wall of the room I hear Bach being played, and those harmonies crystallize my sadness.

Moreover, I think that Louis is entirely unaware of all this; he thinks that nothing has changed, he never *looks*.

Last evening, I had gone out to visit the Laurens:[73] I didn't find them in, and during those nocturnal hours I roamed the streets. I wished that you were with me. Such hours are admirable, and one is astonished. The moon in the sky, but one must be us to see it, for the roofs of the houses hide it and yet the masses look at the sky, an azure parallelogram between the straight lines of the streets. The street lamps light up the sidewalks, prowled by the stale odors of sewers and drinks. The masses are outside, and if you could hear all the laughter! The courtesans are at the street corners, and all nature runs loose. At the open windows one sees women's profiles under lamp lights.

Louis made me disgusted with books. Still, there are other things besides books. The book is not *necessary*. And why must there be books? A question! as Coste would say.

It was the stupidity of the crowds and the vanity of false prophets that caused books to be useful. 'Tis a pity that they're useful.

For actually what good are they?

Hieroglyphics are *enough* to whisper the secrets of a whole science. All the rest is concession. One must not make concessions. Oh to remain pure!

Yet one prostitutes oneself because one was too fond of the others, who are weak, and out of love for them one *explains*.

I leave you now, to see Huysmans. I am sending you this letter, even though it is fateful and the spelling bad. Later on, you will realize that I was right to tell you all these things.

Write to me quickly, for I shall remain apprehensive until I have news of you, my friend, and I will speak to you of Huysmans.

André Gide

Mostly, work. You *must* pass your exam.[74]

---

[73] André Gide met Paul-Albert Laurens, father of Jean-Paul and Pierre Laurens, through his first cousin, Albert Démarest, who had studied with Laurens. Paul-Albert took the young André to his studio in the rue Notre-Dame-des-Champs, and there he met one of his former classmates, Jean-Paul Laurens. Their friendship sprang up again immediately, and in 1892 they took off together for North Africa.

[74] On June 17, 1891, Gide noted: "Wrote Paul Valéry a very long letter." This was the first time he had spoken of him in his *Journal*.

27. Paul Valéry to André Gide

Dear bruised heart, like a bleeding and intoxicated bird, your letter made me ache, and I want to preach.

Louis is a child, you are two children, love him as he is, with his wonderful fire and his will that wants to ravish Glory. Everything that offended you stems, in him, from a higher order. Lull his fever to sleep by the magic of your smiles and your caresses. May he be tranquil between your words. Carry him off to the fields and don't recite poetry. Beautiful poetry comes from the contempt one has for it—which grants it its only originality. He is too fond of the cubic form—it's the sphere that is perfect, the alpha and the omega—neither beginning nor end, the absolute, the Word. Apologize to him for me, I regret my over-sharp letter which struck at his idols. I myself suffer from being monotonous, and I shall soon beg his pardon.

Ah! are my adorations worth more than his! What are they, after all, but an association of ideas?

Well, then, let us all live in the green night to which I bid you come, hand in hand, without thinking that we are one another, but certain of our unity, our perfect fusion into one sole person.

What does Everything matter! Does total art need to appear: one puts it in a star and should gaze upon it! . . .

I have been sick these last days, very tired!

Speak to me of my very dear Huysmans,* whom, *in spite of everything,* I esteem and whom I want to know. What attaches me to him is the honesty of his transports and the integrity he shows. Also his evolution.

But how I regret what is happening! How unhappy I am to see a spirit of defiance growing between you. And because of literature! It's pitiful. It's absurd. Anyway, the heart is no more than absurdity,

---

[75] On the first page of the letter, Paul Valéry wrote, in blue pencil, like an epigraph: MERVEILLE! In the left-hand margin there are three stems of flowers—also in blue pencil—one of which, held by a hand, ends in a corolla at the same height as MERVEILLE.

* *Translator's note:* In a letter posted the same day, June 23, Gide wrote: "I saw Huysmans—it was one morning—I found him in shirtsleeves, trousers, and harsh blue waistcoat. Rather like . . . (?) for fifteen minutes I've been trying to find the words, but in vain. Nothing is more neutral than his face—somewhat bloated—and which shows nothing. We chatted for a while. I don't really know what of it to repeat to you—anecdotes, gossip, etc. Yet he did not displease me: what can one possibly say on a visit like that? One puts on a mask, one plays a part. Anyway, I shall go back there; he asked me to come back. He has extremely curious and beautiful engravings and woodwork—and a cat!"

paradox, and lies, but all of it with a fragrance come from the heavens, and that we don't see.

As for the mute *e,* the only rule of Poetry, the only touchstone, is the place of the mute letter. Remember what I told you about the mysterious flight. Louis did not want to believe me but *pacifique* was what was needed, or another such word.

Out of curiosity, do tell me what de Régnier said about me and WITHOUT RESERVE. I am not afraid of any judgment—as I don't exist.

The *Ermitage* story is very simple. Mazel, who has always been *perfect* to me, placed me where he could in an issue that had already been set up, so that I could be published in June. Anyway, the sonnet was less than ordinary. Louis himself and de Régnier had criticized it.[76]

That's all.

Let us watch the heavenly body Mauclair with interest as it rises to the sound of a bucoliast's flute. We extinguished planets will descend into the circle of perpetual occultation—at least we shall not be alone— until new conjunctures bring us back into sight, while the Star, which is victorious today, will dim and will rejoin the old Moons! . . . Hah! Hah! . . . Hah! (*Laughter.*)

P. Valéry

28. *André Gide to Paul Valéry*

June 29, 1891

This evening, Paul-Ambroise, I shall go and fetch the information you asked for * (yesterday was Sunday and I couldn't do it), and I shall send it to you with this letter which I am writing first, for fear of putting it off yet again. A short note from you, like that last one, will do for me. I know, or I like to believe, that you are busy working, and I am delighted by your zeal.

As for me, I should like to work more, but the outside world is constantly breaking in on my studious ecstasy; I know too many people already, and I want to win everyone's love; that takes up far too much time. Besides, some of them are charming; such as Mockel, such as de Régnier; I think, with respect to the latter, that we shall end by being strangely interested in one another. I saw him after my last letter to

---

[76] Paul Valéry's sonnet *Celle qui sort de l'onde* was published at the very end of the June, 1891, issue of *L'Ermitage,* right before the bibliography.

* *Translator's note:* In a note written on June 27, Valéry had asked for the address of a publishing house in Brussels; the price of *Pages*—a collection of twelve prose poems by Mallarmé; how to procure the June, 1891, issue of *Entretiens politiques et littéraires,* in which the last lines of *Orphée* were quoted and commented upon by Francis Vielé-Griffin; and whether it was *Les Moralités légendaires* he should read of Laforgue.

you, he came, then a sudden card asking me to come and spend the evening of that day with him. We read—excuse us—your *fileuse,* and henceforth I should like him to know you. He, too, prefers "Le jardin maintenant est plus pur sous," etc. What I like to sense in him is how well he "receives" you, how he feels you as someone Real. He told me that what pleased him in you was the feeling of necessary balance and the rhythmical correlations.

Some consider themselves very good because they write poetry with ease, as naturally as they breathe. But we understand, don't we, that the excellence of a poem lies in its resistance, when we want to extract it from its potential. Things must resist us when we want "to do" them, so that they can then resist time when it wants to undo them; they must be *tested.* (I shall give you bits of gold tested by fire.)

One thing distresses him (de Régnier) or, rather, would distress him if he didn't know that you were still so young and so happily undecided—the influence he senses that Mallarmé has on you.

I also read him the sonnet *La Belle au Bois,*[77] which I ridiculously thought you had translated from Provençal, so that both of us, in raptures over it, were astonished that M. de Belle-Visto was not better known.[78]

It was this morning, on rereading it again, that I loved it, and that I became aware of how stupid I was. I don't regret it, for it has shown me that no partiality was involved—when I admired your sonnets. I loved it without knowing that it was yours, that is, sincerely.

But you must have been astonished that I never mentioned it in my last note!

I saw the renowned Mauclair: he somewhat startled me by the look he had of wanting to snap up people's monads. He has, I think, a boisterous and scraggy soul. Yet I could be wrong. He is supposed to come to see me on Tuesday evening; I think he was born for Louis.

We have "had it out" together, Louis and I. We shall have to resign ourselves to being good companions together, or shallow friends; we shall suffer from trying to find any more in one another, because we are unable to give each other any more; the experiment has been made and both of us have suffered enough from it.

You speak to me of *Laforgue!* What happiness if you came to be

---

[77] Valéry's poem *La Belle au Bois dormant* was published in the June 15, 1891, issue of *La Cigale d'or* (a literary review, organ of the Félibrige—a group of poets who wrote in Provençal—established in Montpellier). It was reprinted by *La Conque* in November, 1891, and then incorporated in *L'Album de vers anciens* as *Au Bois dormant.*

[78] A contributor to *La Cigale d'or,* who very likely translated one of Valéry's poems into Provençal.

interested in him! How I love Laforgue! I read him every day: but not *Les Complaintes*. Read *Les Moralités* and especially, in *Notre-Dame la Lune*,[79] the selenic fauna and flora. I'm taking the liberty of sending you this little booklet—and don't thank me; in offering it to you, I give myself more pleasure than I do you. It is one of those books of silence, for two legendary characters like us who eat rose leaves together on old tombs. As for *Les Moralités*, I don't like *Pan et Syrinx*, but *Le Miracle des Roses!* but *Hamlet!* and the entire end of *Parsifal*, and the words of Andromède! However, I don't think you will like the jests under which he hides the shyness of his soul. But indeed you must read *Les Moralités*. Only wait until you have passed your exam or even until you come to Paris, and between then and now, meditate on *Notre-Dame la Lune*.

Do you kow that Laforgue lived at number 2 of our street, and that I should have loved him, and that I cannot help being a bit vexed with him for not having waited for me. Twenty-five years old! that is not an age to die!

As I am terribly afraid that Maeterlinck will have the same lack of *savoir-vivre*, I want to get to know him as soon as possible. I shall go to Belgium in about a week, then I hope to go up the Rhine, to see Cologne and Aix-la-Chapelle. I shall perhaps write my next letter to you from there.

As I write to you, the rain is washing the leaves in the gardens under my window, and the houses and noises grow faint. It would be so pleasant were we here together, saying nothing.

Au revoir. I like you very much.

André Gide

Here are the details: my friend Deman is at 14, rue d'Aremberg, Brussels.

Les Pages = 15 francs and is not out of print.

I am sending you the issue of *Entretiens* that interests you.

I received an astonishing letter from Huret: the youth of Belgium have written the best of articles about me. Do you know that my book is becoming established. Professors in the top form of the *lycée* hold me up to their schoolboys as the book typical of modern evolution (*sic!*) and piles of other things which I shall spare you.

Au revoir.

André Gide

My greetings to the dear aesthete Coste.

[79] Laforgue's *Les Moralités légendaires* was published in 1887. *L'Imitation de Notre-Dame la Lune*, a collection of poems, was published in 1886.

29. *Paul Valéry to André Gide*

[July 4, 1891, in Gide's handwriting]

Dominus, illuminatio mea.[80]

Speaking to you now is a new friend, dear André: the other soul is almost dead.

Do remember that vanished creature; I don't know what is to become of my poor and whirling entity.

For a long time I had accumulated my being. The substance of my thoughts had been devoutly chosen amidst the chaos of things. I had created myself incomplete but harmonic; weak but measured. And now unknown days have arrived.

One look has made me so stupid that I no longer exist:

I have lost my beautiful crystalline vision of the World, I am an ancient king; I am an exile from myself.

Ah! do you know what a dress is—even as a thing apart—especially apart from any oversimple desire of the flesh?

But only the dress and the eye. The idealist is dying. Would the world exist? . . .

And may I thank you for your great kindnesses. You are the best of men.

P.-A. Valéry

30. *André Gide to Paul Valéry*

[P. July 9, 1891]

Dear Ambroise,

You will, indeed, understand little by little that for me being loved is nothing, it is being preferred that I desire. It seems shameful to say, and that is why I have not said it until today, but little by little you will understand that my perpetual jealous anxiety is not so nasty as it would be in others; it is the "more than they do" that I desire, and I suffer while awaiting that impossibility. For me friendship is not a tranquil state.

That is why that sentence of yours which ends your letter: "You are the best of men," has made my tenderness thrill with joy.

Ah! I know very well that I am "the best of men," but to make it understood! There lies the suffering; and sometimes, like a prostitute, my poor soul flutters about, giving the impression of "Just see how agreeable I really am," and will thus be called a whore, until the day when, seeing that it is still persevering, people will understand that it's sincere. Besides, as a pure spirit, from the height of my meditations, I sometimes manage to control * greatly those sighs of an old lovesick

---

[80] "The Lord is my light" (Psalms 27:1).

* *Translator's note:* Here Gide used the nonexistent word *contemner*.

woman and, under the spirit, all such swooning of the heart.

Ah! pure spirits! And now your heart has sung of a new tenderness. Don't think that I blame you for it: let yourself love, let yourself go, for fear of no longer knowing how to be sincere afterward. And then, such joys are still sometimes very beautiful.

As for me, I have never known anyone but Emmanuèle; [81] yet she has forever perfumed my heart, my mind and my soul. Nothing should be scorned but lying, in this world; and one must not say: this thing is art, that one is not. All things, universally, are in Art—or rather Art is in us, and we project it onto all things, even onto banal and entrancing love.

This letter will perhaps reach you on a day when you will think differently,—and I'm distressed about it in advance. The answers in a letter should reach you the very moment they are written. And, specifically, this letter was somewhat delayed, first in my head, then on my table—remaining unfinished. Outside occupations kept robbing me of the pleasure of an illusory dialogue with you.

For example, the other evening, a slow, an exquisite chat at de Régnier's: gathered there were him, B. Lazare, Mockel, Paul Adam,[82] Pierre Louÿs, and myself—and each one in a big armchair, a pipe in his mouth (except for me), we prolonged the charm of words until one-thirty in the morning.

We shall no longer speak ill of Lazare: really I found him charming. We shall no longer speak ill of anyone; really it's useless. Lazare spoke to us of the ternary, the Gnostic heresiarchs; Paul Adam, of magic spells, in fact, of all kinds of magic. I wished that you were there; you would have been amused.

Now, what can I tell you of me?

I'm weary for the country, yet with the tiresome thought beforehand that I shan't know what to do there.

I am irked about my *Traité du Narcisse*,* which I did not write fast enough and which is therefore difficult in coming. I'm writing nothing these days of any worth. And so I play music, or I read: I'm reading all of Shakespeare and have conceived an infinite passion for it. I dream a lot and I sketch out masterpieces in smoke, but the Parnassian scruples, alas, keep me from writing.

[81] The name with which André Gide transformed his cousin Madeleine Rondeaux—whom he was to marry in 1895—into the heroine of *Les Cahiers d'André Walter*. He was to continue to use that name throughout his *Journal*.

[82] The naturalist novelist Paul Adam (1862–1920) contributed to the literary review of the period.

* *Translator's note:* The first edition of *Le Traité du Narcisse* (*Théorie du Symbole*) was to be published in 1891 by Art Indépendant. On June 23, 1891, Gide mentioned *Le Traité* in a letter to Valéry, with the comment: "I would perhaps not have written it had it not been for your words during the evening."

I'm worried about what might have become of Laforgue's *L'Imitation*. Have you received it? Bailly was supposed to send it to me first and I don't know what he may have done? Tell me whether it pleases you.

> Au revoir,
> André Gide

31. *Paul Valéry to André Gide*

[July, 1891]

My dear friend,

I must write to you to calm myself a bit. I am frantic: such a sea breeze is blowing that my hair is damp from it and in the air I inhale the sea!

If you only knew how it penetrates me and what a love *that* is! It transports me and would make me shriek wild things: this is the triumph of an untamable trollop, proclaimed across the waters by vast winds that skip and roll over and roam on the waves! My brain is full of those winds and those glittering waves that whinny; against the furiously splashing foam, the black vessel takes fright.

The sun—over there—must provoke the tempests and the rumbling horn announces formidable combats.

Think of the sharks and the golden porgies languidly fleeing in the glaucous waters. To sleep, to sleep on a branch of that coral, and to see the great star far away through the ocean, like a green and incomprehensible moon. To have the swift and supple movements of those underwater beasts—in order to flee.   P.-A. V.

32. *Paul Valéry to André Gide*

[July 13, 1891, in Gide's handwriting]

O salutaris! . . .

Despite the fact that your letter would seem to disdain what attracts me in friendship, as in everything—the absolute—it is beautiful and good in its ineffable truth.

I should like, dear soul, to tell you* about what I have felt and divined, and about the spiderweb scales on which I weighed a few tears, were it not that thinking back on the past days is as painful for me as the gesture of a wounded man who is curious and lightly touches the sensitive and coagulated bandages under which there is still suffering.

If you only knew how much I suffered and how admirable my transfigured stupidity appeared to me!

---

* *Translator's note:* Here the intimate *tu* form is used for the first time in the correspondence, and from now on (except for Gide's letter of July 14–15 and occasional returns to the *vous* form) it will be used by both throughout.

The most famous thing about these new experiences is that the whole Drama was my own (was? is?). I created for myself the spectacle of Love . . . But this time everything shrieked. The *pure spirit,* the one accustomed to *meditations,* fled, all bitten up.

. . . .

"The Enigma proposed by the mouth of the cruel virgin."
(Pindar, fragment 35)
P. Valéry

I have received nothing from Bailly.

33. André Gide to Paul Valéry

July 14 and 15 [1891]

I received your note, dear Ambroise, on this holiday when the poor souls of ideologists, startled by all the turbulence, take refuge and shut themselves in. Holidays are difficult; however well one's soul may shut itself in, it remains restless: the clamor from out there comes through the closed windows. Your precious note saved me from that restlessness for a while and distracted me from pernicious ennui.

No, don't think that I disdain, in friendship any more than in love, anything that you yourself do not disdain. I am always afraid of some inanimadvertence [*sic*] in my letter, as soon as I mail it; this present letter must make up for yesterday's, and a future letter for today's! Yes, I love the fact that you love, or rather, I love you loving. The state of love, adoration, or ecstasy should be our normal state; we must always have some fervor in our souls, and I am grateful to you for having chosen a painful one. The blood that flows from those mysterious scars makes for the sweetest blooms.

But your heart and your body are still a mystery to me, and I don't know how to speak to you of yourself, although I know that we will agree on all things. I don't know what you call love, and whether for you there is "and the rest," or whether for you that too is love; finally, I don't know what you look for in love and what you know of it—and of the rest. And I fear that one clumsy word from me will make you think that I have not understood your soul, and that I am "another," whereas I am aware of enough different modes within myself so that at least one of them might reflect you. (At times I think that one should be all reflection, the reflection of some seraphic dawn.) I often think that we would have done as well to have chosen some court of love to live in at the time of the Florence plagues. I have often reflected that dream.

Yesterday, I slept until evening: in the morning I had seen Louis, who asked me to tell you that he is working and that you should therefore not blame him for being silent.

But is he working? but does he still know how to work? We have been on the best of terms since we spoke together frankly. I blamed him dreadfully, indicting him in scandalous speeches, too easy, for he blamed himself to begin with. We are now better friends, but really I found his behavior too reprehensible.

Marcel Drouin [83] was the first out of seventy candidates to be accepted for the *licence* scholarship. I don't know why I tell you that; you don't know him (but you will know him some day); he is one of the most faithful and precious souls.

On leaving Louis, I went to a *café-concert;* should I tell you that I now go constantly, I who fled them a month ago and who, as a child, believed them to be haunts of hell. I went back again in the evening.

Paris on a holiday is splendid. A mirage of light, and the gold and tragic dust that blazes round the street lamps! And toward midnight the drunken women, and that smell of prostitution!

Those same songs and all that lewd intoxication convulses me with supreme lyricism. I wildly savor the bitterness of solitude, the quivering regret for caresses, although they were offered.

In the Latin Quarter, at about one o'clock, all that became splendid; the disheveled courtesans, sprawled on the knees of strangers, their skirts pulled up, or, lewd, singing on the shoulders of groups of students coming down the streets. Mad virgins were singing; the cancan was being danced in the squares. In the midst of the laughter, I sat down at one of the boulevard cafés. Certain women were superb; they rolled about on the ground in complete disarray.

Au revoir. I have still things to tell you but I remember nothing. Blame, not me, but Bailly for the negligence that I suspected. I will make up for it as soon as possible.

Next Sunday I shall be with Maeterlinck, I suppose, unless I'm in Brussels, but write to me in Paris all the same, until I give you some other address.

It will perhaps be some time before I write to you, but please don't blame me for it. I like to forget when I travel.

Are you working? I think the fateful hour must be approaching. All my wishes are with you. You'll keep me posted, won't you?

A. G.

---

[83] After studying at the Ecole Normale Supérieure, Drouin was to become a professor of philosophy and then, by his marriage to Jeanne Rondeaux, Gide's brother-in-law. He contributed to *La Revue Blanche,* using the pseudonym Michel Arnauld. He was to be a member of the first editorial staff of *La Nouvelle Revue française,* and the same publisher was to bring out one of his best essays, *La Sagesse de Goethe,* in 1949, with a preface by André Gide.

34. *Paul Valéry to André Gide*

[July, 1891]

Dear blindman,

Do you not feel in your own house or in mine, in that Belgium of Memlinck [*sic*], of Metsys, of resounding Plantains * (and I give these names at random to awaken like chimes in my ears) and do you not ask anything of those old stones steeped in ancient rain which are submerged in the blessedly unctuous water of the canals—drowsy Beguines, accustomed to the bells, Beguines of dead bricks, with battered gables; . . . an iron cross becomes rusty with boredom.

. . . ANTWERP! a Baudelaire all wild and black lies in that word. A word full of spices and pearls unloaded, under a rainy sky, by a drunken sailor, in the doorway of a tavern . . . the pink lantern attracts the Negroes to the sad streets where the woman in underclothes tramples in the mud.

And the prolonged echo of songs in a distant language, aboard boats shrouded in silence.

As you can see, I am letting these foreign words carry me off to you, unflinching.

My exam has come to an end, indifferently but adequately.[84]

My books are open again, but I am still a sleeper awake.

As for other things, I wouldn't have a word to say, as I can't see any more. ". . . What would I *look for* in love?" Myself! that self which slips away and which runs through greedy fingers is the *man* who breaks free every time his soul is startled, by every wound, and who all at once, at certain stormy times, would appear, growing perhaps, or defiling his whole being and the pained spectator who is there.

I should also look for, and have looked for, a manifestation of the outer mystery, an occult correspondence, a harmony of wills.

Adieu,

P.-A. Valéry

I should like these lines to tell you more things than the signs that make them up. I thought for a long time after writing this, and I add that thought to my letter, in a mysterious way. I hope that you will find it.

35. *André Gide to Paul Valéry*

[August 8, 1891]

No, my sweet Ambroise, nothing on this trip is like what you think. No drowsy Beguines leaning over the blessedly unctuous water of the

---

* *Translator's note:* Valéry was no doubt referring to Christophe Plantin (1514–1589), of Antwerp, the leading printer of the second half of the sixteenth century.

[84] On July 30 Paul Valéry passed his second year law exam at the Faculty of Montpellier, with fair grades.

canals; no jewels, no pearls unloaded; no pink lanterns, no Negroes in the streets, nor any woman in underclothes in the doorways; no boats in the silence.

But (the fatal and dismal blindness of eyeshades) someone, myself, leaning over a book, reading first one leaf, then another, meditative and scornful of the rest, who imperiously savors metaphysical pages.

It is very likely that there were Beguines, and bored iron crosses, canals or blessedly unctuous waters,—I even know perfectly well that sometimes, when I lifted my eyes, I noticed landscapes—but now I'm even unaware of the fact that I was traveling.

I noted down this one landscape (I don't remember whether I wrote you about it), here it is, I copy it down:

"Alkmaar,

"My little soul got lost in a garden of tulips and pink lilies; there were tidy lanes between little houses; I wandered over washed mosaics, and in front of the painted doors, little girls, in matching colors, were wiping off invisible spots. Above the roofs strolled the masts of ships; because here, the good Lord created the waters higher than the lands." [85]

And that is all I saw. Yes, I know, paintings too: Quentin-Massys, Memlinck,[86] Van Eyck, and many others, but all that is now of the past. Today I'm in Nancy, for a few days before returning to peaceful Normandy; I am with Marcel Drouin; the friend I've already spoken to you about; the one who wrote *L'Indifférent* in the first *Conque*.[87]

He just entered Normale in first place, took first place in the competitive exam for *licence* scholarships; and took first prize in the main competitive exam. I like it when one is the winner in such things, for Flaubert was right in saying: "One does not scorn that which one is unable to obtain." And one must be able to scorn all those things which are merely human.

That is also why I'm happy that you passed that ridiculous exam. Now take advantage of the fervor you acquired in order to formulate some precious poem; and make up your mind to send it to me. All right?

I leave you for today; my time is still not my own, and I have only very brief moments. I shall say nothing to you today on the question that was raised about love, as in an ancient court; I will not do right by it, and one must do right by such things.

Au revoir.
André Gide

[85] Gide wrote this note on July 23 at Alkmaar. He was to reproduce it in his *Journal,* omitting only "My little soul got lost in a . . ."
[86] [*Sic*]. Read: Quentin-Metsys, Memling.
[87] Using the pseudonym Michel Arnauld.

36. Paul Valéry to André Gide

August 10 [1891]

What modesty veils you from our pure and tender eyes? You disappeared! We are also awaiting your limpid words. . . . You are in silence.

Perhaps before many moons we shall be in Paris, dear friend. And we command you not to know it, in order that our desire, as friends, be blessed and that we find the other friend free of foreboding. We should be pleased also if you would inform us whether *he* is supposed to be in Paris in September, about the 20th, 25th?

Will you be there yourself?

We will, perhaps! and we will write to you about it faithfully, heedless of all the vast secular paths, black with anonymous people, if the lack of friendly souls tortures us. . . .

. . . The only thing that consoles me is the vague silver sound that water makes on tired leaves. . . . Nothing consoles me like that. Art is a toy. Science, crude. Esoterism, the most beautiful of lies. Nothing is complicated, distant, really secret and subtle—except that pale sound of water. Water. This world is as ridiculous as a clock; those stars go foolishly round, not very numerous (thirty-five hundred), not beautiful actually, nor curious. And what do I care about brains, so simple! People, who grow their hair longer, pose on the edge of the heavens, with golden lyres, as so many Orpheuses—because they break up an alexandrine into 8/4 or 3/9 or because they repeat one letter in a line! Horrible!

Our flowers are as stupid as women. The converse is true. Temples are worth nothing except in the imagination. Books! . . are what we are. We rewrite them—therefore, don't need them. Mistresses are dirty or stupid; mammas, inferior. One can drink nothing that isn't foul and barbaric. Only one artistic smell exists—salt—to a small degree, coal. Incense stinks. Death is comically petty. One should end only by exploding! or by sinking right to the bottom on a five-mast ship which would go down vertically with all its sails!

Everything is false! Dissonance splits the ears of my understanding. Language is as impoverished as a widow. Nature, as ugly as if some mediocrity had made it. The other world does not exist, for no soul would ever come back from it. . . . And since nothing is created. . . . The pagans, stupid. The Christians, frightfully ugly; Nirvana: a paradise for beasts. Hamlet would be good if there were no surrounding drama. The mystery does not exist, alas! Poe is the only one. . . . Yet even in him there are a few false notes. Barrès should have his pockets turned out and be bound hand and foot. Scientists reek of the parvenu. Causes and effects do not exist! We create them, Gentlemen! so what does that prove?

Style? Go to see it fabricated, in order to vomit! Artists, you shall go mad! Bourgeois, you are stupid! . . . Who made the universe? I did! God is an atom that radiates. God is principle. God is the Good. God is the Beautiful. God is Three; no, he is Two! God is an Idea. God is! . . . Thus God is a few words. That's not much. . . . Motion engenders number. Force engenders motion. Will engenders force. What engenders will? Engender? Who? Why the moon? and why the minor mode? What is the essence of sadness? whom does one cry for here? . . . The devil is sleeping after his meals. He is aging. . . . Ah! everything is the desolation of boredom! There is nothing strange, nothing! [88]

This is a night of insomnia.

Adieu.

P.-A. Valéry

37. *André Gide to Paul Valéry*

Château de la Roque [P. August 25, 1891]

Dear Ambroise,

I should like all your letters to be written during such nights of insomnia. That last one is admirable, but were those the thoughts of only one night, or have you spent all these days turning over in your mind such sad and stagnant sludge? We should really spend a night together, perhaps with some Aesthete to make a third, a night in November, when—sincere and agonized—until late dawn, we would go thoroughly into its sadness, its sadnesses. We would perhaps come up with some profundity, but the agonizing part is that, alone, it's not even profound—it's so stupid as to make one weep, nothing more.

Every night I joylessly write some deplorable verse, free verse, alas, which afterward I try to believe has been given order by some new metrical system, for free verse is absurd;—but the alexandrine is even more so. That Parnassian perfection, so completely artificial, makes me sick every time I think of it, and still it is the only one that's satisfying.

At certain times, I find that it's ludicrous to try to restore mystery to things which no longer have any. We are the remakers of dead virginities. We are like children who frighten themselves in mirrors. We are like children who want to jump over their shadows. We're playing handball. We contrive to surprise ourselves, and we play at being astonished at everyday things.

Things amaze us no longer; that's why we are sad.

Now listen to this: Louis returns to Paris on Saturday (tomorrow). I wrote to him the day before yesterday to find out what his plans are,

---

[88] Here the French reads: *rien de!*

and whether or not he now intends to stay in Paris. I shall let you know his answer.

I don't think I shall be back to the rue de Commaille before November 1,—but do give me enough notice. I'll come and spend a few days in Paris for the great pleasure of seeing you there. Yet one thing saddens and somewhat frightens me, a coincidence which, between two kinds of happiness, will force me to choose the rarest. I say this *very confidentially to You:* Emmanuèle is to come and spend some time with me, toward the middle of September. I am very much afraid of having to choose between you two. But won't you remain in Paris for some time?

Judging from the beginning of your letter, I fear that you did not receive a letter from me, written exactly a week ago.

Ruysbroek annoys me. He is a despot, not an adviser, like the One of the Imitation; he wants us to give ourselves up to him, and that displeases me. I'm weary of Schopenhauer.

It has been raining for so many hours on water which had already fallen, that it begins to have a certain charm.

Adieu.
A. W.

38. *Paul Valéry to André Gide*

[September, 1891]

Just a few hours after my Latin * was mailed, your letter arrived. I shall not be up there until the 17th or 18th. And I do not wish you to lose either a minute of Pan, or a second of Her, because of me. I forbid you to be jealous and I love you for it.** Do love me a little. . . . I should point out, apropos of one of your asides, that *I* NEVER forget. Not being much of anything, I don't divide myself up, but each of my real friends has me COMPLETELY! You are, however, the only one to whom I say certain things. People, many people, describe me as not very *sentimental* or not sentimental at all, as not very *philosophical,* but rather as a little abstracter of aesthetic quintessences. I admire them for knowing me so well. I am thought to be gentle, I am violent,—but absent-minded! I am thought to be lighthearted and merry—I am boredom and despair personified! but I smile ineluctably. I never tell an intruder what I think but rather what I assume would please him or nettle him, as the occasion requires. I never divulge my soul in verse or

---

* *Translator's note:* On September 10, Valéry had sent Gide a short note in Latin.

** *Translator's note:* On September 9, from Belle-Isle in Brittany, Gide had written: "I'm jealous, Paul-Ambroise! I am frightfully jealous. I *want* to be *there* when you are there. Otherwise, you will forget me, I know it."

in any other kind of literature (except this kind, which is not literature), for writing! does not mean making one's self blush, or confront-
ing indifference—but rather the ambition, to begin with, of grabbing
hold of an ideal reader and unemotionally dragging him off—or of
dazzling him, dazing him, conquering him by the higher Truth and the
magic, yes, marvelous! force of creating anything one wants with little
signs like these! Ah! what a magisterial mystery it is! what pride of
some artistic Hermes, to put down on paper with fabulous wiles the
words soul, tears, emotion, etc., and to make a *very intelligent* man
believe that his life is less stupid, and his being less relative! and thus
obtain the veneration of that Subject whom, in fact, one had merely
wanted to drag off, as a slave, to the banks of funereal rivers, among the
DEAD! I shrug my shoulders when blindmen speak of the Goncourts'
callousness, of X's impassibility, of Huysmans' acephalia, etc. As if it
were easier to define an *objet d'art,* an emotion of the highly keyed
senses, than to spin out limp phrases about a small flame one has not
even seen, a subtle fire called Psyche—and actually, to do no more than
prettify and dissolve in rose water the few true relations and few
coincidences that have been known for ages!

I have scoured all the roads, called for help on all the horizons. One
corner of my past life—forever unknown to All—has shed light on the
beating of the little beast. Exasperated sensuality! Science bored me, the
mystical forest led me nowhere, I have visited ship and cathedral, I have
read the most marvelous of writers, Poe! Rimbaud, Mallarmé, have
analyzed, alas, their ways, and have always met with the most beautiful
illusions, at their point of origin and birth. Where will I find a newer
magic? A secret of being and of creating that surprises me? You will smile
here, thinking of my poor attempts? If you only knew how much—
really—I detest them! My great future poems are seeking their form and—
it's sheer madness! No, you see, in passive as in active art, I have found
nothing but reasons for anger and disgust! To begin with, all those who
study man in himself make me vomit! Only the Church has an art. Only
the Church relieves one a bit, and detaches one from the World. I don't
want to go on speaking of it—you find that I've already gone on too long—
but this should be said, shouted: We are all little boys next to the liturgists
and theologians, since our greatest geniuses, Wagner, Mallarmé, bow
down—and *Imitate.*

. . . You can see that you must not be jealous. Friendship, your stainless
word is still the only thing that filters down to the depths of me. Friend,
your manifestations toward me are the purest apparition of a Truth, if
there is one. And your letters are still bells from my little native country.
So then, I remember! Your jealously rings out deliciously, the bad dream
subsides . . . yes, it is indeed that! In the days of old, in the days of old,

when I was a man, before literature, before stupidity—before the cloud . . .

P.-A. Valéry

39. Paul Valéry to André Gide

Paris [P. September 25, 1891]

Friend, more than ever I need and am hungry for a very long letter. I shan't see Louÿs until Saturday noon, for he too had fled yonder, toward Brittany.

I am somewhat panic-stricken. This Paris which I have seen once again and detest more and more flows round me like a river, and it is a Lethe seething with resonant oblivion.[89] The crowd rules, invades one's brain, and the talent here seems to me to have the desperate arms of a drowning man who struggles against a treacherous current—that which submerges the inner temple and makes the individual a thing of the world, whereas the contrary should be true. You don't understand. So much the better for your soul.

You—elevate your spiritual beauty, love in the sublime distance.

I await a very long letter.

P.-A. Valéry

40. André Gide to Paul Valéry

La Roque [September, 1891]

My dear friend,

You must have met with great disappointment in Paris; this door closed; Louis gone. I suffered for you.

Louis, to prepare a childish surprise, did not want to advise me of his trip to Brittany until he got there and after you had already left Montpellier. As I did not have your new address, I couldn't write to you the note of consolation I had in mind.

Now Louis is there, isn't he—and I am perhaps unwelcome as a third party.

That Paris I flee makes me fear for you. It stirs up the stinking sludge within that one tries to ignore. Active life there is sometimes so mad that it becomes beautiful. As it still amuses me too much, I'm unable to despise it enough.

Have you seen Cluny,[90] Rops,[91] and the rest, the pottery from Egypt and

---

[89] Paul Valéry arrived in Paris with his mother on September 19, on the occasion of his brother Jules' taking the competitive examination, or *agrégation,* in law. Jules, eight years his senior, was to become dean of the Faculty of Law at Montpellier. Valéry returned to Montpellier with his mother on October 24.

[90] The Cluny Museum.

[91] The painter Félicien Rops.

Greece, the treasures of the Cathedral and the flamboyant stained-glass windows of Sainte-Chapelle? [92]

I imagine you looking at these things, more Ambroise than ever. I also imagine you on the boulevards, dazed, feverish, and agonized. Then came Louis, who will jostle you out of your sadness and force you to be merry. . . .

I am constantly distracted from my letter: my family is chatting right next to me, and that kind of thing disturbs me. I shan't speak to you of myself, because to do that I should have to look at myself, and I don't dare to yet. I am carried along by powerful emotions, but I have gradually become so indifferent to the amount of human happiness they contain that I have not succeeded in discovering whether they are sweet or bitter. I am satisfied that they be strong.

My tasks, however, are asleep in desk drawers. I am not of the opinion that fleeting emotions should be put into poetry; everything that lives in time can be no more than transitory. But you're the one who should tell me about all that.

I remember that, in a letter, you exclaimed about the splendor of the word "burn." I now think about it constantly. And at night, when I find myself in my room, in the silence I am as fervent as a great candle.

I plan to see you in Paris. I commend to you one of our brothers in Mallarmé and Wagner—a real one—to whom I shall now write, to whom I shall speak of you. His name is Camille Mauclair. Did Louis mention him to you?   A. G.

41. *Paul Valéry to André Gide*

12, rue Gay-Lussac, hôtel Henri-IV
[October 6, 1891, in Gide's handwriting]

Finally! the wild refuge of a café on this luminous and stupid boulevard has offered me some alien paper and a pen that belongs to Everyone—so that I can insult you.* Since I have known you, I have experienced one minute—on the rue Vineuse—when I should have liked to have had your letters with me, in order to reread them and throw them out in the street, intact. I was furious—I am calmer now but sad to have heard the word *Madness* pronounced—with regard to certain *intimate* and *hallucinated* pages written by you and addressed to M.[93]

---

[92] The main event of Valéry's stay in Paris was his first visit to Mallarmé. The day after his visit, he noted down his impressions. Henri Mondor was to disclose their significance ("Le Premier Entretien Mallarmé-Valéry," in "Valéry vivant," *Cahiers du Sud*, 1946). Valéry himself wrote: "I am pleased to see that yesterday I had already weighed everything he says."

* *Translator's note:* Throughout this letter Valéry uses the conventional *vous* form.

[93] Probably Mauclair.

So, you are capable of writing, to certain others, such words, and such appreciated words! Jealous, then grieved—for after all, you have the right—you have the duty, if certain others attract you, to tell them secrets and to prostitute yourself—unmasked prostitute—drunk with belonging to everyone who may come along.

Burn in the hollows of all the Temples: but anyway, in the name of the higher Truth of bygone days, may the words of yesteryear remain born forever. Verily, I say unto you, I don't know whether one should have more admiration for your debauchery or for the vigor that you radiate, and by which you have achieved it.

I shall stop now.

If I see you presently, then I shall speak more clearly—if I dare to—and I shall tell you so many other things—less tragic—like having seen Louÿs and having seen certain others and certain books, and Paris.

Paul-Ambroise Valéry

42. *André Gide to Paul Valéry*

La Roque, October 7, 1891

What are you so angry with me for, Paul-Ambroise? Because I prostituted myself with someone else? But you know well that my soul is constantly in heat; it must take its fill. Don't be too angry with it for going everywhere to beg for tenderness. Was it not you who just a while back advised it to "burn"?

But this rage suits you. I'm pleased that you got into it,—in spite of the fact that I don't understand it very well. I assure you that I don't feel guilty; and if what you reproach me for is giving myself to someone who is not worthy of it, too bad for him, I shall do it all the same.

But you must explain what you mean: it's time that we saw each other. You shall tell me what I have done wrong and everything that is being said behind my back; I'll not leave you alone until you have forgiven me.

Do excuse all these participles; it's you who muddle my style.

And do know that I love you enough so that you can let me love the others a little.

For I love you very much, you know it perfectly well.

André Gide

And do answer my letter of this morning right away.*

---

* *Translator's note:* The next published exchange between the two is a postcard from Gide, written on October 15, informing Valéry that he would meet him in Paris the following day.

43. André Gide to Paul Valéry

From La Roque, still [November 3, 1891]
Solemn and sonorous woods.

I no longer can, I no longer dare to go back. Paris frightens me. I'm beginning to understand you, and your terror of the city. It rouses so many thoughts on the surface of the brain that one is diverted from deep thoughts. One wants to live too quickly; and that's worth nothing. Besides, I don't trust myself; and I know that deep within me, lying not so dormant, is that old concern about success. . . . Here, I am a pure Spirit. Day and night I roll about in abysses of transcendency. I have just read eight volumes of George Sand.

They made me disgusted with love (I already was a little) and with all sentimentality. And with myself, as an individual.

I long to speak to you; I think I understand you better.

I realize that intimacy is only desirable and only possible with a very few people. (I who wanted it with everyone!) Is intimacy even desirable? What is it?

Is not the feeling of Presence enough? Knowing that the other is there. That there *is* another.

Up to now, I wanted to *make friendship* as one "makes love."

It's ridiculous. It comes from the fact that I don't want to make love. I shall keep this, and break myself of the rest.

Pure Spirit! "in a higher atmosphere." All passion, all emotion, which is not transcendental is contemptible. Συμπαθειν[94] itself is something rather cowardly. Sympathy is the recognized weakness of the creature who is not sufficient unto himself. One must be sufficient unto one's self—with God.

Poe has conquered me. I have been reading him every day, and every day he has grown. Today I find him colossal; and if not he himself, at least his type. But I think he is one of the rare beings who has fully realized his type.

Schopenhauer now. I find him too sprightly, too clever. He lacks "rhythmic balance," and besides, he is too interested in persuading. I preferred Kant. But Schopenhauer will have been my initiator.

My *Narcisse*[95] is finished. I don't know what to think of it. It's highly polished, and I should not be able to change a thing without changing it all—but I think it is limited.

Will it please you?

At any rate, the effort I put into it is not lost, for it unraveled my entire aesthetic, my ethic, and my philosophy. And no one will stop me from thinking that every author *must* have his *very own* philosophy, ethic, and

[94] To feel sympathy for.
[95] *Le Traité du Narcisse.*

aesthetic. One can't create anything without that. A work is but a manifestation of that.

Have you read Balzac's *Louis Lambert?* I reread it every year. I find it tremendous. I even find that it's really well-written. Nothing has ever made me so dizzy as that vision of Louis Lambert's in the dark room, nothing—I don't think even Poe—and heaven knows! . . .

What else? I read the whole day, and I meditate by the fire.

We are on the best of terms, Louÿs and I: he writes me good letters. I'm happy about it, for if we're not on the best then we're on the worst of terms.

With some mutual concessions—how well we get along, all three of us!—how well we will get along!

I'm writing to you with difficulty, my fingers frozen in this large drawing room badly heated by a country fire.

Adieu.

Those are the thoughts of one day. Tomorrow, in Paris, I shall again be that ambitious and vain speculator which I fear I am. But I'll find my salvation!

Adieu.

A. W.

44. *Paul Valéry to André Gide*

[November 7, 1891, in Gide's handwriting]

Dear spirit,

Your familiar beauty haunts me, and I long for you more than you do [*sic*]. When will you cross my garden with the light step of a man preparing a surprise (so admirable, that it strikes me dumb,—do you remember?). Friendship, you see, is being a little like the good Lord to one's friend and appearing, knowingly, at just the right moment. You said terrible things about intimacy and sympathy, you meant to please me, but I assure you that I cordially detest anything that might ring false, for no one has so good, so perfect, an ear as I in such matters. Only one kind of sympathy exists, that which is made necessary by higher laws, that which is a chemical affinity, a correspondence perhaps, with some former marvelous unity. "And Above . . ." If I dared to violate that splendid entity revealed through you, the unconscious universal soul that animates you, I should say to you: "Tomorrow, at a certain hour, you will think of me, all of me, you will act as if you were me, and I, you; *You will live me,* you will know me, you will have me. And I, likewise inflicting on my being the surprise of an unknown, I would know you at the same hour." So that we may more skilfully draw near to the common flame and the world, and grasp, perhaps, with delight, the veiled truth of being and of difference, and go down once again into ourselves, more enlightened.

Louÿs wrote me a letter to tell me that he wrote me a letter to keep in his drawer. You get the idea. I'm tempted to insult him a bit, more especially as he is putting an idiotic sonnet,[96] which I made the mistake of leaving with him, into *La Conque.* If you see him soon, you can do it for me. Ah! if I had had the time to slash it to pieces! But Paris flew by like a train. One *feels* much better in Montpellier, and one feels like one's self again.

A word of metaphysics. "Question," as would say the aesthete Coste (who, having come upon Dr. Ménard, completely gave away your anonymity. Tableau!).

Is it not true that transcendental idealism is hardly plausible in this position? Saying that the individual self creates the world is enough to affirm the existence of the non-self.

P.-A. Valéry

Here is a sonnet written straight from the pen.[97] It amused me to see what my pen could do. *Lege.*

> Bathylle de Lesbos que frise un doigt servile
> A de sa jupe iris [*sic*] . . . déconcerté
> Tel pli trop peu naïf dans le miroir tenté
> Et le voile qu'amuse le beau geste habile.
>
> Voici son rire en l'air éventer le flambeau,
> Gai de voir sous la tresse obscure qui le cingle
> Éclose la beauté par la rose et l'épingle
> Du pied bleu de saphirs au sein gelé dans l'eau.
>
> Le poète sourit, Bathylle, dans ton ombre
> Et dévore à mi-mot des grappes dans ton ombre
> Sa lyre, en noble bois d'ébène pur, se tait.
>
> Car, vibrante! aux échos des étoffes profondes
> A tes amants magnifiques elle chantait
> Orphée antique mort par tes mains furibondes!

45. *André Gide to Paul Valéry*

De profundis. Friday [December, 1891]

My friend,

I shall come, yes, I shall indeed come at last, if only *at last.*

I'm getting stuck in appearances, while awaiting the evening when, near the black swans in the pool, we shall chat about things, real things. I am still correcting, but for the last time, the proofs of *Narcisse,*[98] in

---

[96] The poem *Au Bois dormant,* published in *La Conque* of Nov. 1, 1891.

[97] A sonnet that remained unpublished until the Gide-Valéry *Correspondance* appeared in Paris, in 1955.

[98] The first and very limited edition of *Le Traité du Narcisse* (*Théorie du Symbole*) was published by Art Indépendant, with a white cover bearing the words *Traité du* and, underneath, a drawing by Pierre Louÿs representing a narcissus. It was to come out again in 1892, and was not to be republished until 1899 by Mercure de France, in *Philoctète.*

which I now find no more than two bad sentences, and I'm indolent enough to leave them.

I'm so tired that I wish for the repose of sleep more than for that of work; and I have nothing left in my heart but silence.

Wilde is religiously contriving to kill what remains of my soul, because he says that in order to know an essence, one must eliminate it: he wants me to miss my soul. The measure of a thing is the effort made to destroy it. Each thing is made up only of its emptiness . . . , etc.[99]

For three months I have been dreaming of a symmetrical drama, in which puppets would evolve reciprocally, in which everything would hold together in a necessary dependence. In which there would be an artifice, or an art, of subordination. I shall come and develop it with you.

Still more treatises on heraldry; * the comedies of Ben Jonson; Swinburne and Poe; but mostly Wilde, who talks and whom I take to be Baudelaire or Villiers, at the end of meals during which he has made me drink, meals that last three hours, with Merrill [100] and P. L. or else in Montmartre at Aristide Bruant's [101] with Marcel Schwob and a pimp.

Oh! these last weeks I have been reading the most detestable of books, it is called *Là-Bas,* and it is by Huysmans. . . . And I should continue to defend him? . . . ah! I would rather leave you. Au revoir.

Your reciprocal

A. W.

Remember me to the aesthete Coste, again and again, for I think of him constantly, as I do of you, you silent man.

---

[99] In a letter to Valéry of November 28, 1891, Gide mentioned that he had been seeing "the aesthete Oscar Wilde, Oh! an admirable man, admirable." Wilde, almost always accompanied by his young friend Alfred Douglas, frequented Mallarmé's *salon* and most of the symbolist circles. He was to have an ambiguous but unquestionable influence on Gide, who—after having known him in Paris—met him by chance in Florence and then in North Africa in 1893. Several pages of *Si le Grain ne meurt* are devoted to him, and testify to the determining role he was to play in Gide's sexual emancipation.

Shortly after having written this letter, on January 1, 1892, Gide was to note in his *Journal:* "Wilde, I think, did me nothing but harm."

Ten years after Oscar Wilde's death, Gide was to publish *Oscar Wilde, in memoriam* (Mercure de France, 1910).

* *Translator's note:* On November 15 Gide wrote Valéry that he was "studying heraldry!"

[100] The poet Stuart Merrill (1863–1915), author of *Les Gammes, Les Fastes,* and *Les Quatre Saisons.*

[101] The *chansonnier* Aristide Bruant (1851–1925), author of *Dans la rue* and *Sur la route,* songs and monologues.

46. Paul Valéry to André Gide

[P. December 5, 1891]

My dear friend,

Apropos of the insights of Wilde (in your letter, in which I see him as a symbolic mouth à la Redon,[102] swallowing a mouthful and mechanically transforming it at once into a satanic aphorism), two words:

When I think of you, I am afraid of the entities that surround you—what are you doing but adding, to the ponderous illusions already imposed by the senses, a whole world of *puppets?* We artists fear, like the devil himself, all philosophies inspired by logic, logic being merely the supreme lie, the sole appearance, the very essence of deceptive appearance. The determinism that your drama would invoke, however *logically* TRUE you construct it, is a monstrous negation of all beauty. And why? Because the whole interest of it would be graspable and consequently would belie the necessary desire for goodness.* A drama that would be a pleasure for the faculty of classification and abstraction would be an object of horror, an act of damnation, even a mockery of the *Drama of God.*

A curious thing! I too was thinking of a Drama the day your letter arrived. But *every time,* absolutely every time that intention comes to light, I am solemnly disconcerted by the thought that all Drama is impossible, after the Mass. Whoever says Drama thinks exotericism, spectacle. It is Art's only appearance before *everyone—everyone.* And the liturgical drama is Perfection—in Perfection.

I write a Drama! *etiam Hamlet* or *Tristan and Isolde*—or *The Persians.* But then:

Who will give me a total crowd, a crowd of all the sexes, ages, ranks, thoughts, a crowd that has come on the vigil to repent and to tell all its soul to a holy man; it has fasted since midnight and, called by the bells, quivers in the marvelous naves. As a prelude, peace, the difficult serenity obtained that morning,—as a denouement, participation in the divinity, the miracle bestowed upon each one by communion. And during the whole time of the ceremony, the beauty of ancient words, the gesture, the organs, the emotion that swells through each minute of the mystical duration, the swooning from enthusiasm, the small death that catches at the throat during the elevation, then the Being. It is the extraordinary spasm of ecstasy, the masterpiece of all the arts, the Flesh torn, then annihilated, by the Power of Thought alone. Eh? What Poe ever got that effect? Is it or is it not the supreme wonder of Art, the pyramid placed on its point, nothingness dissipated by so many nothingnesses?

[102] The painter Odilon Redon (1840–1916), a friend of poets (Mallarmé, Valéry, Francis Jammes) and illustrator of their works.

* *Translator's note: bonté* in the published text, not *beauté.* Probably a misprint or a misreading.

I repeat until you're stupefied that we had better sleep after that; and I insist that it is the masterpiece of Preparation, *The House of Usher* of all the existing centuries.

. . . In short, I may say that all Art is that which gives form to those celebrated words: *Et eritis sicut dei.*[103] It is difficult opium and nothing more! It comes perhaps from the Devil, yet Everything that wanders from that way is but formless and chaotic.

Sentimentality and pornography are twin sisters. I detest them. But the ghosts of them can be beautiful, beautiful always. The ghosts of them, that is, their invisible presence bending the flowers, disposing the stars and governing the cadence of the waves of the sea.

I'm sorry. I've been rambling on for too long, at the mercy of a cigarette, on foul paper. I have need of an unequaled indulgence for having spoken so much in the smoke, as if you were there, after dinner. Do excuse the ugliness of my hazardous words, and give me the hand that can absolve.

P.-A. Valéry

47. *André Gide to Paul Valéry*

Thursday, Christmas Eve [1891]

I'm coming soon. Please forgive my silence: since Wilde, I hardly exist any more.

I shall tell you all about that; I hope for a long evening together. Where, how? I'm worried about our meeting. My uncle C. Gide is so little settled himself that he can't take us in; and then, it's mostly for my grandmother that we're coming, and she is in Uzès. So we shall go first to Uzès: I'll write to you from there and will come as soon as possible.

See you soon; I hope to find near your silent soul a peaceful oasis after all this fluttering about.

Au revoir, my friend.

Your
André Gide

[103] "And ye shall be as gods" (Genesis 3:5).

— 1892 —

48. Paul Valéry to André Gide

[P. February 15, 1892]

Friend,

Thank you for the charming words about my *Drames;* [1] still, I had the feeling that they were an unparalleled flop.

That's why I had not sent you a note along with them. The end is absurd, impenetrable—it bothered me a great deal. Also, I was feeling too much remorse . . . Your short visit here is a very bad memory for me. I was so stupid—enough to make you flee? and not one good hour of absolute communion. Not one intimate hour of that beautiful fresh nakedness of the soul, no friendly Galateism. We perhaps lacked some star in the sky. . . .*

Now I have a slight fever. I belong to a "club" of friends in which one evokes the spirits of the furniture. These nocturnal séances are rather astonishing.

And poor C.! He recently had an interview with Péladan [2] at Nîmes—yesterday, I found him *adolente* in an armchair with a nasty little bottle on the table and a hypodermic needle—so I was most distressed. It appears that one dies very quickly from it.

Then, you can guess what the other matters are. The whole thing is changing perspective. There were one or two scenes of the Mass, rather exciting, with—at the Elevation—a concentration of will on a head of such hair!

But let's not talk about it. I am awaiting *Astarté* [3]—in which everything will be very beautiful. Vivat!

P.-A. Valéry

[1] *Purs Drames,* published in the March, 1892, issue of *Les Entretiens politiques et littéraires,* founded in April, 1890, by Henri de Régnier, Paul Adam, Georges Vanor, and Francis Vielé-Griffin, and published by Edmond Bailly. It lasted until 1893. (In a letter to Valéry dated Saturday [February, 1892] Gide had written: "They [*Purs Drames*] are perfect, new—an absolute delight.")

* *Translator's note:* To this, Gide answered, on March 2: "True, neither of us talked very well in Montpellier; to talk at appointed and arbitrary hours is fine when one has merely something to say. But we had everything to say, and the hour took its revenge for being violated."

[2] Péladan (1858–1918), called Le Sâr, was a novelist, art critic, and author of esoteric essays.

[3] A collection of poems by Pierre Louÿs, a hundred copies of which were privately printed in 1891. He was to give the same title to a collection of poems published the same year by Art Indépendant.

49. André Gide to Paul Valéry

Munich, Sunday [P. March 13, 1892]

Today, a holiday in the city; white sun on the snow, and white and blue lights. The armed forces * are parading in the streets.

As you know, one must be in Paris to tell about Munich, and for the memory to become idealized.

I'm waiting for your clear seascapes; your filigrees of laughter on the azure of the waves. But you're not working anymore! I am afraid of you—for you. Tell me, what has become of all *that?* Where will it lead you?

Here, one lives in images.

Adieu, I'm tired from having yawned for almost four hours. A patriotic play so lavishly produced that all the other theaters had to close in order to lend their actors. The settings, as in the city, without any highly colored atmosphere. No, all delineated, juxtaposed shades, without a vibration to unite them. Colored prints, throughout. No actors; extras—and as a central unity: "Vive Bavaria! forever." It all took place at the time of Barbarossa. The bored audience left before the end. I, who remained, am stupefied. I'm sad as well, and that's why I am writing to you, so that you will answer quickly. Write to Paris, I don't yet know where I'm going to be.

Adieu. I feel horribly faraway. Write quickly.

Your friend,

André   Gide

Have you seen that Mauclair is writing in *Le Figaro?!*

50. Paul Valéry to André Gide

[P. March 18, 1892]

Dear faraway,

Louÿs, also, is trying to put me to shame for not working. Do you both really think you can? I shall answer him presently . . . in the way that I *must* answer him.

To you, who knows me from more frequent association, I don't want to repeat my usual—absolute—words. You know perfectly well that there is no point in writing so as to be silent, and merely to repeat one myth—or another. (I am still awaiting my ** *Narcisse;* it concludes on about that note. . . .) I meditate, and try to purify myself, so that death will be less *physical* and less hard. One must not beget the stereotyped, must one, and we are all so threatened by it.

* *Translator's note:* The French text reads: "force aimée," obviously a misprint or a misreading.

** *Translator's note:* The published French text reads: "ton *Narcisse."* This is doubtless a misprint or a misreading, for on March 6 Valéry wrote Gide a short note thanking him for his *Narcisse,* and on June 13 (cf. Letter 53) mentioned that his own *Narcisse* was "reaching *wayward* proportions."

Thank you (as an interlude) for your dedication in *La Wallonie*.[4] You and Louÿs are incomparable friends. I don't deserve you in any way, and that's why you must not be surprised if *I* have not yet dedicated anything to you. Your affection and that of two or three others are the only works of mine I like. *Except for you all,* I am hardly that "charming shy young man" spoken of by the POET [*sic*]—unfortunately.

I am much aware—too aware perhaps!—but I only like artists who are. Nothing would be more painful to me than to be considered an "occasional" rhymester and writer. Art is a second life for me, my works being the family, or the game played at night.

Coste (who, last night, spoke on occultism at the town hall) thanks you for having sent him your book.* To write! he claims that he cannot now or ever.

What a fine issue of *La Wallonie!* exclaims Louÿs. These Belgians reproduce *La Fileuse* over and over again, it becomes a spinning wheel! And with that, *Arion*,[5] jolly bad! an experimental sonnet.

From you, the exquisite rainy dawn,[6] from him, a polychrome marble,[7] from Régnier a long allegory.[8] We're sustaining a real fugue in four parts.

Are you going to Bayreuth?

P.-A. Valéry

51. *André Gide to Paul Valéry*

[Paris, P. April 26, 1892]

From here, I envy your home—at the back of a garden—behind so many flowers. A door that is a closing; here doors are openings through which one circulates. No time to read anything but the Goncourt's *Journal*,[9] or to taste of anything but an ever-increasing annoyance with intruders. I am becoming "impossible to live with," having nothing more to say to them

---

[4] The literary review *La Wallonie* was founded in 1886 by Albert Mockel (1866–1945), a Belgian poet and critic, who took a great part in the symbolist movement. In the January-February, 1892, issue of the review, Pierre Louys' sonnet *Astarté* was published, dedicated to André Gide, along with two poems by Gide: *Lagunes,* dedicated to Paul-Ambroise Valéry, and *Octobre*.

* *Translator's note:* On March 3 Valéry wrote to Gide, asking him to send Coste his *Walter.*

[5] The same issue of *La Wallonie* contained Paul Valéry's sonnet *Arion* (republished two months later in *La Syrinx*), and in the bibliographical notes *La Fileuse* was quoted.

[6] An allusion to the last line of Gide's poem *Octobre:* ". . . Qu'une aube pluviale luise à travers la vitre."

[7] "Him" designates Pierre Louÿs, and "a polychrome marble," *Astarté*.

[8] A poem entitled *La Gardienne.*

[9] The editing of the Goncourts' *Journal* (memoirs of literary life since 1851) was to be completed in 1895. A few fragments were just being published.

and nothing more I want to hear from them. Each day I find that I am bored with yet another thing that had amused me the day before: that's how one grows old. I am alarmed at seeing how few things hold any interest for me today—although they are all interesting, in fact. Talking, or writing and receiving letters (Oh, not yours—but new ones), bores me stiff.*

I no longer think of anything but what I want to beget; perhaps that's why I can't stand all the rest; they're distractions.

And I still haven't the time to settle down to work, because when I do, it will be for a long time. Tomorrow my board;[10] three days later, Munich again for a month, then two weeks in unknown museums, then back to Paris, but this time not seeing anyone.

I read *La Faustin*[11] and found it enchanting—in spots; but if I were going into exile and could take only one of the Goncourts' books with me, I really think I should choose *La Maison d'un Artiste*.[12]

You spoke to me of *King Lear*,** and I never answered: yet I know nothing that I like better. Emmanuèle and I read it together, both of us in an empty room, a few scenes every night, before coming back to laugh with the others. We had never been as shaken by anything. This year, we also read *Hippolytus*[13] and Aeschylus' *Trilogy*.

Paris exasperates me; one can do nothing great in such agitation; one can't even write to you satisfactorily.

Mallarmé, Heredia, Régnier, and around them, all the others; I'm exhausted.

Yesterday, Louÿs read me the last poems that you sent him in a letter, exquisite poems: he read them to me only once; but I feel that I prefer them. I shall speak to you of them another time.

An almost mystical composition is going to come out in an exceptional issue of *La Conque*.[14] Your two dedicated pieces make a friendship ring between my poems and Pierre's.

Now I have a complaint to make about you; when you write to me, you

---

* *Translator's note:* As Gide had already admitted to Valéry in a letter postmarked March 21, 1892: "One should do nothing in life but write books; how everything else annoys me!"

[10] Recruiting board. André Gide's military service had already been "postponed" because of poor health, and he was about to appear before a new recruiting board.

[11] Published in 1882.

[12] Published in 1881.

** *Translator's note:* In a letter to Gide postmarked March 3, 1892, Valéry mentioned that he had reread *King Lear*. "One scene is incredible—it is the pure triumph of all literature—perhaps!"

[13] By Euripides.

[14] This issue was never published.

must tell me what has become of all *that*. Are you writing, are you yielding, what are you doing? You don't realize that it worries me a great deal. I can tell that the whole affair is very important to you. And do please give me news of your mother. Louÿs informs me that her condition still worries and saddens you. I should like to hear about all that from you alone.

I'm sending you these pages because I had to write to you, but they're so slapdash that I fear they may annoy you. But we're friends, aren't we, so that we shall never "be vexed with each other."

> Your
> An. G.

52. *Paul Valéry to André Gide*

[End of April, 1892]

Your very impatient letter makes me feel like copying it down for you with delightful laziness, so that you understand that the same is true here. . . .

And: "Each day I find that I am bored with yet another thing that had amused me the day before: that's how one grows old . . ." tempts me. And I've even been having some Ideas these last days—or shadows of Ideas—but time gives out along with patience, and July with its cudgels[15] is approaching.

Last night I felt that if I had had my friend at hand, I should have done something wildly mad. I have been so mean these last weeks that yesterday I could have wept over the flies—but they are very skeptical, knowing that they're worth nothing.

Then for two good hours I was brilliant: nothing but the very spiritual sea, a swaying sky, and in little sparkling bounds a holy Victory of Samothrace draws near, on her marble galley, rocked by the most limpid wave.

Then a rage of analyzing everything, a pica[16] of conscience, an aura of extralucid somnambulism. Finally, a yawn. . . .

I'm a bit weary of embellishing everything but my boredom, and after having thrown drops of Ocean on the sun, I turned to the right to come back.

---

[15] *Juillets de triques,* an allusion to Valéry's coming examinations in Law, with a recollection of Rimbaud's lines in *Le Bateau ivre:*

> *Quand les juillets faisaient crouler à coups de triques*
> *Les cieux ultramarins aux ardents entonnoirs.*

[16] Craving for unnatural food. From the Latin *pica,* or magpie, an omnivorous bird.

As for *that whole affair,* I detest it: because of her a certain poem recently broke between my fingers, and now it's the end! I must be good and study my Law. The Medusa disappeared a few days ago to some noonday bluish dwelling place, where her sea-hair out of the odyssey will find a good summer rocking-chair unaware of my existence, while the child plays (and now I'm really interested in her child, though it's unformed). We would have been so happy! Romance and hazy moonlight. Ah! stupid! All that, André, is unawareness, it is the misfortune of not understanding keenly enough or rather of not *feeling* what one understands—almost.

For that whole business I deserve booing and rotten tomatoes, except in the second act, when my guardian angel dictated to me those beautiful lucid words which, carefully kept in writing, will be my private glory tomorrow and a kind of encouragement in the future to gesticulate better, and to recite my part better.

I, very reasonably, nearly destroyed myself two or three times (perhaps I shall consider it tomorrow as well) for simple reasons: to begin with, so as to appease nothing; then, and contradictorily, for being so silly, the same as everyone else and altogether human: which is the height of bad taste. A realization which, by its very existence, redeemed my own, since I hastened to analyze exactly how I *should* have differed, at those moments, from the others. Whence a *theory*—that is, life for two weeks.

In honor of her impending return, I am studying Law (not certain!). I'm still afraid of a particular fatal interview—the first one, which will take place at a *Charity* affair! where, perhaps, I shall have to make a pretty little speech, with an almspurse in my hand. I am very capable of fainting or of doing something foolish physically, a small possibility that nearly happened several times—on simply meeting in the streets, which have been terrifying every since . . .*

Here is a page that will end with you yourself yawning, so I shall stop. Tell me about your board and what happened. You speak of my poems— and I can't remember which?

My mother now sees very little, and I dread even more the next visit to Paris with her. It's sad—there is no other word—to see her saddened, and sadder when she plays at being obscurely gay—*gropingly*—to pacify us. Adieu. I await your violet words.

P.-A. Valéry

It's very foolish. Mauclair dedicates an intense and *black* sonnet to me: *Pentacle,* and I don't know what to do. I have nothing to dedicate to him and don't feel like answering him now. Will you help me devise an

---

* *Translator's note:* Gide's comment on this whole affair, in a letter of May 5, 1892, was merely: "O Lord, deliver us from all Medusas, etc."

experiment in simple telepathy or suggestion at a distance, like that of Hennique-Desbeaux? [17]

53. Paul Valéry to André Gide

[P. Montpellier, June 13, 1892]

Poe, and I shouldn't talk about it for I promised myself I wouldn't, is the only writer—with no sins. Never was he mistaken—not led instinctively—but lucidly and successfully, he made a synthesis of all the vertigoes. . . .

I am no more than a silly student these days. After this last exam, I see vague directions.

Perhaps I may go to Italy. . . . Not certain! I'm not very keen about it. Then Paris—to find some hole where I could scratch out words on official paper. . . . To live according to the absurd. We shall keep an eye on that.

Christ is in the delights of the tomb at last. All the follies and the maintaining of one's image before the public are now useless: one lies down.

The silence, in which his bones are at rest and will shine—is sweeter to him than the first steps he took on the cold waters, when he realized that he was not sinking—and Chance!

I imagined a strange theory of mathematics. Very symptomatic of me. It is probable that I shall give Louÿs nothing for XIII.[18] I really cannot. Yet I will [*sic*] have a fine theme. . . .

Ah! let's forget it!

My famous *Narcisse* is reaching *wayward* proportions (not in space, but in *pitch*). Therefore I shall never write it. It is now fairly complete. But it must be perfected *poetically;* composed and, mainly, versified. At this point—hang it all.

I shall end:

Don't forget that if my letter doesn't *want* to correspond to yours, it's because . . .   V.

54. André Gide to Paul Valéry

Montigny, (Côte-d'Or) [P. July 12, 1892]

My friend,

Mallarmé has given me your poems; since he criticized them, he must esteem them.[19] I was delighted by a few that I didn't know; some of them are much less good—that is, in comparison with others of your own.

---

[17] An experiment made on June 11 and 12, 1891, by the writer Léon Hennique and Emile Desbeaux, the former in Paris, the latter at Ribemont, in the Aisne. (Cf. *Les Annales des sciences psychiques,* 1892 and 1893.)

[18] An issue of *La Conque*. But that literary review was never to have an issue No. XIII.

[19] Pierre Louys had transmitted to Mallarmé the poems sent him by Valéry.

On reading them, I imagined them published, but Mallarmé, when I saw him again, didn't seem to think it desirable.

I spent all my time alone, almost, even though I was in Paris.

Every morning in Auteuil at Jacques Blanche's:[20] he has just finished my portrait.

Evenings, very exalted work and hollow aesthetic dreams.

Henri de Régnier was about the only one I saw,[21] in addition to Mallarmé, whom I decidedly cherish.

With Henri de Régnier I plan to roam around Brittany in the month of August; we shall leave on the 15th and shall return at the beginning of September. At Belle-Isle, at Camaret, we want to live, look at the sea, work.

Yesterday, I left sunny and dusty Paris; I am at Montigny, on the Côte d'Or, with my friend Quillot,[22] who sends you greetings. I got up very early; the fields are moist with dawn, my work enchants me and irritates me; I think of nothing else and cannot read.

Your exams?

Tell me everything.

And when you have taken them, you will write a play in verse *for me.*

Love,
André Gide

55. *Paul Valéry to André Gide*

[P. July 13, 1892]

Dear lively one,

Louÿs and You are beastly Semites: one of you, for having underhandedly and covered with a cloak of distance, dared to present my vague alchemies to Mallarmé,

the other of you, for having dared even more, in not repeating to me textually the precious and pure panning I deserved from the Master. Louÿs is completely mute. Whereas you merely hint. Whom shall I kill? All joking apart, you are loathsome. If I knew Quillot better, I should have you poisoned. Speak then, with no fear of stating every lamentable word.

[20] The painter Jacques-Emile Blanche was to remain a friend of Gide's throughout his life. In addition to several portraits of Gide, he painted portraits of Mallarmé, Barrès, Marcel Proust, François Mauriac, and others.

[21] At that moment Henri de Régnier was one of the friends André Gide most gladly spent time with. He liked the subtlety and refinement of Régnier, who was four years his elder and had already published five collections of poems.

[22] Maurice Quillot is the author of *Nihilisme sentimentale, L'Entrainé, Le Traité de la Méduse* (an essay on transcendental mysticism), and *La Fille de l'Homme,* with a preface by Pierre Louÿs. In the top form at the lycée Janson-de-Sailly, he had been a fellow student of Pierre Louÿs and Marcel Drouin. He thus became friendly with André Gide, who was to dedicate *Les Nourritures terrestres* to him.

Happy pastoral creature, I send you love and if I had the time, I would take you by the arm and really tell you a few things.

I trust You.

Paul

Regards to Quillot.

56. *André Gide to Paul Valéry*

Château de La Roque, near Cambremer (Calvados)

July 25 [1892]

In the name of that which is now only a pale thread, and which I saw this evening come up over the calm lawn, greetings. The memory of you is indissociable from this fairyland fruit.

Mallarmé admitted to me in low tones that he has no "sense of the moon." Here is what he said about your poems—and don't have me poisoned: "I'm surprised that with the tact and knowledge of poetry he sometimes shows, he leaves, here and there, some that would seem to me *facile.*" The remark surprised me. And that's about it.

As you asked to have me poisoned, Maurice Quillot wrote you a letter which, when one knows him, is charming. Did he send it to you? I fled from his house in a great rush; for since both of us were absolutely alone in the country house, we were becoming lascivious, and my friend provoking. The evening of my departure I arrived at Pierre Louÿs' and found him even worse. Finally, I got to La Roque; at least I'm alone here. What a business!

And those exams? Write.

I'm losing all patience with a very arduous task which, even before it is done, I feel is absurd; moreover, it is one that won't please you, and this distresses me. It's my *Voyage au Spizberg.*[23] Have I spoken to you about it? Since you asked, and in a "flattering" way, I sent you my poems. You have said nothing to me about them. I should like very much to know if for you they are poems, if they exist in any way as literature. You know that if you think so, I would be absolutely delighted, if not, I will grieve very little, so you can speak out.*

---

[23] Parts of *Le Voyage au Spitzberg* were published in the March and July issues of *La Wallonie,* entitled "Voyage sur l'Océan pathétique" and "Voyage vers une Mer glaciale." The entire work was to be published by Art Indépendant in 1893 as *Le Voyage d'Urien,* its definitive title.

* *Translator's note:* On July 30 Valéry answered: "As a general criticism, you somewhat overdid the soul and souls bit. . . . The language is charming, perhaps not rigorous or mad enough. But I repeat to you that you are the only one who has done in verse (the XIVth) what Beethoven has done in music." The poems under discussion here are *Les Poésies d'André Walter.*

I'm reading the old *Lancelot du Lac,* which bores me—but what a beautiful thing is Goethe's *Iphigenie!* "It is indeed like a statue," etc.

Adieu, I am daydreaming in a hammock and am sick from having suddenly smoked too much. I like you a great deal and am your

André G.

Who is this Joachim Gasquet who has been courting me? [24]

How unmercifully Griffin attacks Féline [25] in *Les Entretiens.* Did you see?

Griffin told me to ask you urgently for a "poetic reading" for his review. Can you give him your bath of Des Esseintes? [26]

57. *Paul Valéry to André Gide*

In Genoa, *since last week* [27]

[P. September 21, 1892]

André dear, I envy your good and untroubled work. Life here is madness, thousands of brainless festivities, dances on ships, arts to eat all the day long. I spend many evenings with an extraordinary collector, an Englishman called Mylius, smoking in his house, which is a kind of Cluny looking right out over the sky and the sea. This man owns wonders that would make Goncourt die of jealousy and that are used, in living and

[24] The poet Joachim Gasquet (1873–1921), who wrote *Les Hymnes* and *Les Chants de la Forêt,* founded *La Syrinx,* a small literary review published irregularly. In 1892 Valéry's *Episode, Les Vaines Danseuses, Arion,* and *Baignée* were included.

[25] The poet Michel Féline, the brother of Valéry's Montpellier friend and neighbor Pierre Féline, contributed to *La Plume* and wrote *La Mélancolie de son Bonheur* (1921).

[26] Probably an allusion to a text of Valéry's on the character in Huysmans' *A Rebours.* This text, which has remained unknown, was never to appear. Valéry did not publish any study on Huysmans until March, 1898 ("Durtal," in *Mercure de France*).

[27] Through his mother, the daughter of Giulio Grassi, the Italian consul in Trieste, Paul Valéry came from an old Genoese family. Whenever he visited Genoa, a city he particularly loved, he stayed with his aunt, Mme Cabella, wife of the Belgian consul general in that city.

Valéry left Montpellier on September 14 with his mother and brother. It was during this "Genoese" visit that the "well-known *nuit de Gênes*" took place, and not in August, 1892, as has been generally thought. That stormy night, a night of insomnia and revelation, Valéry sensed the vanity of literature and gave up all ideas of having a literary career. His daughter, Agathe Rouart-Valéry, related his confidential remarks on the subject in *Les Cahiers du Sud* ("Paul Valéry vivant"— 1946): "A fearful night—spent on my bed—the storm everywhere—my room dazzling with every flash of lightning . . . And my whole fate was being decided in my head—I was between me and myself."

Jules Valéry, in his *Notes,* which were written there and then, mentions a terrifying storm during the night of October 4–5. That date would seem to be the right one, even though Paul Valéry had decided on November, when twenty-five years later he tried to recapture the past.

sleeping, quite idiotically in a habitual dandyism, beautiful in its indifference.

Here, I look at nothing, in fact. Italy is so much a part of me that I can't
even give you the general tonality of it. I got particular enjoyment from a
ballet—a completely Italian feast—vaguely greeted a few paintings, the *St.
John* of Da Vinci (brother of the Parisian one), etc., some Van Dycks, but
all that annoys me *here* for it seems banal. In my uncle's house itself, when
I come out, there is a twelfth-century chapel in the stairway, and the walls
are covered with marble creatures, angels and bulls.

I go to the little streets, to the gardens, to the spring waters—just to live!

I admire your fertility, you already have a *Complete Works*. I am still
holding mine back; I'm forced to. My sonnet in *La Syrinx* dates from
February, it was badly maimed. Example: *bouche* for *boucle*. Adieu. I shall
be in Paris on about October 15. Where will you be stationed?

Your darling
P. V.

℅ M. Gaetano Cabella, Genoa (Italy)

58. André Gide to Paul Valéry

La Roque [P. October 18, 1892]

Dear Ambroise,

When will I see you? It's still true that you're coming to Paris, isn't it?

I'm thinking of returning on November 1; on the 15th, I'm off to exile in
Nancy. In the worst division and in the worst of barracks.[28] I'm afraid I
shall come out of there in the state of a perfect noumenon. If before my
entombment we could peripateticize together for a few hours, in those
Luxembourg Gardens where we already have memories in common, or
else in the Tuileries watching the leaves fall, I think my coming exile
would not seem as hard to bear.

I didn't write to you in Genoa, because I have never been there—and
mostly because all my thoughts, which up to then had been so painfully
organized, became all mixed up again—and because all those days I was
living the most plaintive of elegies. Afterward, I went back to work, and
the hope of seeing you again made me keep putting off my letter. We shall
talk, I prefer it.

The first two parts of my voyage are finished; I'm working on the last.
La Wallonie asked me for everything I had written up to then; the issue
must have come out, although I have no news of it. . . .

Almost nothing to tell you; sometimes I see more clearly, sometimes less

[28] André Gide, who was declared to be "good for service" by a Parisian recruiting
board, was sent to Nancy, where, after a few days in the barracks, he was discharged
for reasons of health. He kept a very unpleasant memory of those days (cf. his
Journal of that time).

clearly in life, but always more clearly in our art. I am reading Leibnitz's *La Théodicée,* which, by proving Christianity reasonable, makes me bored with it. I have read a lot of Goethe, and more constantly than many. The last books of *Wilhelm Meister* are the most boring works by an intelligent man that I have ever read. Reread *Le Cousin Pons,* which I really think I find the best of all Balzac. Its manner is masterful and truly classic. . . . And nothing else.

Adieu. Do write to me about our meeting in Paris. I send you greetings and am your

André Gide

— 1893 —

59. Paul Valéry to André Gide

Paris [January, 1893]

My dear André,

I have two excuses: one, that telling an old sailor like myself about your seas [1] authorizes him to speak about literature with you, a fine writer; two, that there is no one behind me in this room, that since I am actually alone, here as elsewhere, my opinions are gently ascribable to the not very dangerous madness of oneness. . . .

I have therefore a few observations to make on your beautiful story, observations that are necessarily provoked by the fact of knowing you. . . . The principle here, rarely grasped with such purity, is that of being your friend, of knowing—through approximations and indeterminates—your *formula* a little; then, in the lines, smelling you out, seeking you, and finally perceiving what of you is in them, and what—forced, deviated, learned or not remembered—would seem to interfere with recognizing you, my friend, and to become the object of harsh judgment authenticated by the very mistake of pure logic from which you draw the pretext—a strong one—of coupling with joys *that are not fundamental to you.*

You will come upon my manias again, you who love obsessions. Don't reproach me for any of the following, for apart from the fact that it is restricted to my "humble opinion," what I point out there is precisely what is not you—or so it would seem to me. Finally, one suggestion . . . which I shan't mention until further on.

A) Here is the text: One hundred pages. Seventy-two hot—in all senses and giving a general sense, twenty-eight cold—same comment. A page, a

[1] This letter is about *Le Voyage d'Urien,* which was to be published by Art Indépendant in 1893.

paragraph, a sentence, even a word taken *at random* give the impression of *intentional* symmetry in the detail of each one. The original division is corroborated. We thus know that the author wanted symmetry. What kind? A symmetry of detail, and thus necessarily a general symmetry of an elementary nature.

On the other hand, the book is composed of $8/10$ *description* and $2/10$ *ethics*. But thanks to certain clearly perceptible tonalities in the $8/10$ d, one *may* say that the author intended the proportion e/d to be, not $2/8$, but rather about $\frac{3 \text{ or } 4}{8}$. Here a natural and twofold question. The legitimacy of the descriptive portion. *What* is being described? and why? Idols of what is *conveyed,* etc. The justification of this hypothesis = the second part of my question = the legitimacy of the "ethical" portion. Symmetry of a *false* symmetry, assertions of a moral or philosophical nature in the absence of their constructions. Therefore ALLEGORY. . . . The descriptive part (d) had to be carried out and contestable since the ethical portion (e), established in the same way, without its atmosphere, was parallel to it, etc. Whence we deduce the antagonism, obvious only now, of the precise work in a whole series of sentences—with the vacillation of a series of *invocations,* instances of *syntactical* reserve, approximations. With again the result that the skeleton of the book is twofold and does not correspond exactly to all the modulations of the initial intention, and that side by side with what the author felt, one sees what he intended.

In two words, the nature of the book is to be *successive* and *discontinuous.* In it you used notations that have long been familiar to you, for example: ice, purity—fervor, heat. But you must not stagnate in them for too long . . . any more than in the rather sad effects of the "landscape of the soul."

B) More in detail, do note:

1. Brutalities that should, I think, be linked to the ironic tone in several places, as being part of the same intentions. The purpose—at least, the most *apparent* purpose—of such things being to FINISH OFF, somewhat artificially, the book as a whole, the effects of the book.[2]

2. A certain . . . fragmentarism [*sic*], or taste for the detached piece, counterparts of which can be found precisely in that of the blunt sentence and the word taken in itself as *effective* by itself, the latter tendency giving at the same time very legitimate and complete effects no less than others that are too pronounced to operate, at other times. The danger here being the propensity toward plays on words in the category of . . . metaphysics —through infinitesimal distortions.

3. The tones are generally well thought out and carried out. At times one comes across a very felicitous and very appropriate imitation of the

---

[2] In the margin Valéry wrote: "p. 20, 21, 60."

characteristic *boredom* of travelers' relations (monotony of different land-scapes quickly traversed).

4. The images are often a bit . . . coarse . . . , resonant, I might say. Certain of them very beautiful. Not that of Novalis.

5. Diverse echoes: Flaubert, *passim*. Barrès. Maeterlinck. In some places almost . . . *Vathek!*[3] (Were you thinking of it? I'm curious to know.)[4]

6. The style! Of an incomparably high standard and integrity, but to quibble: not *variable* enough in intonation and words—not *differentiated* enough. A very regrettable overindulgence in inversions—and in the word *autour,* joined to another.

7. The work somewhat visible. . . .

8. O psychology.

Denis' decorations[5] are interesting, but their sequence is not faithful enough to the book. There are not enough *inner* differences between those of the first part and those of the second. Finally, his knowledge of the *directions* is perhaps inadequate, his means not very varied—that is, false in too many cases, with enchanting exceptions. Now I repeat that you made too great an effort (I believe it) on behalf of your book—not enough on behalf of Yourself. You wanted to embellish it with everything that seemed to you beautiful—but beware of Literature (*idola libri*). The subtle relations in a work are (at least I feel they are) of a terrifying exactitude. Must not be falsified. Let us fight shy of Pascal's false windows (22, art. VII).* In nine cases out of ten that is how one goes wrong: mathematicians give cruel examples of it—they who do such beautiful things—and who know not what they do.

I have finished. You have put up with me and recognized me. You will find me . . . anything you like. I could have gone on longer, after all. And when we glance through *Urien* together, I shall tell you how I read it and about some beautiful pages I noticed in it. Don't forget either that what one says about a work one says only with regard to what one has grasped. And one grasps what one can, what one already possesses as clear and formed.

Also, I have thousands of explanations to give and to ask for—also, why did I write all this?

P. Valéry

I shall be at home tonight at eight-thirty, tomorrow also, in case you should like us to devour each other.

---

[3] *Vathek* is an Arab tale, written in French at the end of the eighteenth century (1787) by an Englishman, William Beckford. It was published in Paris, and reprinted in 1876. Stéphane Mallarmé was to write a preface to it.

[4] Again in the margin, in Valéry's handwriting: "p. 57, 61."

[5] The painter Maurice Denis illustrated *Le Voyage d'Urien.*

* *Translator's note:* Brunschvicg edition, I.27.

60. André Gide to Paul Valéry

Montpellier [March, 1893]

Dear friend,

I am getting a bit worried; why, before leaving, did I not take back all your letters which, alas, I had lent you. If I had not a very rare confidence in you, I should be afraid that never would I see that correspondence again; I know, of course, that you'll return it to me one day, but I should have liked to have been able to bring it here with me; it would have taken your place. Out of the most exquisite of habits, the sentimental habit, I look for you at every moment, and I talk only to those who have known you and speak to me of you. My first evenings here, I climbed up to the Peyrou in order to watch from the height of the terraces, with their black swans and their stilled pools, the sun set and the distant sea smile. Then I wearied of that very solitary promenade.

This time I have not seen the museum, I have not seen the tomb on which we chewed enchanted roses. I have not walked under the trees in the evening, as we used to do. I have not seen Coste and am afraid of seeing him again. I live in the anticipation of leaving and of bathing in the sea. In three days I shall take off, from Cette or Marseilles, for Spain, where I await my joy from the sun.

Is Paris still as unbearable? What is everyone doing? What are you doing? Are you publishing lots of things? How will I find you when I return? I imagine that Louÿs is vilifying me in his talk: out of carelessness, I wrote him such a friendly letter that he got angry. For him to be decent, I have to beat him as I have never beaten women. There are days when it's tiresome, when you would gladly hold out your hand; but as soon as you relax, he lashes out at you. Oh well, "it can't be helped."

Write to me while I'm still far away; here I have no time to do anything; but how I should like to read a letter in your handwriting.

I am your
André Gide

Do give Mme Valéry all my respects; and give all good wishes for success to your brother.

61. Paul Valéry to André Gide

[P. July 24, 1893]

Dear friend,

For me your first letter is the cold glass of the really wettest water there is, water found on the ground, in the country, in a hole, bent under weeds.

I was going through an unhealthy season—it's when I think I'm solitary.

I am so alone! When my head works, I'm delighted actually, and thanks somewhat to that isolation. But once the wind has fallen, there is nothing beside me. The communications have been cut. Atrociously alone. You know too well (alas for you!) how my expansive experiments have failed—very rightly—in every direction. For lack of approximations. That it all led me elsewhere and electrified me—is true. But to think that I have actually never known Satisfaction, fulfilment, not even the slightest form of spreading out and settling down. . . . I beseech the stones around me. They are rocks! (All this is vertigo—which is gallantly dispelled during the Day, but the Day is not continuous.) I feel that one favorable being would make me live, would prolong my existence by a few centuries; as if I were changing my old consciousness for a new one. Note the point: dreaming of such communions is of about as much interest as dreaming of a boot. But living that dream while, at the same time, dreaming of something else, is illuminating.

If, for example, I had held R.[6] between my hands, within reach of all my spiritual mechanics, machines of wild delicacy and enormous strength for weighing, decomposing, and constructing—moving, I should have jeered at the conquerors and the aeronauts, the scientists and the architects. . . . I would wager that the mistake many people make concerning me is to suppose—in spite of everything—that I have a *literary* ulterior motive, to believe that through the restriction I profess and the renouncement, I am aiming at some *new genre*. I can easily guess at such sophisms, in great part because I know they *must* be formulated. But those people may be forgiven, for they know neither Me nor R.

In addition to these beloved insulations,[7] I indulge vaguely in grammatical speculations. Schwob[8] forced me to read Paul Claudel's *La Ville*.[9] A book the description and statics of which would be very amusing and . . . pressing. Adieu, dear fellow. You are lucky to be in your nest. God knows when I shall see trees! and seas, above all!

P. Valéry

62. *André Gide to Paul Valéry*

[August 24, 1893]

Dear friend,

Where will this letter find you?

Will you have seen the sea, or will you still be moping around in rooms?

I have lived a lot; that explains my silence; for three weeks I could do

---

[6] Rimbaud.

[7] Here a neologism: probably a state of isolation on an island.

[8] Marcel Schwob (1867–1905). Passionately interested in medieval studies, historical research, and linguistics, he was the author of *Le Cœur double, Le Rio au masque d'or* (short stories), and *Le Livre de Monelle* (poetic prose). He was a contributor to *Le Mercure de France*.

[9] The play was published in 1893 by Art Indépendant.

nothing but take life easy, or try things that diverted me from thinking. Family and friends are the reason for it; during the entire time they stayed here, I could do nothing but attend to them.

Yesterday I got back from Brittany where, as soon as the others left, I had to stay for four days.

Now I feel nothing but calm sadness, and anticipation of the future.

Your letter is the bitterest of any you have ever written me; and because of that I find it the best; what you were lacking—am I wrong?—was that call to another; what the other lacked was feeling called. One has to wait frightfully long for an answer; and that is why I well understand those who prefer to call loudly rather than unerringly. One comes out of one's solitude only with the help of an illusion; but one must consent; there are those whose pride makes them reluctant to consent to being dupes. Those are the most haughty; how could they not be unhappy? The sad thing about them is that they are above complaining.

But to see the sea again would be enough to console them; and even never seeing men again, so long as they could be replaced.

It amuses me to write you these words, which are as approximate as possible. And yet I know you're right. But do you ever think how sharp every limitation would be, without that approximation to make it crumble? One does everything—even makes love—while thinking a little about something else—and with what results!

Forgive me: I have been talking nonsense; I should have spoken to you of Saint-Malo in the moonlight and the gray, green and brown polders. But I think I shall have plenty of time next year to talk about landscapes.

I am very much your
André Gide

63. *Paul Valéry to André Gide*

[P. August 26, 1893]

Paris is beginning again.[10] I am here alone, seeing sometimes and often Clignancourt, Saint-Denis, which I like, and the little boats on whose glass bottoms I stretch out close to water that seems to be bottled, smoking, reaching the Alma bridge in order to smoke again with Régnier, amusingly.

Last night (oh! discursively) I recognized an old and dear acquaintance on the boulevard, the Russian Kolbassine,[11] one of the rare men "comme il

---

[10] Paul Valéry came back to Paris, this time alone. He was to return to Montpellier in October, after having attended the funeral of Mac-Mahon.

[11] A professor of Russian extraction, *agrégé* in philosophy (then teaching in a Montpellier secondary school), to whom Paul Valéry was to dedicate *La Soirée avec Monsieur Teste* when it was published for the first time in *Le Centaure* in 1896.

faut," a real thinker, whom I led back here to sit down and talk, talk, talk, until the next morning—a real spree—about everything, about our travels, a scene out of an astonishing comedy in which the conversationalists give the impression of knowing everything and of crossing, in an allusion, spiritual leagues. . . .

It has been centuries since we have seen you. Or Louis (who is in Paris, I know, brought here suddenly by the news that his brother was named minister plenipotentiary and one of the international commissioners of the Egyptian Debt, in Cairo).

While awaiting some departure or other, I live about like this—drifting. . . . In order not to think, I spend days on mad calculations, mechanically, or on horrible fantasies. Then hours in the streets, riveted in front of a jeweler's on the rue de la Paix, or transforming the comforts of expensive hotels and the steel arcades.

Electrified like a metal by having noticed all these disorders on the basin of the earth, which go from Paris to India, and continue to kill still more in the south of France, then over Italy, bleeding on the world throughout the year like a snake of horrible energies—linked to what completely new whirlwinds? who knows? I feel in my being the influence of certain comets, and my "dominant visions" of the moment follow the great slope of vast numbers, the obvious movements of nations and individuals distorted by some precession of the equinoxes.

There you have a lot of approximations. Eh? The approximations of a galvanometer. Good title.

And if I told you that I admire—as a littérateur—the pages of a geometrician, that nothing, neither Rimbaud, nor . . . reality, has given me the *view,* the deglutition of the sea—as did opening a Laplace [12] at random, the other day, at the page on flux and tides. *Extemplo,* the gurgle and the swaying came to me, the steel-gray color, the swelling and the headlong escapes to the West. The word: syzygy! The smell of that thingamabob that moves and shines between azimuths, coordinates, parallaxes, etc., the height of the sun,—everything.

For extraordinary reading I've had Poe's *Lettres d'amour,*[13] something which for me, you realize, is dizzying. But we shall talk about that another time.

Adieu, write very quickly to your
P. Valéry

All my respects to Mme Gide, to whom my mother would like you to please convey her greetings.

---

[12] The mathematician-astronomer.

[13] *Lettres d'amour à Helen* was translated much later by Cecil George Bazile and published in Paris in 1924.

64. Paul Valéry to André Gide

[September 28, 1893]

I see rather a lot of Louis, as you must have perceived from the simple jokes he provokes. This leads me to write a remark: Louis has a way of influencing me—an extraordinary power of irresistibility, half that of a woman, which lasts while he is there—and enough when he is not so that I don't even *wish* then to exert some method of arrangements, permutations, or analysis on this relationship and this gift—and that is indeed the most surprising thing of all.

I haven't told you about his discovery of a bartender who is something of a genius, or how, one beautiful night about a month ago, we were brought together by him on the rue Rembrandt, H. de R.,[14] R. de B.,[15] and myself, delightfully then abominably intoxicated by thousands of American drinks which the Man in the white jacket had been bringing us, periodically and learnedly, since midnight. A real chemist, who managed to mix champagne and nutmeg with eggs, and finally, to offer us that incredible Last Drink[16]—made of every imaginable liqueur—and which tastes like clear water—and which knocks you out.

Et cetera.

I live more than ever in vagueness. My situation is becoming grotesque. And in addition, I'm not fit even to think about it.

I am watching the disintegration of a friend who is dying of a little-known type of syphilis, and the ruin of that individual—a heap of the most intense sensations and magnetically controlled actions, yesterday—is rather chilling. Everyday—however—anesthetic libraries give me a few hours of peace, during which the reading of formulas, malaises precipitated into dizzying arrangements, go round beneath my eyes for a long time. Finally, I prowl about.

I have not received anything from you for many weeks? When are you coming? and with what manuscript? Apropos, you should look into a rather curious coincidence in the last Poictevin,[17] certain pages of which (except for the extravagant words so dear to him) give the impression of having been written by you. Or rather, perhaps a similarity of atmosphere. . . .

Yours,

P. V.

---

[14] Henri de Régnier.

[15] Robert de Bonnières.

[16] In English in the original.

[17] Francis Poictevin (1854–1904), a friend of Villiers de L'Isle-Adam, Verlaine, and Mallarmé, author of collections of tales: *Derniers Songes* (1888), *Heures* (1892), *Ombres* (1894), etc.

65. André Gide to Paul Valéry

[October, 1893]

I am taking care not to write to Louÿs; since I have kept silent, he has written me a mass of charming letters; I read them more or less according to the days, according to his style, but I no longer get upset about them.

Although this will perhaps make you smile, I cannot help but find his prose exquisite, and when I reread his life of Meleager,[18] I can't feel altogether angry with him.

Seeing a friend die of syphilis is something that can happen to us every day, given the preposterous people we know; we would do well to prepare ourselves for it. Last year I saw a friend almost die of orchitis, or at any rate no one was sure what it was, it was so enormously complicated. Etc. Au revoir. Expect to find me at your door late one of these afternoons at about five.

Your
André Gide

66. Paul Valéry to André Gide

[November 27, 1893]

Your mother, André, from whom I finally got your address,[19] asks me not to write you anything too exciting. She tells me that you are ill. Consequently I shall manage to stop at information and questions, without raising my fingers in the air and singing about the *Flamma pura, tersa, clara*. I am in the most prohibitory of Montpelliers—and only Régnier dares write to me.

I often see your friend Rouart.[20] We get along very well on painting. As for the rest, flabbergasted, he has already bought *Les Illuminations* and Poe: mine is a broker's glory. He showed me a certain work: *La Tentative amoureuse*.[21] I have still read no more than the notes—and two or three snatches within. I swear to you that for me you are horribly difficult to understand. I often wish that we were together, and that you would give me a word-for-word explanation.

[18] Pierre Louÿs prefaced *Les Poésies de Méléagre* with a life of Meleager (1893).

[19] Gide was then traveling in North Africa with Paul-Albert Laurens. Having fallen seriously ill in Tunisia, he reached Biskra, in Algeria, where he was treated for a lung disease. His illness explains his silence.

[20] Eugène Rouart (1872–1935), son of Henri Rouart, the famous collector of modern French paintings, friend of Degas and Manet. He was then studying at the School of Agriculture at Grignon. He was later to direct certain great agricultural enterprises and to become a senator from the Tarn-et-Garonne. Like his father, a friend of painters and poets, it was he who put André Gide into touch with Francis Jammes in 1893. With the latter, he joined Gide in Biskra in 1895. *Paludes* was dedicated to him. He himself was the author of the tale *Vengeance de moines* (1892) and the novel *La Villa sans maître* (1898).

[21] By André Gide, the first edition published in 1893 by Art Indépendant.

R., who is somewhat like an ingot, confesses that he is toiling. A moment I consider so paroxysmal that seeing someone in it, especially him, would affect me were it not for a calculation—accurate, after all—which gives rise only to the ludicrous. I know what I mean.

My reading—rare: one very good *History of Materialism* by Lange.[22] A rather curious *Essai sur le principe générateur des constitutions politiques* by J. de Maistre. And above all, the fascinating *Electricity and Magnetism* by the last great theoretician (dead), Maxwell. I say it's *fascinating*. A book completely made up of a primordial, initial metaphor, then just formulas and diagrams—an extraordinary illustration. I'm wasting a lot of time, in addition: games of chess *cum* Kolbassine.

From Louÿs, nothing. From X, Y, and Z, nothing. I say that of all the centuries, the eighteenth pleases me the most. All we have today are *diffused lights* (*largo sensu*).

I am terribly worried about my situation, a fact that doesn't change me. Yet I'm very sensible, two or three *purely* material and simple things are absolutely necessary to me, would be enough for me (I think), and I don't see them in the offing. O objects! some definitive wallpaper? when?

It is fortunate that we . . . ! but you don't agree with me.

I think then that I like you very much. Keep warm.

P. V.

General Delivery, Montpellier

67. *André Gide to Paul Valéry*

[Biskra, November 27, 1893]

Dear friend,

What silence! I am in Biskra; [23] aren't you in Montpellier? I have just been very sick, and I'm living in Biskra now, not as a "tourist" but as a convalescent. I'm sorry that I was not able to cross the great desert of Souf and Djerid. My lungs broke down even before I could reach Gabès, and it was by way of Constantine, not by way of the South, that I managed to reach Biskra, where I am sadly vegetating. At least I made two marvelous, unforgettable crossings, and I so wished you were there, parallel to me, in the other berth, which was empty. Portholes are marvelous eyes through which nature looks at you.

I shan't tell you anything about my trip because I don't think you approve, but I think that traveling, also, is an art and that it can become amusing. I tasted grief that I had never known before; I amused myself by

[22] *Geschichte des Materialismus* (1866) by Friedrich Albert Lange (1828–1875).

[23] This stay in Biskra was to have great importance in André Gide's moral evolution: it was there that he became aware of the deep exigencies of his nature, and freed himself of all the constraints he had thought he had to comply with until then. He was to devote long passages to this stay in *Si le Grain ne meurt* and in *L'Immoraliste*.

living only with the officers, and I now recall really brutal festivities. I have often missed Paris. Because of you now, I miss Montpellier a little. I'm worried about the fact that you're there, for then what is happening? It cannot be that nothing is going on, and you owe me thousands of details. So write me something as long and complicated as your sad and learned life. Tell me what has happened to all that, all that about which we spoke so much. In Montpellier someone is looking for you, one of my most charming friends, you will recognize him by his figure of a "lily! and one of you all, etc." and by his hair which seems to have been made by Monet. A silk scarf round his neck; bent, awkward, and exquisite. His name is Eugène Rouart and he is presently lodged at Miss Twight's, on the boulevard Case-Neuve.[24]

You can talk about lots of things with him; he is very "in the know." I myself am no longer, and I worry in vain about knowing what's happening. When I know what's happening to you, I shall be greatly satisfied by that in itself. Adieu.

Write to me. I am your
André Gide

68. *Paul Valéry to André Gide*

[December 8, 1893]

Did you find my letter at the post office?

You say: "very sick," I don't know what to think. Where are you sick? Why? After all, you are in the sun and you were at sea.

Yes, the berth—the other berth—is indeed freedom. In a room, the best you can do is to try to put everything in that is necessary to thinking. There you have everything. Your words revive it [*sic*] in me. You know, I am left with almost nothing but a "vision," a delirium. And after having played with the landscapes of books and engravings, all I can see is a moving *hectare* of the Pacific, a desire for the little wave that grows and dies and does what it can—in the equinoxes. One must take a clipper to get there. Yet Kolbassine insists that we go to Batavia. He talks about the Island as if he had made it or simply as if he had been there. All the details. I am letting myself be tempted. I really think that there, more than anywhere else, one is nearer, not nature (or stupidity), but the Cosmos. There are earthquakes, cyclones, the sky, etc. The trouble is that we haven't a penny.

. . . My life, my dear André, is neither "sad nor learned," alas! It is saddened these days by the sudden madness and suicide of one of my best friends—who was somebody. A young lieutenant in the naval artillery (the one to whom I *showed* Mallarmé at Fontainebleau), the most well-balanced boy in the world, suddenly went mad, and carried away by a

---

[24] Gide did not yet know that Valéry had already met Eugène Rouart.

childhood dream of mountains and hiking, took off for Annecy and killed himself there. I went to Nîmes to bury him the day before yesterday, etc. How vile the solemn customs of modern life are! Sickening barbarism and idolatry!

As for me, I'm doing nothing. I have caught a glimpse of something rather new, I think, to organize—first to find. You might call it a (little) Treatise on Complexity or a Theory of the Instrument giving a way of resolving . . . etc., with an appendix on the generalization of the three analytic quantities in constructive operations. One German word says it all. But I am unable to work on it. At times, I dream of having an army of workers, whom I would have think about, and purify, everything I have glimpsed. For relaxation and in order not to waste our Sundays, we would use those days to construct buildings on land and on the water.

Adieu, Wanderer, forgive me for so ineffective a letter. I see M. Rouart rather often. I believe he'll be something *good*. But when will I lose the silly mania of showing people that I don't think as they do? Yet another thing to forgive me for and to what a degree!   P. V.

— 1894 —

69. André Gide to Paul Valéry

[February, 1894]

Dear friend,

Although I am quite as ready to blame myself for this silence as to complain about it, the truth is that I was waiting for an answer from you, or was one letter lost—mine? yours? My last one gave you some explanation of my condition, as you explicitly requested. . . . I am now better, perhaps because of the splendid weather we have had until today, which is why I am now writing to you. Had it continued to be fine, I should have been outside long ago.

Nothing, absolutely nothing to say, although my life is very full; yesterday I watched, even helped with, an enucleation: the eye hanging at the end of a thread, cotton in the empty socket, horrible! horrible! a horrible death! There are two doctors here whom I sometimes accompany on their rounds.

My mother has come to join me.[1] I think you know that. I am bored with Algeria; before long, I think I shall be able to get back to Tunis. Before long means three weeks, I should say.

---

[1] In *Si le Grain ne meurt* André Gide tells how his mother, warned about his health by Paul-Albert Laurens, turned up unexpectedly in Biskra to take care of him.

Adieu. Some news, please. I myself have forgotten how to write but am still your

André G.

70. *Paul Valéry to André Gide*

[February 26, 1894]

My dear friend,

The mail is complete chaos. I no longer understand anything about our letters. You speak to me of yours in terms that remain obscure to me—therefore I haven't received it. And I have no idea which is the last one you got from me.

But even if nothing had come, you can be sure that I would have written to you regularly if . . . if my situation had been better. Enough that I tell you about the current knot.

Primo, I am leaving for Paris next Saturday.[2] After four quite useless months of Montpellier, during which my desire to return to Paris, the local pneumatism and thousands of stupidities have putrefied [*sic*] me.

Secundo, my mother is unreasonably affected by it—and while I have never shown this to anyone—it weighs heavy, it's hard.

Tertio, if I leave, you can imagine why. My life is an apple, a fig, but as long as I have it, I must be satisfied in it, I must look for a paid job—*establish* myself, and I leave very worried—I know the difficulties, those that welter in my mind and those that circumstances create. Paris, which I prudently desired, now means struggles of no interest, indubitable disappointments, things that trip you up. It serves me right, one might say—and it's true, *publicly*. Think, my poor André, that I am haunted by oblivion and tranquillity alone, that I have a savage need for *security* in every sense—and for a certain kind of company—for non-isolation. Long ago I killed every ambition, every paradise, every possible future. I have long accepted everything, but I am reaching the limits of my power to bear uncertainty. A petty example: I need books. I should like to have a few indispensable works on mathematics—not only am I unable to buy them, never asking for money at home (and besides, they are very expensive books)—but even if I had them, I should not know where to have them, having no place of residence, no lasting harbor.

And if I dared to stretch my concern to its very limits despite the bad effect, I should say that even with things at their very best, even settled down in Paris and well settled, my fate would still be somewhat crippled with rheumatism.

A convalescent like you will laugh at my lack of wisdom—and from his point of view, he will be right. But from mine, I cannot help but not be

---

[2] In effect, Paul Valéry did return to Paris on March 3.

wrong. My God! I do think an ordinary observer would judge me harshly. He would read my letters and what would he see in them? Constant complaints, a gentleman of twenty-two who has already been grousing for a long time—yet who sometimes claims to be right. The same gentleman, so gloriously gifted with dissatisfaction, disparages 999/1,000 of everything created. Irresistible argument—incontrovertible sign—*he* has created nothing, has he? He complains but he doesn't compare his fate with so many . . . , etc. He speaks of his research, of his *ideas,* and cannot even resolve a not very difficult situation, actually, etc. . . .

Well, my dear fellow, you will be the judge. It's because I believe you won't think about me in such a way that I have again filled up a sheet of paper with my troubles. Now really, if I feel strongly about all that, could I speak to you of anything else? And really, again, our written and spoken meetings are thus not very gay! Now and then you must find my judgment irritating, my letters unbreathable. Yet you know, or please know if you don't, that behind the iconoclast which I sometimes am, the vague, isolated builder that I also find in myself, there is, above all, the . . . or rather a feeling of existence, a very sensitive consciousness before which *everything is equal.* I mean, which does not divide itself up, which suffers or which soars, undivided. A strange basis: at all times of perturbation, when the general wave of life comes back to that geometric point which I wanted to be as a child, the images in my mind are always a sea, where I use up the last minutes of a life or a vigil. I then merge my existence with that whole country of open sea, and I feel myself dissolve. That, for me, is what others call feeling . . . and I am, through the very abstract of constructions or analyses, the influence or the distortion of that dream. And yet it is there that the forms of friendship or love, at their moments of exaltation and possession within myself, bathe, come to an end of bathing also.   P. V.

In Montpellier, 9, rue Vieille-Intendance
In Paris, 12, rue Gay-Lussac

71. *André Gide to Paul Valéry*

[Biskra, March, 1894]

My very dear friend,

Please write to me as soon as possible, the letters take so many days to come and your last one worried me so. Besides, I myself didn't answer as quickly as I might have done. What has become of you? Are you really in Paris? How far astray will this letter go in search of you, as the one before last surely did? For in my uncertainty, what address could I have put on it? Hotel Courtès? general delivery? or in care of E. Rouart? I forget.

Address your answer: "Tunis, General Delivery," and write quickly, for I don't know where I shall be after this. I am awaiting some information on "the state of mind" in Italy. Can a Frenchman, who is not Barrès, live there in peace? Perhaps you yourself have some valuable tips. . . .

But please don't be afraid of speaking to me at length about yourself. I am not in the least concerned about knowing whether others are more to be pitied than you. The fact that you are to be pitied is enough for me. As for advice and consolation, I feel as little capable of giving it to you as you, I think, are anxious to receive it: this partial silence, on the advice of friendship, will not diminish the latter. Yet how I should like to speak! If I were there, what would I advise you? What you yourself would tell me to; it's up to the friend to say what he prefers to be advised. . . .

I am constantly afraid that in Paris some unknown *vortex* will snatch you up, and that from the very beginning of any involvement whatever, you will do very little to escape it. . . . Never have I felt the vanity of my words as much as with you. It always seems to me that I'm throwing my letters to you into a vacuum; there would be nothing particularly curious about it if I didn't have the impression that our friendship was a very real thing, which I am now unable to do without, although at the beginning my being did not feel the need of it; yet it will always remain a mysterious thing to me, a relationship between two incommensurables.

Write to me. Where will your mother stay? Is your brother happy with his new job? Are you not able to consider each hour as anything but important, and will you never bring yourself to waste a few of them, sacrificing them so as to be useful to yourself? Answer and answer quickly, please.

Your friend,
A. G.

72. *Paul Valéry to André Gide*

Paris, 12, Gay-Lussac [3]
[P. March 19, 1894]

You see, dear friend, I am here and your letter, your dear letter, will get an immediate answer, mine—but not its own [*sic*].

I am writing to you between two errands so that this note will get to Tunis on time. . . . And it can be no more than an offer of thanks and a word between people whose trains meet and pass.

I am waiting here for some vague post at the World's Fair of 1900. I'm not counting on it at all. Heredia received me kindly and *spoke* of attending to it. Since my arrival, you can imagine the loss of time, the dealings: when I come in, I have one minute devoted to frenzy, before

---

[3] André Gide was later to recall the room in the rue Gay-Lussac, with its "special disorder" and the blackboard on which were drawn figures and mysterious words (*L'Arche*, October, 1945).

falling completely asleep under the eider down. In a spasm of time, I again see my things, my true race. I know that I do not come from here, that I shall end gently by enduring, by letting things slide. At times I feel that my life has not yet begun, that the events described in my favorite moments are on the move and will ring out—unless they did so a long time ago.

But none of that has any worth. I know too well that I am incommensurable, as you say, with too many people and things. I wonder if they all have as strange motives of development as I.

Ah! in writing to you I now find again the salty tang of the bracing mornings of old, I remember.

I think you can go to Italy—to Florence rather than to Rome, to Genoa rather than to Naples.

If you go to Genoa, let me know and I shall recommend you to my family there.

A word: I am watching the cessation of what we call literature. Half-unconscious, that end—momentary. One feels that nothing justifies a continuation. Do you remember when I seemed to be going too far playing Kassandra [*sic*]? Well, in addition to the inanity of what is being done, disappearances are literally taking place. The existence of individuals as typical as Mauclair, for example, are signs staring us in the face. In order for that particular one to have been produced (and others as well, actually), the mechanics of the century must be in deep transformation. But I haven't the time today to inquire hypothetically into how it functions. And so what! . . .

Kolbassine is right: Batavia and a chessboard.　　　　P. V.

When will we see each other, my friend?

73. *Paul Valéry to André Gide*

[May 25, 1894]

You write to me as you do to Z or, rather, to X,* and I deserve it—probably.

I admit to you that I am weary of the people around here, you can see them,—they haven't changed,—and yet I pretend to associate with them, for actually, once a week I need man, and I go out to speak to him, a kind of brothel.

I'm thinking of going to London. My confused day is responsible for that, and I shall go soon. It's stupid, obviously: it would be better to return, *ahead of time,* to my research on the nature of space and directions, to my architect's dreams of building vast cities and parks, to the movements and numbers of a jostling and mechanical English Channel; besides, today my eider down fascinates me, *primo,* because we are having cold winter

---

* *Translator's note:* The last letter from Gide is No. 71.

weather, *quarto,* because it is a "very nice girl," like a streetwalker, and doesn't resist being sculptured alive, giving enormous pleasure to a physicist-artist's fingers, that of a beautiful model, firm and elastic: Light.

If I go to London in June, it will be for a short month. There, I shall write a drama around the oarsmen of Oxford or Cambridge. They will make love with one another on the river, will smoke a lot, and, bare-armed, will show their savagery, boxing, thus capsizing their boat, overloaded with jealousy, beautiful youth, and sport.

Do you want yours on Dutch paper or on Japanese vellum?

What has become of that tedious, beautiful Italy? and you in it? I command you to write a little less to everyone and more to me, who knows nothing. Speak at least of the Medusa [4]—and promptly, or I shall forget you on London Bridge.   V.

74. *André Gide to Paul Valéry*

Florence, 5, *via* Montebello
Monday [May 28, 1894]

It's true; I wrote to you as I did to H or X; but that you deserved it is false; but it's true that you must forgive me, because I was horribly bored, and yet thinking of you, I had no desire to write to you, and yet I thought I should, so that you would know that I was thinking of you.

But now I am bored no longer; on the contrary. I wrote to Régnier that I would probably soon return; that is becoming false; it's cold everywhere, even here, and the pleasure I find is the only thing that keeps me from suffering too much.

Florence is admirable. I haven't any idea of what you know of Italy and whether you ever came down farther than Genoa? Florence explains you to me—a little—inexplicable. I have spent the whole morning visiting it in front of Medusa, whom my friend,[5] I think, is going to sketch. But nothing here is more beautiful than the Santa Trinita bridge; I live in the Uffizzi Gallery, to which I have brought your letter.

What you tell me about your eider down enchants me, it reminds me of both the "dear little pillow" of Marceline Desbordes-Valmore and of the story of that angelic maniac who was excited only by unfolded white napkins; he inflated them a bit, imagined the folds, the little tunnels—entered rutting and got the whole thing over.

My dear friend, I am writing a modern novel.[6] I rejoice each day not to

---

[4] A term used by Gide and Valéry to personify the first woman who excited Valéry, and then any woman who interested them. See above, Letter 52.

[5] Paul-Albert Laurens, who has not left Gide since he took sick. Gide's mother returned to Paris alone.

[6] *Paludes,* a short fragment of which was to appear in the January, 1895, issue of *La Revue Blanche,* was to be published the same year by Art Indépendant, with the subtitle *Traité de la Contingence.*

be spending it in Paris; what are you doing? apart from modeling elastic down? I should like to see you go to London, more generally let us say: I should like to see you. In Paris, is Hérold still spreading gossip from one to the other, and is Mauclair still professing the same admiration for what he does?

I feel like never coming back; but when is Régnier to be performed? I hope that at least he's playing himself.[7] . . . Try to find somewhere the tale of a reception at the court of Baghdad, of an embassy from Constantinople, by the caliph Moctadar. It's stupendous. I say "try to find," but I have no need of it; it's for you; and anyway you already know that story, you who know everything. As for me, who spends the day walking in the sun, I am finally becoming extremely ignorant, and if you are writing poems, you shall have to explain them to me.

Sono tuo.
A. G.

75. *Paul Valéry to André Gide*
London, No. 10 Highbury Crescent at Madam de Rim [*sic*]
[July 9, 1894]

I thank you for the bridge [8]—although I could not like it more than I do those on the Thames.[9] These structures, you know, are somewhat close to my heart, and if I felt something other than the slight beginning of disgust, I would tell you why. In this order of ideas, one must immediately rush to general speculations on the structure of things and to particulars like mine of this winter, so as not to remain in the commonplace or the descriptive— that madness! I won't elaborate. Besides, having written to Régnier about these landscapes, impossible to begin again (you know me). However, I shall pick up one point from that letter to the poet.

The City suggests to me that: some day such a place, and its men and its setting, will no doubt be regarded as we regard historical things, combustibles, things in the cinders of which we see the flame; yes, my friend, commerce, and nothing in our times could be more passionate, more "true to life," more sublime than the commerce there. And with irony, for example, I note that no artist ever sets foot in it. Therefore, he wouldn't understand anything about it. A Zola! . . .

I believe that there we have the most profound mechanism of this age, a beautiful feast of complexity for the mind. I haven't had the time to think

---

[7] The Théâtre de l'Œuvre, in 1894, staged a dramatic poem by Henri de Régnier, *La Gardienne,* which appeared in *Poèmes anciens et romanesques* (Art Indépendant, 1890).

[8] Paul Valéry is probably alluding to a postcard sent by Gide, and which has not been found.

[9] He has been in London since the beginning of June. He is living with the second of his maternal aunts, Mme de Rim.

about it. It struck me. I am just advising you of it—but not claiming to do any more.

I have never seen anything more boring than the Parthenon friezes. I promise myself to get a rise out of the first Christian who mentions them to me. It would be so easy to show him his own idiotic inebriation!

Good-by! [10] write quickly so that I have your letter before leaving—that is, before the end of the month.

I'm supposed to go and see Meredith [11] one of these days.

P.

76. *André Gide to Paul Valéry*

Saturday, Fiesole [July, 1894]

From under the trees, where I am getting into country habits, for I'm never at the casa, I write to you with the same pencil I used yesterday to copy down your new address: it was to send you a few photos of da Vinci's works, which I am now afraid to entrust to the mails and which I shall bring to you later on; but I am also afraid that you know them and that they will be of no value to you.

Apropos of London, it was in Florence that I met one of the rare Englishmen I know: Oscar Wilde,[12] who was hardly delighted by the meeting, for he thought he was in hiding. With him smiled another poet of a younger generation. I had two vermouths and listened to four stories. He was leaving next day; that was four weeks ago.

I didn't tell you about it because you were in Paris and would have repeated it! But now that silence is easier, I still ask for your silence.

At this point, my pencil is giving out and I have no knife with which to sharpen it.

Sunday

From the same place as yesterday, I continue my letter. The need I have had, throughout this whole trip, of walking a lot for my health, has given me a horror of rooms; my only desire is to leave them; impossible to remain seated in front of a sheet of paper or a book, I no longer understand, I am no longer interested, impossible to write. Whence the stupidity of my letters. My last to P. L. must have irritated him, although we are presently on the best of terms. You told me that I write to you as I do to Z. Walckenaër [13] complains about my silence; he's wrong, and so

---

[10] In English in the original.

[11] The English poet and novelist George Meredith (1828–1909).

[12] Wilde was accompanied by his friend Alfred Douglas.

[13] André Walckenaër was closely related to André Gide's maternal aunt, Claire Démarest. "For three years, the whole time I was in Paris, André Walckenaër came to my home to spend from two to five with me—every Wednesday—unless I went to his," Gide was to write in *Si le Grain ne meurt.* It was to Walckenaër that he dedicated *Florence, Naples et Syracuse,* in *Feuilles de route,* 1899.

much the worse for him, since I just wrote to him. I think of nothing but leaving for Cairo; were I in better health I should go to Batavia. Houses with windows, men wearing hats, women who go to confession, annoy me. I dream of Africa where I had a terrifically good time. I shall return there as soon as the temperature is favorable. Did I tell you that I am now on my way to Switzerland? for treatment, not for pleasure. All the news from Paris makes me happy not to be there, and Pierre Louÿs' "Everyone" reminds me too much of everyone and not enough of Banville. Au revoir; I send you regards and wish you luck.

Write: Geneva, General Delivery, or 4, rue de Commaille, if you don't write immediately.

Your
A. G.

77. *Paul Valéry to André Gide*

Paris, July 14, 1894 [14]

Here I am in Paris again, dear André, and in a state of incomparable sadness. Moments I shan't tell you about have gone by, now I miss London like a fool, the French get on my nerves. If I had the cowardly habit of writing a diary, I should note down: "This evening, dined in ten minutes, went upstairs again to smoke, choked with boredom and, somewhat later, a touch of anger." That, that is what all my days have become.

Yesterday, I vomited all my papers out onto the table, hesitating between two propositions: 1) crumbling them into little balls; 2) classifying them. I seriously debated it. I wanted to classify them! I was sure I would stop immediately, which is what happened.

Then, I set to thinking about politics.

Among the really indispensable books that no one will write, I often glance through, in my mind, *The History and Philosophy of Ingenuity*.

The remarkable void of English literature surprised and charmed me. France has two little doors through which one may pass in order to still do something a bit new. The pity is that no one perceives them or troubles about them. The real pity is that we have one reader out of ten million who judges for himself. Moreover, the unfortunate young man who wishes to be that reader and who lives in the provinces is forced by his age to take, mechanically, a point of view contrary to those around him. . . . Ten years later, when he might reason, he is disgusted forever with reading anything but his newspaper and the twenty volumes he espoused at nineteen. This is past history, but I have witnessed it.

Two days ago I wrote a rather long letter to Mazel congratulating him

[14] Paul Valéry, passing through Paris, was to return to Montpellier on August 2.

on an article about Education. Note that being a fool when it comes to literature and even in conversation never prevented anyone from writing a good article. Moreover, it's not the first he has written, outside of ART, that has pleased me. *Naturally,* I don't agree with him. Still, all our R. de G.'s [15] and our B. L.'s,[16] who are such great philosophers in the eyes of the crowd below and such glorious littérateurs for those who reason a bit, would never have done much with the theme. For me, who am as far from being a littérateur as from being a philosopher, and even from being anything at all—even, alas, a clerk anywhere—the two important points are the only two a pedagogue has never thought of. Education of the senses. Preparation for puberty. That cannot be found at Sorèze,[17] or at Henri-IV,[18] or at Eton. Whence, in part, the strange world in which we live, and the high proportion of the number of stupidities and idolatries everywhere, in one's private life and in customs, writings, and laws.

Painting. In 1894 there are still people of taste who take some kind of interest in Rossetti [19] as a painter, and some . . . in Burne-Jones.[20] Which leads me naturally to announce to you the marriage of our *friend* Coste.

I don't know whether I wrote to you from London. I don't think so. At any rate, I'm enthusiastic about it, or rather, I have a feeling of possible enthusiasm should the occasion arise. It was, above all, the City, the commerce, which attracted me and which I have not had the time to study. The atmosphere there is one of machine rooms or the inside of a heart. Our heroes are there. And while we go to Loyola, to Tristan, to Perseus, to see passion and calculation more easily than in the court of assize—that corner is preparing to obliterate from the impression of our times any other glory and any other movement.

Realization: during that recent period in which I read, studied, and wrote poetry, I should have cut out my tongue and cut off my head rather than think and say that. Remember our promenades in Montpellier, and all the nonsense I said and the enormous pleasure of walking together (for me, at least). It has stayed with me to such a degree that the mere idea of seeing you again stirs me. But when? It seems to me that we have known each other for twenty years.

Pierre must be with you, and I envy him. I admit that I never think of our relationship without surprise. I have known him for four years. And I don't know him any better than I did the first day. He has behaved with me in such a way that I could blush with generosity. One of my worries is

[15] Rémy de Gourmont.
[16] Bernard Lazare.
[17] A secondary school directed by Lacordaire, who died there in 1861.
[18] A well-known lycée in Paris.
[19] Dante Gabriel Rossetti (1828–1882), the English painter and poet of the pre-Raphaelite school.
[20] English painter and designer, pupil of Rossetti (1833–1898).

not knowing how to repay him for it. More especially as I have never said a word that gave him any pleasure, and I have never complimented him, and I don't much approve. Where I'm difficult *is that I implicitly ask my friends to act against their nature.* That is a misfortune that comes from my torments—you have known them—you are almost the only one who has, except for one other person who took care of me and takes care of me from a distance.

I should add that for three years I have neither corresponded nor conversed with Pierre. Every meeting turns him into fleeing quicksilver for me. At such times I admire a few of my other friends who are decidedly very patient and charitable. This can be read by him as well as by you.

Upon reflection . . . Someone who knew me a few years ago saw me again just recently, and found me very changed—like a seed that has not produced its own plant, but another. I answered her: "My dear, I was then a pleasing young man, careful to avoid any friction with people, and I became quite the contrary very quickly. I was enthusiastic and believed in a few words—I fed largely on books and on ideas held by my fellow men. Today everything *must* come from me. I agree to nothing that I don't understand and I translate the word *work* as *find.** Learning, reading, toiling on some piece is not work for me. I should think myself a lazy man if I wrote encyclopedias, for writing in itself or browsing is a pretext for not *finding* anything."

And here I have already consumed half of this July 14. All right! [21]   P. V.

78. *André Gide to Paul Valéry*

BEAU SÉJOUR. HÔTEL SPLENDIDE; VIEW ON
THE MONT-BLANC; TERRACES—SHOWERS,
FUMIGATIONS—MASSAGES, GOOD FOOD,
FOREIGN LANGUAGES SPOKEN.

Champel, July 16, 1894

Dear fellow,

The fact that you wrote on July 14 makes your letter even more excellent, for the moral obligation we all feel of doing absolutely the most amusing thing possible on that day gives me enough proof of the pleasure you took in writing to me.

As for me, I have found nothing more amusing than sending Pierre Louÿs off to Biskra with his fatal companion. [22]

---

* *Translator's note:* The French reads *"travail* par *trouvaille."*

[21] In English in the original.

[22] Gide was taking a cure of hydrotherapy for his nerves at Champel, in Switzerland, on the advice of Dr. Andreæ, a friend of Charles Gide's. It was there that he read his *La Ronde de la Grenade* to Pierre Louÿs and Hérold, who had come to see him on their way to Bayreuth. (Cf. *Si le Grain ne meurt.*)

Twice in this life, up to now, I have powerfully tasted that joy of feeling my *will* laugh: the first was at a barber shop where I had taken Quillot, whom I had convinced to have his mustache cut off.

But nothing is worth the joy of the day before yesterday: it was not on Pierre that my will alighted, it was on Hérold, for Pierre, as soon as he saw me again—(we had been widowers for eighteen months)—thought of nothing but breaking away from Hérold [23] and was returning his tickets for Wagner, and as soon as I spoke to him of Biskra, spoke of nothing but rushing off there.

What amused me was convincing Hérold that he had to rush off as well: both left for Marseilles yesterday morning. They arrive tomorrow at the Maison des Pères Blancs,[24] where Hérold will never manage to finish *Les Victorieux*,[25] because I am introducing him to some women.

Dear friend, I shall see you soon, but it will be for a short time, for I am coming to Paris, but I am coming for only two days. Did you receive a letter from me in London? I wrote to you there from Florence. Your letter of the 14th arrived here immediately after the glorious departure of our friends; I was therefore unable to tell Louÿs what you told me about Pierre —wonders—and that extraordinary phrase which explains *us* in our relations: "I ask my friends, implicitly, to act against their nature."

My nature, it seems to me, has changed: I am less *crouched*. Do I deserve to be congratulated by you for it, or is it to the stars that I owe being so much [*sic*] happy? I am as happy as one can be, with the perpetual feeling that tomorrow I shall be even more so. But what does that prove? the excellence of my morals, my stomach, or my foolishness?

Dear friend, I embrace you as a friend, for that indeed we shall have known how to be.

I am for you
André Gide

79. *Paul Valéry to André Gide*

[August 25, 1894]

I think the East would like to have me. Not that Quillard has answered me,* but yesterday a gentleman wrote me that there is a job I am welcome to as a tutor in Cairo. I refused. As Constantinople is not coming through,

---

[23] Pierre Louÿs never managed to shake off Hérold, who was to follow him all the way to Biskra.

[24] Where Gide and Paul-Albert Laurens had been lodged.

[25] A dramatic poem that was to appear in 1895 (Art Indépendant).

* *Translator's note:* On July 27, 1894, Valéry wrote Gide: "[Quillard] has almost convinced me to go to Constantinople with him. There is an opening at the school he is at."

going to the vassal state displeases me. Anyway, all that could hardly be called *positions!* Eastern postures.

If I were rich—*today*—do you know what I would do? Lead a physical life! I would put myself under the discipline of oars, dumbbells, and horses. And I would do nothing but that and swim from morning til night. Today, only the rich can have muscles. On leaving for London, I had intended—avowedly, but without having thought it out—to *write* a little drama about a few muscle men. It ended with some unexpected boxing in a rowboat in the middle of the river. They capsized, and all managed to swim off toward the white twigs and the salad-like jumble of water lilies on the banks. Curtain. Rouart was pleased with that little play when I told him the story. The interest of the thing was to create three male embodiments. There were no women. The drama had only a skiff sailing about, with three or four diverse and silent females aboard. That was part of the setting, and like the rest, served only to provide conversation.

I recently reread *Le Discours de la Méthode,* which is indeed the modern novel as it might be written. It should be noted that subsequent philosophy rejected the autobiographical part. However, that is the point that should be revived, and one should thus write the life of a theory as one wrote, far too often, the life of a passion (in bed). But that's a bit more difficult—for, puritanical as I am, I insist that the theory be more than trickery, as in *Louis Lambert.* . . .

Do you know Wronski?[26] I am skimming through him again, that madman, a great genius besides, but mad. Chimes in his head!

Adieu, my old André, and write; I have need of that and of answering.

P. V.

80. *Paul Valéry to André Gide*

Paris, 12, rue Gay-Lussac[27]

[November 10, 1894, in Gide's handwriting]

[On the envelope, Gide wrote admirable, underlining it twice.]

Dear André,

You have issued me an accusation[28]—and it is my turn to be given, by you, that Thermidorian title which I have so often, in low tones, bestowed on others: Enemy of mankind. . . . The only thing that surprises me is that it took you so long to at least say it. But before answering or rather picking up your points, some information:

---

[26] Hoene Wronski (1778–1853), a Polish philosopher who, exiled in France and writing in French, tried to give a mathematical formula of creation and developed the idea of the creative spontaneity of every individual.

[27] Valéry returned to Paris on September 11, with his mother and brother, who—on October 30—went back to Montpellier, leaving him alone.

[28] The previous letter from Gide has not been found.

I have been in Paris for about a month. I have been nervous here and sick three days out of six. On top of that came thousands of difficulties of the maddening sort. The last one dates from yesterday: Régnier, with a goodness and nobility that stabbed me to the heart, having learned that the post of secretary on *La Revue de Paris* was not filled, tried to get it for me. A slight delay ruined everything. I had the most stupid fit of rage possible.[29] It increased as I became aware of it. The misfortune was that this little difficulty coincided with a physical state of which I have had enough, enough, enough. The imaginative consequence of that, in me (headache, etc., and disappointments), became at once a proper bombing of London—English blood, like bad wine, in the Strand, flowing all the way to the Thames. But, then, my good sense was asleep.

Now back to our diplomatic exchanges. I shall go about it unmethodically. Thus I take your letter, and having read it:

1. A confidential question—in code. Did you not receive a letter from Rouart shortly before, mentioning me?

2. As an abortionist or emmenagogue of books and letters, or antimaieutical! I answer quite freely that I have always begged the people with whom I converse to take no heed of my feelings—which is very easy— then, not to accept any part of my theories without testing them logically; moreover, I have always repeated that I could never conceive of a *general* theory: a theory that is not personal is independent of the theorist.

3. That takes care of the *quia corrumperet juventutem*.[30] Let us go on to the individual:

I know how one can judge me, for I know what I have shown. The fact is that if my friends or groups of my friends were put in a room and asked a question about me, the diversity of the answers, the very contradictions in them would be curious, I think. I could assign at least one name to each of the following opinions: I am considered a poet, cracked, rational, mystical, heartless, disparaging, too mistrustful, too confident, too frank, dissembling, amusing, pedantic, etc. I forgot flighty and ponderous. And all that shows me some jolly bad reasoning that is rather general and as clear as the day.

What I know is that I feel I'm really too different—not perhaps that I am more so, but that I feel it and *tend* to feel it more than anyone else—from other people. Do you remember: I told you that I gave up my ideas as soon as others had them. That is still true. I want to be master in my own house.

---

[29] Somewhat later, on November 22, Paul Valéry, in a letter to his mother, again mentioned his regret at having failed to get that job.

[30] "Because it would corrupt youth."

. . . But how am I distressing, and to you, my friend, who would seem to say that your letters are disdained, that I don't understand you, and that the primary motives of my acts escape you?

Remember that you have been almost my only confidant—*the whole time,*—that often the only rest I had was writing to you and reading your letters during the painful weeks when I had trouble going from minute to minute—and even at this very moment! What you should reproach me with is having wearied you by my incessant, useless complaining, but is it not somewhat mitigated by the fact that you are the only one to whom I let myself do it? I have suffered enormously from isolation. If you only knew how I regretted your absence, if you only recalled some of the comments of old, some of the former moments!

My dear fellow, for a long time I have been living in the ethic of death. This very striking limit gives movement and life to my thoughts. I believe that, since the fanatics, few men have worked from this charming, intoxicating, and liberal basis. All that I have really wanted, I have wanted with my eyes fixed on the word: End. I have always acted so as to make myself a potential individual. That is, I have preferred a strategical life to tactics. Having at my disposal without disposing. The goal of this was inner, imaginative balance.

What struck me more than anything else in the world was that no one ever saw anything through. Once, before having read the same words in Goethe, on the quays, I said this absurdity: "One must have an impossible goal." Well, I know all that is nonsense—but as a feeling, such nonsense is, determines, and even underlies any poetic spirit. It must not be made into a theory. It must be satisfied or explained, or both.

I have reinvented many things. Other men, for example. I have punctured honestly the notions that were muddling my mind. I have wanted to throw my boots in the face of words instead of shining them. I have made and am making systems that are absolutely to measure, theories in which there is a place for my corns, connections which for me are the convenient elevators, water, and gas of reverie or analysis. I have scrubbed my windows, I have scratched off the nascent pride of which I've never had much, in spite of appearances, perhaps.

I have written bad poetry, which has taught me the recipe for good poetry. And I have detested Flaubert—as a cat detests a dog.

There are my crimes and my bad instincts. Judge me. I am as capable of loving as anyone else, I even know how to put in a certain novelty and violence. But patience I lack, mediocrity makes me sick, and vagueness kills me. I would adore someone whom my mind had not decided to suppress at the end of six months. Woman or man.

Finally—between you and me—do you know what I see, and what our relationship is? I see, I feel, that we love each other, but each of us shows the other what terrifies him the most, you a kind of Paradise—and me a certainty of Hell.

Ah! give up Switzerland! and come.

Valéry

81. *André Gide to Paul Valéry*

November 11, 1894

Dear Ambroise,

Exquisite creature,

Your letter is just the one I was waiting for; you can see that I am answering it immediately; I have not yet even taken the time to reread it. For now, let us add this preface to my letter of yesterday; I was thinking about you too much to be satisfied with the vague and overly abstract image that you were becoming, although still living, perhaps changing, certainly functioning: I distrust all silences; they are a cover for metamorphosis; I experienced that when I myself was keeping silent. I wanted the most dangerous of things, which could come about between very few people and which anyone other than you would not have wanted. . . . To test a friendship; a desire to feel it resist, thus feeling its power. Among all my still unwritten letters to you, I chose the painful letter, that's all, in order to know what you would say, feeling yourself accused by me, my accusations being, if not false, at least reversible. (This one will remain, in spite of you, *quia corrumperet juventutem*. One must be either stupid or conceited not to find one's self half-witted compared to you: you seem to take pleasure in it, and in order not to feel grieved, I must at least have some cordiality.)

In answer to that most painful of letters, you write me the best of letters. Both letters will be of importance to us. Don't expect me to write you any more painful letters, I've had enough, but understand that I expect from you even better letters; never could I have enough. (I should like to be with you for a time, in a hayloft, childishly,—or below deck on a ship, with lots of dry biscuits to nibble on, in a corner with very little space to crouch in, a good deal of darkness, and the noises of water for the silences.)

. . . It is by instinct that I never see things through (and because it's too difficult, this said in a low voice). I like only vicious circles. I think that what is important for each one is to know whether he has really put on all his own skins, one after the other, and not too much of the clothing of others; whether, when nude, he had not been too cold, and whether, although dressed for some masquerade, he knew how to behave and afterward turned out his pockets completely to empty them of the opera glasses and pralines. Perhaps, during the masquerade, you think too much of the coat check . . . but then, I have no idea . . . forgive me.

I feel too happy to find any flaws in "my technique for living," as G. Kahn [31] says. Besides, I still adapt it every day.

"A state may be voluntary without being free," said Leibnitz, among others, and it's rather banal, but here is what is not banal: working to make all one's states *voluntary,* whether one is under compulsion or not. (That is not acceptation—on the contrary—it is the choice after the test, the counting of one's chickens after they're hatched.) There lies my wisdom, and I say wisdom, for that is what one generally calls recipes for happiness.

Your system would drive me mad or to suicide before a week was up; for me your wisdom would be madness. . . . But let's change the subject, for I approve.

I am living here completely alone in a "Rainy country." [32] I have still about five months to go if I can stand it. People call me the *Foreigner;* how right they are; yet I still belong too much to the landscape (reasons of health, walking, breathing); I am waiting for the snow in order to lose my footing—the isolating snow.

An unbearable book is still keeping me from transcendencies, but I have almost completed it. You know, it's called *Paludes,* and I gratified myself with it.

Rouart was not the cause of my last letter, but his perpetual conversations about you obviously contributed to it. . . . Don't accuse him; gentleness, friendship, he has every good feeling for you. He contributes to our friendship.

A deplorable business, that secretaryship which misfired—too bad—but how nice it would have been!

Obviously I should like to see you again. You say you're sick: What's wrong? Is it a matter of bromides? of camphor?—or of sailing the seas? Speak. Write to me as you did this morning.

I am your
A. G.

82. Paul Valéry to André Gide

Paris [P. November 29, 1894]

I saw your mother this afternoon, and she told me all about your Algerian adventures—those fit to be mentioned. I note in passing, and as a

---

[31] Gustave Kahn (1859–1936), poet, novelist, and critic, author of, in particular, *Les Palais nomades* and *Le Roi fou.* One of the first adepts of free verse.

[32] La Brévine, a health resort in the Swiss part of the Jura mountains (canton of Neuchâtel). In *Si le Grain ne meurt* Gide was to say: "One must have lived in this region to understand the passages of Rousseau's *Confessions* and *Rêveries* that refer to his stay in Val-Travers." He was not at all happy at La Brévine and was thus to explain his antipathy: "In fact, I missed Biskra."

former littérateur, a word (an epithet, sir) she used which amused me, so that I kept it in mind for some time. She described the sunset on the objects in Biskra as being . . . this and that . . . and—*printanier!* I saw it.

I pester Bailly regularly.* But can a horsefly hurt rubber? Question!

Paludes cannot be printed before mid-January, at the earliest. Printers are refusing work at this time. (Says Bailly.)

I saw Rouart Sunday. Nice as ever. He is so taut, that boy, that he can't contract. What fun! My weeks are filled with visits, vague occupations, taking out ladies, etc. In the space of two weeks I saw *Madame Sans-Gêne,*[33] *La Fée Printemps*[34] (a black drama at the Ambigu), heaps of Folies-Bergères, twice the Théâtre de l'Œuvre (the most tedious of all), *Monsieur Alphonse,*[35] etc. Then I saw a doctor about my little arabesques of pain, a contraction of the pharynx, etc. He promoted me to a male hysteric. I saw that he himself didn't understand. He prescribed rest, rest. You idiot, I thought, there is no rest! I live as I can, and am unable to live any other way. I then walked immediately over to Mallarmé's, and the whiskey in the bars led me back to my door with my hysteria—my *male* hysteria.   V.

83. *André Gide to Paul Valéry*

La Brévine, December 2, 1894

Dear friend,

Don't be surprised that I have still not sent you the manuscript: there is no end to ending *Paludes;* the beginning is helping me to get the end; besides, it is pointless to part from it as long as I have not received the specimen pages which would at least prove to me that the task is begun. And if it won't begin until around the middle of January, I shall be there.

I live in the expectation of spring—a morbid expectation; I think that around April I shall become a chameleon or a buttercup, or a fragile boat like . . .** The cold weather is horrible; one feels well begrudgingly, the sky is purer than in July, and I write on the ice.

Poor hysteria! don't speak ill of it; it's the most amusing of illnesses. . . . In our old age we shall ask each other: "Did you have a little pocket of ice above your knees? stains in the blue of your eyes? see

---

* *Translator's note:* On November 21, 1894, Gide wrote to Valéry, telling him that he had sent the first chapter of *Paludes* to Bailly, his publisher, "in order to have a specimen of it in print," but that he had had no word from Bailly as yet.

[33] By Victorien Sardou.

[34] By Jules Mary.

[35] By A. Dumas fils.

** *Translator's note:* "bateau frêle comme . . ." An allusion to Rimbaud's poem *Le Bateau ivre.*

imaginary rats running round the floor? find it impossible to swallow your saliva? and impossible not to drink a whole decanter in one gulp? have ideas that toppled over? no feeling in your shoulders? unmotivated congestions? . . ."

"What they need," someone says in *Paludes,* "is fresh air. . . . I know perfectly well that there is the Luxembourg. . . ."

. . . But all that, I think, can be cured only by satisfaction of the flesh— even more perhaps than by that of the mind.

Beware, at least, of bromide: it's hard to forget, and it keeps you from finding your words. Once, because of the stupidity of doctors, I had to take basins of it,—I hold it against them terribly. The same resentment against chloral, etc.

I know well that one does not thank a friend for this, but that's just too bad, I shall do it all the same: thank you for that visit to my mother. She is timid, clumsy (in spite of seeming too sure of herself), and will have had trouble showing the pleasure you gave her. . . . I quote: "Saw Valéry, who paid me a good, *long* and *friendly* visit (I underline that which is underlined). It seemed to me that his face was not so bumpy as it was two years ago; can it be that he is not as agitated, not as feverish? . . ." etc. And this, now, from one who signs E. R.:[36] "Saw Valéry—transformed." And farther on: "Sunday at lunch and during a long afternoon, Valéry was marvelous."

And I don't see you! How sad. Au revoir, but then, see you soon. "Be in good health" and don't transform yourself too much, so that I shall still recognize you.   A. G.

84. Paul Valéry to André Gide

[December 2, 1894]

I wanted to write this morning to a little girl I like. But I spent the evening in such a way that I shall answer your letter only. I spend my time with a young girl whose fundamentals I promised to respect. I seized this rather rare opportunity with delight and we make love not without ecstasies—but she with her dressing gown and me with my clothes on, unopened. Her virginity is all-knowing. But my experience is learning things. It is as curious as a Jesuit postulate: *de peccatis per approximationem, quum visus manusque unice denudantur.*[37]

All that takes me endless time. I had promised myself to write something for Louÿs. A colloquy. It didn't last long. Once the theme was decided upon and the difficulties understood—I put it away in the shed of easy pleasures and never thought of it again.

---

[36] Eugène Rouart.
[37] "Sins by approximation, when only the eyes and the hands are bare."

As for those transformations, bah! phoo! pshaw! It's the weather that's changing. There will perhaps be some transformation the day the *climate* itself will be changed. A secure life, possible patience, exciting combats, what a beautiful telegram to send you! But without that!

Besides, what can I do? Personal principle.

Lemma: I am very aware.

Principle: I see nothing but variations everywhere. Thus, given m days or hours, during $3m/4$ I'm not worth a sou. Leaving $m/4$. That quarter of m is divided as follows:

During a fraction of it, I am completely involved in *my* theories. (I have no time to set them forth. It's a special analysis that I sometimes found rather satisfying.) Another fraction of it is devoted to sort of scientific speculations. An extension of ideas, the logic and psychology of sciences such as mechanics, or analysis, induction, etc. At other times I dream of nothing but diplomacy and the practical conduct of affairs, strategies, or else of the arts, of cities, of manual work, or else of some literary applications, thousands of essays.

Finally, a strange, inexplicable corner, about which I spoke to you at length in a fragment of my antepenultimate letter, which I never sent. It consists of visions of wars, on land and sea. I give myself up to them madly at certain times. I have no idea where they come from. I only know that they have existed ever since childhood. The regularity and the force of them surprise me. I *feel* the weight, the pure shape, the energy of the cannon and the shot. I imagine flights of armored ducks buzzing under [*sic*] the seaports. Then cartographic terrains, with lines of men (the row of men is my inductive triumph, I deduce extraordinary things from it). Do you know Da Vinci's bombardment drawings? There you have it.

I am therefore obliged to work (!) in irregular spurts. I saw Huysmans yesterday at his place, messing about with proofs that he can't bring himself to send back. His novel *En route* treats the question of the Trappist monks. The truth about the Trappists. Demolition of the fable: "Brother, one must die!" It seems that doesn't exist.

I shall call on Bailly again. But, from what I hear, *Paludes* is a *roman à clef?* Very much yours,   **P.-A. V.**

85. *André Gide to Paul Valéry*

Thursday, December 6, 1894
Business letter

Dear friend,

Have you a minute? Can you do me this favor? Rush over to the offices of *La Revue blanche*,[38] try to find out how far they've gone with the

[38] *La Revue blanche,* founded in 1889 in Belgium, taken over in Paris in 1891 by Alexandre Natanson, with Lucien Muhlfeld as managing editor, played an important

typesetting of the pages of *Paludes* (1st chap.) and, if possible, prevail upon them to use the enclosed text, in preference to the one I gave them. The *text* itself is not changed, but you'll see that the indications of "paragraphing" are so numerous that the distribution of pages will be changed. You should therefore advise Natanson of it, and please, dear friend, be so kind as to correct the proofs yourself, or if none of it has yet been set, ask Natanson to have these pages given to the printer of the review.

What happened was that I realized the dialogue was too compact and needed to be spaced out.

If it's too late for it to be gone over or overrun, well, it can't be helped, but I shall be sorry. It has an unfortunate appearance.

If I don't write directly to Natanson, it is because all that is complicated, annoying, and requires a great amount of good will.

That is why I appeal to you, *caro,* hoping that one day you, too, will send me proofs to correct. (For you know that as soon as I have returned to life, I'm going to have your poems printed, if only for myself.) [39]

I count on your diplomacy as a friend to make my apologies to Natanson for all the bother; tell him, besides, that when I pass through Paris I shall come and thank him and apologize for myself.

Paludes was finished yesterday. And since through some inexplicable good luck and thanks to you, I believe, Bailly managed to send me the galley proofs of the first pages without making me wait until January, you shall receive the manuscript, as we had agreed, very shortly. You will then be good enough, since you were good enough to agree, to take the manuscript over to Bailly and get it moving as fast as possible. And: discretion, discretion, please. Don't you yourself try to read those horrible pages. They are not filled with any finicky esoterism, but I have too much to correct on the proofs and the manuscript may be *deceiving.*

Did you receive the German translation from Freddy Westphal? [40] . . .

I am your
André Gide

---

role in French literary life from 1891 to 1900. Collaborating on it were Régnier, Vielé-Griffin, Dujardin, Kahn, and Mallarmé, whose *La Musique et les Lettres* and *Déplacement avantageux* were published in its pages in March and October, 1894, respectively. André Gide was to follow Léon Blum as its regular literary critic. The fragment of *Paludes* to which Gide alludes here was to appear in January, 1895.

[39] It was not until twenty-six years later that Gide, with the help of Gaston Gallimard, was able to carry out this plan for publication (*Album des vers anciens,* 1920). Three years before that book was published, *La Jeune Parque* was dedicated to him.

[40] Alfred Westphal (1869–1928), a friend of André Gide's, a native of Montpellier, author of a one-act play in verse, *Hylas,* founder and director of the newspaper *L'Ere nouvelle.*

86. *Paul Valéry to André Gide*

Monday [P. December 11, 1894]

I have read *Paludes*. I shall devote tomorrow to changing it to my liking. And, since I'm lazy, I shall dictate the passages I want to insert to the Angèle [41] who spends twenty hours a day with me. What bothers her are the quills. Typically feminine! But for the cuts, Walckenaër will make them, with sickly shrill noises. I was rather grieved—should I admit it?—not to find myself in that clan of almost intimates, in which Hérold plays such great roles. Perhaps I am there and so well described that I didn't see myself. . . . [42]

It amused me last night to unfold the manuscript, then to read it at one go until around midnight. I shall say nothing about it, except that certain corrections and patches worried me a little because of the printers. There are, for example, fragments of sentences, the same but different, that you kept at the same time. Likewise, the linking of pages on glossy paper, etc. But *Paludes* would not be *Paludes* if you didn't do a lot of work on the proofs.

Tuesday

Your mother lent me a book: *L'Intrus* [43] (translated from the Italian), which is not bad. I also found a little book which enchanted me (moderate that verb) and to prove that to it, I bought it; it's *Faraday as Discoverer.* [44] When we see each other again, if we can live together a bit this time, I shall speak to you of some vague work I have undertaken these last days of the year, work which, in spite of all the strikes and the continual intrigues, has begun to take shape.

But for the last month I have been stacking weapons. On the floor above me lives my Angèle, and I am with her all the time, finally taking great pleasure in thinking of nothing. I am becoming rather gentle again. It's rejuvenating me. . . . Good old marshland fevers!

V.

---

[41] Name of the author's girl friend and confidante in *Paludes*.

[42] Actually, Gide did not paint Valéry's portrait in *Paludes*.

[43] *The Intruder,* by Gabriele d'Annunzio, translated into French by Herelle in 1893.

[44] By John Tyndall, translated into French as *Faraday Inventeur* by the Abbé Moigno in 1868.

— 1895 —

87. Paul Valéry to André Gide

[P. January 3, 1895]

My dear André,

I am working unenthusiastically on my article,[1] and it's snowing. The whole thing is going flat. Poor Da Vinci will have a bad time of it. It will be written without sun and without inclination. I have emptied out on the table all my old notes, all the albums, notebooks, and backs of envelopes on which I wrote only the important word I understood.

I'm going to do a serious job of spinning it out, which would make me sick to read. Fortunately, I have only to write it. I am beginning to grasp that trick of padding. I shall do a fragment on architecture (old loves), one on mechanics, one on fortifications, etc. Somewhere I shall put in a point of view on the theory I should have liked to expound seriously, *punctiliously,* and all the important points I have established and written down.

Then all the trappings, all the rhetoric (what I call filet mignon with potatoes), a few quotations to cheat on some lines, and that's about it. Imagine, fifteen pages of *La Revue* = the length of *Le Voyage d'Urien,* for example.

What contempt! one must subject the great Flying Man to such formats. How many times have I seen him, from the Peyrou, crossing from the sea to the west, breaking the circles of the pure sky. He was experimenting—in the air—on his machine, which had become inseparable from him, but in reality, on *me.* Was it to teach me how to read? What an alphabet! The kind of thing in which being stuck in the mud means being stuck in the treetops. Adieu. I shall plunge back into the magma of dead words, the skins of ideas and the fat of rhetoric. Keep warm. I thank your uncle very much for his booklet.[2] As I read it, I thought the whole time how I should prefer to make a watch, or to calk (in Malta), than to dilute minutes in ink. How is your cousin? *   P.-A. V.

[1] During a visit to Marcel Schwob, Paul Valéry spoke very brilliantly of Leonardo da Vinci. Léon Daudet, who happened to be there at the time, saw to it that Valéry was asked to write an article for *La Nouvelle Revue.* It was to be *L'Introduction à la Méthode de Léonard de Vinci.* In 1919 *L'Introduction* was to be reprinted, with an additional "Note et Digression."

[2] Charles Gide published two booklets in 1893 and 1894, entitled respectively: *L'Idée de solidarité en tant que programme économique* and *Conférence sur le contrat de salaire et les moyens de l'améliorer.*

* *Translator's note:* On December 28, 1894, Gide wrote Valéry: "My little cousin Paul Gide [son of Charles Gide] is very sick."

88. *André Gide to Paul Valéry*

[P. January 27, 1895]

Dear friend,

I am impatiently awaiting a letter from you. I shan't be able to receive it in Algiers, where I shall claim it (if it is there already), for three days.

Everything annoys me, and I am acting like the insomniac who turns over to fall asleep. Impossible to find a place to live: overly expensive hotels or badly ventilated hovels.

You can tell P. L. from me that thanks to him, and since I can no longer associate it with him, my life interests me no longer: What is he doing? Where is he? How stupid he is to have thought me cruel. Or is it I who am stupid. . . . Tell him that it was a misdeal, and let's start the game over. We have been playing whist long enough.

Well, it can't be helped. I dreamt of Biskra: I want to see if I shall be mocked by things even there. At least there I know the house: I know the depth of the bed and how the windows open.

O saisons! ô châteaux![3] Spare us from seeing symbols again; my gestures are becoming solemn, as if men communicated with Nature through me. And I am getting to be a prowler. End of youth.

A word, to be obliging:

The young people of Aix and Marseilles are founding a journal (a "Social paper," more appropriate). They informed me that you were among those in whom they had the greatest hopes. I said no; they said I was wrong. So here are the facts: I gave them your address; they will send you a large red poster, and perhaps a letter along with it. They want you to agree to your name appearing in it, and some Tuesday to intercede with Mallarmé, I'm not certain why . . . but probably to assure him that the review is just what is needed. . . . Ah! and they also want Kolbassine's name, but you alone know the spelling and the address.

Write in care of: Léon Parsons, rue du Village, Marseilles.

What news of your Da Vinci? What news of everything? I'm hungry! I'm thirsty! I know nothing.

Your
A. G.

89. *Paul Valéry to André Gide*

[P. February 4, 1895]

My dear André,

I finally have to send this letter to the rue de Commaille, you're so forgetful about giving me your addresses. Moreover, that is why I haven't

---

[3] The first line of an untitled poem by Rimbaud (*Poésies*).

answered you. Your mother wrote to give me news of you, and I learned about the beginning of those vicissitudes, the end of which I already knew from you.

Da Vinci couldn't be in a worse way! I think I have to begin the whole thing over again. It's a nuisance! With pleasure, I showed it to Drouin (an honest and charming counsel) who, at about the thirteenth page, called my attention to the fact that I was not speaking of Da Vinci. I knew it only too well. But what can one say about that creature? I shan't describe the style, it's terrific. *Ex.:* "And now we come to a remark worthy of attention." That's how *Paludes* should have been written.

I can tell you a place to live, a wholesome hotel. It's between the rue du Bac and the rue de la Planche.

A word, not to be obliging:

I cannot join the staff of a Socialist journal, since I got the idea of soon applying for a job with the Ministry of War. It would be a case of Fénéon II.[4] In addition, if I have to write, I can see doing it only for money. Very important things depend on that post and on those paid articles: a home, a gilded armchair, muslin curtains, a good stove, books, and the possibility of going to London twice a year.

Moreover, must we hand Kolbassine over to those apaches? I am always afraid he'll get carried away. If he began writing, chances are it would be about politics, and from that to getting the sack, being turned out, is not a very big step, only a tenth of a millimeter.

P. L. is in Seville, 9, Plaza de Pacifico, Hotel de Paris.

I shall give him your message, but not without fear. Go and find him. Screw his Lola! Tell him that he was seen stealing into a brothel in the Calle Molliena, etc.

I have squabbles with Stéphane from time to time. Recently, I made him rather indignant on the subject of Villiers' grave. I said that I found such attentions absurd, idiotic, I withered the funerary superstitions of the Parisians (who are the vilest people on earth). Another time, I told him, and this embarrassed him quite enough, that glory = dough as a motive and that I even put it lower down on the list, for one can be highly aware and have an eye on dough, it's fit to be talked about, and even more; whereas in the case of glory, one must really be dazed by error to pursue it, etc. He must consider me the hen who hatched a snake.

Adieu, dear fellow, I leave you to your heat waves, we are under white shit, hypnotized by the roofs. **V.**

---

[4] The idea of taking the competitive examination for the job of draftsman in the Ministry of War was suggested to Paul Valéry by Huysmans, whose job with the Ministry of the Interior allowed him a great deal of free time. He thus took the examination after a visit to Montpellier in April and was notified that he had passed in June. The example of Félix Fénéon, arrested the previous year at the time of the anarchist hostilities, recommended caution in his contributions to the press.

90. André Gide to Paul Valéry

[Algiers, March, 1895] [5]

Caro,

It is rather tiresome that after having waited so long to write you, I now break the silence to complain. Anyway, through Drouin, Laurens, or Rouart, you must know that I have kept equally *silent* with the others; it's merely a matter of some obscure graphophobia. If I now want to complain, it is most certainly not about you, but about the exasperating P. L.,[6] who dares to call himself Hubert* on the pretext of his "straightforward friendship."

Since every time we meet I have a little less confidence in him, here—out of fear that he may distort them—is an account of a few facts, the repercussions of which can still be felt.

And if that sentence has already given you the impression that I'm going to tell the story badly, forgive me and listen all the same.

And, first of all, let me state that complaining is stupid; then let me say that I am not even very angry about what happened. This time Louÿs wanted to lay all the blame on himself, so that I came out of that inevitable quarrel satisfied. My blundering behavior in Paris and my near stupidity had left me with a taste for reopening the question and almost made me want to make amends. Your letters to Seville were clever, I think, for soon after, and without my having said a word, Louÿs made the first advances. The telegrams, which at the beginning were sent at long intervals, suddenly became very urgent, on both sides, and what supremely induced me to meet the monster in Algiers was a message in which he claimed to be "very ill." In such cases my mission is to rush off.

In Algiers it is not too difficult to find a wild-eyed Pierre Louÿs, his mustache absolutely fierce, looking exasperated, and not so ill that he can't run around the Casbah in search of women. In order to be agreeable, I went along with him three times, and we shared rather well the tasks of love. I had been surprised at the little emotion I felt upon seeing him again; I was expecting a keener, more naïve and sudden joy; and I think the same was true for him, judging from the effort we made at first to re-

---

[5] It was a few days before, during this stay in North Africa, that Gide came upon Oscar Wilde by chance in Blida and came under his influence to such an extent, especially as regards his sexual emancipation.

[6] Pierre Louÿs, recovering from an illness, had spent the winter in Seville, and had left there to join Gide in Algiers. "We had not been together for fifteen minutes when we began quarreling . . . It was about everything and nothing . . . Decidedly, we could no longer get along, no longer bear one another." (*Si le Grain ne meurt.*) They did not break off relations completely until the following year, when Gide was to refuse to contribute to *Le Centaure.*

* *Translator's note:* The writer's friend in *Paludes.*

inflate a feeling that had decidedly gone flat. In three days I had a lot of trouble hiding and calming down an annoyance, a contempt almost, that was caused by his being constantly on his guard against me. Decidedly, in him social conventions replace and negate any truth. Questions of greetings and tips are taken as seriously as matters of caesuras and accent, and friendship does not come until after it has been proven. Finally, the fear of appearing to be what he is or what he is not, especially the fear of someone being disrespectful to him, makes him into a puppet who is almost unable to move without the help of outside strings and who has almost none of his own impulses any longer. Those disputes with hotel proprietors and bellboys, that haggling over a five-cent cigar, that perpetual assertion of his rights, and even to that insatiable desire to spend when one has nothing left but other people's money—finally, that mixture of conversation in the style of Scholl,[7] Bonnières, and especially Mendès[8]. . . . —all that, and his intransigence, his lack of understanding, his insulting authority—I stood that for three days. The strange and only interest of that very long (!) promiscuity was to feel growing within him a mad desire to make me scenes again—and it didn't fail to happen. Apropos of some stories I told him, he cracked insulting jokes—but I didn't want to get angry at that for he would have come out on top. Then there was something more peculiar still but so silly that I remained completely calm; you heard how he spoke of Maurice Quillot when we lunched together (it was nothing, but it was already significant), then that tiny scene he made about our saying *tu* to each other. . . . It was still nothing, but remembering that, you will better understand what that turned into when, annoyed at the fact that I seemed not to hear since I wasn't protesting, he made a point of discussing all my "friends," those who are not also his, in such a way that I was unable to tolerate it indefinitely. You were involved too, although very, very slightly and in a way that would have gone unnoticed had it not been added to the others. But since he made a point of joining the most unpleasant adjectives to the names of Walkenaër, Laurens, and Rouart, I finally, apropos of the latter, told him something very calm, I hope, something similar to this . . . well, too bad . . . I'm not sure of the words and I don't care a hang, but approximately: "When someone calls you an imbecile, I get angry, thus for the same reason, and knowing that Rouart is my friend, do understand that I find it very unpleasant to hear you discuss him like that." It was less stereotyped, it was most certainly not any more brutal, and if he has kept silent ever since, if we never meet again, it will most certainly be more because of his annoyance at seeing that my relations with Rouart

---

[7] Aurélien Scholl (1833–1902), novelist and playwright. His published works include *Les Nouveaux Mystères de Paris* (1867) and *Le Roman de Follette* (1886).

[8] Catulle Mendès (1841–1909), a Parnassian poet, novelist, and playwright.

have continued through all the scenes he has made to break them off.

Moreover, feeling no resentment against him—and I feel almost none— implies that henceforth he is considered a creature without any *real* personal *value,* without any personality and quasi-irresponsible, or some- one who interests me but little, or someone who acts according to motives of which I cannot approve. *Amen* and so be it and it can't be helped. It will have taken him quite some time to understand that his friendship is not irreplaceable and that he is not, despite everything, my best friend.

Met Coste this morning; couldn't avoid the collision, nor could I refuse an invitation to lunch.

I am reading D'Annunzio's *Intruder* and I am admiring.

I don't like Algiers, but yet I wish you were here in a little café with no seats, where we would chat, stretched out on mats, adjusting ourselves to the shape of the walls, playing chess or, when it's too hot, checkers.

A café to which Pierre Louÿs will not come because it is far from the women's quarter, a café that Pierre Louÿs does not know and to which Pierre Louÿs has never come. Ever since "the event," there is where I withdraw, draw myself out, stretch out, and hide out; there I am the only *roumi;* * there is where I spend two or three hours every afternoon, doing nothing; and one hour again every evening. Without smoking it, I breathe in the stupefying smell of the hashish that the others smoke, in a large water-pipe from which each draws but one puff and then passes it on. And when my turn came, the first day, I very happily inhaled down to my diaphragm and then spent two hours thinking I would die from sweat and nausea. The Arab musicians play monotonously on their little two-stringed lyres, others gently strike the skin of strangely shaped drums with the tips of their fingers; from where I am, one can't see the street, the opened door protects me from it; but stretched out on the mat, I let the tip of my red shoe show out—so that if Louÿs passes by he will see it, recognize it, and go away.

Will he have seen it? Has he passed by? I shall never know, I guess, and that is no longer any concern of mine.

What else shall I tell you about the café? A nightingale's cage hangs in the shadow, under the archway, but it's empty. Cats of all ages move about; the people there don't read newspapers and no one awaits *Paludes;* the Arabs who sit around are almost all regular customers, and I am getting to know them; they don't give me much of a feeling that I bother them, and I deserve it, for I know so well how to smile at them sweetly and greet them religiously; in order to please them, I take off the shoe on the foot that's placed on the mats, keeping the other shoe on the tip of the other foot only as a scarecrow.

What am I doing here?

* *Translator's note:* A Christian, in the language of Arabs and Moslems.

I am awaiting a little money that will allow me to return to France. I shall be there, I think, around the beginning of April, and in Paris around mid-April.

Your
André Gide

91. André Gide to Paul Valéry

Grignon [9] [May, 1895]

Dear friend, send me news, please. I don't ask for a long letter, unless writing it pleases you more than it tires you; but I left you so ill, so tired, and with so many worries that I must hear from you, if only a few lines, but lines that tell me whether or not your sleep and you are finally getting on, whether or not something is succeeding in your life, exams or the new review (what a perfect toast you proposed!),[10] and whether or not I grieved you too much those last days together—write me *that,* dear friend, that most especially—and write that you forgive me if I troubled you with how very much my sentimental worries and the uncertainty of my life, which is *decidedly* at stake each new hour, have monopolized my thoughts, so that, even during the hours I live far from M.,[11] I still think only of her and with fatiguing steadiness. It will soon be seven years that I have been awaiting such hours; the anxiety, although it finally led to happiness, was no less taxing; but those are temporary torments; don't think that being a lover makes me *any less your friend.* WRITE TO ME.

The park is splendid; with this great cloudless heat, the horizons become vaporized, the acacias are about to bloom; in the blaze of day, the folioles from the young elms rain down; one enjoys a kind of physical bestiality, like after one has had a lot of beer to drink, one pisses and shits in the leaves; then one gets up full of caterpillars.[12]

Rouart is exquisite; his affection has delicate possibilities; it develops and matures. We speak a lot about you, I love to feel him love you and hope that you are pleased with his tenderness. How unsatisfactory our meetings were in Paris! Great worrier that I am, tormented by too much happiness. Say when you plan to come here. If nothing happens, I shall stay four more days, then four days in Rouen—then *indesinenter* [*sic*] Paris . . .

Your
André

---

[9] André Gide went to see Eugène Rouart, who was then finishing a course of instruction at the Grignon School of Agriculture.

[10] Probably at a dinner with young littérateurs.

[11] Madeleine Rondeaux, Gide's fiancée.

[12] Paul Léautaud, who was to become acquainted with a copy of this letter, had a grievance against Gide for speaking so vulgarly and was to quote the terms used in this sentence, somewhat distorting them (*Entretiens radiophoniques,* Gallimard, 1951, p. 372).

92. *Paul Valéry to André Gide*

[May, 1895]

My dear André,

There is nothing new. Ever. I have come to note some rather curious variations in my condition. But I no longer have any confidence in those moments of confidence. I now know that every two weeks I have some physical discomfort. It's my monsoon. I don't work any more. From time to time I polish the brass, I tripolize [13] my habitation in order to watch it become oxidized all over again. Besides, I can work only on difficulties, and the ones I'm able to find come to a very small number, which are well known and with which I shall never have done.

You know that the direction of my mind was chosen precisely in accordance with the various difficulties involved in a certain number of questions. I have always gone straight to what is important. So that I am caught between what belongs to me and by that very fact disgusts me, and the rest—which is not mine and which discourages me. I know what I have found. I have in hand two or three hundred problems, resolved or not, which people always juggle away. I think I am able to bring anyone into them. And at that point he must answer or disappear. I am the one who will disappear. There are times when I should like to have someone to educate, to strengthen. (Laughable and true!) I am stupid enough to miss having experimented with a method and a few ideas, an experiment I shall never make. Were I now to have some holy peace, perhaps I should plunge back into the great mental game. . . . I realize that I have become like an alcoholic. When I think of the vigor I used to have occasionally, I become fully aware of my present disability.

May I ask you not to worry about me and not to lose a spark of your feelings over me: 1. because such moments are rarer than the troubles of your friend, and 2. because there is nothing to be done about the latter.

Au revoir, my dear fellow, my old André, read Virgil to Rouart, *I am rushing off to Hérold's!*   V.

93. *André Gide to Paul Valéry*

La Roque, Wednesday evening
[P. May 30, 1895]

Dear Paul,

My mother is ill, and I am afraid it's serious. Will this letter arrive soon enough to cancel, alas, the one I sent you from Evreux? *

---

[13] A neologism Valéry derived from the name of a cleaning product, "Tripoli" polish.

* *Translator's note:* A letter of May, 1895, in which Gide had invited Valéry to spend some time at La Roque in order to work in peace and to rest.

Marie,* who sat up with my mother these last three nights, is not at all well herself and, in this big house, is not really equal to all that has to be done. I can no longer ask you to come, it would add too much to her fatigue.

Write to me so that I may feel you are my friend. I need affection and am very sad.

Your
André Gide

94. *André Gide to Paul Valéry*

Friday morning [May 31, 1895]

Dear friend,

My mother is dying. I am very sad and very alone. Our doctor is going to come from Paris. My family has been notified.[14]

Your
André

95. *Paul Valéry to André Gide*

Saturday [June 1, 1895]

My poor André,

This morning Rouart gave me a telegram to read, the one of which I had a foreboding. Ever since your letters, I have been thinking of this horrible thing, and you were never out of my thoughts all yesterday and last night. I send you love, I feel everything you feel. I am completely at your service.

Paul

96. *André Gide to Paul Valéry*

Cuverville [P. August 15, 1895]

Dear Paul,

I would reproach myself a great deal for my silence, were it not that I reproached you even more for yours; for in Montpellier, not yet a soldier,[15] you must be at a loss for what to do, whereas here I have everything to do, and please understand that no one could be busier.

Dear friend, I have been living with your article,[16] surprising myself at understanding it so well, and digesting it slowly.

---

* *Translator's note:* Mme Gide's faithful Swiss maid, whose real name was Anna Leuenberger.

[14] "I was anxious to watch over her alone. Marie and I helped her in her last moments, and when her heart finally stopped beating, I felt my whole being sink into an abyss of love, guilt, and freedom." (*Si le Grain ne meurt.*)

[15] Paul Valéry was about to do his reserve duty of "twenty-eight days" of military service.

[16] *L'Introduction à la Méthode de Léonard de Vinci.*

"Circumstances" will keep me from going to Montpellier after I'm married.[17] I therefore don't know when I shall be able to have the pleasure of introducing my wife to your mother. Please at least give her, from me, the news of my approaching marriage and offer her my respectful good wishes. Remember me also to your brother. Dear fellow, write to me, please. In a few days, I shall go and see the Charles Gides at Noirmoutier. Continue to write to 4, rue de Commaille—your letters will be forwarded from there.

> I am your faithful
> André Gide

97. *Paul Valéry to André Gide*

[P. September 23, 1895]

Dear fellow, on my return from some most exhausting maneuvers, I find your letter, along with a hundred others. A Madagascan kind of heat, marches at noon and sleeping on the ground or on the hateful straw of stables (two weeks without undressing), have fagged me out. As a finishing touch, I see, upon returning home, trunks all packed and an impending trip to Venice and Genoa that I could very well do without. I am off the day after tomorrow, still completely battered.[18] I thank you for the pin * in your letter, but I confess that I still don't understand a thing about what I read. Rouart's brother wrote me a charming letter, but I judge it as such still by approximation: I see nothing at all, I sleep. You are getting married on the 8th, but where will you go then? Come through Genoa around the 20th. I have not sent you the booklet and manuscript,[19] for lack of everything, but they will come.

I should offer you lots of good wishes for your marriage, but all my intentions have been thrown out of gear by those twenty-eight days, their psychophysiological consequences and this departure.

> Love.
> V.

[17] On October 8, 1895, André Gide was to marry his cousin Madeleine Rondeaux.

[18] Paul Valéry had just taken part in maneuvers in Lorraine. Having returned to Montpellier on September 20, he was to take off again, a few days later, for Genoa, via Valence, Grenoble, Modane, Turin, Venice, Trieste, Padua, Milan, and Pavia. He arrived in Genoa on October 8.

* *Translator's note:* In a letter to Valéry postmarked September, 1895, Gide wrote: "I have cut this quarter of a page for you out of a recent letter from [Drouin] and at the end I've pinned on a few words that are missing from the sentence. As you shall see, your article is still on our minds."

[19] Of *L'Introduction à la Méthode de Léonard de Vinci.*

98. André Gide to Paul Valéry

[P. October 3, 1895]

Dear friend,

I have finally received your booklet.[20] I am getting married in a week and, completely bewildered, can only write you a word. Your manuscript has also arrived as a most charming gift, so intimately friendly, and the strongest invitation to memories. Dear Paul, forgive me for thanking you so inadequately: I am stupefied by these preparations for getting married, and I think that as soon as the ceremonies are over I shall fall into a six months' slumber, which I shall sleep off in Venice, Corfu, Capri, or what have you. Our objective is to reach Venice by way of the Engadine; it's perhaps stupid. . . . Where are you? Where will you be? What news of the Ministry of War?

That trip you mention worries me. Your mother wouldn't by any chance be in Montpellier around October 16?

I should take great pleasure in introducing my wife to her; write to me, for if Madame Valéry is not there, I don't think we'll make the detour, having already seen the Ch. Gides at Nîmes and then having to reach Geneva. Meanwhile, please give her my respectful best wishes.

Your

And. Gide

Drouin is plunged in Rimbaud up to his meninges.

99. Paul Valéry to André Gide

Genoa [P. October 9, 1895]

Dear friend,

You must be married, you are perhaps en route? I should have liked to give you some sign of life on this occasion, but I no longer know where I am. I'm completely dispersed. Maneuvers, departures, and going through so many cities, it all has bewildered me. Finally, I have been stagnating a bit in Genoa since yesterday. I picked up a Christ by Da Vinci for you in Milan, the same one again. You shall have it when you want it, but where? I have no news from the Ministry, I am vegetating before returning to Paris. My mother is with me. She is sorry not to be able to meet your wife. I don't think you'll come through Genoa before the end of this month. It would be the only point in common.

I have been to Venice and to Trieste, not very sensitive on the whole to anything but (I shall know later on) a few Tintorettos and the gondola, a kind of sleepy, funerary, etc., hansom cab.[21] Milan exasperated me, as always.

[20] *L'Introduction à la Méthode de Léonard de Vinci.* An offprint from *La Nouvelle Revue.*

[21] In English in the original.

The little thinking I've done, since my departure, has been of a military nature. A rather curious phenomenon—due perhaps to my twenty-eight days. "A very zealous corporal," they put on my record, and indeed I had one man stuck in prison and another in the disciplinary companies (with great difficulty, I may add).

However, look:

[Here Paul Valéry drew a diagram.]

going over this line on this plain must be maddening in strategy and tactics. It's the most exciting chessboard in the world, and with the incompetency of Bouvard, I *saw* only "military crests, turning movements, dangerous zones." Just think, the posts in this country are called Lonato, Verona, Peschiera, Castiglione, etc. Now with that trifle of history we once took in, and a few memories of shooting with blanks, I constructed a MECHANICAL or PSYCHOMECHANICAL view, trying to fuse the *terrain,* still so interesting, the individual, and the complex of *individuals* = the army in an organized composition. Imagine what the algebraic or pseudo-algebraic expression of the whole would be, with the values that might be given to irregularities in the field, geological laws, productive regions, and the very shifting of races according to the given surface relief of a Lombardo-Venetia.

You grasp the aesthetics of it, at once. And I'm speaking to a newly married man! My dear fellow, you know well that I shan't write to you without sending you all good wishes for . . . and for. . . . Please tell your fiancée [*sic*] that you have a friend who is a good enough friend to you to cut out the epithalamiums. He reserves vague things for indispensable occasions. I shall tell you quite frankly that I am distressed at knowing there is no hope of seeing you for centuries, and that you are very right to become befuddled in far-off countries and to flee us. (Don't go to Constantinople, it's frightfully boring.)

Adieu!
P. V.

100. André Gide to Paul Valéry

Cuverville [P. October 10, 1895]

Dear friend,

Thank you for your card.

I have already been married by the mayor and in a few hours will be married by the minister.

On passing through the rue de la Vielle-Intendance—if I do go to Montpellier—I shall drop off a gift for you, a box of compasses.

If you write to me (and you will write to me), send your letters to the rue de Commaille, whence they will be forwarded to the right place.

Not long ago I wrote you a short note, which I hope has been sent on to you, but perhaps the postage was insufficient. Forgive me.

Your friend,

A. G.

101. Paul Valéry to André Gide

[P. December 6, 1895]

My dear André,

I have finally just received your marvelous box of compasses! You are completely out of your mind, you need a guardian, I assure you. I am your dancer, your stables, your collection, I cost you no end of money. You have given me all that's needed to build the world. Ah! if God had been equipped like that! what orbits, lord! what kinds of electricity! Men would perhaps have had somewhat more precise minds. But the Illustrious Geometer created himself. At thirty, he knew only the Postulatum and he died on a cross that had only one perpendicular—suspecting that with a second, the whole thing would have been f—— up. There you are!

My dear fellow, I am involved in a singular adventure, which I shan't "commit to paper." You can guess: it has nothing to do with Krafft-Ebing,[22] it's very healthy—morally.

The point is that I'm not doing a bloody thing, satisfied just to see, nearby, Hérold, who is shaping Sakountala;[23] Pierre, who is inventing horrors; Mauclair, who . . . (I shan't commit it to paper); Régnier, who hides, prints, and grows younger; Schwob, very *happy,* very nice, more informed than ever, who *produces;* Mallarmé, who distresses me because people are distressing him; and everyone who eats, drinks, evacuates, and delivers, each of them giving to one or another of those verbs the dominant value of stigmata.

I wait, sometimes impatiently, to be asked to work, and it doesn't happen quickly: I dream of impossible gadgets: I become the inventor of New Year's Day toys of no possible use, in the metaphorical sense; I don't resist dining at Fontainas'; I gallop through the museums, in order to digest; I spend an entire afternoon listening to Walckenaër read me one of his next articles on Childhood, I make honest comments, I smoke, I get bored, I exhaust myself at night, I exercise with dumbbells, I broke two watches, I begin to work out calculations, I go back to my system, I meet Louÿs at the

---

[22] Author of the well-known treatise *Psychopathia sexualis,* dealing with sexual inversion, published in 1886 and translated into French in 1895.

[23] *Sakuntala,* a heroic comedy by Kalidasa, adapted by Hérold as *L'Anneau de Çakuntala* and performed on the stage of the Théâtre de l'Œuvre on December 10, 1896.

d'Harcourt,* and I wait as naïvely for the reviews to ask me to write something as for an appointment at the Ministry. Anyway, time goes by, the days become oxidized, and now and then, a terrific trumpet call that lasts for a second.

At every moment *in life* (!) we are in the pose of acrobats after every great stunt. There we are—standing solidly on our legs, a smile on our lips —and suggesting, out of graciousness, to the audience or to ourselves, that nothing extraordinary has happened. We have returned to equality. We object: "That was nothing. Nothing painful. . . ."

Have you read Rimbaud's prose at the end of the edition of *Les Poésies?* [24] Those unpublished texts are miraculous (let's be accurate!). They are astonishing Illuminations, the best. I should like to spend two hours with you and them. You would give me the strength to think and speak about them, and we would again have drunken orgies—as in the past—you know, when each of us, on his own, read *Le Bateau ivre* for the second time. Come, come, let's keep calm. No speaking to the helmsman.

Paul

(Write) ∞ and again (Thank you) ∞.

102. André Gide to Paul Valéry

Florence [25] [P. December 15, 1895]

My dear Paul,

Although I left for Venice, I have arrived in Florence, where I find your letter, five days stale.

I saw Milan, which I hated beforehand; I walked under the arcades of red Bologna; I ate sausage and I drank chocolate. I crossed the Apennines by way of the old carriage road, where from village to village the inns have marble plaques bearing the name of Garibaldi, who passed through the region at a time when there were no other roads. A thick fog obscured all the landscape except the trees along the edge and the slopes of packed snow. The fog opened over Florence.

I love Florence. After what you wrote me about your great boredom when faced with cities, I feel a bit ashamed to confess my joy.

"Here below" it is always less sensible than boredom; I make a secret of it in front of you, as if it were some shameful enjoyment, some vice, and before I show myself to you, I arrange to have wrinkles.

---

* *Translator's note:* A café on the Boulevard St.-Michel.

[24] Léon Vanier had just published Rimbaud's *Poésies complètes,* with a preface by Verlaine and notes.

[25] Gide was to assemble his impressions of this trip to Italy, and then to North Africa, in a book entitled *Feuilles de Route,* published in 1899 (Impr. Vandersypen, then Ed. du Mercure de France).

At sixteen, we would have been able to wander over the roads together, we would have had the sea at our right, the lonely East * at our left, and before us, at a great distance, some venturesome inn in which to try our luck at satisfying all those hungers. At night we would have pressed our faces to the windows, to see families preparing for happiness; and we would have gone down the chimney into rooms that otherwise were too calm, and we would have frightened the people who were about to fall asleep. In the morning, before dawn, we would have had a swim and we would not have had headaches.

Now, we have too many millstones round our necks, and we are awaiting too many answers. Have they come from the Ministry? from the review? . . . Thank you for the one concerning the box of compasses. Move the world, my friend, and may I be your place to stand. I am beginning to try and corrupt the young by preaching Nomadism, I shall see what comes of it with Camille Mauclair and the Belgians. Besides, they're charming, friendly, and make sowing possible. Mauclair writes me good letters and sends me wishes for happiness; I am far enough away from everything so as not to be irritated by anything but myself, and I find Mauclair charming. No, I don't know the new Rimbaud texts.

Adieu.

Your
A. G.

— 1896 —

103. Paul Valéry to André Gide

A Saturday [P. January 11, 1896]

Dear Friend,

I read an excellent piece of yours in *L'Ermitage*.[1] Then I reread it. And, far from any objections, forgetting the meaning of your words, I spent a long time tasting bit by bit the pleasure of loving you, the imperceptible fatigue of remembering ** our meetings, our emotions, our very clearly defined differences,—and your goodness in my changeable mind and La Roque.

---

* *Translator's note:* "l'orient désert" (Racine, *Bérénice* 3.4.).

[1] *Ménalque,* a fragment of *Les Nourritures terrestres,* which was to come out in 1897.

** *Translator's note:* The French text read, "*te* rapeller," probably either a misprint or a misreading.

You know that I am not acquainted with your God, and that I cannot seek one for myself. Alas! I am not a man of God or a man of the country. Ecstasy and grass never overexcite me for more than half a day.

We have buried Verlaine.[2] And we also took advantage of the occasion as much as possible. After the speeches, fifteen of us sat down to eat in a bistro at the Clichy gate. And we were so gay that the dead man must have been sorry he was dead. I was between Mauclair and Beaubourg,[3] both of whom depress me a bit. I therefore spoke very little, no more than what politeness demands. Yet I'm about to join them. Perhaps I shall start to do a lot of scribbling. Who knows? I see that time is going by and that no stable job is coming my way. I am hurt, I have been foresaken by my intimate diversions, and as I look round me, a digust for furnished rooms and brief visits takes hold of me. A black mood, in particular, disturbs my logic, I repeat mechanical expressions, onomatopoeias of sadness and rancor. And well! when one has so much loved light! . . . (Even in the strangest theories about it.) So, I should like to sell blackened paper. And as luck would have it, I don't have one idea, not even a subject for an article!

I have often felt like reading my portrait in one of your books, a portrait that really resembles me, under one of those strange names you find, which give the impression of a false nose. But then would I recognize myself? Besides, I would be suitable for literature only in very exaggerated form. And it would no longer be me at all, for I think I dwell in a very unstable equilibrium or in a meeting of tastes which is never in perfect equilibrium but which swings round a middle position. I should like that because of your way of writing. For me it would be the best thing to remember you by and the most accurate document.

The portrait is a genre I have wanted to tackle. I had a series in mind for *La Nouvelle Revue* with rather peculiar names. (Degas,[4] Poincaré,[5] etc.) But there are difficulties. I know that Mauclair is going to write about Degas, and in addition, that this annoys Degas. Poincaré is difficult to do

[2] Verlaine died at the home of Eugénie Krantz, rue Descartes. He was buried the day before Paul Valéry wrote this letter, January 10, 1896. A religious service was held at Saint-Etienne-du-Mont. A great number of men of letters accompanied the coffin to the Batignolles cemetery. Speeches were made by Coppée, Mendès, Moréas, and Barrès. Mallarmé's long farewell speech, which began thus: "The grave loves silence at once . . . ," provoked the sarcasm of the *chansonniers.*

[3] Maurice Beaubourg (1860–1943), novelist (*Contes pour les Assassins,* 1890; *Dieu ou pas Dieu,* 1906) and playwright (*L'Image,* 1894; *Les Menottes,* 1897; etc.).

[4] Degas (1834–1917) was a friend of Henri Rouart, the father of Eugène Rouart. That is how Paul Valéry came to meet the painter shortly afterward. However, the study he was to devote to him, *Degas, danse, dessin,* was not published until long after Degas' death, in 1938.

[5] The mathematician Henri Poincaré (1854–1912).

without knowing him. He interests me a great deal, for he does hardly anything but articles on psychology, from the point of view of a mathematician. It is quite to my taste. I have had that constantly in mind since my new Testament. (The Gospel leads us there, says Euclid!) Only *He* does it with the most fascinating logical genius, being the great old boy that he is, and he deals with particular points. And I, poor cripple and ignoramus, I, on the contrary, have discovered only the mathematical ABC's of it and should like to concentrate on the reality of thought. I have often thought that knowing him would be precious to me, that a monthly conversation with him would help me make great headway—and perhaps would not be altogether useless to him—but would it be free? And anyway we have nothing in common. And I wouldn't dare raise objections to what he says.

I want also to dig saps beneath the publishing house Quantin. You know the collection of art books they have. Since they have done "Arms" and furniture, there is no reason that Boats not be included. With skill, one might slip in a very sober Naval Aesthetic, with engravings and galleys on a scale of 1/1,000, and almost nothing of what I once liked to speak of by that idiotic name, and which means nothing to me any more. As you can see, I'm building galleons in the air, the sign of a bad time.

Louÿs leaves Tuesday for Athens, by way of Italy. You shall see him at D'Annunzio's in a few days.

Addio, carissimo. Penso che mi avrei perdonato l'ultima mia lettera. Nessuno conosce piu di me quel acuto dolore che danno la forza e la debolezza in tempi troppo brevi unite e strette. E poi ho avuto tanti disgusti e tante speranze fallite che la mia mente s'inaspre tutti i giorni e che la mia ragione non vuol piu ragionar.[6]

Amicissimo tuo,
P.

104. André Gide to Paul Valéry

Naples, January 24 [1896]

Caro,

You did right to answer my letter, I was so upset about you; and especially as I realized how silent I was in the face of your pain. One only consoles imbeciles. I know it from never having consoled anyone but myself, and I smiled in advance, along with you, at the silly things I might have told you. Nothing has any value in such sadness but the persistency

[6] "Adieu, my very dear fellow. I think you will have forgiven me my last letter. No one knows better than I that intense suffering caused by strength and weakness so closely combined in too short a time. And then, I was disgusted by so many things and disappointed in so many of my hopes that my mind grows desperate each day and my reason refuses to reason any longer."

of friendship, and I was happy that your letter, in its confidence, showed me that you were aware of mine.

I hoped to see you again, the story of our relationship seemed to me clearer than ever. I have hovered round you for a long time. The recollection of our first meetings in Montpellier has a charm that I find in no others, a very special charm, almost independent of us it was so helped along by the season, the avenues from the Peyrou to the Botanical Gardens, Narcissa's tomb and our age. I find that only the close of meals at La Roque has, in our relationship, an almost comparable charm.

In your last letter you refer to it again, and I am so touched by that. Really, were you able to like *Ménalque?!* [7] I wish to be *sure* of your praise, and I have such a perverse mind that I more willingly believe your criticism. *Ménalque* doesn't please me; I did a slapdash job of it for Ducoté, who had asked me for a text in a most particularly urgent fashion. It is an advance rehash of my next book, [8] on which I count to justify my next exile. I had to blur and smooth out everything so that it would not be too apparent that although every little paragraph may seem to involve all the rest, the rest was not at all meant to follow. But my book will be better, and *Ménalque* will not be recognizable. In it I am cutting up my fodder into small slices, and I admire how many little pieces it makes! I hope that afterward I shall be able to allow myself a book that is somewhat seriously sad, for Melancholia, in this one, will come out rather badly. Each day I learn to eat my hay more directly, and a certain share of sun, grass, and water is enough for my daily intoxication. I have rediscovered the enchantment of Florence, the boredom of Rome, and the nervous irritation of Naples, and in addition I have understood more and more that only the desert really pleased me; I am obsessed with soon going back *there,* and certain nights it keeps me from sleeping. Piles of books in preparation await an approaching retreat; I have given up writing while traveling, but as soon as I get back to France, I think that writing will make me give up all "the rest."

How do you expect me to write your portrait *already,* you, the least fixed of men! Have you managed to make your two ends meet?! Are you not still undecided about yourself? The types in *Paludes* are all tied up like Punch and Judys; none of them are still developing. And take all those around us. . . . How many among them, having had no *childhood,* give any hope for their reaching a *mature* age? Hérold, Bonnières, Souza, [9] Quillard, etc. I exclude Griffin, I think, but hardly Régnier, who nevertheless pleases me more. . . . On the contrary, Drouin, you—indeed, you would

[7] Published by *L'Ermitage* in that month of January, 1896.

[8] *Les Nourritures terrestres.*

[9] Robert de Souza (1865–1946), a poet and critic, was to publish, from 1896 to 1898, *L'Almanach des Poètes,* with contributions from the major poets of the time.

not have been in your place in *Paludes*. If I write your portrait later on, it will be long, subtle, and very tragic. Adieu, I am not writing well and my nerves are completely on edge.

Your friend

André G.

(The end of your letter—in Italian—is absolutely exquisite, write to me.)

105. Paul Valéry to André Gide

London, Grenville Street, 15 W.C.

[P. April 2, 1896]

My old André,

I have been in London for two days, your letter reached me yesterday. Really, I live in a most peculiar way! Sunday morning, I receive a note from someone unknown, telling me to come to England at once for some work. Tuesday morning, I arrived in London, at nine o'clock. At eleven, I was at work. I entered a new world, which is still not very clear to me— which might interest me if I were not so overwhelmed with tasks the whole day. I rented a room near my employment. I live absolutely mute and alone, except during the hours of explanatory meetings and discussions and orders. And I come back immediately afterward, abruptly cut off from my previous life and from any thoughts other than . . . technical ones. At English hours, a maid brings me some vile food—Oh! vile—I eat while watching the fire, and I have my mind constantly on very solemn affairs. Sometimes, I make faces in the mirror in order to at least act as if I were laughing, in order not to be too serious the whole time. Since I am rather shrewd, I rather quickly understood what it was all about. I immediately wanted to perfect my work and make it more efficient. I don't know whether I have yet been understood. Let me tell you that I am in a mechanism of infinitely able people. Thanks to my job (as a confidential agent), I have learned some very important things. I have in my hands some rather powerful documents. Please don't say a word about what I'm telling you: I awoke on Tuesday with, in front of me, one of the thousand parts of a colossal machine called the Chartered Company,[10] which is acquiring all of South Africa. It's the most extraordinary politics. The general public knew nothing about it until the Jameson affair and the events in the Transvaal. You have no idea what the power, the depth, the wisdom, and the brutal clarity of these people are. They're always right. I am aware of their *ethics*. In France no one will ever understand them. We shall always fall short of the situation. I am acutely sorry that I'm still a bit

---

[10] On March 30 Paul Valéry wrote his brother that he was leaving for London to do some translations. He had been asked to work for the publicity department of Sir Cecil Rhodes' Chartered Company. He was to remain there only four weeks.

scatterbrained. I still can't clearly connect my observations (almost unconscious) of today with my tables of ideas and my conceptions of keen logic. . . . That is why your letter * stupefied me a bit more. I am twenty thousand times the earth's radius away from *Le Centaure* [11] and from everything. Your letter appeared to me to have been written by a man from some extinct civilization and one difficult to imagine. . . . Ah! the strange impression when I arrived, with absolutely no idea of what they wanted of me, anxious, in fact, and when my employer put me under close arrest, as it were, in a room where a Negro from Mashonaland served me in silence, where I was astonished at the shelves of books on tactics, books on travel, treatises on gold mines, general-staff manuals, etc. Then taken to one of the heads of it all, out-thinking him—and showing it. I hope to be very well paid. That's what they promised me. I believe I should get a hundred and twenty-five francs a week, which for me is rather nice. . . . In spite of everything, I am anxious to regain my badly paid idleness. Well, perhaps these work days will bear fruit!

I shall perhaps be in Montpellier in a month. But who knows? perhaps I shall be in Pretoria! or in Rhodesia! Write to me very quickly—but to my address in Paris—it's safer. It is understood that all this is just between us until further notice. Please.

PROMETHEUS (ravished by fire) **

106. *Paul Valéry to André Gide*

12, rue Gay-Lussac [P. May 18, 1896]

I must write to you, my dear fellow, so I need not have to go back over everything again and again. You are really the only one I like to chat with. The others amuse me in patches, etc. And besides, you are the only one

---

* *Translator's note:* On March 25 Gide wrote Valéry a note from Biskra, mentioning the new review *Le Centaure,* and with the postscript: "Do you want to play Prometheus in my next novel?" *Le Prométhée mal enchaîné* was to come out in 1899 (Ed. du Mercure de France).

[11] *Le Centaure,* a de luxe quarterly of literature and art, edited by Henri Albert, with the collaboration of Pierre Louÿs, André Lebey, A.-Ferdinand Hérold, Henri de Régnier, Jean de Tinan, and others, concentrated on the young writers published by the Librairie de l'Art Indépendant. In it André Gide was to publish *La Ronde de la Grenade* and *El Hadj;* Paul Valéry (under the initials V. and P. V.): *La Soirée avec Monsieur Teste* and two poems: *Vue* and *Eté.* The first issue was to displease Gide to such a degree that he was to refuse to let them print *Les Notes de Voyage,* which had been promised for the second issue. That incident provoked something of a break with the group, and a definitive estrangement from Pierre Louÿs. (*Le Centaure* presented lithographs and engravings by J.-E. Blanche, F. Rops, and Fantin-Latour.)

** *Translator's note:* "Ravi par le feu," written in pencil, has obviously a number of meanings, given Gide's postscript in his letter of March 25. See the translator's note above.

with whom I don't have the feeling of "should" and "have to." I had two other friends like that, but between them and me there was always a kind of veiled war—for such reasons! and then friendship and the rest were buried together in the sand by the years.

I felt like writing to you about trees. Thinking of you, I saw the greens of La Roque rolling behind in the barrel of my mind. Then I forgot you for the plants, I admired the plane trees, the birches and others. I have known for some time that the tree is the one thing in the world that does not yet bore me. (I am speaking of what one can see—and I am speaking also of very tall trees, with a light and rather smooth bark. Horror of callused trees.) The sea and waters in general make me sick—because of having overindulged. That leaves me with the tree and my well-known "whatevers," which always lead me to vague inventions that I express for others in terms of their clearest results, and for me, in a more than cryptographic language, mixed with scientific terms and "idiosyncratic" representations.

Anyway, it seems to me that beautiful trees give me pleasure, and I don't see myself being happy except together. (Solecisms.) They are to one's feelings like a good breath of air at just the right temperature, or like a perfect bed, becoming one with the back of the body and giving you the idea of spreading out your limbs.

I'm ruminating. Griffin writes me a beautiful letter to thank me for my dedication. Summer! rock of pure air! Bah? I'm re-ruminating. I feel like making some experiments in *Le Centaure,* a vivisection actually! But I lack an adequate subject. I have always felt (since 18.., the great era) like inventing the story of an old boy who thinks—since no one wants to get to work on it—and I should like to do a study for that. A histology of one end of it, giving the processes in the raw. If I were sure that I'd find it diverting, I would get to work on it.

Meanwhile, I am rereading *Candide* and being reminded of the night table in the hotel at Honfleur. This evening, a big dinner of centaurs with all the poets, at the d'Harcourt, and "no one will be witty but us and our friends!" *

All my respects to your wife—and to you nothing at all: you have already consumed four of my pages.   P. V.

107. André Gide to Paul Valéry

La Roque [May, 1896]

Dear old Paul,

A dirty trick has just been played on me. I arrive here to patch up some of the roofing, which is letting in water and rooting the crops, and to take

---

* *Translator's note:* "nul n'aura d'esprit hors nous et nos amis" (Molière, *Lés Femmes savantes* 3.2.).

part in the municipal elections in the capacity of a three-day-old councilor. And, quite in spite of myself, oh woe is me! I am appointed mayor on the first ballot, by an overwhelming majority![12] People who never saw me before! I never did *them* any harm! Well, the world is really cruel. Today, I have a bad head and a raging fever from having breathed in for so long the smell of their filthy drinks. You can't imagine what it's like. All of them are three-quarters eaten up by alcohol; the sturdiest of them began to pass out in the middle of the council meeting, and it would not have taken much for him to die on the spot; he was weeping mostly at the thought that he might perhaps have to cut down; some of them are so far gone that one or two drinks is enough to destroy them; the children are born idiots, contorted, or can no longer even be born. All the same, I begin my duties by receiving two illegitimate ones. The worst of it is that it's rather rare and that no one even wants to be born any more; a little sensuality would save them. I'm going to bring in some Aphrodites. The former mayor didn't know how to sign his name, and my deputy mayor, one who *doesn't* drink, can't even read. Tomorrow, I shall have to throw out of the presbytery a parish priest who plays nasty tricks and is bringing discredit upon the Holy Office.

I was hoping to rest up here by working; all that exhausts me and is ruining my *Nourritures*—I no longer dare sing the praises of intoxication.

All the same, the wistaria is in bloom, and it smells jolly good in the stairways.

I am withdrawing from *Le Centaure* (and you should do the same, my dear old Paul). I read this first issue in amazement. The pages by Régnier, by Louÿs, and my own are good (Hérold's also), and I even like Louÿs' and Régnier's very much. Tinan, Lebey, and Henri Albert are charming, but their writings do not please me at all, and the unfortunate thing is that, since all three of them take the same direction as Louÿs' and as mine in that *Ronde*, Régnier's short pages and yours and Hérold's overly severe tale are not enough to get rid of the impression that this review is a rather flat invitation to debauchery and a branch of the fourth page of certain Saturday newspapers. The rest just seems to be there as gilding, and the *art* in it is no more than a vague pretext at justification. The pages on travel that I could give them, in losing any value of seriousness, would appear as nothing more than reporting for the amusement of snobs, etc.

Finally, if it pleases Louÿs to found a school and pleases Hérold to baptize it, it suits his disciples L., T., and A.[13] just fine to follow along

---

[12] André Gide, at twenty-seven years old, was then one of the youngest mayors in France. He was to officiate for three years.

[13] Lebey, Tinan, and Albert.

and settle right in on de luxe paper, but singing along with them doesn't suit me at all, in that one sings out of tune when one doesn't sing the same melody. So, you withdraw as well and you will see . . .

At first, I thought of asking you to be kind enough to inform the others of my resignation, but that might have been disagreeable for you and I preferred to write quite frankly to the other collaborators. You shall tell me the effect it has. That will amuse me; give particular care to your account of it.

A long letter to Tinan (which you are not supposed to know about) and a letter to Albert, which greatly amused me to write in a lingo into which he will be able to read anything he likes. I am writing likewise to Régnier and to Hérold.

Poor dear old Paul, I should like to talk to you. I am sad and bothered after having read those columns, etc. Those drinking bouts were the last straw, and intruders are at me continuously. Here, I used to own a peaceful spot in which to forget the rest and work delightfully.

. . . O! solitude, soothing vastness of the desert, etc.

Caro, I like you and already wish to see you again.

Your
André Gide

108. *Paul Valéry to André Gide*

Friday [P. May 22, 1896]

Your Honor,

All my congratulations: Balzac's *Paysans* are now yours,—and you remind me of that lovely comment made by Stendhal, who exclaimed in a small town: "How sublime it would be to have a trial here. If only I were a rich Englishman . . . , etc." Pass a decree against *Le Centaure* right away.

We, André Gide, mayor of La Roque-Baignard, given the law of Prairial 7, year VIII, etc.

Have decreed and decree the following:

Art. 1.—The importing and peddling of *Le Centaure* is forbidden within the boundaries of the commune.

Art. 2.—The rural policeman is intrusted with executing this decree . . .

And now let's talk about politics.

I have not yet seen P. L., H. A., J. de T. I have seen H. de R. and A.-F. H.[14] Your resignation is having a most disastrous effect on those two gentlemen. It surprised me and delighted me, and at the same time

---

[14] Pierre Louÿs, Henri Albert, Jean de Tinan, Henri de Régnier, and André-Ferdinand Hérold.

bothered me a little. I find it difficult to hand in my own. 1. It would seem like a conspiracy. 2. We would have no idea what was going on, especially you, who are so far from their operations, even in Paris. 3. You have realized from my letter that I intend to make some experiments. It is possible that I shall be led quite *naturally* to imitate you in these trial essays, for I don't intend to forbid myself anything. (Like the others.)

Now I have something more ticklish to tell you: I have heard it said that your wife is responsible for your determination. I pass this on very confidentially. Remember that you know nothing at all about it, but *be aware of it* and come and chat with me on your return. You shall have to play your cards right, for you must not ignore the fact that *people are going to talk*. I'll write you about what I observe this afternoon at *Le Centaure* and about how I am greeted. I'm tempted to act in certain ways that you will understand. I feel like taking two or three of our friends and collab. aside and *cutting them to the quick*. I'm enticed by this opportunity to speak some truths (if I dare to express myself . . .). I would be more blunt if my situation didn't force me to be *itchingly* compromising. But I want to tell them once more "what *is*" and jeer at "what is not." I cannot stomach the fact that frauds, ingenuous schemers, or skilful rhetoricians flourish in so comfortable a security—when you, my old André, knock yourself out *creating* yourself, not to mention certain others or myself. I have told you hundreds of times what I would do if everything didn't tie me down. I note with pleasure that you are taking the right way—you who are free . . . —the highway! * Last night I dined at Griffin's with Mauclair, Fénéon,[15] Dujardin,[16] Thorel,[17] Hérold, Vallette,[18] and Emile Laforgue.[19] After dinner we discussed a mercurial edition of all Laforgue; they had brought over a few more of his manuscripts, and it amused me to glance through them while the others were busy talking. It was there that Hérold *announced* to me your defection, etc. *Aplati sunt!*

Ieri sono andato da Enrico, *il quale dopo avermi parlato di tuo affare, mi disse parecchie cose* curiose *circa il successo e l'avvenire di P. L. Ne parlava con certi scherzi rialzati di complimenti, una lingua che capisco assai bene. E la prima volta che si sfoggava un po' su questo soggetto in mia presenza.*

---

* *Translator's note:* The play on words in French is: *"le bon chemin . . . le bon chemin de fer."*

[15] Félix Fénéon (1861–1944), great scholar, art critic, and upholder of free verse and "modern" painting (Bonnard, Dufy, Matisse, Seurat, Vuillard, etc.).

[16] The poet Edouard Dujardin, one of the forces behind the symbolist movement, founder of *La Revue wagnérienne.*

[17] Probably Jean Thorel, playwright, novelist, and poet (*La Complainte humaine,* 1899; *Le Joyeux Sacrifice,* 1895; *Gillette,* 1902; etc.).

[18] Alfred Vallette, editor and manager of *Le Mercure de France.*

[19] Brother of the poet Jules Laforgue.

Che terribile cose si farrebero se si farebbe diplomazia! Ma troppo minuti
sono gli oggetti, e troppo vicine della propria esistenza, la consequenze.[20]

Friday, 5:10 P.M.

I am writing to you from the lair itself, where nothing is happening.
Only Hérold, Tinan, Albert, and myself are here. The motives for your
resignation *refuse to be understood*. What weakens your effect a little is the
success of the issue, which is selling rather well. It is continually in
demand. I saw Rouart around two o'clock, and I shall probably go to La
Queue on Sunday.

If anything happens, I'll let you know.

When are you coming back?   P. V.

109. *André Gide to Paul Valéry*

[July, 1896]

Dear Paul,

Here's my face; so that you don't forget it. Forgive my silence, a sign of
mental convalescence; however, I have been working and have almost
finished a tale ("which shows my inclinations") about that epigraph:
"Dans l'Orient désert quel devint mon ennui!" * Because Paris and
Montpellier are not the only places one can be bored, still I think it's always
due to recollections. You who have a good memory, speak to me of what
has happened. For my part, I remember just exactly enough of yesterday to
realize that today is very similar to it. How did you find your mother? Do
you plan to stay in Montpellier much longer? Are your writings coming
along?

Drouin all but lost his wits reading Maxwell. *We* are having a dialogue
with our conscience. I'm reading Nietzsche, who bores me a little. In the
woods, I killed a few vipers; I am horribly weary of the green of trees and
lawns. Yesterday, I went back to Honfleur, where one day I did not look
for you [*sic*]. If I had some idea of what might interest you about me, I
should write you better letters, but with you I feel altogether too stripped of
guile, I'm left with no more than a sickly nakedness. I should prefer to still
be running about on a beach, and when noon comes, we would swim
together. Tell me if you're still taking swims at Palavas, in the evening,

---

[20] "Yesterday I went to see *Henri*, who, after having spoken to me about that
business of yours, told me some *curious* things about the success and future of
Pierre Louÿs. He spoke about them with a kind of banter spiced by compliments,
in a language I understand rather well. It's *the first time* that he talked somewhat
freely of this matter in my presence. What terrifying things we would do if we
were in the diplomatic service! But these subjects are too insignificant, and the
consequences too close to their very existence."

* *Translator's note:* "In the lonely East how my torment grew!" (Racine, *Bérénice*
3.4). But here Gide takes the word *ennui* to mean boredom, not torment.

with Coste, and if there are any intrigues in your life elsewhere. Au revoir.

Your
André Gide

110. *Paul Valéry to André Gide*

[P. Montpellier, August 4, 1896]

Dear André,

Your portrait is good, especially the flyspecks of light between the palm trees, and your trousers, which are admirably cut. You tip over a bit, but anyway, it's fine. All your clothes are excellently designed. Also the cape, and the softening effect of light on its left shoulder is perfect.[21] As for the face, I know it! Ah! my old André, I'm frightfully bored! I'm doing some work for *Le Centaure,* a sickening piece of filth that I am plodding through with disgust, without even having the courage to prepare it. I write it bit by bit, going I know not where.

But no matter! I'm furious at missing my swims, for the weather is humid and I'm in fear of getting neuralgia. I confess that here Ubu himself loses all his savor. Shith* isn't good. It's stupid.

And finally, I've come across an old friend here in whom I have great *intellectual* confidence, despite all the trouble and agitation I spoke to you about three or four years ago. We have talked a lot. The people who once knew me are not very sure of me. They are rather surprised (to use the diplomatic style) that I am doing nothing *concrete.* They know that I'm interested in many things, I am considered to have a ravenous curiosity, but well, I should, etc. To add up: this opinion is held by Louÿs, Kolbassine, and the friend in question. What would you think if people were to settle your hash like that? Note that there is no point in saying dreadful things in answer. That would be easy as could be. But I am not indignant, because, being the party concerned, I distrust certain optical illusions that occur when personalities intervene. Moreover, this is an imposing tribunal. Not to mention that you think the same thing, probably, and if so, it's a supreme court!

Well, once we dismiss the countercarte, which, I repeat, is easy—and once we dismiss also the serious value of this opinion, which is based upon obviously false premises—I am left with nothing but rather acute sadness. That's what it is to prefer friends to a public. Don't my friends, then, believe in anything but public approbation? Do they, by any chance, feel particularly wronged because they are preferred to everyone? It's strange.

---

[21] A photograph taken in Biskra by the young Arab Athman. It shows Gide wearing a beard, a large felt hat, and a cape, leaning against the trunk of a palm tree.

* *Translator's note:* Ubu, in Alfred Jarry's Ubu Roi, instead of "merde," says "merdre."

Well, so much the worse for me! I mind my own business, I live on my own, I don't know how to write a book. I know, in a way, how to stir up a few things here and there. I know well that I shall never achieve anything, but what is one to achieve?

I sincerely ask my friends if I have often violated our IMPLICIT pact. If I haven't sometimes told them interesting things, if I haven't suggested, if I haven't asked, that they be of good faith, if I haven't made known to them my research—imploring them to have precise objections, declaring as worthless any words of praise or blame, laying myself open to the point of doing unto them, at the risk of friendship, what I would have them do unto me. Not one answered me. . . .

What saddens me is that I shall have to go on more alone than ever, and wall up the rest of the windows. It's very hard, when even now I work with a fair amount of disgust, and when I have but one pleasure left—or rather one anesthetic: my association with a few people.

They shall drive me really wild.

Good bye.*

P.

111. André Gide to Paul Valéry

Cuverville, near Criquetot l'Esneval
[P. August 29, 1896]

Dear old Paul,

No, you know perfectly well that I am not of the same opinion and that I have never exclaimed, even within myself: "He must have some goal in life." To be sure, I think that, often, the belief in a goal is something of an assurance of happiness, but that's quite another thing, and you know it as well as I. But as a matter of fact, the more I go on, the more I find it presumptuous to hear you reproached with that by people whose *goal* is transitory, constantly overshot and constantly shifting (or else whose goal is to *succeed*)—to hear them reproaching you, whose unity or unification of research is extraordinary; you, who for years and years have been working "in the same direction," etc.

I claim that they don't understand what they mean when they speak of another goal, and that if they were cornered, they would end by giving as arguments some grotesque or contemptible truisms. I sometimes think that in the desire several of them have to see you *"choose* a goal," affection plays less of a part than the egotistical desire to know you as a *famous man*. I am not at all convinced that your "ethic" rules out producing, but rather that it disdains producing and considers it useful only as a notation that compensates for memory and makes new research possible; it would seem to me that one has only to know you a little to understand that. Then, into the

* *Translator's note:* In English in the original.

bargain, there are the *kindnesses* of friends, the solicitation of reviews, the need for money, for respect, for not seeming like a Buddhist in the eyes of one's mother, etc., and I confess that I greatly count on such factors for my personal delight. . . . But enough . . . Neither you nor I will be surprised if your ethic doesn't lead you to happiness. One does not always choose one's telescope because it shows a rose-colored moon; at least, that is not what you wanted, and I congratulate you on having agreed to pay with much happiness for the permission to seek the truth. I am somewhat ashamed, near you, at admitting to myself that I have often taken black for white, but the world thus appears to me all the brighter! Idols make happiness easier; the iconoclast must resolutely know, etc.

My poor old Paul! May God keep me from asking you to worship false gods! For my part, I have always in my closet some little idol before which I console myself for the loss of the others. I haven't been swimming either. The weather is dreadful; we've lighted a fire. The cold is nice for warming up, the rain for reading, and shith for staying at home. One great change in my existence is being without a piano and giving my hours of scales and trills to hintellectuhal [*sic*] work. I am becoming intelligent; soon I hope to have some visitors; meanwhile, I am writing a tale that bores me a little because it's retrospective.[22] I have no news of anyone except M. Drouin, who is evolving a metaphysics on the fourth floor of Cuverville, while I write on the second. The Laurens sometimes bicycle over to see us from Yport. It's the only event in the week. I am reading Dostoevski and Lachelier's *Du Fondement de l'Induction.* Au revoir, dear old Paul. Remember me respectfully to your mother.

Regards from my wife, and I am your

André Gide

112. Paul Valéry to André Gide

[P. Montpellier, September, 1896]

Dear friend,

I wanted to write you immediately after that most excellent letter of yours, which did me such a lot of good, but I was unable to. Everything is all wrong. I am submerged in neuralgias, insomnias, and all the rest of it. I have spent agonizing nights. I don't know whether it's the weather or something else, but this entire month has been very hard. I think we are all going up to Paris by easy stages—via Bordeaux, etc.—around September 20.[23] My family will spend a month there, I think.

Your letter is exceedingly accurate with regard to everything concerning

[22] The tale is *El Hadj*, which was to be dedicated to Paul-Albert Laurens.

[23] After his stay in London, Paul Valéry went back to Montpellier at the end of July. He was to return to Paris at the end of September, with his mother and brother, taking a touristic route: Carcassonne, Toulouse, Bordeaux, Poitier, Amboise, Blois, Orléans.

me. There isn't one term in it that I hadn't thought about during various periods. It makes me very happy, for I sometimes find that I am defenseless and in the grip of all the vagaries so bothersome in friendship, because of the fact that *the more I understand and the more I understand myself clearly,* the less I am able to explain, and to explain myself, clearly. I don't know why you have put such "blind confidence" in me; you give the impression of being a connoisseur of melons! And note—it's rather funny —if I credit your insight regarding that confidence, I become at once, *ipso facto,* an individual of unmixed vanity! It's extraordinary.

I am stammering more and more with M. Teste. I am as disarmed as possible. *Le Centaure* is pestering me,[24] the old boy bores me—I don't know what to stick into it—at those times when my neuralgia leaves me free to be merely stupefied. Yet besides the style, composition, and masonry that are lacking, I think I have put in two or three curious things—but on close inspection, they are anything but *literary.*

You must take into account that this is my first essay about an old boy, etc. A kind of novel (without a plot). Moreover, whether out of disgust or lack of time or lack of talent, the *effects* I wanted to get ended by either being eliminated or worthless. Therefore my *mechanical* attempt is dying out, failing. Write soon. What is Rouart doing? and Drouin? I give you up to the infernal gods for having dropped your piano. Frankly, it's madness! I predict that you're going to exhaust yourself. Were everything that is not my basic concern taken away from me, I'd explode!

I read the *Fondement de l'Induction*[25] coming down from Paris, in the train. I haven't reopened it since: I have no idea what's in it. I shall reread it this winter. I have received letters from about everywhere, not very exciting. You can imagine.

Au revoir, all my respectful regards to your wife. I shan't tell my mother that I'm writing to you, she would make me add at least two lines of you know what. Therefore . . . , etc.

P. V.

Ceremonious greetings to Drouin, P. Laurens (the elder), even the younger. Is Rouart still in that Cheese-Land (S.-et-O.)?

113. André Gide to Paul Valéry

[End of September, 1896]

Dear old Paul,

It appears that I must have an *ex libris* for my edition of *Le Mercure,*[26] in the manner of . . . , etc. And I don't know how to draw. Would it be a

---

[24] *Le Centaure,* Vol. II, 1896, was to publish *La Soirée avec Monsieur Teste.* In the table of contents we find the names of Hérold, Régnier, A. Lebey, Gide, Henri Albert, Pierre Louÿs, J. de Tinan, and J.-M. de Heredia.

[25] J. Lachelier, *Du Fondement de l'Induction,* thesis, 1871.

[26] An edition that was being prepared of *Les Nourritures terrestres.*

great bother to you to concoct some little thing of the right size (about that of a 50 c. coin) and bring it to Vallette. I should be very pleased, as a friend, if in that way you would personally protect my book. Except for a c..., I would leave you free to draw what you like, but I think I should prefer a little owl like this:

[Drawing of an owl.]

. . . but better . . . and without halftones.

O you who draw, I send you love rapidly since I have not yet received *Monsieur Teste.*

I am your . . . (who would like to be respectfully remembered to your mother) . . .

André Gide

114. André Gide to Paul Valéry

La Roque [P. October 4, 1896]

Dear friend,

I am writing you at once [27] . . .

I think you must resign yourself to no longer being, from this point on, a superior being and to simply writing "little masterpieces." I'm looking for a word for *Monsieur Teste,* now I find it: *incomparable.* Enough. What surprises me the most is that it's interesting; I mean that one gets caught up in it and that its taste is so good it makes one hungry. It can only be read all the way through. But it's so *satisfying* that I can't imagine anything else, and I should gather that along with the article on Da Vinci and four or five letters from you as a preface, your "complete works" are concluded. One thing is lacking perhaps (?). A few words from Teste to just anybody, his way of ordering a dinner. Does he only speak to the Intelligent Man? How does he speak to the others? The only criticism I dare make to you is about this sentence (p. 37):

"Je n'apprécie *en* toute chose que la facilité ou la difficulté de *les* (*accusative*) connaître."

You understand what I mean. It would have to be "la facilité ou difficulté (qu'elles ont) *d'être connues."* The syntax would be that of an elephant, but still, it's not as incorrect as that of your sentence.[28]

At least, so it would seem to me . . . (?) answer me on this point.

P. 43, four lines before the end, correct *souffrir,* and at the bottom, *évidente.*[29]

I can keep the proofs, can't I? I consider *Teste* primarily as a little code of ethics.

I'm happy because (if they paid some attention to it) this would make it more difficult for certain others to write. Everything in it is, I think,

---

[27] Gide had just received the proofs of *La Soirée avec Monsieur Teste.*

[28] Valéry did not take Gide's comment into account.

[29] These were typographical errors.

equally good, but M. Teste's falling asleep is more terrific, literarily speaking, than all the rest. And the account of the first meetings in the café. Anyway, the beginning is . . . anyway, you know better than I . . . As says Heredia José: "After that, you can write anything you want: drama, novel, sonnet, elegy. I know it will be good. . . ."

All sorts of respectful good wishes to your mother from my wife and myself. I am your friend

André Gide

I should willingly kill M. Teste.

115. *Paul Valéry to André Gide*

[P. Paris, October 5, 1896]

Dear friend,

I don't know how to make kowls! I send you some vulgar animals, but don't forget that these specimens would be photographed and that the fatter and more vulgar they are, the better. I am even to the point of regretting the small size necessary for your mark, because in playing around with the theme of snails, I saw some very amusing possible combinations. For example, a frieze * of this kind:
[Drawing of four snails in single file.]
or else this subject (better done):
[Drawing of only one snail twice as big.]
The snail delights me for it has its mineral shell, or the normal thing, and its mucous flesh—remarkable, very formless, very separate. It is a very simple complex: almost ridiculous. And then it has such astonishing feelers, in which the visual and tactile sensations seem to be merged and whose length is a kind of function of sensation.
[Drawing of a snail's feelers.]
I can also make you a sea horse. But really the diminutive size of the final *cachet* forbids all combinations.

Your letter on *Teste* came just in time. I confess that a rereading of those ten pages left me with an unfortunate impression. One of something done with elements that I find good, actually, and fairly well sifted, and the whole of which is deplorable. I know perfectly well that I wrote it bit by bit and without any idea of it as a whole except for having to fill twenty pages with my handwriting, with the help of notes that were linked to one another. But anyway, a true feeling of discouragement and *political* uselessness (if you see what I mean) came over me. Further emphasized by a day spent with P. L., during which I was really conscious of *not having written* any *literature* for four years. And yet I write, I now can't do anything else! You know why. And yet, also, I write, but I must do something else, the very thing that might be of some use to me.

---

* *Translator's note:* The published text reads: "grise," not "frise," but this is possibly a misprint or a misreading.

Your observation on the sentence, p. 37, is radiant! But I confess that I understand nothing about syntax! "toute chose" would at least have to be made plural. I don't at all agree about those words from Teste to just anybody. Given the *scope* of the short story (?), it seems to me that nothing should break the sphere of complete intellectuality in which the narrator himself moves. . . .

What bothers me is not having arranged the same elements in any satisfying psychological order.

And then, the conversation is too broken up, and a bit stupid. But enough!

This evening I am dining at Rouart's (he won't know how to tackle me, and from the very beginning I shall enthusiastically and sincerely praise the last exhibition of Degas).[30] In the last issue of *La Nouvelle Revue* do read the TERRIFIC article by General Dragomirov on the use of side arms. It really shows rare intelligence and he is a general who, with such a subject, makes no bones about putting in four pages on logic! [31]

My mother sends both of you all her greetings, I almost forgot to put that in, out of Testism.

116. André Gide to Paul Valéry

Cuverville [P. October, 1896]

My word, dear fellow, I was about to write you . . . when your letter,* this morning, nearly kept me from it.

At the same time, I received a letter from Hérold informing me that *Les Perses* is coming to the Odéon Thursday evening.[32] Therefore I shall leave Cuverville, which anyway is swampy, on Wednesday, and would you like to lunch with me, anywhere, before I get to the Odéon? Perhaps you have "family obligations"—in that case, let me know by letter and let someone know that I shall lunch at the d'Harcourt—because I don't at all like eating alone before a "performance."

Why have you been sick? . . . still acting rashly!

And I, too, found myself behaving like a chest-maniac again for sixty-four hours on end. Anyway, I hope to be able to greet Mme Valéry before

[30] Paul Valéry had asked Degas, through Rouart, for permission to dedicate to him *La Soirée avec Monsieur Teste.* Degas refused. Valéry probably would not accept defeat. But finally, Degas confirmed his refusal, which is hard to explain in any way other than that he distrusted a young writer.

[31] The October 1, 1896, issue of *La Nouvelle Revue* was almost entirely devoted to Russia, on the occasion of Nicholas II's visit to France. General Dragomirov emphasized the role of the will in combats, "a role far greater than that of reason and its derivatives."

* *Translator's note:* The last published letter from Valéry is No. 115.

[32] A translation of Aeschylus' *The Persians* by A.-F. Hérold, performed, with music by Xavier Leroux, on the stage of the Odéon on November 5, 1896.

she leaves Paris; meanwhile please give her my respects, etc. Was it really my uncle who sent you that article? I am dumbfounded. . . .

I'm expecting a colossal uproar in my family on the publication of *Les Nourritures;* [33] I'm working on it with a good bit of exasperation. You are called Angaire in it, unless you prefer some other name.[34]

Never has going back to Paris amused me so much. By the way, do read Dostoevski's *Idiot.* Before I speak to you about it, I want to finish *Karamazov.* But up to this point, I find it almost very bad, full of devices and . . . interesting. So read *The Idiot.* I have read *Monsieur Teste* several times more. One curious thing: it's easy to learn by heart.

Au revoir. Until Thursday, your old

André Gide

— 1897 —

117. Paul Valéry to André Gide

[Paris, P. January 1, 1897]

My dear old André,

Did you receive a box that I sent off to you a few days ago? If you did, was it in good condition? I'm questioning you so that, if need be, I can take action against the low-down scoundrels who, possibly, managed to lead it astray. (And we give them the benefit of the doubt.)

Have recently read Mallarmé's article on Rimbaud,[1] which he passed on to me—and which is rather unfavorable and sly.

Good wishes, etc.

Valéry

NOTES ON "EL HADJ." [2]

Isolated promontory, vast mystery.

---

[33] Gide's mother had been strongly opposed to the title. Cf. Yvonne Davet, *Autour des "Nourritures terrestres"* (Gallimard, 1948).

[34] Angaire, who was no more than an episodic character in *Le Voyage d'Urien,* where he is mentioned only three times, was merely named in Book IV of *Les Nourritures terrestres.*

[1] In the May 15, 1896, issue of the North American review *The Chap Book,* Mallarmé published an article on Rimbaud, with a portrait of Rimbaud by Félix Vallotton. He wrote, in particular: "Everything would most certainly have existed, afterward, without this notable passer-by, just as no literary circumstance really paved the way for him." Cf. Mallarmé, *Œuvres complètes,* p. 512 (Bibl. de la Pléiade, 1945), and Henri Mondor, *Rimbaud ou le Génie impatient* (Gallimard, 1955).

[2] *El Hadj,* or *Le Traité du faux Prophète,* had been suggested to Gide by his last trip to North Africa. Written in 1896, it was to be published in 1899, in *Philoctète*

*

Important comment: the characters and the subject are so fused with the lyrical prose that they are *perceived* with difficulty. They seem to be drowned in some inflation. *Ex.:* El Hadj's very interesting perplexity on the death of the prince does not come through. One is not perplexed, for one feels that the flow of the sentence alone will effortlessly unravel the situation—automatically, as it were. A sensation in the reader that should be avoided, since it demolishes all of literature.

*

Strange, the lack of reality in this tale, corresponding to its lack of the fantastic. Thus it is possible but not at all probable. The most important character in it is, at bottom, the masses—whom we don't see.

*

Beware of that which can exist only out of enthusiasm.

*

Proportions exceedingly well observed, general arrangement very agreeable. For all that, style a bit unrelated to what it says. You chloroform the words before placing them in position.   E. T.[3]

118. *André Gide to Paul Valéry*

[February, 1897]

Dear Paul,

Sunday! The workmen are resting, and the house is calming down. I gave up living, for want of any place to live. It was appalling. Six days of restaurants, of fleeing. Protecting any attempts at work, in some refuge or other: libraries, cafés, mercuries[4]. . . and having to supervise the whole thing, to keep my wife from doing it and tiring herself out—and then, she supervised the whole thing all the same and is very tired, naturally. How I found the genius to finish my book, I don't know, but it's finished. So now there are the proofs. And then, Mockel wants me to write poetry for Mallarmé, it's cruel. And then, Souza for *L'Almanach;* singing of animals that correspond to one particular month—as if animals didn't live for twelve of them and Souza for many more[5]. . .

(Ed. du Mercure de France). The style of this tale is very special. In it Gide attempted to lengthen the sentence by a kind of arbitrary resumption of it at the point when one might have thought it was concluded. In Letter 152, of July 6, 1899, Valéry, in commenting on *El Hadj,* reproached Gide with that style.

[3] Edmond Teste.

[4] An allusion to *Le Mercure de France.*

[5] An allusion to *L'Almanach des Poètes,* of which Robert de Souza was the editor. This almanac consists of a series of texts, each corresponding to one particular month extolled by a poet.

I think I'm going to decide in favor of neurasthenia, because otherwise there is no way out.

If only I were writing to you on a table, I should have told you about the anguish at *Le Centaure*. I nearly negotiated a stupendous deal—that of bringing Griffin into *Le Centaure* under the nose of Louÿs. . . . Even better: it was agreed with Albert that he would do the *next column* (the one Tinan had written before), and then Griffin ran off to Naples— therefore nothing done and status quo. Adieu for today, dear Paul. I am tied up in knots from nervous irritation and can hardly write. I think I'll see you soon in Montpellier. Take energetic care of yourself and don't return to that Parisian menagerie too quickly. Please give your mother respectful good wishes from my wife and myself, and our regards to you.

I am your
André Gide

O! Write *Le Système.**

119. *Paul Valéry to André Gide*

[P. Montpellier, March 15, 1897]

My dear André,

I am meditating in the bosom of all sorts of things, and of the family, with a tremendous wind just two steps away on the windowpanes. *Mallarmé*[6] is immobilized; will it progress any further than the two first pages I have written? That's what comes of wanting and not wanting, of knowing that, *all the same,* one will serve no purpose. I reflect for my own pleasure, but the more I reflect, the further I get from any usefulness, the only rampart against possible stupidity on *the outside.* I am furious when I think that I still have that (the stupidity) of becoming irritated, at least implicitly, at the discovery (and it happens often) of waste, of a bad return in a business, in a book, etc.

I have discovered, this evening, that I am unconsciously working with history, in my own way. I am now reading de Maistre—and not without pleasure. To read that and Stendhal, which is quite the opposite, is exciting. The bouquet of our former politics makes me good and tipsy. As it happens, I read by chance five or six very toxic works on the period 179...–184... In history, I don't care a rap for facts, and that will last as long as someone does not show me the impossibility of conveniently substitut-

---

* *Translator's note:* In a letter postmarked February 22, 1897, Valéry wrote Gide that he was almost tempted to "just go ahead and publish *Le Système.*"

[6] A study on Mallarmé that was never to be completed. It was not until after Mallarmé's death that Valéry was to devote numerous texts to him, all of which make up Volume L of his *Œuvres complètes: Ecrits divers sur Stéphane Mallarmé* (Gallimard, 1950).

ing any one event for any other. *What proves to us today that N. B. did not win at Waterloo* except the accounts? No necessity. For all the facts are "perforce" uniquely *imaginative,* that is, without *resistance.*

Reading de Maistre (such a great writer and for me juicier than a *chateaubriand*), I am perfecting (sometimes *a contrario,* or else in agreement with) my ideas on a certain subject. . . . Governing is as lost an art as building or stained glass. Current affairs and the stupid philhellinists have no meaning. All current history is dominated by fear, which plays right into the hands of the charlatans in Athens and the Socialists in Paris. It would be curious to show, step by step, how clear ideas become rare, how little one reasons about the simplest things. As a matter of fact, you once supped on my fury about that. The glaring truth is that for x years we haven't had either a minister, or a diplomat (or a literary Statesman in literature). And I'm not bringing in my preferences!

I am going back to 1820.

I have learned that you uncle's son is extremely sick.[7] In any case, I shall go and see your uncle tomorrow. I am thinking of soon returning to Paris. But for the first time, the idea doesn't appeal to me.

Your

P. V.

120. *André Gide to Paul Valéry*

Hôtel Palumbo, Ravello, near Naples

Good Friday [April, 1897]

Dear old Paul,

We were not able to stop in Genoa; did not even have the time to see if a letter from you was awaiting me at the post office. (If there was, let me know so that I can have it forwarded here.) We arrived at midnight and left again at noon, after having got extraordinarily lost, not in the streets of the port, but in the upper city, whence we at times had a view of all Genoa and the coast, which compensated for our fatigue and the storm clouds. Our visions are added to those of last year—simply—and form a very homogeneous recollection. Rome alone seemed to me *far* more beautiful than it had two years ago. Naples, the same—just as beautiful—but with no surprises; the coast, just as beautiful, etc.

I say that so as to seem natural to you; the truth is that I find everything more beautiful, but as I had already found everything *very* beautiful, etc., it could become tedious.

With *Lucien Leuwen* and *Les Mémoires d'un Touriste* I became captivated with Stendhal—or Stendhal violently captivated me.[8] It took all

---

[7] Paul Gide.

[8] We owe two studies on Stendhal to Valéry: a preface to *Lucien Leuwen* (Champion, 1926) and *Essai sur Stendhal* (La Pléiade, 1927).

the tedium of *Rome, Naples et Florence*[9] to get somewhat free of him.

If *Lucien Leuwen* interests me somewhat less than *Le Rouge et le Noir* or *La Chartreuse*, it's because the characters he presents, prompted by political *opinions* I don't very well understand, are never more to me than chess pieces whose significance I don't exactly grasp. It's so amusingly subtle that every hint should be understood; the allusions escape me. I can tell between the lines how much this book must have pleased you.* It did me too, and he educates me because, at every line, I resist. Today, I prefer Stendhal even to Balzac. Perhaps tomorrow I shall find that his art is somewhat that of a preparation; in the first act he's perfect; from the second on, he lacks fatigue (the reader's is there), scope; he remains subject to his method and continues to analyze. . . . That's fine for the memoirs of a tourist, but for a novel . . . I . . . and well, bah! I may add.

We are in Ravello on a most extraordinary terrace, but with a foreground that soothes me; the ink, as you can see, is very bad; I no longer understand a word of the Italian spoken around here. . . .

Dear fellow, let us talk business.

Here are some questions:

1. How are you? *a*) Health. *b*) Relations with deputy. *c*) *Mallarmé* article and other literature.

2. How is Schwob?

3. . . . P. L.?

. . . I received from Kahn the enclosed letter, which bothers me slightly. Consider this sheet of paper a voucher of authorization; see if there is any reason to do something; I should prefer that they leave me in peace; I don't know of any actor and have written nothing for the recitation, therefore act as you will, but by now it's probably too late and the whole thing has already been decided.

. . . My *Nourritures* is another question altogether, and what is happening matters greatly to me. You who have a foot, an eye, and an ear in the place, will you please give me a few pointers? How is it progressing?

I am writing to Vallette and asking him for the first sheets so that I can write the dedications. Vallette will send them back to the stitcher. Each book will be wrapped, with the name for each dedication written on the wrapping. I shall send a list on which there will be an address for each name. And now this is where your devotion comes in, if you're willing:

[9] Editions Delauney, Paris, 1817.

* *Translator's note:* To this Valéry commented, in a letter of April 19, 1897: "As for *Leuwen*, which I adore, I'm going to forbid you . . . to say anything about it but words of praise. I like M. de Stendhal because he writes as we speak to *ourselves*—that is, as I often speak to myself. And he is so reasonable. On the other hand, he is almost the *only* writer in whom I can bear the love passages. I find written love odious, except in Beyle."

make sure that everything has been done properly, then see that the books leave immediately by way of . . . (what do you call that? . . . in the tobacco shops . . . costs 25 cent., I think) but not through the Bidot agency, which loses everything en route. Also, do your best to be certain that Vallette's little clerks don't sell the dedicated books (I suspect them). Vallette will charge my account with the difference between the two systems of shipping. That's better than letting half of them go astray. Then, see to it that they don't dawdle about shipping them to bookstores, etc. Finally, I know that out of friendship you will do everything for the best, and as a bonus you shall have a beautiful copy on de luxe paper.

And all the gratitude of one who likes you very much.

André Gide

121. *Paul Valéry to André Gide*

Paris [P. May 3, 1897]

My dear fellow,

Your book is well on its way. I have had no hand in it, actually; you know that prominent man Vallette, he has an answer for everything; besides, he knows everything I can tell him since you have already told it to him. I have given Kahn *Solstice, Avenue,* and a third piece of yours for the Odéon.[10] When the time comes, I shall work with the actor (I'm trying to get de Max or Rameau). What you tell me about your wife is rather alarming.* What is the nature of her ailment? Aren't you making her travel too much and tiring her out?

P. L. is in Paris, with his not very pretty but extremely irritating Moorish woman, who speaks a good sugary kind of French. Their place is splendiferous, with a study that is half studio; bay windows, open sky; at the back, hollowed out, bookcases painted purple. I don't like the colors used.

In the bedroom (if I dare put it that way), electric lamps on all sides and especially on the floor, like stars for the perineum.

I spent an exquisite day yesterday in the delicate woods of Compiègne. It has been a long time since I've breathed like that. And no ideas, it's now my way of being happy. When you compare that state of cleanness, which is self-sufficient, to the other,—ideal, terrible, and impossible: that of being

---

[10] *Solstice* and *Avenue* are both from *Les Poésies d'André Walter.*

* *Translator's note:* On April 27, 1897, Gide wrote Valéry: "My wife has not been well for a minute the whole time—in fact, not at all well. She is recovering a little and that may make it possible for us to leave Ravello in two days. I'm counting on the air of Switzerland as a stimulant. We shall get there as soon as possible, with only an eight-day stopover in Florence. . . . I'm too worried about my wife's health and too busy taking care of her to do anything at all, either work or reading."

happy for one moment, as you imagine, during that moment, all the best ideas you have ever had, all your possessions simultaneously, and being the master of your own house.

The furniture of the château drawing-rooms had filled me with importance. The furniture of the forest made me physically spiritual.

I have learned that I may be appointed to the Ministry from one minute to the next. Good old Huysmans has been perfect.[11] I like him very much, not because of that, nor even because of his talent—the thing that led me to him and that will always hold me aloof from him—but he is someone who has been *tempered*. I know what I mean! A certain nausea came over me at the idea of this necessary thing (the bureaucrat). I calculated the advantages. My great failings and my great fits of anger went to my head again. ME AND THAT . . . ! I thought. Luckily I had a sedative in hand. It was enough to repeat, one key lower: me? me? . . . And since physically we were all right, we came to terms. The kind of person who does not want to make up his mind, who is enraged by the invariable, who would dread giving permanence to a thing he had found for fear of losing patience next day, either for having done it or for not having been able to repeat it—*had* to go through that. And it will happen again.

Read (or rather galloped through) the Prince de Talleyrand's *Mémoires,* published a short time ago by de Broglie. Fine preface by the aforesaid prince.

Skimmed through Mauclair's *L'Orient Vierge.*[12] It's the most elaborate handbook of foolishness that ever existed, and is being brought out, this time, by Adam (who is marrying a Jewish Eve, Muhlfeld's sister-in-law).

When those gentlemen have brought forth a *Vie d'Henri Brulard* or a *Leuwen,* then we can talk. But before, they should forget the whole thing.

It appears that I infinitely intrigue H. de R. (That's what it is to be a simple soul.) I have been told repeatedly that he finds me mysterious. And that didn't seem mysterious to me. The foolishness of all French humanism since 1830 is such that wanting to throw it off means taking the risk of being called everything imaginable, even that (the most slanderous) which has been told me repeatedly and which again I have written above. The funny part of the story is that I am *awaited*. I am looked upon as a reserve regiment; everyone wants to see what will come of *all that*. And that very

[11] On May 5, 1897, Paul Valéry was appointed to the War Ministry, in the Artillery Department, as an assistant draftsman. Huysmans, who was himself in the Department of Criminal Investigation, had advised Valéry to become a civil servant so that he could write his works in peace, and he supported his candidacy. Cf. Valéry, *Huysmans* (Ed. de la Jeune Parque, 1927) and *Le Souvenir de Huysmans,* in *Tel Quel,* II (Gallimard, 1943).

[12] "An epic novel about the year 2,000," which was published in Paris in 1897.

opinion is the rudiment of all one must think to be completely in the dark about me. They're the same sort of people—and in fact, it was the same individual—whom I have heard go into ecstasies about Poe, almost solely because of the *French* and the *sound* of Ch. B.'s [13] translation!

Without any doubt, if so many problems didn't exist, and if a few logicians didn't divert one's attention—one would choke from pure and simple contempt. Let us therefore be accused of mystery and let us be considered insensitive. On good days, I wouldn't exchange my nerves for theirs.

Tuus

V.

122. *André Gide to Paul Valéry*

Friday, the 21st [May, 1897]

Dear Paul,

Well, it's done; now you are jugged in the Ministry! I just learned it from your mother, whom I didn't know was already back from Genoa; on the off chance, I knocked at her door; a happy reunion! Everything in connection with you seems to give her such joy; she told me that these first days at the office have been hard . . . Poor old Paul, stick to it. Reread *Lucien*.[14] (I shall return quickly to Paris and give it back to you.)

I had to come to Montpellier for a few days (from the day before yesterday until the day after tomorrow), my aunt, ailing and sad, was belling for me. I left Madeleine and her sister in a small village near Geneva, where I shall rejoin them on Monday.

Then we'll make our way to a sulfur spring in the Jura, which should patch all of us up.

Write to me, General Delivery, Geneva.

How is P. L.? Has the Moorish woman already been received at the Heredias'?

I am writing a few bad poems and preparing a few good dramas.

Impossible to write you better than this. People are talking all around me, I am being summoned from every side. Do you have my book? Does anyone have my book?

If only one could write the articles one's self! (But then I imagine it would be a new book.)

How are the Centaurs? and you? and the Odéon? Adieu, dear old Paul, I am not so soft-headed as my letter would give you to believe—but weary all the same and living in the expectation of another state of things.

Au revoir. I am your

André Gide

[13] Charles Baudelaire.
[14] *Lucien Leuwen.*

123. Paul Valéry to André Gide

Ministry, etc., Monday [P. May 24, 1897]

Dear André,

I won't speak about my mood, I am absolutely going to pot. It stands to reason since I've been earning the livelihood of a slug.

What a fine form of torture the objective impossibility of thinking, and consequently of working, can be, for here we work the whole day, for seven deadly hours on end, and afterward I walk for two hours, and then I eat, and at desert I fall fast asleep from fatigue. Add to that the gastralgic tedium of breakfasting at nine and dining at seven-thirty.

On my desk I wrote down a sentence from H. B.: [15] "Society pays only for the services it sees." This directed to me, an old boy who has often been passionately fond of society, and who always stupidly dreamed of perfecting it.

Yesterday, I was at Valvins,[16] lured there by the most charming invitations, naturally. Mallarmé alone is really so simply Mallarmé that one ends by being that way too.

In the evening, after rowing and drinks (always too many), a rather smutty dialogue both very interesting and very serious. There I read your letter with regard to *Un Coup de Dés*.[17] "It really sounds like him," said S. M.[18]

Furthermore, the sky was full of extraordinary *coups de dés;* which meant that having to take the train back hurt me even more.

I do not have your book;[19] nor do a lot of people. Fanny has it. The opinions of those who do not have it are very divided.

As for the Odéon, I fear that neither you, nor I, nor Claudel (whom I had invented for them because I had just read his *Agamemnon*[20] with

---

[15] Henri Beyle.

[16] Mallarmé's summer place, on the banks of the Seine, in the department of Seine-et-Marne. It was there that the poet died a year later.

[17] Mallarmé's *Un Coup de Dés jamais n'abolira le Hasard* had just been published in the review *Cosmopolis*. Gide had written immediately to Mallarmé from Italy on May 9: ". . . It shows such literary audacity so admirably and simply done; it seems to arrive there like a very high promontory, strangely jutting out, ahead of which there is nothing but the night or the sea and the sky full of dawn. The last page chilled me with an emotion very similar to that provoked by some symphony by Beethoven. . . ." Mallarmé answered on May 14: "Ah! Dear Gide, what literary generosity you have and how much this letter sounds like you! . . ." Mallarmé was to give a set of proofs of his poem to both Gide and Valéry.

In 1913 Gide was to lecture at the Vieux-Colombier on *Le Coup de Dés*.

[18] Stéphane Mallarmé.

[19] *Les Nourritures terrestres* (Ed. du Mercure de France).

[20] Aeschylus' *Agamemnon*, translated by Paul Claudel, was published in Foochow, in 1896, in a limited edition, privately printed.

interest) will live out this year. Next Saturday will be the last, and God knows what sort of Mr. So and So's will take part in it.

Besides, I see all that through an opaque windowpane since I've been here, in this confounded *Artillary Department*.

P. L. is not very well, it appears, he has bronchitis. But I know nothing specific, it has been a long time since I've seen him. And who do I see?

I'm glad you saw my mother. She finally knows me to be "settled down!" All that's left for me now is to marry, it's clear.

I have been thinking these past days: that by unearthing a monster, or a deluded young girl, endowed with liquid money, and acting like all men with clear ideas, I would get myself out of the Ministry! I would regain my mornings, and I would again render invisible services to society!

—Yes, but what would X think.

—Nothing bad, if X knew how to work out the rule of three.

—By God, by God!

It's dazzling that from now on all my ideas will be dominated by this one: to leave here.

As Pascal said: "Everything in relation to Jesus Christ."

The idea that in twenty or thirty years I will perhaps still be *al medesimo sito*[21] stupefies me. Unfortunately, I have always accustomed myself to "bearing" things. In all I do, I am too fond of acting only when it's a safe bet, and I can only enjoy what is safe. Also, I become easily indignant—as you know—at those who make statements without protecting the approaches. That naturally is beyond me.

Write to me quickly, at length, and to the point. And try to come back. On my way home from the factory, I would sometimes stop in and see you at five.

Give me news of your wife. At bottom, it's rest that she must need the most.

Have you clear views on the existence of Drouart, Rouin,[22] etc.?

I am totally in the dark about them for the moment.

Your authentic
P. V.

124. *André Gide to Paul Valéry*

[P. June 4, 1897]

Dear old Paul,

Vallette tells me that I left you off the list of books to be shipped.

1. You have a de luxe copy![23]

2. Do forgive an oversight that was, I think, motivated by 1., since I

---

[21] In the same place.

[22] Meaning Rouart and Drouin.

[23] One of twelve copies of *Les Nourritures terrestres* printed on Dutch paper.

made a small personal list which meant that seeing you once was enough. I'm coming back before too long (in about twelve days) and will make amends. Meanwhile, take a copy *ad libitum* and ask Vallette to please stick it on the author's account. I sympathize with your imprisonment; do tell me how to go about seeing you. My wife is decidedly much better; as for me, I'm suffering from bad nerves and a bad heart, one because of the other, I think. All the same, the intellect is holding its own. The weather is devilishly hot. Nothing to say; little work; I am swallowed up by correspondence for stupid little affairs. I am playing quite a lot of piano and writing poems, hoping to do something else; but I don't know what, so I sit down at the piano again, and I write poems again.

> Au revoir, dear fellow, see you soon. I am, etc.
>
> André Gide

125. *Paul Valéry to André Gide*

Monday [P. Paris, July 5, 1897]

My dear fellow,

I have been so very late in answering you because I didn't get your letter until this morning. Imagine, it went down to the Aube and found another employee by the name of Valéry, who is there on holiday, and who opened it and sent it back to me with his apologies. Anyway, I congratulate you, as well as Drouin, as well as your wife, and I don't know your sister-in-law so as to make it general. When is the wedding? [24] I shall write to the fiancé as soon as possible.

Yesterday, I meant to write you at length about other subjects. But I tired myself out terribly on a bicycle, and a woman, in the evening, therefore . . .

I, in turn, reread *Leuwen* and found still other "beauties" in it. Among those others, he is really the son of his father + his mother.

Now, I must sift out those of the author's opinions which have become commonplace and without interest. There are some.

I think that an important point in Stendhal is the following: he had a solid psych. theory, not good, not very adequate, but fixed (Helvetius, *Correspondance avec Pauline Périer*) [25] and, in addition, that theory, defective from the point of view of analysis, was very good for a clear view and especially for expression—therefore literary. Anyway, it made it possible to classify all observations very quickly. Anyway, it had a fixed central point, a base of operations that was well marked out. *In such a case,* one can set about being witty, just as witty as one likes—but not before.

> Au revoir, I am overwhelmed with work.
>
> Your
>
> V.

[24] Marcel Drouin was to marry Jeanne Rondeaux on September 14, 1897.

[25] *Œuvres complètes,* Impr. Didot, 1795, Vol. XIV, *Lettres.*

126. Paul Valéry to André Gide

[P. Paris, September 21, 1897]

What makes your little Baedeker [26] amusing is that it has a bit of everything. There's a d'Annunzio, there are sooks, Donatelli, and fruits that are in fashion. (*Cur?*) The whole is perhaps too consciously written; and the impressions not original enough. I sum up these two criticisms (so habitually written by this hand): one too often senses the movement beginning. Just as often, you stop it, and only one sentence of it is left, but the feeling remains. You will answer at once: "It is not a book," and well, hang it all. . . .

Now that I have bowed down in silence and have no more to say, I shall proceed to other subjects.

First of all, I am doing nothing (to begin with eternal things, things eternally of no interest).

Saturday night, a singular impression of the February '96 kind (at that time, my departure for London). I shan't describe it, it is merely of conversational interest. Well, it was a two-hour interview in a squalid but very electrically illuminated garret of a big hotel, with an individual whom I misprize and prize greatly and who, every time I see him, has the same effect on me as tickling on the bottoms of one's feet, a frightful pleasure. . . .

You have perhaps received a review entirely devoted to X . . . [*sic*]. And to think that the practice of begging is forbidden! Public childishness is unforgivable. We have come to the point of no longer reflecting on anything that is unwritable; I think that this habit eliminates in its customers two-thirds of the possible mental operations. There's a profound review! And I repeat yet again that the judgment passed on literary people would change extraordinarily if one perceived, beneath the product, the true psychological plan of its construction. And such a glimpse is not impossible, in the general case, especially for contemporaries.

Moreno [27] has been very sick these last days, and is still not at all well (peritonitis). Naturally, don't write to S. *Non oportet.*

And then, I daydream among my files, or in bed. I turn in very early, with two or three books. I read until midnight, then comes reflection or wandering, until I fall asleep, and I wake up very bloated, and swollen. Last night, for example, I was drowned by a word, the word: unpopular (?). Then, I thought very naturally of the "delights of lost causes" which produce the de Maistres and great beings like Berryer le Vieux, [28] and so many ridiculous people who please me from a distance.

[26] *Les Nourritures terrestres.*

[27] Marguerite Moreno, who was to become the wife of Marcel Schwob.

[28] Nicolas Berryer (1757–1841), lawyer, counsel for the defense of Marshal Ney, father of Antoine Berryer.

I now note that a foul sign of our times is the disappearance of such advocates of collapse. For instance, the literary critics, who know that inevitably a "generation" *will come into its own* through the simple play of time, irrespective of its value and its ideas, have become very facile, very flowing. It's true in politics, in which so many groups have come to power that . . . It should be considered alongside this most curious thing: the mechanical creation of illustrious men, with the help of traditions and of anyone at all, by a country like ours. Why it's positively terrific. Examples abound. For instance, Mr. H.; [29] for instance, Pasteur's successor—and on the other hand, five-sixths of the Academy of Sciences. In literature they instinctively look for someone to treat like Hugo; or they create for themselves a Balzac II, a Shakespeare XII. There will be a Maeterlinck XXII and there are Verlaines and anti-Verlaines like popes and anti-popes. Marat was already a Brutus, Napoleon a Caesar, Louis XIV a Jupiter.

Theorem. A dynasty is a metaphor.   V.

— 1898 —

127. André Gide to Paul Valéry

Nice, Villa Arson (for a week)
January 7, 1898

Dear old Paul,

Since my wife declares that you will detest her if she doesn't get me to write you, I shall do my best. My wife is ailing, as she often is; she has a cold, not a bad one, but bad enough to make me give up Africa. Besides, nothing could be better for my work than giving it up. We are thinking of spending the end of this winter in Rome. We're waiting in Nice for our letters to be sent us from Biskra. Almost nothing to say about Switzerland; pure and icy air; there, you patch up your body while exasperating your mind.

An admirable arrival in Marseilles; the joy of that light of Provence, which I love.

We arrived before six in the morning, and took a carriage which led us to the Prado, where a sunrise was being performed.

In the evening, at dinner, a card was sent over to me, on which the name M., preceded and followed by quantities of initials, at first left my mind a complete blank. "Monsieur Valéry must have spoken to you of me. . . ." he began, in the waiting room where I had gone to find out who he was. . . . And vaguely, I remembered the awful nut whose travels you

[29] Probably Hugo.

told me about. The only way I could get rid of him in Marseilles was by inviting him to lunch in Nice. Anyway, he's a rather good sort, ludicrous and somewhat overbearing, but almost pleasant, and he takes you exceedingly seriously. I tried out some conversations on him and some assertions I was not yet quite sure of, he's a practice piano. He said to me: "Valéry! Ah! Valéry! etc. Now allow me, Monsieur Gide, to show you how admirable . . . etc.," and again: "Last night, as it happened, I was emerging from the arms of a charming woman . . ." I was naïve enough to ask him if he came from Paris, because of which, when he answered "No, from Cairo," it suddenly appeared to us so obvious that my wife began to laugh. He could be more interesting, but showed me a pocket bicycle which is something really practical . . . etc.

Au revoir, dear old Paul. Signoret [1] (whom I haven't seen but who knows that I'm nearby) has asked me whether the gentle and sad Valéry is still smiling. . . . If you are smiling, dear old Paul, may it be in *La Revue des Deux Mondes*. It is a wish I make for '98, and many others along with it. If you write to me, don't fail to speak to me of your little dealings. *Prométhée* and *Saül* [2] have not yet progressed a line, but you know that I am still very cordially your

André Gide

128. *Paul Valéry to André Gide*

Saturday (without delay)
[P. Paris, January 15, 1898]

My dear fellow, thank you for your excellent letter! Your Signoret * highly amused me, more especially since I once saw him, didn't speak to him, though. I am very nervous. I wrote a long, very *reasonable,* and exceedingly defensive letter to Montpellier. I still have no answer. . . . Then yesterday I accompanied Moreno to the Théâtre des Pantins to see

---

[1] Emmanuel Signoret (1872–1900), an eloquent and enthusiastic poet of the classical type, author of *Daphné* (1894), *Vers dorés* (1896), and *La Souffrance des Eaux* (1899), founded in 1870 (at the age of eighteen) a poetry review of mystical tendencies, *Le Saint-Graal,* of which he was both the managing editor and (often) the only member of the staff. In it he published, the first year, Verlaine's Catholic poems. In January and March, 1898, he devoted long articles to the writings of André Gide, particularly *Les Nourritures terrestres* and *Le Voyage d'Urien.* In 1908 Gide was to bring out a collection of Signoret's poems, for which he wrote a preface (Ed. du Mercure de France).

[2] *Le Prométhée mal enchaîné* was to come out in 1899, and *Saül* in 1903.

* *Translator's note:* On January 12, 1898, Gide wrote Valéry a letter describing Emmanuel Signoret as follows: "He's a bit too short, that is, a bit shorter than I am, and suffers from the drawbacks of poverty: a questionable beard and hair, ugly skin, etc. (I am naturally speaking only of things a little free water would straighten out.) His hands, just glimpsed and very small, seemed to me astonishing. The palms (am I wrong?) had absolutely nothing on them but the two transversal lines."

Ubu performed by themselves.[3] Between two of the acts (if I dare put it that way), I went to the bar, a small ordinary room that was packed. There, belly to belly with Quillard and Hérold, those gentlemen spoke of a huge proclamation that should come out in the next *Hermès* against the army, the government, the generals, etc.[4] A very lively discussion had taken place before dinner between Gourmont and A.-F. H.,[5] the former being on the right side of public opinion. You know how the opinions of our fine revolutionary comrades and friends have a talent for annoying and exasperating me. I therefore didn't breathe a word. But probably my features, which are still badly educated, *gave the time of day,* for Quillard had the goodness to warn me that he was taking the responsibility for the controversial pamphlet and that *it would not compromise me in any way.* Which I answered with a dull grunt. You can imagine my inner cocktail. Then, my feeling became clarified into a sharp point. I have promised J.-K. H.[6] an article on *La Cathédrale* as soon as it comes out (the 31st of this month). I am quite determined not to put a line in *Le Mercure* if this pamphlet "sees the light"—and it will, either in February or in March—so? And I am bent on writing the article, which certainly won't amuse me—but it's due and promised—and I want to write it *solely* to try and please the author alone. To get some low satisfaction, I had a diabolical idea, I took two steps, right up to the flat belly of Fénéon; mutual civility; and I told him that I should probably come to *La Revue Blanche* and bring him some copy. If all this takes place, I'm going to change my name. You can very well see to what degree the "vaguery" (!) of all that disgusts me. Can those revolutionaries who never promote revolutions jeer at military men who never make war? And they protest against outraged justice, misunderstood humanity, and so forth and so on. We see individualists who are not even individuals, and all those eternal cocks who want to make omelets without breaking the inevitable eggs! The merest Jesuit knows a thousand times more about it than they do, the

---

[3] Alfred Jarry's *Ubu Roi* was published in 1896 by the Editions du Mercure de France. Two stormy performances were given by the Théâtre de l'Œuvre in December 1896 at the Nouveau Théâtre. Here Valéry is alluding to the few performances in January, 1898, organized by the Théâtre des Pantins, 6 rue Ballu, in Paris.

[4] The Dreyfus case had just reached its culmination. On January 13, 1898, two days after Esterhazy had been acquitted, Emile Zola wrote his famous *J'accuse* in *L'Aurore.* That day 300,000 copies of *L'Aurore* were printed and all were sold. Every day, lists of protesters were printed in *L'Aurore.* Among them were Hérold, Pierre Quillard, Camille Mauclair, Alexandre and Thadée Natanson, Charles Péguy, Gustave Kahn, and Paul Langevin.

[5] André-Ferdinand Hérold.

[6] J.-K. Huysmans. Valéry's article was to be published in the March, 1898, issue of *Le Mercure de France.* It was entitled *Durtal* and discussed three books by Huysmans: *Là-Bas, En Route,* and *La Cathédrale.*

merest wine dealer understands it better, since all that is basically no more complicated than a bookkeeping operation. Seeing a country left to chance like this disgusts me. Among other things, and we must make no mistake about it, we are on the way to acute anti-Semitism, which might become the cause of extraordinary agitation. The state of excitement all the Jews are in is remarkable, understandable, alarming. On the other hand, the state of mind in the army ranks must be curious. Anyway, the radicals and Socialists are fanning all the flames. Whereas in power, that is, in the Chambers and in the Cabinet, are people who are forced to reckon with all those elements, and who want to keep them all. Climbing up a bit higher, one sees nothingness and the weakness of Republican principles in all its scope. The formless remains of the reason of State disputed in the *free* press, every bit of the social domain open to the expansion of every idea, by virtue of the following curious paralogism: "Every idea can be valid. A valid idea is necessarily good for everyone. Absolute freedom for every idea." Now there is no direct or simple relation between such things. Nothing is so curious as to see the Socialists, for example, basing their reasoning on the theory of evolution. That is to say, a hypothesis as hypothetical as possible, and in any event necessarily confined within the realm for which it was constructed, can and will lead to the bumping off of a lot of people, etc. Nothing is more superimposable on the quarrel of transubstantiation or the word ὁμοιούσιος[7] (if that's the one?).

Well, I'm boring you stiff, and very rightly you are laughing at me. But these questions leave you cold and you take off, whereas I do nothing but come upon them again and again.

The Semantic thingumajig * is the article I wrote about the book *La Sémantique;* I am most dissatisfied with that thingumajig, and mixture.[8] It came out in the January issue of *Le Mercure,* where you can read it in the column *Méthodes,* if you feel like it.

I am looking for someone to bore and am not finding my match. I really need one. At this point, when by chance I think over my contraptions and systems, I would need to expound them orally in order to untangle various things that are all involved within me, get them clear, and finish with them. Writing can't help me with that, for I stop at once, seeing the difficulties, the slightest ones, whereas the spoken word would force me to move on, a big point. Anyway, I would thus be forced to see it as a whole. But the bored person required has not yet been born.

[7] Of similar appearance.

* *Translator's note:* In a letter postmarked January 11, 1898, Valéry wrote Gide that his "Semantic thingumajig has come out," to which Gide answered on January 12, "What in the devil do you call your 'Semantic thingumajig?' "

[8] A review of the grammarian Michel Bréal's latest book: *La Sémantique, science des Significations.*

One of these past evenings, I set to work, *sub lumine,* writing the beginning of the following tale, which I shall never finish, for it's too difficult. Given one of those women who sleep for two, three, or ten years on end, one assumes (most gratuitously) that she dreamed the whole time, and that upon awakening she can tell about her dream. Now for two, three . . . , ten years, she has had no sensations: thus one might study the impoverishment (or something else) of the datum with which she fell asleep. It's a problem of transcendental imaginary psychology, which is very hard even to conceive. The successive zones of the deterioration of images, etc., the variation of thinking, which became gradually void, would be curious to write on. I got carried away by the theme for ten minutes. Then, with no enthusiasm, I wrote a few lines of the beginning, which in fact were foreign to the problem, then I stopped. But, something very typical, I filed that statement in order to study it at leisure, geometrically, and outside all literature.[9]

Yours, and my regards to your wife, to whom I plan to write, if I may, to thank her for her fine deed, as soon as you have a permanent address, in Florence or elsewhere. I won't ask you to go and see my family in Genoa this time, for diplomatic reasons you can imagine. But if on your return you pass through that beautiful Genoese spot, let me know.

Your somewhat mellow
Valéry

129. *André Gide to Paul Valéry*

18 Piazza Barberini, Rome
January 18, 1898

Whatever rush you were in to write me, the rush I was in to reach Rome was even greater; your letter was sent to me here from Nice. It's fortunate that I am not in Paris; you probably would prove to me that I'm absurd to be so carried away by Zola's letter,[10] and I should find that disagreeable; on the other hand, I would be so exasperated by seeing X. or Y. agree with me that I might perhaps change my mind; my character does not allow me to have opinions except in the provinces, and that's why I believe they are mistaken; in fact it's for that reason they interest me, etc. (is there a direction in which such talk could not continue?).

. . . We have rented here, for three months, two bedrooms, rather well located, and a *salotto,*[11] which is an icebox; from the bedrooms you see, on a square that is rather well designed, (mostly riffraff and) a Triton who spits water through a shell; the thin stream of water he spouts rises very

[9] Valéry was to call that study *Agathe.* He often alluded to it in these letters but was never to finish it.
[10] The one published by *L'Aurore* on January 13, 1898.
[11] A drawing room.

high, so that the sun still hits it when the Triton, the basin and half the square are already in shadow. I love this square and have long wished to live on it, failing to be able to rent Beyle's admirable flat, although now its view is obstructed partly by Crispi, partly by others. The annoying thing is that for meals we have to chase into town, for we weren't able to find any suitable place to board. I readily allow that there is nothing thrilling about these bits of information, but today I have nothing else to say, having spent my two days in Rome attending to such matters.

It would be amusing to see you on *La Revue Blanche;* [12] it's there, too, that *Le Prométhée mal enchaîné* will be published (unless something unforseen occurs); [13] I hope to finish it here, if the fine piano we have doesn't interfere.

I should have liked to see *Ubu,* and especially the audience. When traveling, all that is rather irreplaceable, and one can hardly say that—conversely . . . Next time, do speak to me again of Hérold, Quillard, or anything else you have at hand. . . . Yet I am not pleased by everything you tell me; one can perfectly well be an individualist without being an individual, damn it! The former expresses the desire to be the latter, and the latter doesn't really care a rap for the former.

Au revoir. Yes, indeed, I allow letters to my wife, and she thanks you for them in advance on condition, she says, that she doesn't have to answer them. She still has a little cold and is rather tired, but feels better and sends you friendly greetings. I am your

André Gide

130. *Paul Valéry to André Gide*

[Paris, P. February 14, 1898]

My dear André,

I have come to the end of a devilish week during which I constructed in great haste a mishmash on *Durtal,* a nameless thing, due, rushed by *Le Mercure,* where I finally brought it yesterday, in fact I finished it on the spot. [14] Well, it's done. The most annoying thing is that I again had complete insomnia, which at this point has lasted for five or six nights and does me in. I regret having had to work in great haste every night; I hate it, especially for something I actually couldn't get a hold on at all and which developed only on paper, barely. I regret it because at the conclusion of that performance I began to get somewhat interested, that is, to rediscover things I had formerly thought about the subject + their connection with the current trend.

---

[12] Paul Valéry was never to write for *La Revue Blanche.*

[13] *Le Prométhée* was to be published not in *La Revue Blanche* but in *L'Ermitage,* in 1898, and was brought out as a book by Le Mercure de France in 1899. It is dedicated to Paul-Albert Laurens.

[14] The article on Huysmans. See above, Letter 128, n. 6.

All this explains why I haven't answered you sooner.

This morning I received a *Saint-Graal* which shows that we still have some genius, but with Golberg [15] and others—well really! one prefers perhaps to be simply not stupid but separate. I have come to think that that luminous nut is just dandy, even though he seems as ignorant as a fish, crafty and gullible *ad nutum*. His f—— stupidity is really phosphorescent.

What enraptures me about his case is that: he's like a diagram, or a puppet of the "Great Poet" type. Emmanuel [16] sums them all up, and when he proclaims it, he tells an undeniable truth. If one takes a distance from the question of results, the perfecting of such and such fragment, etc. . . . one can see in him the concentrated juice (ideas or lack of them, ways of associating, etc.) of the more or less gigantic—*id est: vague*—lyric poets. He has everything that goes into them. Like them, he is an image-mill, who turns and knows not what he mills. All that is very pure, very pleasant, and easy to demechanize in the above-mentioned.

Do you know about the great fashion? On sale are little live turtles, as big as forty-sou pieces, with fine stones and bits of gold on their backs. A very fine gold chain fastens them to the necks of women, on whose breasts they roam about and, I'm told, make their BM's or die, as their little hearts desire.

It's Des Esseintes. It appears that beetles are also used, but I have seen only turtles.[17]

At Durand-Ruel's I bought a few photographs of Degas' works, thus violating my anti-iconic principles, but I haven't been able to keep much order *in myself* * any more, since I've been here.

People are still annoying me everywhere with the D. Case. God knows when it will be over. I'm spreading the good word as much as I can, that is: of what possible importance are insects eating each other up? Let us seek true freedom, that with which we may provide a man in charge of the State.

Shortly, anyone will be able to rise and will have a party. Let us wish for

---

[15] Mécislas Golberg. In answer to an unknown correspondent, André Gide wrote, on December 12, 1932: "Dear Sir, Who was Mécislas Golberg? A political refugee, I believe, of doubtful origin, of uncertain religious persuasion (probably Jewish), a strange Bohemian, who looked half-starved, a kind of *illuminé* of great intelligence, who had an unquestionable gift for literature, to which his many writings testify, but whose life and thinking showed great disorder . . . ; he was seen mostly at the side of Emmanuel Signoret; they upheld one another in their poverty through a kind of mutual admiration, which caused Golberg to say, at the bedside of the dying Signoret: 'Console yourself for leaving, dear friend, *I* am staying' . . . ; that simply means: 'Poetry is not dead; I am here.' "

[16] Emmanuel Signoret.

[17] An allusion to the turtle of Des Esseintes, the extravagant character in Huysmans' *A Rebours,* who kept it at home and had its shell covered with precious stones.

* *Translator's note:* In English in the original.

a brutal, disinterested man who will keenly sense the interesting things that need to be done. But, at bottom, I have little hope. Perhaps if we looked into it adequately, we would see that the machine is finished and that they have broken everything, thrown out everything, except the individuals who remain nude and null.

Your
P. V.

131. André Gide to Paul Valéry

Arco, Tyrol [P. May, 1898]

Dear old Paul,

It seems to me now a frightfully long time since I've written you. I have no excuse; it is what a psychologist would call a "trait of character"; that's all right with me, but it's a most objectionable one. I long for Paris, for you —for everything. We are still detained by an inhalation treatment which Madeleine is finishing up here and which is working so well I wouldn't dream of cutting it short.

Arco is a rather objectionable little winter resort where the Germans speak Italian and vice versa, ostensibly because it's on the border. The menus are in French. The annoying thing is that it's horribly far away.

To avoid Switzerland, we plan to return by way of Munich, then Strasbourg, Nancy. Three stopovers—the one in Munich extendible at leisure because of Wagner, whom my principles do not allow me to hear in Paris.

What news of you? What news of everyone around you? I killed off Saul the day before yesterday. You will have to explain to me the tactics necessary to get this masterly work on the boards. But you'll have to explain it to me in person, for it will be amusing to discuss it together and our meeting is now a question of days.

Madeleine has asked to be remembered to you. If you want to write me again, do so in care of General Delivery, München.

See you soon, dear old Paul.

Your
André Gide

132. Paul Valéry to André Gide

[P. May 6, 1898]

My dear returning spirit,

Don't come to see me yet. For the last month I have been as ill as possible, and unrecognizable. Since then I have seen no one, absolutely no one—except the people in the Ministry. All society fills me with horror, and conversation I find impossible.

When you arrive in Paris, write me a note. And if I feel better, I shall come and see you—if not, I'll wait.

I am really going through the mill. Well, it's just too bad. There is no reason, actually, for things to be any better.

Your

P. Valéry

133. André Gide to Paul Valéry

Cuverville, near Criquetot-L'Esneval

[P. July, 1898]

Dear Vale,

I'm sad that I left you feeling ill; I would have stayed with you if my wife, also ailing, hadn't made me so anxious about being a long way from her.

At any event, we are both awaiting you and preparing your cure.

The weather is fine, very fine, but it's not the usual *season,** and despite the sea air blowing as hard as it can, I miss La Roque's abundant meadows.

It is fortunate for both of us that we said a few words apropos of *Saül* yesterday morning. You know perfectly well that, while I dread your looking over my work, you are one of those whose opinion matters most to me and to whom, as you can well imagine, I want most to show my big production. That's why I was so gravely hurt by what I took to be intentional indifference on your part. It may have spoiled somewhat our meeting on the 14th, imperceptibly, for out of a touch of pride unworthy of our friendship, I had promised myself not to be the first to speak of it and to wait for you to be the first to ask for *Saül,* before giving it to you. I might have waited a long time, if you yourself, etc. . . . Now all is well, and I am having the manuscript sent back to me here so that you can finally get to know it.

Here is the train schedule. Come as soon as you can; have Julia ** give you a certificate advising you to breathe in a little salt air.

I like you, dear old Paul, and await you.

André Gide

P. S. 1—Would you be so kind as to bring me a box of quills such as one finds under the Odéon. . . .

P. S. 2—[accompanied by the page of a timetable]. The express that leaves Paris at 6:52 in the evening goes only as far as Beuzeville, therefore if that's

---

* *Translator's note:* In English in the original.

** *Translator's note:* In a letter postmarked May 27, 1896, Valéry wrote Gide that Julia was "the very devil of a young man and doctor—one of the three people who have perhaps read . . . *L'Introduction* [*à la Méthode de Léonard da Vinci*] from cover to cover."

the train you take (once you try it, you'll make it your own),* let me know enough in advance so that I can pick you up in a carriage at Beuzeville.

134. *Paul Valéry to André Gide*

[P. Paris, July, 1898]

My dear fellow,

I take my leave of *Saül,* with whom I have just spent an hour. This drama puzzles me to such a degree that I reopened my Bible. I thought, before reading it, that the fable of Saul was merely a pretext. I now see that, on the contrary, it is the veritable backbone.

In short, the general tone of the play seemed to me . . . how shall I put it, humorous. (That's not the word at all, nor is ironic, but something between the two. . . .)

That tone is fortified by Saul's madness, which is made ambiguous by his violent pederastism, and impassioned by the David-Jonathan dialogue.

I have still not really understood the king. He is perfectly clear in the play with relation to the action. He is not, with relation to me, to you, to us. I am trying to find some of Saul's ideas in me.

I appreciate the trouble you must have taken to make it clear. It's frightful to work on theater for any mind that skips a little and devours its thoughts. You have to spell out for people everything that is seen in the twinkling of an eye. That's the devil of it.

This leads us to consider those gentlemen the Demons. I confess that I don't know how you'll deal with them on stage, even if Cremnitz [18] weren't there. Chiefly the one who takes off all his clothes.

I find them a bit too frivolous.

If the king had not lost his mind and all his sense of government besides, a dozen kicks in the backside would have rid him of that little hostile press.

(All the foregoing was written at random, and so is all that follows. It is as if I were leaving the theater. Just joking.)

Let us make some objections in order to restore some of our importance.

I think two or three phrases should be crossed out, for they might provoke inopportune laughter.

I shall make one criticism concerning Saul's madness: *it is dramatic madness.*

The whole play, at bottom, rests on the immoral and opposing loves of gentlemen. Actually, the queen could almost be eliminated. I find the barber Arabian and pleasant.

Jonathan's end is not—obvious enough. He is struck off wordlessly. That will seem obscure.

* *Translator's note:* The catch phrase of an advertisement in France: "l'essayer, c'est l'adopter."

[18] Maurice Cremnitz, art critic and poet.

I protest energetically against Saul's words addressed to the audience. That, never. Don't you agree? etc.[19]

The very end is a bit Shakespearean, no objection. But one must not be reminded of Shakespeare, who upsets all reasonable judgments of plays. Indeed, people have a stock image of him.

From a somewhat paroxysmal point of view, I regret that there is no SUPREME showdown between the three lovers. True, it's an altogether different method, which would have led to closing up three acts (in the style of battalion training) and making the drama square-cut instead of rectangular. True, as regards theater, 1. I know as much about it as a fish; 2. I infinitely approve of the genre *Francillon* by Dumas fils (from the viewpoint of the general pattern).

All this clearly indicates to you that I am about to go to bed and cough a little.

I shall look into *Saül* again, and especially, now that I've seen it as a whole, certain scenes which, as I went through, asked to be examined more closely.

Your
Paul Valéry

I reopen my letter, having just heard of the Drouin birth.[20] I shall write. I learned today that I have tomorrow and Friday off. I made up a telegram to tell you: "I'm arriving with *Saül*," but foul weather is keeping us here, after much hesitation.

135. *André Gide to Paul Valéry*

[Cuverville. P. July 26, 1898]

Dear fellow,

I was not able to thank you any sooner for your pens and your letter because I was in Alençon, where I just became an uncle. I stayed there longer than I had originally planned, for my sister-in-law was not feeling very well—phlebitis, etc.

To come back to *Saül:* if the demons won't work out on stage, too bad— I can't eliminate them; I should thus eliminate the entire play.

As for the words addressed to the audience (at the end), that is up to the actor; if it's painful during the first rehearsal, nothing is easier to take out.

How are you? You no longer speak of your arrival; it's annoying, because now the family is going to flock to Cuverville. Were you at the

---

[19] Act V, scene v: "*Saul moves up toward the footlights, facing the spectators. His voice is heard above all the noise:* 'Before leaving, I should like to sum up in a few words' (*noise of the demons increases*). 'Be quiet, you roisterers! Can't you see that I'm speaking to the audience!' "

[20] That of Dominique Drouin, André Gide's nephew and godson.

Ministry during those recent hot days? In Alençon we thought we'd pass out.

And *Agathe?*

Au revoir, old Paul; I shall probably soon spend some time in Paris and will come to see you if you're still there.

What has become of my manuscript?[21] Is it you who has it?—or Chanvin,[22] or who? or is it in the mail?

Please let me know, and if it's you who has it, do send it back to me, with the necessary precautions.

Your
André Gide

136. Paul Valéry to André Gide

[P. Paris, July 26, 1898]

My dear fellow,

I'm sorry that Chanvin took the manuscript from me before I had time to tri-read it. At bottom, I still have no strong opinion about *Saül*.

As I see it now—in other words, rather vaguely—there are points I am unable to elucidate, and I realize that I would have needed an hour of exegesis, with you present. Hérold is very satisfied with it (but we don't hunt for the same truffle).

Anyway, certain elements of very good theater may, must—in print—escape me altogether.

I continue to believe that the drama would gain by being shortened. I can visualize a good scene with the devil, somewhere in the last third of the play—on the sand—but what is your devil, or devils?

Are they classical? the filthy blackguards of the Middle Ages? Are they evil little imps, Voltaires à la Goethe? They, at one point, gave me (yours) the lovely impression of extremely black statuettes in dry, dark sand. Compromising statuettes, alas.

What really bothers me in your play is its "perverse" and "disquieting" nature. I was surprised by it. Once the subject of παιδεραζειν[23] was given, I'd have been willing to wager that you'd treat it differently. I'd have thought of some long-standing conversations on this point.

So that while reading, I had to fight against a preconceived idea that wondered at getting involved in the historic story of Saul.

I also think that, at times, the recollection of Mr. W. J. Shakespeare, M.A.,[24] influenced you somewhat artificially (that is, outside your subject).

It was an anticipated danger. I feel like writing three pages here on that

[21] *Saül*.

[22] Charles Chanvin, a friend of both Gide's and Charles-Louis Philippe's. He appears with Gide, Henri Ghéon, Eugène Rouart, and Athman in a painting done by Jacques-Emile Blanche in 1900.

[23] To practice pederasty. The exact Greek verb is παιδεραστειν.

[24] Master of Arts.

very troublesome Englishman. I am holding them in. But if one were to write a "Study on the Current Use of Shakespeare," considering him quite simply as a practitioner or a technician who had arrived at a certain degree of knowledge about his spectator, what should be considered as usable today? Think about that.

You can see how vague I am, at bottom, in what I say about your play. But I have not reflected enough about theater: the tricks of it are unknown to me, and what makes me turn away from it is that one has always to be concerned with hitting N individuals *at the same time,* that is, bringing one's self to use only averages. In a word, it seems to me impossible to go the whole way in it, as if one were quite alone.

By the way, I shan't come to Cuverville since I am leaving for Montpellier on Saturday or Sunday, until August 15.

You haven't told me whether Mme Drouin has recovered.

Your
Valéry

137. *André Gide to Paul Valéry*

[Cuverville. P. July 27, 1898]

Dear fellow,

I am annoyed that you *t.d.o.*[25] without having come. As it happens, Cuverville is available as of next Saturday. You should therefore put off your flight to Montpellier for two days.

Something really terrific would be for you to take a ship at Le Havre and reach Montpellier by way of Marseilles. . . . I tell you that because you like the sea, but it would kill *me.* . . . So you will come, won't you? And let me know if your train goes no farther than Beuzeville, so that I can fetch you in a carriage.

I found a wealth of interest in your last letter, which arrived a moment ago. A conversation would have done no harm. I'd give you the impression of talking nonsense if I said that what makes *my* demons different from the others is that they are not outside Saul. I see them, with regard to Saul, as filling the part of an orchestra for a ballerina in the manner of Mallarmé, that is, explaining his silent monologues. Physically, you see them very well —black on sand—and as statuette-like as possible. They should be played by a band of little circus clowns completely swathed in black,—thus never, or always, appearing naked.

. . . Shakespeare?—? O! obviously—but how is it possible to imagine anything that doesn't more or less recall Sh. without, by the same token, eliminating the scenic effects? All I can say is that I don't believe that Sh. collaborated on *Saül.* If *Saül* recalls the stamp of W. S., it's because there is no way of ever, or anywhere, imagining *means* other than his. Yet certain

[25] Took days off. French: *p.p.c.,* or *pour prendre congé.*

scenes—namely, those with the demons—are, I believe, very far from him. And then, you must understand that the whole of *Saül* is no more than a vast monologue, all of which unites only to explain his character, that character being, I think, hardly Shakespearean. We shall have to find time to talk.

As for Chanvin, I believe he has made off with my manuscript. I don't even know his address in Germany, and yet I'm beginning to need that manuscript very badly.

Au revoir, dear fellow.

Do try to come.

I am your
André Gide

138. *Paul Valéry to André Gide*

[P. Paris, July 28, 1898]

My dear fellow,

Do understand that it is impossible for me to come to Cuverville now. I have only two weeks to give the family, and my mother hasn't seen me for a year! If I had a month, all would be different. I dream of nothing but Normandy and greens, and I am going down where the temperature this year is +96°! That leaves the sea.

As I write you, I am most perplexed. . . . Yesterday someone called my attention to certain extremely serious facts concerning espionage, and mentioned to me a name and details that are at once fantastic and precise. On turning it over in my mind, I see that one unquestionable point emerges. I thought of informing the "competent authorities" in order to ease my conscience, but in these difficult times, full of gaps, in which it is too easy for the most important services to be publicized and handed over to malevolence and schemes, getting mixed up with committed parties is not an attractive prospect.

The information I received is curious, for the tenor of it is more precious than the detail. In any event—while remaining obscure about it—I can tell you that in current affairs, for example, the most committed and most boldly maintained interests are not what everyone thinks. Whatever the *pretext*—the *theme*, developments, and *contrappunto* come from the OUTSIDE by means of a scheme that really struck me. The same is true for certain previous affairs in the realm of general politics.

But what can I do? These are times of cowardice and fear in all circles and—especially—no goal, no will, no time in sight. There is suicide in the air.

I suffer from seeing a rather glorious boat becoming a drunken boat, springing a leak, and running aground continually.

Au revoir.
Valéry

139. André Gide to Paul Valéry

La Roque, September 8 [1898]

Dear old Paul,

This heat frightens me; what overwhelms us even here must be intolerable in Paris. How do you bear it? Does the Ministry devour you anew each day? Alençon, in a sheltered plain, concentrates the sun horribly; not a breath of air; Marcel [26] did his twenty-eight days of military service in a small office; it was killing.

My sister-in-law is being cooked as she lies in bed; she still has a long time to go; but the phlebitis is abating. The little one is puny; four times too intelligent and nervous. Between Cuverville, Le Havre, La Roque, and Alençon, we are wasting a tremendous amount of time. Here, I am not very free; on the pretext of my being mayor and a landowner, etc., everyone considers that he has the right to help himself to my hours; I have to supervise work; give advice; reprimand; append my signature; all things that someone else would do just as well.

I have absolutely no news of Tinan.[27] His article in the last *Mercure* made me think he was better. Give me some information when you write me.

What has become of *Agathe?* Au revoir, dear old Paul; this letter would not have been as brief if I dared to talk about politics; but I dread talking about it. . . .

And am thus all the more cordially your
André Gide

140. Paul Valéry to André Gide

[P. Paris, September 10, 1898]

My dear fellow, I am prostrate. Mallarmé died yesterday morning.[28] I received a telegram from his daughter last evening and am now writing to all quarters.

Last night, when I was unable to go to bed, I felt all the affection I had

---

[26] Marcel Drouin.

[27] Jean de Tinan was very ill at the time and died later that year.

[28] Two days before, on September 8, at Valvins, while he was working, Mallarmé, who was suffering from a simple case of laryngitis, had a serious choking fit, and recovered after a few hours of rest. But during the evening, as if he had had some foreboding, he wrote his "will" in an almost illegible handwriting. The next day he began to feel ill again. The doctor was called and came at once. But Mallarmé died suddenly, during another choking fit.

Valéry later wrote: "A telegram from his daughter informed me, on September 9, 1898, of Mallarmé's death. It was one of those thunderbolts which first strike at the core and take away even the strength to speak to one's self. They leave our appearance intact, and we live visibly; but within us is an abyss. . . . From that day on, there have been certain subjects for thought that I truly never considered again." (*Stéphane Mallarmé*, in *Variété II*, Gallimard, 1930.)

for that mind—and the more I tried to fathom it, the more I felt his death within me.

The funeral will take place tomorrow, Sunday, at four o'clock.

Your

P. Valéry

141. André Gide to Paul Valéry

La Roque-Baignard [P. September 11, 1898]

Dear friend,

Mallarmé's death fills me with great sorrow. . . . Can't you send me some details?

He is the only writer of yesterday who allowed us to admire him.

I can speak to you of nothing else today; I know how you loved Mallarmé, and sense, from my own sorrow, how great yours must be.

I am writing to Mme Mallarmé.

Adieu, dear fellow.

Your

André Gide

142. Paul Valéry to André Gide

[P. Paris, September 26, 1898] *

My dear André, here are the details. Writing them down will relieve me a bit, since for the last three nights I haven't slept, I've been crying like a child and suffocating. Well, I have lost the man in the world I loved most, and, in any case, with regard to my feelings and my way of thinking, nothing will replace him. With him I had got accustomed to an absolutely filial familiarity, under his own guidance. And then, he understood all sorts of thoughts, and my most singular deviations found a "precedent" in him and, when necessary, support—opinions notwithstanding. All that is irreplaceable. Six or seven weeks ago, I spent the day there.[29] He seemed to me weary—he was all white—and his little boat, still roped up and floating, was, he told me, forsaken. We went to his room to talk. He showed me some drafts of his *Hérodiade* in progress, etc., changed his undershirt in front of me, gave me water for my hands and then perfumed me with his perfume. In the evening he and his daughter accompanied me to the Vulaines station, under circumstances—night, stillness, and three-part talk —that were unforgettable.

Friday evening I came in late, around eleven, and found the telegram from Geneviève. "Father died," etc.

---

* *Translator's note:* From the context of this letter, it would seem misdated. It must have been written on September 12 or 13 and perhaps mailed somewhat later.

[29] The account of that last visit to Mallarmé was to be published by Valéry in *Variété II* (Gallimard, 1930). It is one of Valéry's most moving texts.

I shall skip that night, one of the most frightful I have ever known, along with last night. In the morning I telegraphed to his friends in Paris, I wrote to you, etc.

P. L.,[30] at the very last minute, did not want to go out there. I left with Régnier and Heredia, I let them go off to lunch and I was at the house.

I don't know if you are acquainted with the spot? Here is a little sketch:

[A sketch of Mallarmé's house.]

A indicates where the coffin was placed; a few people were arranging it with flowers. I put a wreath of roses at the head. It's in Mallarmé's room.

I had barely entered the garden when his daughter threw herself into my arms, weeping and saying: "Ah! Monsieur V., Papa loved you so much!" Then I saw his wife as well, and in what a state! But the poor girl who sacrificed everything for her father and who formed such a pure and delicate group with him, a spiritual "marble"!

This is how he died. It was an accident, and unique. Ever since Monday he had had a case of tonsillitis—of no seriousness—but, that being a weak spot, he went to bed. Friday, the doctor came to see him. He felt better (naturally) and wanted to get up. While he was chatting with the doctor, a glottal spasm killed him outright by asphyxiation; he drew himself up, and fell back dead. It appears that such cases are exceedingly rare. This deadly spasm had hardly any relation to his sore throat. Perhaps he might have been saved if that minute probability had been considered and everything had been ready for an emergency tracheotomy.

He died at eleven in the morning. His daughter claims that at the one supreme moment, he understood and gave her a look. Ever since she told me that, I see the look.

Gradually, people began to arrive. Catulle, Roujon, Dierx, etc., the Natansons, etc.—rather a lot of people, actually, filling the garden, and aside from me, I think, everyone wore country clothes, dressed for cycling, etc.

We went to the church at Samoreau in frightful heat and then to the cemetery, which is charmingly located: he would have the same view there as from his window.

Roujon[31] spoke with great emotion and said what was necessary about settling the future of the two women.

Then, Quillard forced me to move up near the grave and say farewell in the name of the—Young People! And I was absolutely unable to utter anything but indistinct mumbles, I was choking and no one understood

[30] Pierre Louÿs.

[31] Roujon, director of the Beaux-Arts, was one of Stéphane Mallarmé's faithful friends. Among those present were also Rodin and Renoir, accompanied by Mlle. Jeannie Gobillard, Berthe Morisot's niece, who in 1900 was to become the wife of Paul Valéry.

the four sounds I emitted any better than I did. You will find mention of that in today's papers.

His daughter's last public throes took place, then she was taken away and we left. All that came back to me last night and, as I could no longer breathe, I got up, inhaled some vapor—then a huge storm broke out, and I slept for an hour.

Please keep this letter, which is an accurate description of yesterday. I shall ask you for a copy of it later on, for I have neither the inclination nor the courage to write all this down for myself now.

Your
Valéry

143. André Gide to Paul Valéry

La Roque [P. September, 1898]

Your letter was awaiting me here (I had gone away for two days). Thank you for having written me all that; your sorrow finds in my heart a deep echo that surprises me: for the last three days I have been able to think of almost nothing else. The fact that I could not be there causes me great sorrow; perhaps had you informed me by telegram? . . . But no; even so, I should not have had the actual time to come back; having spent all day Saturday in Le Havre for the christening of my nephew, I didn't learn of the news, from the papers and then from your card, until I had returned here. I went upstairs to weep in my room, thinking so much of you, and of that man's whole admirable life. I did my utmost, considering the five different addresses given by the newspapers, to find out where to send a telegram and letter. . . . But my great shyness had always kept me from speaking to Mme or Mlle Mallarmé, so that they barely know me. . . . I'm counting on you, dear friend, to give me information: if by chance something must be done . . . even anonymously, for them, I should be happy to be able to lessen my grief at having recently given Mallarmé himself such small proof of my tenderness and devotion. I had not seen him since the time we visited him in connection with that protest in the *Mercure*.[32]

Yes, dear friend, I thank you very much for your letter; it is sadder than I ever believed a letter from you could be; and what you tell me of his daughter moves me . . . fills me with tears. . . . Is there . . . ?

---

[32] On January 15, 1897, for the first anniversary of Verlaine's death, Mallarmé had given *La Revue Blanche* a very beautiful sonnet entitled *Tombeau,* which provoked offensive criticism in *La Plume* from Adolphe Retté. André Gide at once took the initiative of writing a letter of protest, which was published in the February issue of *Le Mercure de France*. As he wrote to Mallarmé: ". . . The recent article in *La Plume* against you made me so indignant that I was unable to refrain from answering back."

Forgive me, dear friend . . . but the solitude of those two women appals me. . . . What a bitter thing, what a bitter thing is glory!

I am writing an *Eloge funèbre* in *L'Ermitage,*[33] and I'm afraid of doing it very badly. The loftiness of those thoughts, so different from mine, disconcerts me—and yet I am so happy to write it, because the latecomers, who claim to love me, take the stand of not admiring Mallarmé. . . . Won't you write anything? Is *La Revue de Paris* closed to you?

Adieu, poor friend. I embrace you tenderly.

André Gide

144. *Paul Valéry to André Gide*

[Paris. P. October 7, 1898]

My dear André,

I have been ailing all week: yesterday, however, I had to take myself off to Valvins, summoned by those women who remain.

The impression I got was tepid, vast, smooth, a mixture of great stillness in that very beautiful country, of my physical aches, and of memories. A long talk, steeped off and on, slowly, in funereal things, sometimes going so far as a laugh—as though it were posthumous—with moments altogether moving.

First of all, let me tell you, just between ourselves, for this must *not be circulated at all*[34]—that I was led to the death chamber and there, on the untouched table, was a paper full of scribbling, written the day before the death, which I was given to decipher. On it I read a statement ordering that none of the papers were to be shown, that nothing new was to be published and that "that big pile of notes, a half-century old . . . which I alone understand" was to be burned. The convulsed handwriting made that scrap of paper terrifying—and next to it were two almost completed fragments of *Hérodiade,* the final work. I was allowed to read them, in spite of the interdiction. One of them—*Le Cantique de Jean*—is in stanzas à la Banville (8,8,8,4), the other is made up of about fifty alexandrines; although I don't remember any of the lines, I have the impression that *Le Cantique* is very beautiful.[35] As you can imagine, I was hardly cool and collected.

The strange and painful impression—on my return in the train—of realizing that I couldn't recall any of the lines of those fragments.

Now, I shall get down to business. I'll be brief and clear.

[33] The October, 1898, issue. Gide was to say: "Mallarmé, oddly enough, *thought before speaking* . . ." and "In an age in which we needed to admire, Mallarmé alone warranted justifiable admiration."

[34] As these facts have long been disclosed by literary history, there is no longer any reason not to print this letter.

[35] *Hérodiade* is in three parts: I *Ouverture,* II *Scène,* III *Cantique de saint Jean.* Only *Scène* was published during Mallarmé's lifetime.

During our conversation, I led those ladies to expose to me their monetary situation. In short, they have about 3,400 francs a year to spend. They are keeping Valvins—at the cost of 400 francs a year. It was at that point that their regrets came through—they admitted that the Paris house would have to be eliminated—and they displayed such grief about it that—really!—I came forward. Thinking of you and of me, I rapidly made a little mental calculation and said, very vaguely to begin with, not daring to go too far, that . . . some friends *had* thought about such things. I saw the pleasure it gave them, I summoned up a little audacity, and I promised to straighten it out for them.

Here is my idea: the Paris rent comes to 900 francs a year, that is, 75 francs a month. It's not so terrible. But I alone cannot go above 25 francs a month. On the other hand, I naturally don't want to appeal to everyone in a body, for that would be indiscreet and consequently would defeat the purpose. So I thought of you. Tell me what you can do in this sense—if you want to. I shall make no secret of the fact that the merit and difficulty of the whole question lies solely in the follow-up, in the REGULAR CONTINUATION of that income, as well as in its remaining an absolute secret.

Answer AS SOON AS POSSIBLE, and give me your advice on this other point: after you, and only after I receive your answer, I shall appeal to the following friends: Dujardin, Griffin, and perhaps Fontainas. I must have people who 1. are gallant, 2. are honorable, and 3. can contribute regularly and be particularly discreet.

Once this scheme is organized, I shall inform the interested parties of it, giving the names of the friends who participate. Whatever your answer, complete silence. I have been asked, by the way, to thank you for your letter. I must now write to various people for the same purpose.

Were you informed of the birth of my nephew, last week? [36]

> Your
> Valéry

145. *André Gide to Paul Valéry*

La Roque [October, 1898]

Thank you for your letter, old Paul. You can count on me; reassure the ladies at once. I am of the opinion that we should apply to the smallest number of people possible, and if needs be, I would agree to take on that responsibility with you alone; but I get a little panic-stricken at the idea of your laying out twenty-five francs a month; on the other hand, I wouldn't dare commit myself to a *regular* payment higher than that of the remaining six hundred francs; therefore, I should advise you to ask Griffin, in whom we have great confidence and whom I really like, for a third

---

[36] Jean Valéry, son of Jules Valéry.

contribution, to reduce both your subscription and my own; † unless you have some serious reason for not asking Griffin. . . . In that case, let's just forget it. Anyhow, reassure the ladies and write me what you have done.

And in any event, count on me and on my discretion. I think we can count entirely on Griffin's. (I don't know Dujardin.) [37]

Take care of yourself, dear old Paul.

I am your friend
André Gide

† I can't give anything *immediately*. The six hundred francs would be "collectible" on two dates (January and July), at the bank that I indicate.

146. Paul Valéry to André Gide

[P. Paris, October 22, 1898]

My dear André,

I have Griffin's total adherence. I am now awaiting an answer from Valvins to launch the affair.

I read your *Mallarmé* in *L'Ermitage*.[38] It's very good, very good. I was most satisfied with it. I note that in such contributions to *L'Ermitage*, you don't object to a little aggression. It's rather curious.

Yesterday I thought back on your *Sahul* [*sic*], as I was reading Renan's *Drames philosophiques,* which was lent me.

One couldn't be better informed than Renan's characters. Unfortunately, their philosophies result in extreme banality.

Having to recite accurately the ideas of others and recite them in the capacity of men who don't invent them = who don't give a damn about them, they seem like a thousand weary professors.

Renan's skepticism comes, I fear, from having failed to discover. People of that kind discover nothing but ways of reciting the minds of others, and manage to bring together politely and introduce to each other pleasantly the originals who sweated blood, etc.

There's a senseless sentence. Figure it out for yourself, or call Renan.

And so, with relation to these things, I thought about *Saül* (I write *Sahul*).

I realize that, actually, I like the play, but what bothered me in it was finding no character to put my mind at rest. The truth is that I don't *feel* King S. And as for you, this is what I think. You chose S. because both king and legend already existed. He was a vehicle for the thing you wanted above all: the special kind of love that directs your drama. But S. is unfortunately mad. No doubt about it, is there? For that reason, the two interesting men he drags about with him, the Rex and the somewhat

[37] The poet Edouard Dujardin, one of the forces behind the symbolist movement, founder of *La Revue wagnérienne.*

[38] *L'Eloge funèbre* was published in the October, 1898, issue of *L'Ermitage.*

special Lover, seem to me very diminished. At bottom, I believe the only role a madman can play in a drama is that particular one (of being mad), and he can hardly be the main character. Hamlet and Lear prove it more than they disprove it.

In the historical theme of *Saül,* there is one lovely aspect which you saw but didn't show sufficiently. It is the growth of David. That's tremendous. It is the extraordinary confrontation—of established power and personal power—which is set up. That conflict is the philosophical basis of the current situation. I keep on repeating it. . . .

I have thousands of other things I could tell you but I have to run. We'll come back to them. In short, your *Saül* appeared to me in a very favorable light, compared to the above-mentioned Renanisms and since I happened to be reading them.

I am enjoying Mardrus [39] these days. He's a prize.

Your
P. V.

147. *André Gide to Paul Valéry*

La Roque-Baignard, October 22, 1898 [40]

Dear fellow,

I am sorry that I wasn't able to find the time to write you sooner, for to my mind, your letter lacked clarity: "Griffin accepts fully," you said . . .

That "fully" frightens me; you must be more explicit. Since the question has still to be discussed between us, here is what I propose:

Solution I		*Solution II*	
You	15 fr.	You	15 fr.
Him	25 —	Him	30 —
Me	35 —	Me	30 —

It is up to him to decide which of the two solutions he accepts. I don't wish to consider any others. Unless Griffin cannot give that much. In that case, I would give more.

Mlle M. wrote me a delightful note about my little article; [41] please tell her, when the occasion arises, that I appreciated it very much. I'm glad you found it good; now it is up to you to speak about the works.

I like the fact that you have come back to *Saül.* You deserve to hear more of my views on it, for I fear that you are sinking deep into an interpretation

---

[39] A doctor and an orientalist, translator of *The Arabian Nights* in sixteen volumes.

[40] Letter begun the 22d and finished the 23rd, which explains that Gide had received Valéry's letter of the 22d before sending his own. [From the context of this letter, there would still seem to be a letter from Valéry missing.]

[41] His *Eloge funèbre,* mentioned in Letter 143, came out in the October, 1898, issue of *L'Ermitage.*

that lessens the play in my eyes by magnifying, in yours, the importance of *the anecdote.* I tell you it is hardly in my mind at all (the immoral offense), and it pleases me only because it limits to those strictly necessary persons a very general matter, the interest of which extends, on all sides, beyond that sad court scandal. You can imagine that I did not carry that subject around in my head for six or seven years simply as a dramatic curiosity and that it must be *interesting* . . . or I'm nothing but an ass.

I agree with you that a madman cannot be suitable for the stage; only reasonable beings should be presented; that is, beings whose acts and words flow logically from a predetermined character. Aside from a few stray words, such, I affirm, is my *Sahul,* and everything that gradually suppresses him can be found IN HIM, shown from the very beginning.

Let us change pens.

If I continue to write drama, I should like to exclude any outside chance; I should like all the movements, peripeties, and catastrophes to spring from each one's character alone, so that each one creates and demolishes his own story. The Demons are there only to mime the monologue; David is there only to represent the inner drama which all vice is: welcoming, loving what is harmful to you.

Two considerations here: I consider the subject very general; but I shouldn't be displeased if people were not of my opinion. I have been reproached enough with my subjectivity in *Les Cahiers, Les Nourritures, Paludes,* etc., so that I may finally treat myself to the pride of apparently having created a type in which nothing of me can be found. One has to do better than just understand what I write in order to tell that *Sahul* is the sequel and the negation of *Les Nourritures,*—as may be gathered from those phrases I felt had to be added to the monologue in the beginning, to throw a little more light on my monarch: "The slightest noise, the slightest fragrance claims my attention; my senses are opened outward, and no sweetness escapes my notice." Later on, the witch says, and he repeats: "All that charms me is my enemy," and the play revolves around that saying until it ends with this other one: "With what shall man console himself for his fall, if not with that which made him fall?"

If this explanation bores you, forgive me: it truly wearies me to explain and defend what I do, because that is why [*sic*] I acquit myself so very ill.

Do believe that I shouldn't have done anything, if you had found my play simply bad; but thank you, old Paul, such was not the case, and that is why I dwell on it.

What you tell me about *Saül* is good especially for this reason: I now wish to speak to you of a new drama which will interest you more than this one (I hope).

. . . .

I just received your letter; well, too bad: I shall send you this one, such as it is, and inclose the money. I am too aware of the tactlessness I would show by dwelling on it, but I am even sorrier not to have written you sooner. I should have liked Griffin to have relieved both of us, not only me, and since it is now agreed that he give 25, please let me adopt solution No. 1. I shall soon return to Paris, and we'll talk it over again, won't we?

Your
André Gide

148. *Paul Valéry to André Gide*

Saturday [November, 1898]

I thank you for your remittance. Vielé, whom I saw yesterday, also gave me his third. I shall refer all of it to Valvins at once. Subsequently, we'll talk over some permanent arrangement of this matter.

This morning, my dear fellow, I had hardly the time to read your eight pages. The weather is damp as a sponge, like some limp, hot end of March. A temperature for vain attempts and leaden legs. Hands as well.

One moves about in an apparently feverish organ.

I really don't know where to hide or what to do.

To sum up:

Health variable. Energy *idem.* Disgusts *idem.* Absolute lack of time, that is, usable time.

Acquired knowledge.—Nearly all the essentials. But that minimum is often inadequate in some particular case.

Perception of those problems I feel I must solve (*!*)—Rather good.

Output.—Excellent theoretically. Very low, in fact.

Balance of acquired habits and broken habits.—Just about maintained.

Observations.—A vague and disadvantageous feeling that nothing one will or might do will pay off enough to seem worthwhile getting involved in. Dilemma: doing what would be useful is a deadly bore; doing what would be useless is useless.

Answer to the dilemma: "There's nothing new about that. You know it's just a momentary problem."

Answer to the answer to the dilemma: *"Well!* * but moments in themselves are nothing, it's the sum of those moments, etc."

Variations of sociability.—Introduction to young L.[42] in my frequent frequentations. Introduction into the relations—rather close—of Moréas (!).

Considerable cooling off of relations with Schwob. Wait and see. Sort out. The reason—politico-patriotico-religious. Profound reasons.

Introduction to a young man driven to despair by love. Serious case. Twenty-nine years old. Very intelligent. Scientist (natural sciences). After

* *Translator's note:* In English in the original.
[42] André Lebey.

short conversation, takes me for a doctor of souls (!). I am writing to him in Le Havre, giving medical advice. I believe I have an effective—but very toxic—product for him to take.

The rest of my relations are continuing. An unmistakably growing intimacy with P. L.[43]

Recent reading.—Skimmed through a book by young Ruyters (*Armide*).[44] Wait and see. Absolutely forbidden to pronounce judgment on an early book. All both good and bad. Letter to write praising it.

An histology textbook. Nothing for it, of no interest.

Ten pages of Machiavelli. Admirable, because confirms in vaguer language an aphorism of old Teste. Also read *La Mandragora*.[45] Some terrific phrases. Play worthless.

Shows.—*Maîtres Chanteurs*.[46] Very great pleasure. Would infinitely amuse Gide.

La Maraine[47] at the Gymnase. First act funny, the rest worthless. An admirable woman here and there.

Ideas to follow up: zero.

Work: idem.

Eternal research: to be continued.

A little progress on work concerned with painting and especially drawing.

Theory on mental operations, continual difficulties.

Marriages.—Rouart. Julia. Mlle. de Régnier, etc. P. L.[48] and I (and Hérold) are the only bachelors left—and another P. L.![49]

Notable conversations with: Moréas, Griffin, Mazel, Degas at Rouart's.

P. Valéry

---

149. *André Gide to Paul Valéry*

[P. November, 1898]

Dear old Paul,

Forced to ask for a postponement. I really have too much to do and am unable to keep the time for you tomorrow. Do let's put dinner off for a few

---

[43] Pierre Louÿs.

[44] André Ruyters, Belgian writer and banker, who was to be on the original staff of *La Nouvelle Revue Française*. He then went to Addis Ababa as director of a bank, organized the Far Eastern departments of the Bank of Indochina, and advised Gide and Valéry on securities in which to invest. In 1898 he published *Les Jardins d' Armide*.

[45] A comedy by Machiavelli.

[46] Wagner's *Die Meistersinger*.

[47] Comedy by Harry Mitchell.

[48] Pierre Louÿs, who was to be married a few months later. See below, Letter 152.

[49] Paul Léautaud, who was to remain a bachelor, or Paul Laurens, who was to marry in 1900.

days. The *Saül* Case will very shortly come before Antoine.[50] O! what worries.

Your

André Gide

— 1899 —

150. Paul Valéry to André Gide

[January 13, 1899 (in Gide's handwriting)]

My dear André,

I now ask you for the fifty-six francs, twenty-five centimes. . . . Dujardin agreed with no difficulty.

Your

Valéry

P. S. I read my *Ermitage* devotedly. *Prométhée* is good. But I am waiting for its end to give my considered appraisal.[1]

As for Nietzsche, well really! It would seem to me (if I got the point, which is still not certain) that you're in something of a hurry to give him unity.[2] For me, he is, above all, *contradictory*. For example, he attacks A by means of method B, and then he demolishes B; and retains both attacks all the same.

Therefore, taken as a whole, there are admirable or naïve or useless things; therefore, one must choose what's suitable and return either to Stendhal or to Descartes, for there is almost no middle ground possible. Often entire chapters are, as your café waiter * would say, tremendously gratuitous. His big mistake, in my opinion, is to want to construct a philosophy of *violence*. The result: it's Mauclair—it's clear!

. . . The most amusing aspect of him is his convinced manner and his

---

[50] When Gide wrote *Saül*, he hoped to see it performed with the actor Edouard de Max—to whom the work is dedicated—in the leading role. Antoine appreciated *Saül* but would not accept it unless Brieux's last play, *Resultat des Courses*, whose staging he had just completed, was a success. Brieux's work turned out to be a flop, and Antoine, penniless, could not stage *Saül*, which entailed great expense and great risk. It was not until 1922 that the drama was performed, at the Vieux Colombier, with Jacques Copeau in the part of Saul, and Louis Jouvet playing the Great Priest.

[1] *Le Prométhée mal enchaîné* was serialized in the January, February, and March, 1899, issues of *L'Ermitage*. It was published as a brochure that same year by Les Editions du Mercure de France.

[2] *L'Ermitage* (No. 1, January, 1899) also contained a *Lettre à Angèle* signed by Gide and concerned with Nietzsche.

* *Translator's note:* A character in *Le Prométhée mal enchaîné*.

concern with ethics—a thing that always tickles me—for actually it's a matter of tricks. He wants to work with ethics, and he doesn't see that the modern foundation of that is *indifference properly presented.* Besides, did you notice the marvelous *gimmick* that goes to make up the *Superuomo?* [3] It allows him to be both optimistic and pessimistic, whence diverse pages, etc., and to be romantic and classical, etc., *ad libitum.*

I am very interested by his ethic of masters, and of slaves, but what a lot of plays on words! Now I forgive him a good deal because he is for "a little more awareness," a former hobby of mine. But it's a kind of ethic or mania that leads me to become engrossed exclusively in the search for forms of thought, mainly those that remained unknown to the terrific logicians of old, to the philosophers who followed them, and especially to those who make the most use of them, artists, imaginers, etc.

That is why Nietzsche "doesn't teach us much directly." The awaited novelty being, to my mind, a combination of the personal—rich, multiple, etc.—and the simple or general.

But a very *suggestive* author, by reason of many very passionate and very different things on one page.

Your
Valéry

You say that he was extolling the unconscious. I don't think so. There are even distinctly contrary sentences. But quite simply, his beloved *Uebermensch* [4] *must* be completely conscious of everything, with all the "advantages" of the UNCONSCIOUS. That's clear, without that he would not be an *Uebermensch,* he would be, in one sense or the other, no more than the magnification of any type at all that was chosen, with or without consciousness. Vacher [5] or Poe, unbounded.

That is how I, personally, would have proceeded to create a character. (Cf. *Teste.*)

But Nietzsche, who is far more of a metaphysician than I,—for I believe that I'm as little a one as is decent,—has remade his God, his Cause, his Strength, his Life, etc., and he took the good traditional road: contradiction.

Only, in him it is not so much a contradiction in terms, *in terminis,* as in things. There is apparently nothing contradictory in defining an animal as a combination camel and snail. But it is possible (probable?) that if you analyzed that mad animal point by point, you would arrive at a particular

[3] and [4] Superman.

[5] Vacher de Lapouge, in 1889–90, taught a course in political science, open to the public, at the Montpellier Faculty of Law: "The Aryan: His Role in Society." The author of *Race et milieu social, Systèmes et faits sociaux* (1909), he gave a prophetic tone and scope to his social forecasts.

contradiction undisclosed by an investigation of the above-mentioned general proposition.[6]

Finally, note that in extolling the unconscious, Angèle's [7] correspondent —at bottom—feigns that quality of unconsciousness but wants nothing of it. (It's rather a hindrance to good writing.) He is for a modified, very constitutional regime, the entente cordiale of Life and Paper. Say it isn't so?   P. V.

151. André Gide to Paul Valéry

[Algiers] April 11, 1899

Dear old Paul,

I found your note on my arrival in Algiers. Inclosed is the money order; I think you'll receive it in time.

Nothing memorable in our travels but five exquisite days in El Kantara; the rest did no more than disgust me with traveling.

If I weren't hoping to come back soon, I would give you a somewhat longer account of my doings; but you'll lose nothing by waiting two week to hear about them: they have no current relevance.

The trip made me actually *feel* the signs of my growing old, that is to say, my menus have changed. Lord! how bored I was from Tunis to Kairouan, from Sousse to Tunis, from Tunis to Batna! I traveled in the same way as one goes through ceremonies of mourning . . . but enough!

El Kantara was worth all the boredom.

And besides, nothing to tell you except (but it's nearly over) that a frightful (as well as cerebral) case of bronchitis laid me low for two weeks. And you?

Au revoir, your
André Gide

I am reading aloud with my wife, in small doses, *Henri Brulard*.

152. Paul Valéry to André Gide

[Paris. P. July 6, 1899]

My dear André,

You are perhaps at La Roque, or perhaps in the rue Ducoté.[8] I am writing to La Roque, which I love.

I received the most recent of your published works and amused myself by skimming through them very quickly, from beginning to end, having a

---

[6] Cf. Valéry, *Quatre Lettres au sujet de Nietzsche* (Cahiers de la Quinzaine, 1927).

[7] It was Gide who gave that name to the imaginary woman, first a character in *Paludes,* to whom he presumably addressed his critical articles in *L'Ermitage.* She appears also at the end of *Le Prométhée.* His *Lettres à Angèle* were published in 1900 by Les Editions du Mercure de France. They were reprinted in 1903 in *Prétextes,* by the same publisher.

[8] Edouard Ducoté was the director of the review *L'Ermitage.*

taste for the cinema and wanting to experiment with style. From that point of view, I re-liked *Narcisse* and *El Hadj*. I also found *Prométhée* appealing, but I am isolating from that gloomy drama the final thoughts, which don't seem to me nearly so good. *Philoctète,*[9] which I knew nothing about, disclosed to me a most interesting Neoptolemus,[10] whose first speech is extremely well written. I expected to see that young man more or less raped later on. But such was not the case. Also missing are Ulysses' last words, I was hoping for something nasty from him instead of his conversion. But: "everyone to his taste," says Bordure.[11]

I took upon myself to read *aloud* Neoptolemus' prelude and a bit of *El Hadj*. They were very good—in spite of the instrument. In those fragments, I was pleased, for, at bottom, I like the "upright" style. But I shall always quibble with you a little about: 1. Overcomplicated sentences—uselessly—in certain cases. 2. Plays on words. I know what I mean, I know what you mean, you know what I mean. They don't mean anything.

Anyway, you'll tell me that now you're busy with theater.

P. L. recently left for Pallanza. He has been ailing since the wedding,[12] but all that is merely hearsay.

I had quite a session at the *Journal* a few days ago, in a little room with Barrès. I ended by getting a bit excited (to say the least!) and I took a slice, good and rare, out of the free man.[13] Granted, he's a delightful littérateur—let's go so far as to say philosopher (unwillingly), but what a want of political sense, what ignorance; and *that* wants to Caesarize! Do you remember what I have always said about him? Our meetings have merely solidified and magnified that opinion. *That* believes, obviously, that Machiavelli consists simply in buying off some and surreptitiously giving arsenic to the others. And, thereupon, we collect gossip and funny sayings. I believe that politics—as a totality—is made up of awfully simple calculations, on the one hand, and of flexible nuances vis-à-vis people, on the other. But, above all, absolute precision in partial objectives, and I would almost add: never make known the great and sole Objective. In our times, things are so lacking in subtlety, so little dependent on personalities, and so well known in their separate states that it's possible to become very competent, and a rather good prophet, providing you never take your eyes off a map of the world and read the English newspapers from time to time.

---

[9] The play *Philoctète ou le Traité des trois Morales,* dedicated to Marcel Drouin, had just been published by Les Editions du Mercure de France, at the same time as *Le Traité du Narcisse, La Tentative amoureuse,* and *El Hadj*.

[10] Achilles' son, who goes along with Ulysses to recover Hercules' bow from Philoctetes.

[11] Captain Bordure, a character in Jarry's *Ubu Roi*.

[12] *Nôce*. Pierre Louÿs had just married Louise de Heredia.

[13] An allusion to Barrès' novel: *Un Homme libre* (1899).

Ideas are readily accepted, and impossibilities are revealed in no time. A few statistics on trade and population and—well—some principles should go along with the *Times* and the atlases.

What's terrifying in France today is that it would be impossible for any new power whatever to work in a consistent and sustained manner. Nearly the whole machinery of the country would have to be made over, and perhaps we would even have to wait a generation. For anyone who keeps informed as to our decline in most realms and who follows the footprints of the Frenchman's growing disenchantment with existence, there is only one—strange—thing to keep him from concluding: "We're damn well finished, I'm leaving," and that is the expectation of the unexpected that has sometimes occurred in this country.

And without that? . . . For you're damn well finished the minute you don't give a damn.

The kind of politics I was speaking about should say to itself: "Let's see, how far can we go? Assuming that everything continues as it is: What do we achieve? Who will pay out this budget tomorrow? Who will fill in these columns? Who is in debt to me? To whom am I in debt?" and finally, this question, which I consider most essential: "On what has France a monopoly today? Organization, numbers, military or naval power, courage, money, a mad desire to grow rich?" What a tableau we could draw up, with nothing but unquestionably established facts!

Ex.: Who is the head of State? . . .
  Who is powerful in France?
  Do the French wish to grow?
  Is exportation increasing?
  The debt?
  Are we afraid of the . . . and the . . . ?
  How do we rank in . . . (sciences, machines, etc.)

Your
P. Valéry

153. *André Gide to Paul Valéry*

La Roque, July 11 [1899]

Dear old Paul,

Enclosed are the provisions.

Respectful greetings to Valvins.

Your previous letter interests me. Barrès is a failure. He has great charm, but is not worth much. Had he known the extent of his attraction, he perhaps would not have launched out into assertions in which so little of it is involved. Yet he's the one who writes the best articles of the so-called nationalist kind, but for all that, one has to pick and choose. Have you read the booklet by his Maurras? It is entitled *Trois Idées politiques.* (That is to say: Chateaubriand, Michelet, Sainte-Beuve.) The style was very *arresting*.

It would appear that the above-mentioned Maurras has just attacked Signoret in *La Revue encyclopédique*. At La Roque we get only echoes of echoes. Signoret has intrusted me with answering! Fortunately, I haven't managed to get hold of the article. I am rereading M.'s [14] *Arabian Nights* with the greatest interest, and I see with delight that he has taken my few corrections into account. For instance, the marvelous sentence: "They tempted one another mutually by making signs of copulation with their eyes," is mine. Admirable accounts of the kalenders.[15]

You speak discerningly of *Philoctète*. *Plays on words* are indeed one of my worst intellectual failings. It's a kind of skepticism. I believe and hope that it will disappear. Very pleased that you like my style, etc. Thank you.

I am presently extracting *Candaule*,[16] slowly and with difficulty; remember, I spoke to you about it. I shall perhaps ask you to read it before I publish it—unless I'm forced to give it to some review before we meet again. I am leading the most peaceful and puritanical of lives here. No spirits, not even wine, tea, coffee, etc. Up at six, a long period of work—scales and exercises on the piano; the annoying thing is that since my work has been going well, sleep has not. As soon as I've blown out my candle, I am besieged by belches of work.

Au revoir, old Paul. Think about writing some poems for December.

Your
André Gide

154. Paul Valéry to André Gide

[P. Paris, July 12, 1899]

My dear André,

I received your "provisions" this morning and thank you for being punctual. Mardrus, who had popped up two days ago, left for the sea yesterday. In September the second volume will come out. The Nathans [17] predict profits of from 100,000 to 150,000! The fact is that Volume One is already in its fourth printing. Your copulo-mimetic sentence is excellent, it tempts me to make the sign and suit the action to it.

Do work. It's time; France is producing nothing but translations: Nietzsche, Harun, and that stupid Wells, with whom Davray [18] has been flooding us, and that amusing Kipling. But it seems to me that our best

---

[14] Mardrus.

[15] The calenders are wandering dervishes who belong to the Arabic Sufi order.

[16] See below, Letter 169, n. 2.

[17] *Sic*. The Natansons, who managed the publishing end of *La Revue blanche*, and brought out the Mardrus *Arabian Nights*.

[18] H.-D. Davray was the critic in charge of English literature on *Le Mercure de France*. He translated the major works of H. G. Wells, including *The Time Machine* and *The War in the Air*.

literary periods have been those in which excellent translations were published. Nietzsche claims that the genius of France is female: she bears ideas but doesn't beget them, a role he attributes to the Jews, the Romans, and the Germans. Yet we have had a few males. But which is it better to be? Which has the greatest pleasure? Here, the female. For my part, I think I prefer the male. Besides, all that belongs in the category of vague ideas. Apropos of vagueness, I note in passing that a vague idea is the one most generally understood—and you're considered obscure as soon as you become precise. (Cf. X, Y.) That's because there are degrees of understanding, and most people fancy they understand more often than they do. In other words, if they are made to think through an idea which they *feel* they have altogether grasped, they begin to stammer.

I am rotting over a fragment of *Monsieur Teste*,[19] similar to aged Roquefort, which I promised a long time ago and which is as spineless as can be. You know my fate. Everything that amuses me is a bloody bore to the public, without exception, and no one does as badly as I the things that don't amuse him.

I am still not sure what use to make of my meager holiday and my infinitesimal means. If I did what I should, I'd have to divide myself up between Genoa, Montpellier, and the Aveyron. It's absurd.

Your
P. Valéry

155. Paul Valéry to André Gide

[P. Montpellier, August 2, 1899]

My dear antique,

I am in Montpellier for the moment and am dying of the heat, notwithstanding swims in the sea. In a few days I shall go to the Aveyron, where I'll probably be bored stiff until the end of my shortened holiday. Then I shall sweat in my office, etc.

I brought here, with no illusions, some manuscripts in progress, *Teste* and the Chinese, and I'm letting them sleep.

I should have liked to have done with those two monsters quickly, so as to deal with other things, but we are being bored together.

On July 14 and 15 I went to Valvins. Several observations on this which I shall communicate to you buccally.

Mlle Morisot and her cousins were there. We spent some time in the woods, and painted water colors on the banks of the Seine.[20]

---

[19] *Teste en Chine*, which was never completed, but which, thirty years later, was incorporated into *Le Yalou* (privately printed in 1928 and then included in *Regards sur le Monde actuel*, 1931).

[20] Berthe Morisot (1841–1895) had married Eugène Manet, the painter's brother, and had a daughter, Julie, of whom Stéphane Mallarmé was the deputy guardian.

I miss my mother, who is in Italy. I found it difficult to go there for so few days. Moreover, I should doubtless have needed special permits.

I hope you have read the Jammes in the latest *Mercure*.[21] But—doubtless —with eyes other than mine.

I am filled with hate for visibly manufactured naïveté.

Madrus.* Cours Pierre-Puget, 79, Marseilles. But he is at sea. In any event, that's where to write.

See you when?

Paul Valéry

156. *André Gide to Paul Valéry*

La Roque, in extremis
Sunday [end of September, 1899]

Dear old Paul,

Are you free on Monday, October 9, from 6:00 to 8:25? Send your answer to Cuverville, near Criquetot-L'Esneval, S.-Inf., if it should arrive on the 7th or 8th, and to La Roque if it should arrive before the 5th (not inclusive). I shall only spend eight hours in Paris and want to console myself in two hours for two months of silence; that's why I am booking you so soon. We'll dine together at the Gare de Lyon, as we did once before (Gare de l'Est, I believe).

If, in your letter, you don't specify a place to meet, I shall await you at 6:00 in the station restaurant. When you leave the Ministry that day, however, don't fail to check with the *concierge* as to whether a note has been left for you or whether I myself am there waiting for you.

My silence has been inordinately prolonged because of the delay in my return to Paris; I began three letters to you in the last week; I just threw them out. Drouin gave me news of you, and almost the only reason I was writing you was to ask for news, since, except for the slow construction of my *Candaule,* nothing new has occurred either within me or around me. See you soon.

I am, etc., your
André Gide

Julie Manet and her first cousins, Paule and Jeannie Gobillard (the future Mme. Paul Valéry), continued to live in the house built by Berthe Morisot, 40 rue de Villejust (the future rue Paul Valéry), after her death. Paul Valéry had met Jeannie Gobillard for the first time at Stéphane Mallarmé's funeral. He saw her again at Eugène Rouart's wedding, and met her often on visits to the Mallarmé women.

[21] Francis Jammes' *Conseils à un jeune Poète,* published in the August, 1899, issue of *Le Mercure de France.*

* *Translator's note:* On July 24, 1899, Gide wrote Valéry asking for Mardrus' address.

157. Paul Valéry to André Gide

[Paris, October 16, 1899 (in the
handwriting of Gide, who added in
pencil: "The pencil marks are mine.")]

My dear André,

I received your wordless remittance, and from that silence I concluded
that you had seriously begun your cure.

After having left you a short time ago, I burned a cigar over various
thoughts on subjects that had been interrupted by our meeting; once home
and in bed, I left all that and went back to the very place of our
conversation. Meaning, of course, mental place.

You had rubbed my nose in my trouble, and at first I re-examined that
disgusting faculty of mine, agreeing with the previous conclusions on the
subject. The real name of that trouble, which continually checks me, is
irregularity of strength and mood. My means vary fantastically according
to the moment, and I find that same discontinuity in my body. I made as
much use of it as I could, and I think there is absolutely no doubt that part
of the results I managed to achieve are due precisely to that way of being.
But regularity alone makes one powerful and efficacious. . . . My present
existence has, as it were, confirmed that state by reason of its being
absurdly distributed, thus introducing artificial breaks in my current (to
add to the rest!) and, moreover, an accumulated annoyance due to office
hours. Anyway, nothing can be done in this respect: I am a pitching kind
of creature.

With regard to the exercise of my critical faculties (in the worst sense of
the term), I grant you that I should perhaps have limited it to my own
delight. I attracted attention to my void, by using the leisure it gave me on
extremely simple observations about my contemporaries. But I get the
feeling that my defense must be harder for them than my objections. I have
only to answer, and it's the simple truth: "You never realized that all I
wanted was to be contradicted. *You cannot deny that I have always given
reasons and that they were not always bad."* [22]

That aggressive kind of sincerity, of which I now tend to rid myself
since it did not give me what I was looking for in adopting it—that is to
say . . . terrible and extreme intimacy—made me realize that I was not a
social animal but rather—uniquely and tremendously—a sociable one. By
extreme intimacy, I mean the state of knowing a few people to whom one
can really say everything, and in which one would secure the comfort of
conversation between active thoughts, without reminiscing kinds of monologues, echoes, etc. We would each look at the other, "finding as we went
along . . ."

[22] Sentence underlined in pencil by Gide.

As for this *particular* contempt, it is altogether justified by the shocking things I have heard said and seen written for the last ten years, and more especially by the *intentional refusal to see what is, in order to preserve the literary talent one imagines one has.*[23] This has always seemed to me admirable and is worth the most intense of infinitely thin and infinitely explicit smiles. Moreover, it may be added to the ignorance and most contemptible contempt of the people we know with respect to endeavors other than their own. They cannot imagine the possibility of seeing frightful difficulties in the very facility of their routine. They can no longer imagine *themselves* once any hope of having genius is taken away from them!—just as a Christian needs his heaven in order to live.

I find, therefore, that I have not had good judges. I find them either self-seeking or incompetent, and I can sense that I trouble their minds—infrequently—with an awkward problem.

You'll say that I, too, keep my documents—secret. But I never said that my ideas were decisive or that I could establish and give results. The little I have published, in itself, shows great distances; it comes out at rather spaced intervals; yet I think it shows a homogeneity of work and of rather unique research. One cannot help but feel that I base my thinking upon something which is at once very blurred and very solid, and which must give the impression that I myself consider it of the greatest importance. Finally, I talk about my work and I talk about it willingly. I even talk about it with the kind of naïveté that causes me to say: "That time I had an excellent idea."

The actual root of the "miscomprehension" can be found in the main tendency of my mind: extension, perpetual generalization. It is absolutely impossible for me to apply myself to anything singular. Today, in fact, I can give you a precise idea of that. For me every specific subject comes down to a series of physical and mental operations expressed in mathematical terms. These terms are invariable, and they are as *thought out* as possible. Now such operations, especially the mental ones, may be acquired. The only difficulty is to analyze thoroughly the given subject in order to reduce it, in every possible case, to a group of positively *dead* elements and to a diagram of a more or less organized series of intellectual actions. Finally, the mental operations are certainly finite and small in number. This system, of which I have given you a very rough outline, exhausts—even now—many things, and although I haven't described its methods and needs in detail, you can see its scope. One of its great advantages is that it cuts down to a minimum my chances of nonsense due to language, for in always putting words back alongside their *signified* counterparts, it does not take them into account at all.

[23] Sentence underlined in ink by Valéry. In the margin, next to the sentence, Gide drew vertical pencil lines.

I must add that my inclination would exist even outside any method. A typical example, in a realm unknown to me—music. If I were a musician, you can tell from where you are that I would think constantly, for example, of all possible melodies as a whole, I suppose. I would be dominated by that. I would try to draw one from the other, classify them, etc.

In short, I don't want generally to see things as everyone else does. I first get as instantaneous an impression of them as possible, then I come back to them by trying to rediscover them through a series of conditions that are unrelated to one another and, consequently, more general than my object.

What becomes of literature in all this? It becomes a problem, an application, but not an objective, and not a fundamental point. In not too long a time this opinion will certainly be common. Medicine, which was an art with everything that implies, with a genius for diagnosis, with the gimmicks and quackery of its practitioners, with the superstitions and fads of the public, finally, in fact, became a particular problem in chemistry.

To sum up this colossal letter, I shall ask you a question. What do you do when:

1. you have an irregular temperament,

2. you believe in certain things that go against the feelings of the public, that annoy people when you declare them or that offend their personal gods (hope, enthusiasm . . .),

3. you haven't the "actual" TIME,

4. you don't believe in what prompts the people around you?

Well, you do as I do:

You work when you can—and so strangely that, if you disappeared, no one would recognize any of your true ideas in your papers.

You display radiant good humor—insofar as possible.

You think what you think and you let the others talk. You praise or you blame according to your mood, for *here,* what is published doesn't count any more, what is said doesn't count at all.

You seek out little, so-called pleasures—vulgar pleasures, since, when all is said and done, you have experienced plenty of sorrow that wasn't vulgar at all.

You leave your ethic, your outward behavior, etc., to chance, for you know only too well that it is of no consequence, since it cannot shake the deepest dogmas.

You talk with anyone, for it comes to the same thing—one ear is worth another.

And sometimes you have the right to scorn comprehensive totalities and well-defined ethics, since you have duly taken them into account, and you have weighed them.

Valéry

158. André Gide to Paul Valéry

Lamalou-le-Haut, October 19, 1899

Dear old Paul,

I am carefully storing away your defense, and, later on, if you die of boredom before I'm dead from pleasure, I will bring out this paper, along with so many others, and will say, as R. Colomb [24] did for Stendhal: "Among the rare beings who have had the good fortune to . . . I believe I am one of those who . . . My deep friendship for him, as much as my fear of seeing one of such rare intelligence misunderstood . . . , etc."

I have turned your letter over and over in my mind, old Paul, and am terribly sorry for being so dazed by my cure that I am unable to take up certain points in any satisfactory way, yet they are questionable. I persist in thinking that there are things and people (me, for example) whose measure you take badly, whose level within you is somewhat off.

"Intentional refusal to see what is, in order to preserve the literary talent" ("one imagines one has" was unnecessary).

1. I hope you haven't included me in, since you *speak to me about it*.

2. One prefers to be, rather than not to be; that seems very natural to me. All my Protestant horror of "lies" does not keep me from understanding that for many it is more comfortable than a "non-lie." Is there anything surprising about the fact that everyone isn't keen on going mad in the manner of Nietzsche? And, anyway, so much the better if it's reserved for the few.

There are a few empiricists for the one scientist who makes use of them. All right. Since you have trouble listening to others, especially when they don't speak, you often believe that you're the only one to think as you think; there are others, I assure you, who ask themselves questions (often, I grant you, not generalized or methodical enough), but chiefly the question of the *sine qua non* of their lives and their own production. *Sine qua non* is often the blinder, and that infuriates me as well; but what little exteriorization you give to your *results* is not made to convince them of their mistake.

If some people don't pursue any further the chemical study that would allow them infallibly to make flowers, it's also by reason of their terror of the unlimited number of flowers they might henceforth produce. In some of them, compromise is more conscious, intentional, and deliberate than you think. Actually, what almost all of them lack is not intelligence so much as method. . . . (There is also the fear of finding it all tiresome.)

I might add, with regard to the tricks, etc., devices, that I don't believe one acquires them without losing a kind of finesse, sensual finesse; Wagner's music seems to me terribly coarse as an art. Through wanting to

[24] Stendhal's executor, who wrote a *Notice sur la Vie et les Œuvres de H. Beyle* (Paris, 1845), and an appendix of biographical notes for *La Chartreuse de Parme* (1846) and *Armance* (1877).

determine sensual pleasure beforehand, his senses lost in refinement. In art there is always something indefinable which the instrument won't be able to grasp, etc. The art of artificial flowers.

A lot to say; we'll chat, but you will triumph because I'll stammer. *You* will be clear and your calculation will work out, but it will be *because* your figures are wrong. Au revoir; I'm beginning to write like Rouart, and that's bad for me.

I am deep in *Bourgogne;* [25] if you know of any others like it, tell me at once. It's terrific.

Au revoir. Always your
André Gide

This cure is making me absolutely idiotic.

159. Paul Valéry to André Gide

October 25, 1899 [in Gide's handwriting]

Dear fellow, I see that my letter nettled you, which gives me the pleasure of feeling you take the offensive. I have long been afraid that you were becoming insensitive with regard to the group we could form together; it seemed to me that we hadn't the time to be useless to one another; and that idea gave me permission to write you a few vague and irritating pages.

You considered the declaration of needs that are personal to me as a judgment on you; and I find that the best of effects. I love you, my dear fellow, because—and among other things—we are faced, wonderfully, with the problem of *differences*. It's one of those questions in life which I passionately watched take shape during many an intimate relationship. You are in one scale of a balance. In the other, you put a woman, a stranger, an imbecile, an intelligential [*sic*], an imaginary genius; you yourself furnish, as well, the support and the beam of the machine. The sensitivity of this balance is singular. It depends on the quality of what you put in the *other* scale. When you, André, happen to be in it, mine becomes more sensitive than ever.

I don't think our differences are at all enormous. What gives them their value is that they seem to me extremely slender (capillary-like), so that to encounter them, we can draw much closer together than most other intellectual pairs. And that, at bottom, is what we have done. We caught a glimpse of the fact—without, perhaps, admitting it—that, in general, everything one of us does is precisely what the other should not do. Every impulse of each one is for the other, a priori, a piece of information about himself, and opposite in meaning. Until I really understood this mechanism, your successive new relationships (for example) positively intrigued me, I won't tell you exactly why. Anyway, I could enumerate a host of

---

[25] *Les Mémoires du sergent Bourgogne* (1812–13), published according to the original manuscript by Paul Cottin in 1898.

points on which this mechanism has functioned remarkably, half unbeknownst to us.

You will note in passing that this suggests the concept of multiple "ethics" which correspond to one another. You imagine a group of people and you postulate the necessity of any one of its members having some one specific "ethic." You then determine all the others, assuming that any one of them will act by reversing, or exaggerating, or omitting the modes manifested by the old boy you chose as a basis, etc.

I believe there was a misunderstanding between us, the mistake of people who want to do away with a precious thing and a basic difference, instead of taking it as the key to their music. That mistake was certainly due more to me than to you: it goes back to the period when I was conscientiously floundering around among your tendencies, with a confidence that comes, only at the beginning, from the use of a general analysis. I would have been absolutely right, had those tendencies been my own, and I did get the better of some of my own. One can say: "I think A and find A wrong," but one cannot say: "You think A and I find A wrong," because you think: A is inaccessible to I. But all these you's and all these I's are robbed by language and, abominably, half done away with. The result was that your you protested against my purely verbal massacre of some of your ideas, as they were expressed. There the blame begins to fall on you; at least, it seems to me that you had—then—only to oppose me, with a simple fact: the irrepressibility of the accused tendencies.

You are mistaken, just as I am, when you reproach me with believing that I alone think *sicut meipsum*. I think in this manner because nothing, really, in the actions or writings of others shows me the contrary. Indeed, that is one of the very points on which I wanted to sound out my contemporary. You know him, those millions of him. Moreover, I was him, and like him I experienced that fear, mentioned in your letter, of finding it all tiresome.

Well, I saw him, at twenty, full of far-reaching ambitions and a certain charm of daring and fear; and at twenty-five, with all the talent you like, but it already had a rancid stink. He is built on ideas that are as rare as they are commonplace, that is to say, not his own. He is so afraid of finding it all tiresome that I find him tiresome. He has a true horror of any change in vision, for he knows that his professional value is tied up with it. Of course, he gets better and better at doing the same thing. (And you, incidentally, are the only one to whom that does not apply.) I know perfectly well that if I had continued to write fourteen-line poems, I would now be writing very good ones: necessarily. That's why stupidity and talent so frequently coexist. It's that same old boy, by the way, who invented genius and talent, like officers and petty officers. He invented Art just as he invented Life, Society, etc., and he'd be a stupendous inventor if all his discoveries didn't tend to dispense with discovering. I myself put the question to him. I ask him if he is willing to find it all tiresome, if he is willing to *overcome;* in short, if he is willing, always, to consider everything that has been done, everything he has done, as *worthless.* And he, who does what he does only so that it be done *already,* who wants to give himself a comfortable past, laughs in my face. I speak to him of power—and he answers me with success.

We talk about literature. I seek an author and I find merely a man—not even a man—a dressmaker. I have an even greater inclination to be severe in that I have known, here and there, a few far more audacious and vigorous individuals, the kind of minds that didn't consider everything as material for a printing press, who asked for difficulties and relied on their dissatisfaction. It was they who spoiled my . . . contemporary for me. I want him to be more maddened.

You speak ill of "artificial flowers" and Wagner. But note—and this is the essence of my system—that although they may not be as beautiful as the real ones, they come out ahead from the point of view of the doing. The mind of the worst sculptor is active; the minds of two beings who make love are reduced to jelly. I know quite well that the happiness of one day and twenty years of research may be equal on paper and in their results —their visible results. But, in the long run—or in the mind itself—calculation comes out ahead, for by its very nature it fortifies each moment.

Anyway, for me there is something real, something . . . endowed with a future, and something viable in that instinct which happened to prevail upon me to move among ways of thinking, more than among thoughts.

In the system of real flowers, life becomes a matter of angling. You quickly come to the point of comparing the value of the pike you caught to that of the time consumed in waiting for it. In the system of artificial flowers, I think it would be almost impossible to lose one atom of time. I know quite well that there is the boredom. . . .

Finally, as everything must be taken into account, I have to own up to a certain bad humor, latent and ever-present. Not so very long ago it was anxiety about tomorrow. Now it's anxiety about today. I am often a bit despondent in the morning upon leaving the place and the moment in which I would have worked well; and every night I look back on the day from which I fell for nothing. Now and then I'm seized by the mad desire to conquer time and to want to find in one second something far more important than all I would have searched for during the whole day, had it been up to me. That mad desire has served me well, but rarely. I fall asleep with something painful in my mind, even if I laugh at myself, saying: "It all comes to the same thing." Or else: "But you wouldn't have done anything." You can see how lucky I am, all the same, to have the kind of head I do, to have no need of "literary accomplishments." In that case, where would I be? It's true that . . .

I am being interrupted, it's preferable. I shall send you this as it is—and it's quite enough.

Your

P. Valéry

160. André Gide to Paul Valéry

Lamalou, October 28, 1899

Let's work the mine! Your letter is excellent and invites me to speak like a cynic. I had better first admit the following: your judgments on that Million, as soon as I feel myself truly excluded, seem to me (almost) very accurate.

And what bothers me in our conversations against Him, is that I can never tell exactly to what point it isn't I, too, who am being attacked; as soon as you lodge me in the annex, I can speak more frankly and play more freely.

Whether a good old cousin of mine says: "Yes, André is trying to find his way. . . ."

Or another: "But, you'll see, when you succeed in one genre, you'll really stick to it!"

Whether P. L. said: "You don't know how to deal with people."

Or whether you said: "You don't spread your nets high enough."

Or: "After *Paludes,* that's not what you *should* have written."

Or again, during our last chat, apropos of a clumsy word *you made me say:* "Ah! yes, there is also the group of those who are awaiting the success that comes at forty-five."

I make little distinction; there is an equal lack of understanding in them all; and if I take your words more seriously, it's because your lack of understanding cannot be excused by stupidity. Or else, owing to the mere fact that I write, must you look at me with a biased look?

Precisely because I win the hostility of others, I *should* win your praise as well; or else my way of acting, writing, and living *must* appear to you as a tissue of practical blunders.

For actually, at thirty I must either have a printing of N thousand, or have the esteem of Valéry (if Valéry is authentic), or be no more than an imbecile (and in that case Val. is too, for writing to me).

You were willing, in your letter, to realize that "our differences are not at all enormous"; moreover, you say a succession of things about me which make rather pleasant reading. . . . And it's to that that you owe today's letter. In it I seem irritated; but the fact that I am a little less irritated explains why I dare to give that impression.

If you don't understand that I am writing to you amicably, and very amicably, tear up my letter, blame my pride, and I shall be able to go back to my hypocrisy. Yet it seemed to me that our *relations* could be more interesting than we managed to make them this past year, and the fact that, from your letter, you, too, seem to suspect as much explains why I quickly, before our next meeting, am plucking and clearing out the thorns that still obstruct the approaches to the mine.

Very much your
André Gide

161. *Paul Valéry to André Gide*

[P. Paris, November 7, 1899]

I want to answer you today but I don't think I can do it as I should, because I'm absolutely exhausted from periods of difficulty and terribly busy nights, things that are beside the point here.

So as not to tire myself too much, I shall merely reread your letter and annotate it.

For example, the sentence:

"Precisely because I win the hostility of others, I *should* win your praise as well, or else my way of acting, writing, and living *must* seem to you a tissue of practical blunders."

Doubtless! say I quickly to the first horn of the dilemma, but the quibble lies in the word: "others." Taking the others as a whole, some of them praise you, *others* attack you. First point, if you charge certain of the latter with a lack of understanding, be fair and see the same failing in some of the former. As a rule, is it not probable that those who attack us understand us (in a body) better than those who praise us? Besides, if you write each of your works *against* the previous one, how do you judge those who like them all?

Basically, then, I make little distinction between those for and those against. As for improving one's admirers—alas! Look,—who could claim to have done it more than Mallarmé? Well, I know by heart the ins and outs of his admirers and the direction taken by their admiration. I see myself among them, and, on that particular point, I prefer myself. Now they—that chosen little group—do not seem to me, in general, to have grasped the most obvious and the simplest principle of the poet's intention, and I personally know very well how different my intention is in being interested in his.

I always come back to the same conclusion: literature can have only three aims—that is, whatever you do, it results in the following three things (each to be considered at its maximum): 1. dough, 2. number of individuals who know your name (and the consequences), 3. personal instruction, by problems of a general nature created by the technique and exercise of the art.

1 and 3 have my sympathies. Anything preferable to 2, except insofar as 2 results in 1.

If you adopt 3, either you give up literature, or you stick with it, but only as something special, episodic. In addition, you are inevitably led to theories analogous to mine, *id est:* the greatest possible awareness and a closer and closer approximation of a calculation. Actually, doing otherwise (in hypothesis 3) doesn't teach us anything, and once the splash of *genius* is spewed up, we're just like anyone else. In other words, our way of thinking has not been affected. Do understand—by way of thinking I don't mean opinions, or a taste for some particular thing, or sensuality applied here and there—I mean a way of seeing all things and a dependency with regard to it. A change of syntax, not of words. A change of country more than a change of regime.

Never forget that in literature the finest book by the finest writer is immediately counterbalanced with the account of a Cook [26] or a Bourgogne, and that the public or reader doesn't have to take into account all the trouble a man has producing Russian campaigns out of his head alone. But his head has to be its own reward. . . .

Therefore, it's true that I don't understand your sport. I find that you think of your public too much or not enough. In fact, I'm sure that you are aware of it. You certainly feel, now and again—how shall I put it?—the sudden need to recover a kind of middle ground that you were fortunately forgetting. On the other hand, it seems to me that an account of your relations would show the same tendency?

I could in no way mistake you for a literary littérateur, copy after copy of whose true portrait, even if he's a Hugo, can be seen at H's Sabbath-day receptions.[27] In other words, I hope and am sure you don't do *that* as one makes sugar or practices medicine or teaches (even enthusiastically). The proof of it is that you work hard not to *imitate* (don't get me wrong! this would need an explanation, I'm using the word here in a very broad sense) and not to *imitate yourself*—and that doubtless you always prefer to interest others less and yourself more.

Note, if I'm right, how gentle the slope is between this way of *thinking* and that in No. 3 above.

Granting this, you can understand how little I understand your sport.

True, I am not made for that kind of understanding. Everything I have done or thought is connected to my existence—IMMEDIATELY. It is strength and weakness. Now, as it happens, this existence, this sense of being or not being, and—especially—this sense of being a certain way (that's the stupendous part!) finds no interest or pleasure in constructing opposing works in order to delude or dazzle the people around. On the contrary, everything disposes it (disposes me) to take on additive properties, to connect its every moment (on condition that it allows them the greatest diversity, and in that line, you have noticed that I don't do too badly!), so

[26] James Cook, *Captain Cook's Voyages,* published in France by Lerouge in 1811.
[27] An allusion to the Saturday literary gatherings at Heredia's.

that I would be able, in this way, to describe the perfect or theoretical state of my being: moments; and—in each of them—*strictly anything;* but, *around them,* a tendency or an art which emerges, without distorting their particularism, and which consists in trying to guess the laws of their transformations or their mutual substitutions—and in proceeding as if those laws were known. I can thus go anywhere. We are not responsible for the ideas that come to us but, *at the very most,* for the fate we decide for them. That, we have perhaps something to do with. The hand we have in it is more clearly conscious of itself. And it's that hand that interests me. The coming and going does too, but what comes and goes leaves me cold, even if it's what the minds of others call an inspired idea or filth or *et cetera,* it's the luck of Job.

Of all possible feelings, the strongest in me is that of *security*—or, if you prefer, infinite defiance. I can have no confidence in what comes and goes. I don't trust it. That's why I have sought more constant things. I don't mistrust them (consequently), that's why I deny myself nothing (in my mind).

Here and now, I can imitate the amusing collection of opinions, in your letter, pertaining to you.

Kolbassine called me "the freest mind that . . ." (fortunately, there was still no Dreyfus! passion would—as they say—have blinded him!).

For Heredia, I am a lazy man. (You bet!) For thousands of others, who are very perspicacious, but not above the belt, I am the gentleman who will never do anything, or the abstracter of quintessences, or a poet who died young, or a fraud, or a bore (those last two are quite correct). For various and sundry, a very original, complicated mind, etc. From other quarters, I have been described as good and as wicked. I have the esteem of M. Ubu. There are also feminine opinions, no less varied. In short, I am the geometric locus of all contradictions.

And what about me, my real opinion about myself? V. is an uneven creature, extremely sensitive, who will never get used to the idea of being what he is, at a particular moment; and who continually disparages himself, lost in the incessant feeling that he has not said his "last word." This feeling proves nothing, but I always have it.

All the above opinions are correct. Especially mine.

. . . .

Let us stop here for today, duty calls. This letter will have neither head nor tail, which is a great advantage. Yet I find it less foggy than I had foreseen at the beginning. If you knew the figured bass that accompanied it, you would perhaps find it more interesting. I am currently facing a fair number of things, I'm not too bored, I'm maddened; after so many internal wars, I aspire after peace, but the means of an honorable peace disgust me, and the enemy who is killing me pleases me.   P.V.

— 1900 —

162. André Gide to Paul Valéry

Friday night [P. January, 1900]

Dear old Paul,

I couldn't possibly make the Ministry tonight in time to catch you on your way out: I shall be there tomorrow, but, for fear that there will be squalls, I'll wait for you in the corner café.

Your
André Gide

163. Paul Valéry to André Gide

[P. Antwerp, June 8, 1900]

My dear André,

Sono felicissimo.[1] I am breathing in an atmosphere of vagueness with as much delight as I once took in fleeing it. Add to that the bliss or vanity of finding that one can suspend a rather old form of discipline.

Through all these moments of a new beginning, I am aware of what I might call a kind of insipid Belgium. Bruges, seen from rather close to, left me undisturbed. Its picturesque quality alone disgusted me a bit. Antwerp has somewhat disappointed me up to now. True, my new state[2] is keeping me from such experiences or riddeks[3] as would be fitting, in order not to be robbed.

But chiefly I am tasting the pleassure of noticing nothing. Yes I am. I look solely, but hardly, within myself, at a kind of elementary reflex of rather old states. This return amuses me *because* I shan't bear it for very long. Otherwise, I should have to begin all over again being stupid, a poet, etc.

At the heart of my suspension between an unknown and M. Teste, there are also a few unquestionable and serious worries. My mother wanted, at all costs, to remain in Paris, and there she is, senselessly, alone in a boarding house! Then, the eternal ghost of the Artillery is tormenting me. Finally, uncertainties and the prospect of moving out, moving in, annoyances, all those bewildering and arithmetic things one calls the seriousness of life. . . .

[1] I am very happy.

[2] In February, 1900, Paul Valéry became engaged to Jeannie Gobillard, Berthe Morisot's niece. Their marriage took place on May 31, the same day as that of Julie Manet (Berthe Morisot's daughter) and Ernest Rouart, brother of Eugène, Louis, and Alexis. The latter was to become Agathe Valéry's father-in-law. Valéry wrote this letter during his honeymoon in Belgium.

[3] A Flemish word meaning wanderings, and in a wider sense, places for wandering. Valéry is doubtless alluding to the "red-light" district in the port of Antwerp.

I have learned, by letter, that your bookcase is really fine. If, as I believe, it's a turning one, and meant to be at the tips of one's fingers, I see it full of my reference works—that is, lots of geometers—an *Henri Brulard,* a *Divagations,*[4] well, my fixed points. You shall perhaps deliver me from the eternal litter on my table. Do take this as tremendous thanks!

Au revoir, my good André. Just think, I can now write you: my wife . . . you and yours, her . . .

But I shan't fill in the blanks this time. I shan't write out what *she* has instructed me to add for "you both" at the end of this kind of letter. It would already sound too "married," I felt. And well, that's how it is all the same.

Your old and recent
P. Valéry

164. *Paul Valéry to André Gide*

[P. Paris, August 29, 1900]

My dear André,

I haven't written sooner because I fancied I didn't know where Cuverville was. I just now thought of Criquetot-L'Esneval. . . .

I am continuing in my position at M. Lebey's.[5] It's pleasant, actually, and limited. Anyhow, he is very considerate of me and sometimes tells me about patches of contemporary history or particular business events, which have a certain zest.

I still worry about what will happen at the end of my six-month leave? There lies the shadow. I have a feeling I shall be exceedingly annoyed if I have to go back to the jail.

Another worry is my wife's health. It turns out that she is very anemic

---

[4] By Mallarmé (Fasquelle, 1897).

[5] Edouard Lebey, director of the Agence Havas. His nephew, André Lebey, a poet on the staff of *Le Centaure,* was a friend of Paul Valéry's. Valéry was employed by Edouard Lebey as his personal secretary, ostensibly for a period of six months. Actually, Valéry stayed on with him until Lebey's death in February, 1922. The following is André Gide's description of Valéry's role: "A confidential job in which Valéry had all the time he needed to exercise his wisdom, his competence in political, diplomatic, and financial matters, his unerring judgment, his integrity, his tact, as well as his exquisite courtesy of manner and the subtlety of his feelings. He spoke of that old man, to whom he became very attached, with great deference: a kind of old Leuwen, he said, suffering from Parkinson's disease, which allowed him no control of his movements. To those who came to see him, he said, holding out a hand shaken by his disability: "Stop my hand, if you please." Sitting in a large armchair, he would listen to the newspapers and Bourdaloue's sermons (which he preferred to Bossuet's) being read to him; but Valéry confessed to me that he often skipped pages. That was to last months, years. And doubtless he learned a great deal with that wise old man, in those ticklish duties which put the practical qualities of his mind to the test." (*L'Arche,* October 1945.)

just now, with faintness, headaches, and other types of discomfort. It reacts somewhat on me, and together we look after each other.

But I had to interrupt the useful work of dictating my notes, to have a clean copy, just as it was beginning to take shape.

I can tell, by looking at this little stack, how bored the potential reader would be if ever I published a critical collection of my *Questiones*. As my aim is purely linguistic, representative, and consists in seeking a convenient figure of knowledge, among an infinity of others that are equally possible, I must do without any metaphysical appeal. I see no good reason why a philosophy or a psychology should give more ideas on the great Commonplaces (Life, Fate, Self, etc.) than geometry.

It's curious that in no professional philosopher can one find a concern with establishing as precisely as possible the connection between words or phrases and internal facts. It's a study that amuses me greatly, the principle of which was suggested to me by reflections about time and by the theory of the construction of geographical maps, that is to say, transformations of figures.

So the theory of words is keeping me busy these days, and it seems to me I've found the principle behind it. You should see the definitions that grammars give for *word!* They remind me of the definition of a straight line, regarding which the geometers, for fear of having to make use of what *is*—that is to say, an image and a rather simple property of that image —invented the most vicious-circle kind of propositions imaginable.

On the other hand, I don't write very often or I rewrite a sentence at the beginning of *Agathe*.[6] It's very hard indeed. But where there's no difficulty, there's no pleasure in writing.

As I haven't seen a living *literary* soul, I can give you no information in that category.

I assume that your wife can now use her arm, and is regaining strength.[7] If handshakes are allowed, I should be happy if she'd keep one for me, or rather two, and even three, since I am several.

But we must not tire her.

Your

P. Valéry

[6] *Agathe* or *Le Manuscrit trouvé dans une cervelle,* a prose work. It has already been mentioned as *Le Sommeil d'Agathe*. Valéry was doubtless especially fond of the name Agathe, since he was to give it to his daughter a few years later.

[7] On July 13, just before leaving for Cuverville, Mme. Gide was knocked down by a car on the Place de la Concorde and was injured. A bad fracture in one arm necessitated an operation.

165. André Gide to Paul Valéry

[Lamalou] October 15, 1900

My dear Paul,

I was hoping to stop off in Paris for a week. A telegram from Rouart suddenly called me to Les Plaines,[8] leaving me no time to see you again. It made me sad, and the sadness is still with me; I know perfectly well that our friendship does not depend on a chat or two; but, although I have long been a friend of *yours*, I am not yet a friend to *you both*, and I have the right to be a bit worried about my absence and my silence. During all this time, you are both living; ties are quickly woven in Paris, and as I'm still a sentimental soul, I am terrified of finding, on my return, that my place has been filled, for having been left empty too long. Yet I remember (and am comforted by the fact) that last year, in this very Lamalou where I am now vegetating for a month, I sent you and received from you the most important of letters, and as a result of resuming our correspondance, our communication was deepened and our relations more clearly defined. So write to me, dear old Paul: I left you at such a strange turning-point in life that nothing has yet managed to assure me that I won't find you changed. But what does it matter: we have almost no idea of what we love in someone. What news of Havas and the War?[9] And what news of your writing? I have learned that you are moving. . . . Speak, tell me all.

I spent four days at Les Plaines, and am now growing desperate at my solitude. My wife, in the meantime, has about closed up Cuverville and is winding up a few arrangements. Her arm is now as "reduced" as it can be; I fear it may remain somewhat deformed, but only slightly. It has recovered its movement and flexibility. She is supposed to join me here; but I doubt that I'll have the courage to wait for her; I'm planning to bring my cure to an abrupt end and to flee. But I haven't yet mentioned it. . . .

Question: is your brother the kind of man who would be annoyed or overjoyed, if I went to see him at Plaisance?[10] I have discovered that it can be done from here. . . . But first, answer me bluntly.

News: Paul Laurens is getting married; a very suitable marriage, etc.[11]

Au revoir; I am worn out, dying of boredom and irritation, thinking confused.

My best wishes to your wife; all my respectful affection to your mother.

Your
André Gide

[8] The name of the country estate managed by Eugène Rouart, not far from Autun.
[9] The Agence Havas and the Ministry of War.
[10] An estate in the Aveyron owned by the family of Valéry's sister-in-law, Mlle Descolys, who in 1897 became Mme Jules Valéry.
[11] Paul Laurens married Berthe Guérin on October 10, 1900.

166. Paul Valéry to André Gide
My dear André,

I am answering your letter, which exudes a certain discouragement, at the very earliest possible moment. Why this cure at Lamalou?

I had written to Cuverville, but probably didn't say anything that matters since you imagine I'm going to bestow on just anyone the armchair, in my inner hovel, that belongs to you.

Nor will *connubium* deprive you of it. Our ties are too . . . abstract for diversity in life to interfere with them, and we interest each other enough to interest each other forever. All our adventures—even that kind of hostile friendship which, during your previous stay in Lamalou, was momentarily ours, and very close—have merely resulted in enormously tangling up a thing or two and in very successfully untangling all the rest. I hope we make very frequent use of clearly defined types whose turn of mind is other than ours, and just as pleasing and as different as possible! Ideally: as *possible* as possible!

The stupid thing in this question, as in all others, is that we have only one word (friends) for very diverse types of reciprocity.

If you like and if you agree, I should say that in a certain sense we are harnessed to the same beam and know each other as such, or are subjects of the same power, that power being placed at a distance from all others as constantly as one likes.

But you can find thousands of better approximations. . . .

Anyhow, what I've written above is probably not clear—it's tossed off—but it's very definite.

I have not yet perceived any change in me other than one of existence, that is, another way of wasting the time one always wastes, in any existence. It seems to me that the rest is holding its own.

Except that I am considerably bored writing *Agathe* as an imposed lesson, given the way the subject has cooled off. I'm condemned to writing retroactively, with no warmth, no objective, no desire, and no pleasure—like a complete imbecile,—an imbecile being he to whom his duty is an awful nuisance, and who performs it. . . .

I am struck by the coincidence of your depression and P. L.'s. They are very different, I know, but less than you two are. Up until now, I had almost a monopoly on those rotten states. The more I go on, the more I feel a slave to the physical, that is, to I'm not sure what, and I thought you were less bound than I to your flesh and nerves. Here is a title worth meditating on constantly (so that it be worth something): theory of the body's disobedience.

I went to *Le Mercure* a few days ago. It's been centuries. Chatted rather gaily but with no interest whatever. It has *become* impossible to indulge in that charming sport, no doubt of it. At times I have a mind to "advertise" for conversationalists, it's annoying. I like people who jump as quickly as I do, and who can forget in speaking as one forgets during certain rapid movements. The true *verbal* analogy with music (if there is one) is the colloquy that permits all transitions and all—discords. But no performers or no music, and none of us yet has the grandeur to perform solos like Mallarmé's.

There's a pleasure that's out.

Bloy just wrote a book against Zola.[12] It's filled with excrement, but there's so much of it the result is almost imposing. Anyhow, I was convulsed when I read it. Therefore, gratitude and glory to the author.

I shall drop this infinitely anharmonious [*sic*] letter, written in the midst of moving, to give *Agathe* an hour before dinner. Do consider it chit-chat which I almost drew out in order to avoid the above-mentioned labor.

This is not a dialogue between you and me, I am still a bit too shaky in the saddle (or chair) to chat comfortably. Also, I am not yet used to my wall and my table.[13]

> Your
> P. V.

I'm certain that my brother *would be delighted to have you at Plaisance* —where he is bored stiff—but, according to the latest news, he seemed to be getting himself mobilized to return to Montpellier.

So write him to make sure, and don't fret too much at Lamalou.

> P. V.

167. *André Gide to Paul Valéry*

Biskra, December 26 [1900]

Dear Paul,

You can imagine how the following three lines in a letter from Marcel[14] worried me: "I looked for Valéry" (Drouin spent thirty-six hours in Paris to attend Paul Laurens' wedding) "in order to see him and to pass on, somewhat belatedly, an invitation from Paul L. Unfortunately, number 64, avenue V.-Hugo has not yet been built. At 54 Valéry is known only by reason of a few stray letters they had to return to the post office!" What gave my wife the idea that you lived at 54? I don't know, the fact remains that, from Algiers, it was to 54 that she addressed a letter to your wife (six weeks ago). It was to 54 that I myself wrote you at about the same time. It is now needless, I think, to try and unearth those letters, but at least don't believe . . . don't either of you believe that we kept silent, and stop being so yourself and yourselves.

[12] Léon Bloy's *Je m'accuse* . . . (La Maison d'Art).
[13] Valéry had just moved to 57, avenue Victor-Hugo, in Paris.
[14] Marcel Drouin.

I have just come back (last night) exhausted from a twelve-day tour in the Souffi. On my return I found my poor wife exhausted from waiting for me.

The hideousness of the country we traveled through was beyond my gravest expectations, but as well as great fatigue, I am left with the kind of intoxication one gets from long crossings, the infinite bitterness of nights without lodgings (or almost), the exaltation of dawns and nightfall . . . (the hardest day, our mules walked sixty-seven kilometers, from six in the morning to seven in the evening, in sand, and at night we had to sleep on the ground), and the evenings, sitting round a fire. Similar to the twenty-eight days of military service, actually—you know what they're like. At Lamalou, my old doctor claimed that the twenty-eight days and the thirteen days furnished him with more cases of ataxia to cure than any intellectual excesses or any sprees. So let's beware. I have no desires other than work, no visions other than my study in Paris. The idea that you'll come to see me at once, old Paul, makes me desire it all the more; I am so tired this morning that avenue V.-H. seems to me at the ends of the earth. If the crossing weren't horrible, I'd sail straight for Marseilles from Tunis, our next stop; but one must reckon with the gods—we are therefore thinking of reaching Trapani first.

Au revoir; address a good letter to Tunis, telling me that you and your wife are fine and that neither of you has forgotten us at all, and I am

your fidus
André G.

And all good wishes to you both for a happy New Year.

Our best regards to your mother.

You are the reason for our going to see Bizerte; I remember what you said about it.

I just found your genuine address in a letter from you, from Lamalou.

168. Paul Valéry to André Gide

57, avenue Victor-Hugo [15]
December 31, 1900

My dear André,

I have been awaiting your address for centuries (your wife's letter never arrived, I shall claim it), I was dumbfounded by your silence, and in the end I thought you were in Paris, you held your peace for so long.

Finally, here is your handwriting, and I am very glad to see it, my dear old André.

Let's chat like people of the last century.

---

[15] Valéry was to live at that address (third floor) from the fall of 1900 to the summer of 1902.

But no. I've been made singularly stupid by December 31.

Nothing much new, and, alas, nothing new about my job, except that I am continuing *apud* L.,[16] without seeing anything definite *nell' avvenire*.[17]

My wife has been feeling very poorly because of a vaccination. The doctor triumphant, me absolutely furious. It's beginning to let up.

I believe there's a coolness between P. L. and me. I suppose I committed some offense against the dear man's imaginary protocol. He has come to prefer an observance of it to simple friendship. In fact, I received an *unassailable* letter from him. I shall try to straighten it out. I'm suspicious enough by nature to think that a friend who comes to see you in cuirass and cuisse is no longer that much your friend.

Whereupon, my dear fellow, not another word. Duty awaits, and I wanted to answer you forthwith.

Wait for the storm to die down a bit and then cross.

My mother and my wife thank you and send you their best wishes.

I send all my regards to your wife. You can't know how much we all love her.

Hugs and kisses in *saecula, -orum*.   P. V.

— 1901 —

169. André Gide to Paul Valéry

Thursday night [P. March 28, 1901]

My dear Paul,

I had so seriously set my mind on coming to see you tonight that, finding I can't, I feel as though I'm breaking a date . . . but at least, please don't read too much into my silence and my disappearance; you perhaps know that I had to rush off to Naples; that on my return I found my whole family shattered by the death of my Aunt Démarest . . .[1] and by lots of other things, so that I have had hardly any time to myself, and now that I might hope to breathe a little, rehearsals of my *Candaule* are beginning.[2]

---

[16] With Lebey.

[17] In the future.

[1] Mme Guillaume Démarest, née Claire Rondeaux, Gide's maternal aunt.

[2] *Le Roi Candaule,* drama in three acts, published by La Librairie de la Revue Blanche in 1901, then republished in 1930 by the N.R.F., was performed at the Nouveau-Théâtre by Lugné-Poe on May 9, 1901. Lugné-Poe played the part of Candaule, and Edouard de Max the part of Gygès. The play was performed again in 1904.

And yet I should like to see you again somewhat alone, before the Marcel Drouins arrive (Easter holidays) and we all get together with them, as they count on us doing. So the first day I can, I shall ring your bell about five, unless you say otherwise.

Meanwhile, I am completely worn out, but very much your

André Gide

170. Paul Valéry to André Gide

Sunday, 57, avenue Victor-Hugo
[P. June 24, 1901]

My dear André,

It is finally decided that I shall foresake the Ministry on the formal and precise promise of a job at the agency.[3] It really didn't take too much persuading to get me to give up the idea of going back, and I have made up my mind. Thus I am building on the unknown, but the known was so tiresome! My mother left for Montpellier yesterday, changing the direction of her worries by moving away. My sister-in-law is still feeling poorly. This paludism is boundless (though *Paludes* gave up on it).

And I myself am dying of the heat here. Steam room and notebooks.

From time to time a resolution claims my attention. And as is my wont, I see it at once in the form of oblivion. I nevertheless begin to implement it, certain that I or some other thing will interrupt it.

For example, a little while ago I wrote at the top of a page: *Definitions.* That title gave rise to a few difficulties. Whence six to eight lines in the eternal notebook that's always open. I came back to my empty page, and I wrote a half-dozen definitions of my vintage. At that point I was interrupted. I got up with the certainty that this was the very end of work that would be most useful, if needs be, to find my bearings in my explorations.

The fact is that I never touch it again. But I have fortunately come to the point of barely taking anything but the present moment into account any more, so that each day I leave behind me a page that I generally never turn again. All that survives of this calendar, I esteem, for it has remained in my mind. To have been so struck by what you've manufactured that you remember it is a kind of sign, actually. Not worse than any other.

Few people at the Mallarmé wedding. I had the glory of taking beautiful Thadée Natanson in on my arm. Mme Mallarmé led the procession with an old general in red and gold, etc.[4]

[3] The Agence Havas, whose director, Edouard Lebey, had just employed Valéry as his personal secretary for a trial period.

[4] Geneviève Mallarmé married Dr. Edmond Bonniot, a habitué of Mallarmé's "Tuesdays" and one of his great admirers. "Beautiful Thadée Natanson" designates the wife of Thadée Natanson, director of *La Revue Blanche*.

I read *Eureka* to my employer. I felt that I was perhaps wrong x years ago not to have written some article or other on Poe.[5] Now I have no inclination whatever to do it. Still, that one has a unique title. He is absolutely the only writer who had the intuition to connect literature with the mind. I deduce this entirely from the following propositions:

Literature is a property of the mind. The mind is *such and such a thing*. Therefore, etc.

One old boy alone discovered that very simple idea, and applied it (only in part, for lack of enough detail, in the minor premise of the above syllogism). If writing has the slightest importance, this idea is as important as Descartes' "take-off." And in both cases, the question is nothing less than one of substituting a general type of research and *hypotheses* for empiricism.

At bottom, Mallarmé did in detail, I mean expression, etc., what the other did in principle. . . . But the field of application is far broader than the notion of *method* would at first suggest, and than any possible particular work.

Today, I can judge what an influence that former persistent reading had on me. . . .

What I reproach, therefore, in most literature is a juggling with things whose scope the author is unable to gauge. This reproach is only personal, naturally; I mean that *that* is the reason for my not being gripped by most literature. Also, what becomes of the sport when it meets up with a reader like myself? I should be very much afraid of a reader like myself. And if I don't write for someone like myself, I am writing in space, I'm shooting at an empty hat, I am not hitting the milieu in which I can *reproduce* myself.

Literature does not suffer objections. That's why the beginning is ticklish, the continuation limited; and the end always false. The whole question is to decide whether there is any point in perspiring over one's paper with an eye to someone who's bloody well not up to making objections. And every author implies a strange faith in that Someone—the eternal Customer.

Needless to say, I was merely speculating. *Le Mercure* will not close its doors on the basis of my opinion. And yet I'm right. How comical it is, after all, to read a book, knowing well that the author couldn't justify three lines of it. Even Stendhal, almost, could be boiled down to marionettes. And yet I love Stendhal, and I'll almost never say to him: "What do I care about that which doesn't resist me?"

Relative obscurity is what gives Mallarmé resistance.

[5] Twenty years later he did write the article, which served as the Introduction to an edition of *Eurêka* (Paris, Pelletan-Helleu, 1923) and was dedicated to Lucien Fabre (cf. *Variété I*, Gallimard, 1924).

Let's leave these noble and gloomy subjects. Avenue Victor-Hugo is deafening this Sunday, for heat brings out imbeciles, all of whom should be bare naked on their innumerable beds.

The more I go on, the more the masses—that is, today, absolutely everyone—disgust me, given that they're no longer any good as a plastic substance. They'll end up shapeless and happy.

Is Cuverville more to your liking than Lamalou? And what does one do there? I, too, am beginning to long for plants, lazy living, and a sea too long foresaken. It seems to me centuries that I haven't kicked my heels in the water, unless . . . intellectually . . . probably . . . but neverthe-less . . . oh dear! . . . Yes, of course! Of course!

Please tell your wife that before leaving, my mother instructed me to send her all possible regards; Jeannie and my sister-in-law would do the same if they were here, but I'm too lazy to go and tell them, and your wife won't be angry with me, because really, I'm too hot.

Write soon, won't you?

Your
P. V.

171. *André Gide to Paul Valéry*

Cuverville [P. July 5, 1901]

Dear Paul,

My wife is impatiently awaiting an answer to her letter (true, you were just as impatiently awaiting, I hope, my answer to yours, and that makes up for it). But can't you really induce your women to come? Your sister would get a good rest; she would finally put an end here to her long-drawn-out convalescence.

And naturally, if you yourself can make it, come along, but let me warn you that from the 13th to the 16th, I shall be wandering around La Roque, where I have "business"; a question of health as well; and the need for a change of ideas. I haven't had many to spare since I left Paris; and those that were turning rancid I discarded and put into the "lecture" I have just taken agonizing pains to write: it's the same one I was to have given for the "Indépendants," the text of which I've messed around with to oblige *L'Ermitage*.[6] If those interested have only one-quarter of the trouble reading it that I have taken to write it, I should consider myself adequately avenged. Well, got to give one's self a reason for being.

And now, I am re-imprisoning myself in my novel;[7] I should have written it at least two years ago; at present, the taste is gone; I don't like the "dry genre" any more; but one is always late in writing; the annoying

---

[6] *Les Limites de l'Art,* a lecture that was to be published in the small collection of *L'Ermitage* that same year.

[7] *L'Immoraliste* (Ed. du Mercure de France, 1902).

thing is that it stops development; there is always something within or beside one's self that is not up to date and that nags. . . .

Ah! so much the better for your confounded Ministry.

Bits of gossip: I received a *Roi Pausole* [8] (1st edition), with "To André Gide— . . . naturally—Pierre Louÿs." The dedication is funny, but the book, hardly; I searched in vain for those well-known changes that were promised. . . .

Terrible heat has been forecast.

And *Agathe?*

Much love to you three from us two, and when you write to Montpellier, choose from among the best greetings a few *ad hoc.*

> Your
> A. G.

172. *Paul Valéry to André Gide*

> Paris, July 14, 1901 [P.]
> Saturday, I think

My dear André,

I am dying of the heat. I urged my wife to go and at least breathe among your trees, but as you have learned, my sister-in-law is still ailing—so the plan is sunk. I should have liked to go with them. It's been so long since I've led a lazy rural life. . . . Oh well!

An anecdote, but please keep it strictly to yourself. Yesterday, after dinner, I went (as I do every evening) to see my employer, whom I found in his little garden facing a spray of water from the hose, and I took the seat next to his. Night was forming. . . . Suddenly he said: "Do you know that you have had an enormous influence on me?" (. . . we protested . . .) "—Yes, on my mind—You have made me go back to religion.—??!!—I have found peace in it and am grateful to you, etc."

It appears that it was the result of my criticism. I was rather touched by that act. But who would have believed it?

Curiously enough, it's not the first time I have had such an adventure. But what strange kind of apostle am I? I must admit I have a passion for the Church. I have not found one screw that doesn't fit wonderfully, nor one piece missing. All the qualities of the ideal mechanism, and first and foremost, the game's being independent of the value of its agents, etc. But that estimation is rather questionable, basically more terrible than heterodoxy or freethinking. Yet that's the effect it has. So?

A storm has blown up, it has finally burst. Nothing is more curious than the noise of thunder. *Agathe* sweats and retreats. I have a feeling I'm going to remove half of my second notebook. In a subject where there is no

[8] *Les Aventures du Roi Pausole,* a novel by Pierre Louÿs, published in 1901 (Fasquelle).

possible order, since, by definition, it takes place *before* any order, I can't manage to juxtapose my ideas. They are so rarefied, rendered irreducible, that I can't close up the arch and get out of a tedious parallelism.

I knew about the *naturally*[9] beforehand. But I don't understand too well, or else it's very far from the state of mind I had told you about.

I am much more satisfied with my eternal little notes than with *Agathe*. It seems to me that I have made quite some progress these days. But the more I go on, the less I see a whole, in the *book* sense of the word. Anyway, on that point I have the absolute conviction that it would be (should the occasion arise) a book for no one. Some are infected by their studies and their idiotic vocabulary. The others would not get the point. My innovation is to make use of conceptions as devices and not as realities, considering, moreover, the diverse conceptions as transformable by one another. On the other hand, a host of related observations furnish me with lots of problems, all of which come down to questions of either duration or language (in the most general sense of the term—that is, any notation). So out of that broad outline I constructed a kind of general theory of notations, which was lacking, I think. I had long observed that, in reality, philosophers have investigated little more than meanings of words. As a result, they teach us nothing clear about the mind but only about the internal relations of language, that language being based on nothing. It's easy to prove. For instance, you would waste your time trying to find in them a solution to the following general problem, which I consider of capital importance: "What does language preserve?" I'll explain. A geographical map, according to the system of projection adopted, preserves, for example, the proportion which the lines of the terrain bear to each other, or the angles of two lines of the terrain, etc. As you see, we don't have such rules for ordinary language. Algebraic language preserves *ad libitum* the *individuality* of quantities and the operations, etc.

But having been interrupted, I leave you. . . .

I thank you very much for your invitation. I have a feeling I would have chatted with you for a long time somewhere in the grass. Too bad.

Give my regards to your wife.

> Your
> P. Valéry

173. *André Gide to Paul Valéry*

August 27 [1901]

Dear friend,

Madeleine had forwarded your letter to me. . . . What happened? Was my telegram misleading? or did you misread it? Marcel and I looked for

[9] Allusion to Pierre Louÿs' dedication to Gide in a copy of *Le Roi Pausole*.

you, then on *Saturday evening* waited far into the night; I am even sorrier not to have seen you, inasmuch as, now, where and when will it be? The news of your sister-in-law makes us very sad indeed; do please let us know how you find her.

Returned to Cuverville last night to find icy winds and rain. Marcel is beginning his twenty-eight days of military service.

Au revoir. All our regards.

André G.

174. Paul Valéry to André Gide

[P. Paris, September 17, 1901]

My dear André,

I returned [10] to Paris yesterday morning, called back only by L.,[11] leaving my ailing wife down there with my sister-in-law. One is in one bed, the other in the other, and as one is directly above the other, they talk through the thin ceiling of pine boards.

For two or three days this shaken holiday threatened to be amusing. A few conversations with Fontaine [12] or Redon, a lovely walk and not a bit of work, even negative. But, to finish it for me, just as my wife's health was beginning to worry me, this rather sudden departure had to take place.

I am making a gigantic effort to write to you, but actually I may almost manage it here, whereas there, I should have dropped the paper by now.

The region is nice with its subdued ocean and bights, which they always call "coves." * On the Royan side, that is, toward the northwest of Saint-Georges, in each cove there is a bathing establishment, some coterie or other, and as they are well separated, each has its own horizon. We have rented a villa quite near the shore, very large and pleasant. Fortunately, I finally came across a doctor who is a gentleman and conscientious, and whose one delight in this region is waiting for October in order to enjoy the sunsets.

Be that as it may, I pressed him hard, and almost induced him to act vigorously. It would seem that his treatment brings results, and I noticed a relatively big improvement.

How often I have regretted not being a doctor myself and not being able

---

[10] From Saint-Georges-de-Didonne (Charente Maritime), where the painter Odilon Redon had rented a villa.

[11] Edouard Lebey.

[12] Arthur Fontaine (1860–1931), uncle of Eugène Rouart, graduate of the Ecole Polytechnique, was not only trained in science but had a discriminating taste for literature. Founder of the Labor Office, promoter of the international legislation of labor, it was to him that André Gide was to dedicate *Le Retour de l'Enfant prodigue,* published in 1907 in the March–May issue of *Vers et Prose.* It was at his home that Léon-Paul Fargue, in 1917, was to read *La Jeune Parque.*

* *Translator's note: conches.* a term used only in southwest France.

to be one! In the case of Paule,[13] I observed her minutely for hours, it's one of the strangest cases and it seemed to me that, had I been a doctor, I should have diagnosed it.

In medicine they are just barely beginning to look into the total functioning of the system. Now all strange illnesses are strange because their symptoms have no visible or anatomical connection, and there is no science of will-o'-the-wisps.

But how we conform to the vacillation of general energy all the same! Life, using units of time, has theorems that are still unknown but that may be guessed. A doctor sees the cranks, pistons, and a little of the metal of the machine, but as for work and power, he still sees nothing. Example: when it comes to the nervous system, in which actually no physiology is visible, the therapeutist sinks into the lower depths where occultists, aestheticians, and philosophers eat their own feet.

Yours,

P. V.

— 1902 —

175. *André Gide to Paul Valéry*

Saturday [P. April 6, 1902]

Dear old Paul,

I shall merely copy out the following:

"Fritillary:

"Etym.: *fritillus:* dicebox, liliaceae family.

"French synon.: *couronne impériale* . . .

". . . moreover, the six sections of the flower are provided internally with a small nectariferous cavity simulating a glass eye or a large nacreous pearl, surrounded by a blackish aureole, and filled with a sweet liquid . . . ," etc.

I thought the "small nectariferous cavity" * would please you.

Au revoir. Regards to your family.

Your

André G.

176. *Paul Valéry to André Gide*

[P. Paris, April 9, 1902]

Dear Horticultural André,

But what is the use of those little cavities? Are they glasses of sugar and water for insects, requisites for a lecture on finality?

[13] Paule Gobillard, Paul Valéry's sister-in-law.

* *Translator's note:* "fossette nectarifère."

Have you read *Fragments d'Huber sur les abeilles?* [1] I don't understand a thing about those monarchic animals, but the above-mentioned fragments are fascinating. I'll give you my copy the day you put a few beehives in your Cuverville. *My* weakness would be spiders. All spiders attract me. . . . Don't worry: I'm not going to reel off any threads here. My notebooks are quite enough. On the days I treat myself well, I see myself running about on a difficult web, sensitive as water, a web in which gross stupidities would be caught, but escape.

I don't know if you know that I have included in my twaddle an addendum (obviously a pudendum) * independent of my ordinary point of view. If I've agreed to it, it's because it came of itself, and was not a deliberate invention.

I have tried (after long and past encounters with difficulties), in my sketch of man, to make use of a conception analogous to the energy of physicists. You can perhaps sense the advantage there would be in representing and unifying everything in "the mind" that appears to us in the form of waste, preservation, successive transformations, instantaneous states, reversibility, etc.

The realization of all that is merely a question of good definitions— initial definitions. Once that's done, the gain would be the possibility of representing, with great precision, the state of knowledge between two given moments.

I spent the little useful time I've had these days in making rather good progress with that endeavor. I shan't go into it in detail. It's tiresome to write out.

Up to now, no one has ever dared bring the noddle into the total energy of the Universe. And, failing to be able to, they've gone so far as to call the phenomenon: mental epiphenomenon. Which is rather comical.

I took another direction. I constructed a special notion for those phenomena by observing that the difficulty is inverse. In the physical world, it consists in finding the unity behind the forms, and *here,* it consists in rediscovering the diversity. The unity is given.

The whole question will be to see whether I succeed in finding my energy, parallel in its laws to physical energy. These types of analogies go to make up the method of physics and have led to that great edifice, general physics—which is no more than a limited pile of purified and perfected concepts.

---

[1] Published in 1829 (Paris, Bureau de la "Bibliothèque choisie"), with a preface by Dr. Mayraux, after a book by François Huber (1750–1831), published in 1792 in Geneva: *Nouvelles Observations sur les Abeilles.*

* *Translator's note:* The play on words in French is: "J'ai annexé . . . une partie (évidemment honteuse). . . ."

Scoff at these lines and lock them up. On that condition, I promise you the energetics theory of syntax.

Your

P. V.

177. *André Gide to Paul Valéry*

[P. July 1902]

Dear Paul,

Tomorrow, Wednesday, at around noon, I'll come to see you if I'm here. But above all, don't upset any plans for me. I wanted to let you know earlier, but I am

your unexpected

André Gide

178. *Paul Valéry to André Gide*

[P. Paris, September 18, 1902]

3:30 P.M.

My dear André,

My wife is reproaching me from the top of the stairs for having refused —disagreeably—to explain my work to you. Having denied that, I shall proceed.

True, I wasn't inclined to talk about it. The state it's in now is ineffable. I have so many different considerations on my mind, so many beginnings or roads are taking shape that I couldn't state them clearly. You know there is no one to whom I would rather confide my endeavors. Glancing together, in a safe corner, through one of those notebooks I keep day by day—and whose only connection is me—would please me very deeply. You can well imagine that, despite my perseverance, I sometimes have enormous doubts about all these boxed-up adventures. I would need to tell someone about them, if only to remember them and to test them better in the rapidity of conversation.

I am to the point where I often talk about them to Mr. L.[2] A monologue in which he is good enough to appear interested.

He asks anxiously: "Have you written all that? —Yes, sir, I have noted it down."

But God knows if I could take the measure of all those ideas at just a glance. You know what it is: the minute observation of mental *truth,* a systematic reducing of *all* language to certain properties, incessant research for unities (as it were) to which all human processes should be reduced. Anyhow, the last few months I have added some new chapters to it that are closely bound up with physiology, and are, as it were, the reducing of

---

[2] Edouard Lebey.

physical facts, indispensable to knowledge, to axioms and formulas. On that I have still much to do, etc. But it means nothing without explanations, precise details, and I repeat: this is not the moment.

That's about it. I'm off to 38 *bis*.[3]

Your

P. V.

179. *Paul Valéry to André Gide*

[P. Paris, December 3, 1902]

My dear André,

On my way back from your place, I realize that one remark or one digression was missing from my whimsical account of "classical" art. Here it is, for it supports my hypothesis a bit, without diminishing its purely conversational scope. . . .

You remember I talked about laws—arbitrary, perceptible, outside the subject? . . .

Well, here's the remark. In the so-called classical periods (antiquity, seventeenth century, etc.), people generally believed in the possibility of the arbitrary. They did not believe—generally—that everything was determined, partial; and precious in itself as a document or a fragment of laws.

So, they added laws. They constructed, a priori, a likeness between the work of art and the natural fact considered as a product of Fatum or else of divine prescience and power.

The situation is reversed. No arbitrary will, a boundless subordination of impersonal laws. Such is the feeling today (I am not disputing it, of course). Well, then, the most ordinary fragment of the most ordinary work of art belongs necessarily to the great mechanism. . . . The modern importance of notes, bits of paper that often take more out of us than books constructed *secundum artem*. Realism. Vitalism. Naturism, in short, all the heresies. Well, then, again, what's the use of composing? It only means uselessly making *forgeries*. We are no longer conscious of the composition, because we *want* to feel or believe we feel the connection of anything to Everything.

And in point of fact—in adding one individual to anything at all—the sum is always COMPOSED.

On the other hand, I think it correct to consider a work of art a logical and psychological forgery. But this view is enormously awkward for art. So?

In truth, I believe that what we call art is destined either to disappear or to become unrecognizable. Art is in the process of not escaping from

---

[3] Avenue du Bois (now avenue Foch), address of Edouard Lebey.

experiments and exact analysis. I feel it and I see indications of it. It won't be long before a certain amount of still undeveloped research manages to do it. Yet if only some awakened element could materially survive today's popular mess.

. . . To sum up, you see what I mean: we know almost too much to be true classicists. Euclid, who was classical science, has himself been shaken after twenty centuries of constant fair weather. His work shows us what constituted absolute classical chic, the rigor of the arbitrary.

Today we must accept the personality—which is holy! Who would want to bow—and why?—to a regulation? Look at poetry, look at music. Talent, on the contrary, is recognized by its power of dissolution. Equality —which is a feeling—results in abolishing that which was common to all men. Death of criticism, owing to talent and lack of discipline.

Etc.

> Your
> **P. V.**

— 1903 —

180. Paul Valéry to André Gide

[P. Paris, February 25, 1903]

My dear André,

I intended to come and see you today, since you're leaving tomorrow.

But I'm dead-beat, I can manage no more than to remain in an armchair, without doing a bloody thing.

Everyone here is like me. They are nothing but played-out creatures. . . .

Give your wife the news I gave you a few days ago. But we are not mentioning it just yet.

My wife is rather tired.[1] Every day there's something new, painful spots, sensitivites that break out, and hide, and disturb her nights, etc.

These are indeed singular modulations. I feel them at a distance.

Needless to say, I am not doing one bloody thing.

See you when?

> Your
> **P. V.**

Are you reading *L'Inconstante?*[2] Have you read *Le Petit Ami?*[3] Will you read *Le Mariage de Minuit?*[4]

[1] Mme Valéry was expecting a baby. Claude was born on August 14, 1903.
[2] Novel by Gérard d'Houville.
[3] Novel by Paul Léautaud.
[4] Novel by Henri de Régnier.

I drank [*sic*] all that, it's perfect.
And yet P. L.⁵ is in Biarritz.

181. *André Gide to Paul Valéry* *

Cuverville, July 2 [1903]

My dear Paul,

The news your mother gave me about you twelve days ago was not so good that I could go on lightheartedly, without worrying about your silence. Here we think of you constantly. My wife is very eagerly hoping for a word from Mlle Paule; ⁶ don't keep us in the dark for too long. If only a few lines to reassure us a bit.

Nothing to tell you about Cuverville. My sister-in-law has been here a week and everything is going . . . normally well. We're expecting the delivery the middle of this month. No news from Eugène,⁷ I hope all is well at his place.

Au revoir, poor old Paul, I fear you must be very tired. . . .

We send all of you our very best regards and warmest good wishes. . . . Love.

Your
André Gide

182. *Paul Valéry to André Gide*

[P. Paris, July 3, 1903]

Dear André,

I was meaning to write you. Everything weighs on me so, I haven't been doing a thing. My wife, who is perpetually tired and under a strain, with almost no respite, is still at Le Mesnil.⁸ I was hoping for a zone of relative peace and calm. It has turned out quite differently.

At bottom, and soon, the difficulty of the return—and, finally, the climax.

And I, physically neither here nor there, remain where I am, worn out, and at the mercy of all ideas and all discouragement.

⁵ Pierre Louÿs.

* *Translator's note:* This is the first published letter from Gide since a four-line note, postmarked October, 1902, explaining that he had phlebitis.

⁶ Paule Gobillard, Paul Valéry's sister-in-law, was nine years older than Mme Valéry. When Valéry married, he did not want to separate the two sisters, who until then had lived together with their aunt, Berthe Morisot, and then with their cousin, Julie Manet. Paule Gobillard, who devoted her life to painting, was to live with her sister and brother-in-law at 40, rue de Villejust. It was there that she died in 1948.

⁷ Eugène Rouart.

⁸ Le Mesnil was the estate, between Meulan and Mantes, that Eugène Manet, Berthe Morisot's husband, Edouard Manet's brother, bought just before his death on April 13, 1893. Then the personal property of his daughter Julie, it was often to serve as the country place of the Valéry family during summer holidays.

I hope Drouin and his wife are more valiant. Of course, they have already gone through these ups and downs. But there is probably always an accelerating oppression that cannot be avoided. Give them my very special regards, meaning that at the moment, we can very easily imagine one another's state.

I received *Prétextes*[9] and *Sanguines*[10] and even *Les Trente-six mille Nuits*.[11] Plurals dominate. I saw Pierre two weeks ago. As I arrived at his place, I caught a glimpse of him in his garden, which is small but close, very close, to gigantic (for Paris) trees; he was happily watering the lawn with a hose, in a frock coat.

He seemed to me in very good health, very old—friendly. I spent a rejuvenated and almost Wagnerian hour with him. We discovered, in chatting, that both of us had spent half the night of April 11–12 watching the eclipse of the moon, with binoculars. He concluded, there and then, that we alone among all our friends, etc. That idea enchanted him. And when an idea of that kind enchants him, one is enchanted and delighted along with him. Isn't it true?

One thing is certain: both of us, taking very dissimilar roads—I think—happened to while away the hours watching them *in person,* through opera glasses, on their parallels. I built myself a kind of astrolabe out of cardboard and I tried to construct an astronomic telescope with just any old lentils.

I should speak to you, in my own way, of *Prétextes,* instead of telling you such idle tales.

Were I lucid, I'd do it willingly, but I am unable to raise my spiritual limbs. Besides, it's a book of criticism, and thus one must begin at the beginning. What a lot of quibbling, my good André; I get bored just thinking of it! It's only in talking that I can rather quickly get to the end of the road I *must* take before broaching the question. It is one of the things that dissuade me from writing, that vast, continuous, stark road, before drinking in safety. Better not to suspect it, but when one does, that's the end: there is no other.

Ah yes, the article on Villiers is capitally interesting. I don't understand, however, the word *imposture* which ends it?[12] In your lectures it's those notions of "great man," "nature," and "art" that lead me astray; and it

[9] André Gide's *Prétextes, Réflexions sur quelques points de Littérature et de Morale* (Ed. du Mercure de France, 1903).

[10] Tales and short stories by Pierre Louÿs (Fasquelle, 1903), which contains *L'Homme de Pourpre, Dialogue au Soleil couchant, Une Volupté nouvelle, La Fausse Ester* [*sic*], *L'Aventure extraordinaire de Mme Esquollier,* etc.

[11] A joking way of referring to the translation of the *Arabian Nights* (*Les Milles et une Nuits*).

[12] The following is the last sentence of Gide's article on Villiers de l'Isle-Adam: "His art then appears to be but an admirable and dazzling imposture."

seems to me that in your judgments you mix up several modes, for example, intentions and execution, etc. I mean that these pages are deep in literary atmosphere. So in me as a reader, a conflict arises between pleasure and profit. (Two vile words.)

I am sputtering hints. All the above is unintelligible but I am elsewhere, and there, I am very worried indeed. Heaps of regards to your wife, whose goodness is really rare, and to you.

Your
P. V.

183. Paul Valéry to Mme Gide

Saturday [December 26, 1903 (in
Gide's handwriting)]

Dear Madame,

Jeannie received your dates. It is I who am eating them. I have an enormous weakness for that sticky fruit, whose half-liquid and almost fleshy sugar is imbued with a special silk round a bone predestined for mouths.

Fruit should be classified like the letters of the alphabet. There are the palatals, there are those which hurt your teeth, the *d's* and the *t's*. Dates are liquid and labial.

I won't labor the point. Since Schwob informed me that I was very complicated, I've had to make up my mind to savor myself in silence. I move my own fleshless pit secretly round in my mouth.

I was pleased to learn that even Biskra was very rainy. I should have envied you too much. The sun, here, no longer exists except in the weather-bureau directory. Everyone is pale. Even literature is the color of de luxe asparagus.

Theater alone is prospering, thanks to artificial lighting. I reckon that anything leads to premières, and that not one play, for months, could *fail*. Flops have become impracticable. Hervieu, Mirbeau, Donnay, Brieux, Sardou, Capus, Caillavet and de Flers, d'Indy, Debussy, Le Roux . . . etc., succeed. Why? I believe talent increases in proportion to possible profits.

My little Rat[13] (still without teeth) is increasing as well. He is beginning to make shapeless speeches. But he can't teach me anything about *that*. The shapeless is my specialty. He, the child, utters straightway what I've so often sought, killing sentences, breaking words, evoking the very prattle of the organs, that is to say, of . . . things!

But André is convulsed, and I am now disturbed by everyone here asking me to add a host of greetings at the bottom of my page. No, no, it would be petty, the ceiling is too low! My signature will stifle.

P. Valéry

[13] Claude, Paul Valéry's eldest son, then four months old.

— 1905* —

184. *Paul Valéry to André Gide*

[P. August 26, 1905]

Yes, my dear André, I have been feeling very, very poorly, and have not yet fully recovered. The slightest effort *knocks me out*. This heart, this liver, these nerves, this brain, the whole business isn't worth two sous. Anyhow, through baths, bed, drugs and time, I'm getting back on my feet without much conviction, and this uncertainty, this lack of self-confidence is not the least of the evils.

I am afraid of pestering you and fear that we did pester you both with our inquiries about seaside inns.[1] It's all your fault. We found the region enchanting. . . . I therefore carefully read your methodical letter, hating, I repeat, to have made you write it, for it implies research and writing, a whole documentation.

All right.

As a result of that letter of yours, Yport and Saint-Valéry are our preferences.

So if my doctor doesn't categorically forbid me those shores, I mean to take off for them directly and alone, by way of Cuverville, as you suggest. I'll come and see you between two trains, the second of which will take me to Froberville.

From there I shall wire the group to join me; or I'll go to Saint-Valéry to look for something better.

That name which resembles mine differs from it *radically*.

In the South (ill-timed), Valéry is a family name. It is a plural form of Valérius, which comes—it's great—from *valere* "to be in good health" (irony).

But in the North, Valéry = Walaric and was the name or surname of a monk who founded abbeys around 800 or 900. I no longer recall the exact sense of the word. It means something like idiotic, simple, rustic. And that takes care of Saint-Valéry.

Now, I'm done in, I shake your hand. I hope, if I come through Cuverville, to get some information about you, since you tell me nothing.

---

* *Translator's note:* There are no published letters from either Gide or Valéry in 1904, and none from Gide in 1905. At this point the correspondence becomes more or less sporadic.

[1] Paul Valéry had asked André Gide to suggest a place on the Normandy coast where he and his family could spend the holidays.

Thank your wife, whom my women are overwhelming with incredible questions, and give her my regards.

Regards also to our Drouin friends and to Domi [2] the wise.

Your
Walaric
(for today)

185. *Paul Valéry to André Gide*

[P. September 1, 1905]

My dear André,

Really, you overwhelm me with precise details. But will they make *me* any more precise? In fact, am I going anywhere? In other words, my doctor, whom I saw again today, has definitely forbidden me to go to the seashore. He has just barely agreed to let me go within five or six kilometers of the foam . . . and he himself advises Arques, near Dieppe. Hang it all, I shall end by very simply taking off for Le Mesnil, and then, I'll see.

This doctor still finds my liver a bit delicate and is subjecting me to simple but tiresomely negative prescriptions.

I am not surprised that I'm melancholic and picrocholic, I am so annoyed and irritated in life. How mad wisdom is! and how all that's true is stupid! Actually, I have practiced, to a rather notable degree, the precept commanding us to seek our satisfactions or distractions only within ourselves.

That's fine. We become simpler, etc. But the liver, which doesn't give a damn about true and false, is injured and swells; and with its disastrous bile, poisons the righteous.

Moral: everything scoffs at us. It is the only point on which ideas, livers, muscles, cells, memory, senses, and unknown worlds are absolutely in agreement.

Adieu, I'm writing nonsense.

Your out of sorts
P. V.

186. *Paul Valéry to André Gide*

Montivilliers (Seine-Inférieur), Ferme
Lemaître [P. September 17, 1905]

My dear André,

When are you coming to see us? Ever since yesterday my whole tribe is encamped here; we're back to the land.[3] I spend my time with my legs. My brain is somewhere or other, I see it only when I'm dizzy.

---

[2] Dominique Drouin.

[3] Paul Valéry and his family were boarding at a farm in Montivilliers, not far from Honfleur. André Gide visited them there.

Our accommodations are somewhat inadequate. We're counting on you, *supplied with table napkins,* a very important point.

When we left Cuverville, I led my wife to Le Havre to spend the night in a hotel called the Amirauté, rather dirty, very dirty, but I recommend it to trained travelers. You have a fascinating view of the outer harbor, and beneath you, the Southampton boat and parrots.

Jeannie, who is not blasé about ports, stayed up late, leaning on the rail, watching the beacons, the lights, the moon and its vapors, the doings and undoings in the life of the port. All this blended in with the impression, still pure, of vast expanses and its [*sic*] deeply rooted masses.[4]

The noble annihilation at Cuverville, Le Havre in motion—these two things delight me—do you know how? Not in any present way, since I am too low, too null, too ill, to reinvent them at the same time as I see them, which is the definition of my pleasures.

But I have the feeling I would take such pleasure in them or would have taken such pleasure in them during some other period, and that evaluation *by means of some other time* is a kind of satisfaction that is curiously different from actual good. Just as a tourist says: "How great this spot would be if it weren't raining."

Drouin must have found me haggard. (A ghost comes back to the names of things it was interested in when alive. . . .)

I found *him* in very good shape and robust. I admire the way he can hold his muscles and pyramids in stable equilibrium. That was called wisdom twenty-eight-hundred years ago.

Anyway, friend, if your cold has dried up, if your trip to Montpellier is canceled, set out again toward the South. Domi and your wife would take the train (with the table napkins) and the Drouins would come down the road with you on their extraordinary reversibles [*sic*]. It's a matter of sixteen kilometers, and you can stop on the way to see if the shadow of the great Anselm still disturbs the site of Notre-Dame-du-Bec.[5]

Regards from each to each.

Your
P. V.

[4] Allusion to Gide's rural estate, Cuverville.
[5] The abbey of Notre-Dame-du-Bec, twenty-one kilometers from Bernay, had as its abbot, in the eleventh century, "the great Anselm," future archbishop of Canterbury.

— 1906 —

187. Paul Valéry to André Gide

Wednesday, March 7, 1906 [P.]

My dear André,

A little damsel arrived at our house this morning.[1]

My wife suffered very much, very courageously, not for very long, from three to nine-thirty.

Regards
Paul Valéry

188. Paul Valéry to André Gide

Sunday [July 13, 1906]

My dear André,

I am just back from Le Mesnil, where I spent thirty-six hours seeing my women and children. When I return to Paris after that endless trip, I'm half dead. I get up at six, arrive at ten, read aloud until noon. It's two o'clock, and I am perishing from rebellious torpor.

Around five I shall again have to get busy on the Russian Duma [2] and the collapsing stock market.

But the heart of my thinking will still be fatigue, the desire to sleep a whole night through at last and not detached pieces, an anthology of dreams (in which you appear) as coherent as if it were due to V. B.[3] . . . Added to that will be—stage right—all the caresses of my little sap of a son, who never left off kissing me (is that good French?) * yesterday.

And that takes care of M. Teste.

. . . With my wife, also yesterday, I paid a visit to Raoul Pugno,[4] a country neighbor and mayor of the place. I mention him to you inasmuch as you're a pianist. . . . And there is one problem.

A strange and deep problem, those virtuosos, who—according to all musicians and all ears that aren't asinine—are in fact artists, stage directors of mute music, exegetists capable of radically transforming a page, and who, however, yet, and nevertheless, almost all have, fantastically, some-

---

[1] Birth of Agathe Valéry.

[2] Russian Council of State, created in 1905 by Nicholas II.

[3] Adolphe Van Bever, who in 1900, in collaboration with Paul Léautaud, published *Les Poètes d'aujourd'hui,* selected poems, with bibliographical notes and a bibliographical essay (Ed. du Mercure de France). Valéry appeared in it but not Gide.

* *Translator's note:* "qui ne me quittait pas de baisers."

[4] The renowned pianist (1852–1914), mayor of Gargenville, from whom Mme Valéry was taking piano lessons.

thing *mulatto* about them. I don't see them as white. They're never very subtle.

And for all that, if I were asked, a priori, what one should think of a person who extracts a very alive being from such and such sonata, concerto, or prelude—or who reconstitutes the beast of those fixed abodes [*sic*]—I would call for singular intelligence—a reader of bad faith and very good will—thus a man several times more able than the task itself would require.

As a matter of fact, *he* is charming with his fat belly; and his furniture, brought back from concert tours, is worth all the admiration he happily wants us to have for it.

I have to admit it, I give in. True artists are like drunkards; inspiration is everything; lucidity is its negation. Art flooded with light is a pure invention. The little of it we've seen is merely experimental; mustn't dream of investing our capital in it.

I received a small volume from Ghéon.[5] And the fact that his singular poetry did not leave me indifferent makes answering very awkward. You feel at once that his "temperament" is too poetic to *execute* verse, it's the libretto of a nervous system. Difficult to say, but I should like to make him understand that *that* interests me.

And as for me, here I am at the end of a fat notebook. I shall buy another in the same way as one changes a canary's cage. I should very much like to know what you are doing and in what state of mind you're doing it, but I won't ask you to write me about it until you have made me guess.

Your
P. V.

189. *André Gide to Paul Valéry*

Cuverville, Friday, the 17th
[August, 1906]

My dear Paul,

How unhappy I've been about not writing you! The excellence of your letters increased my desire and my regrets; I was shapeless and felt nothing inside me but worries. The one I nursed the longest was that of having allowed your mother to leave without seeing her again; had I been capable of writing, she is the one I should have written to first; then you, whom I painfully imagine in red trousers, dying of heat and discipline.[6]

Now, listen quickly to this: I am coming through Paris on Monday. Since I have baggage to take to Auteuil, it won't be very convenient for me

---

[5] *Algérie,* a collection of poems (Brussels, Monnom, 1906). The poet and playwright Henri Ghéon (1875–1944) was to be on the original staff of *La Nouvelle Revue Française.*

[6] Paul Valéry had just done his "twenty-eight days" of military service.

to come to the rue de Villejust first; that would force me to return to Saint-Lazare immediately afterward. Can't you come and pick me up at the station (train from Le Havre) (11:11 A.M.)? We could lunch in the neighborhood. If I don't see you when I arrive, I'll try and come to the rue de Villejust around one-thirty.

Your
André Gide

190. Paul Valéry to André Gide

[P. Paris, October 9, 1906]

My dear André,

I have been wanting to write you since I got back. But my occupations, my kids, and two days of malaise were against it. . . . I find Paris hateful, this time. I didn't want to come back, and this childishness persists. When I sleep, I have nightmares, and am not enough in control of myself to profit from them in the morning.

. . . Once again, I am re-faced with my accounts and—being in the unfavorable position of one who can't count up the seasons by his completed writings—I must revive the most forgotten of the dead, those that have turned to pap, to dust, and to mummies.

On the road I thought of nothing at all, except the rain, the beginnings of which I could read on my handle bars.[7]

Lillebonne and Tancarville are worth nothing. After them, the large trees begin. At Villequier I lost my way, and then, straightened out, I thought I had lost my way. There is a fantastically steep, dark, and winding slope that leads to the village. Delightful road along the water and then Caudebec. Go to Caudebec. A quay I saw in a tempest. The Seine thrust back, roaring, a pink-gray spotted with shells and occasional pigeons. At the right, a magnificent low terrace, trees, and M. de Caumont's[8] balustrade, and, perpetually above a patch of water outlined by the quay, twenty-five very mechanical sea gulls playing at looking for their dinner, and whirling, not taking any account of the hurricane, round a center, always the same, like a cluster of gnats. They seem to mime the hunt, for one never sees what they catch.

Terrific church and streets. But the final *shape* of *constructed* things no longer attracts me. I am too concerned with things *under construction*.

Very comfortable hotel, excellent bath, very mediocre cuisine—all of which can be explained by the frequent presence here of the English.

Met an intelligent man who sells jewelry, books, and postcards at the

[7] Paul Valéry had just spent some time at Cuverville, having come on a bicycle. He was then a bicycle enthusiast, and rode around the Bois de Boulogne every day.

[8] Probably an allusion to the Norman archeologist Arcisse de Caumont (1802–1873).

foot of the church. He led me to his junk shop where I hoped to find a book or two. But nothing. A conversation.

Next day, made for Saint-Wandrille * in tiresome and harmonious rain. I didn't go in, almost put off by the uninviting farmers who have the keys. But I found it beautiful. Very Benedictine site: and from there, on a very wooded, very winding, very hilly, very quiet path almost in the mountains, I went to Yvetot—worthless. Admirable bakeries, I might add.

Finally Motteville, where I took the train.

Two names: on the road from Honfleur to Tancarville, a café is called: Café de la Pissotière à Madame.

As for the other, it's the Mont du Cul, and well named! it knocked me out.

The Cuverville salsify is terrific; it has caused me to make my peace with that vegetable.

. . . Went back to Rimbaud last night. Ten years ago . . . Still bowled over. Really, that blackguard guessed and created literature that is still *beyond* the reader. But let's not begin or begin again.

> Your
> P. V.

— 1907 —

191. André Gide to Paul Valéry
> [*Pneumatique*] ** Saturday [P. October 19, 1907]

Dear friend,

The two of you are going to get soaking wet.

Listen; you are perhaps not unaware of the fact that I have commissioned three statues from Maillol! [1] Should the occasion arise, try and find out whether he's working on them. One of them (all three are intended for the bottom of my stairway) is merely a perfected and enlarged version of an exquisite statuette he exhibited last year (terra cotta) at Bernheim's. You might tell him, moreover, that I am returning to Paris and plan to visit him one of these days.[2]

See you Monday, dear friend.

> Your
> André Gide

---

* *Translator's note:* A well-known abbey near Rouen, founded in 648 and now occupied by Benedictine monks.

** *Translator's note:* An express letter, transmitted by pneumatic tube.

[1] For his brand new house, the "Villa Montmorency," in Paris.

[2] André Gide finally acquired two works by Aristide Maillol: a small bronze representing a seated woman and a plaster-cast bas relief of a couple.

— 1908 —

192. Paul Valéry to André Gide

[P. Paris, March 8, 1908]

My dear André,

Your card made me burst with envy.[1] I'm even vexed with you for being there, in a country I shall perhaps never visit again, or if I do, what will become of that sort of brilliant harshness, that mixture of defense and surrender, achieved in 189...? Tremendous *appetite* and profound laziness.

No message for Genoa, unless you need something. Nothing is left for me there but debris and so many reasons for mourning. If you do go, send me some picture postcards—from Nervi as well.

Don't stop in hotels at Nervi, I fear they're very tuberculized. They have also poisoned that entire coast. Go to La Spezzia. One can Stendhalize by the Croce di Malta, away from the main road.

If you go to Genoa, try and eat popular things, even in the streets. I recommend the *piè,* or boiled chestnuts, and the *farinata,* a huge delicious pie, ever so thin, made of chick-pea flour . . . Oh dear, I should like to be there with you.   P. V.

193. André Gide to Paul Valéry

[Genoa] March 10, 1908

My poor dear captive,

Well yes, here I am! and very ashamed to be here, or at least to be here without you; for this is *your* country, I know it and feel it, and when I think of you, I get the impression I'm committing a kind of adultery with the landscape. Forgive me!

But at our age, alas! one melts only on the surface. Besides, it is still winter; as regards foliage, only that of last year: olive trees, pines, and holm oaks. As many Germans as Unter den Linden![2] You would suffer a lot from that, I think; the Frenchman has become a *rara avis.*

Nothing is more out of place here than the article I am preparing for Rouché on Dostoevski (correspondence).[3] The little virtue I should need to write you at length is taken by that. Here are a few pictures, really

---

[1] Gide was then traveling in Italy, and above all, was meaning to visit Genoa, Valéry's favorite city.

[2] "As 'Under the Linden Trees,' " a well-known avenue in Berlin.

[3] *Dostoïevsky d'après sa Correspondance,* an article that was to be published in the May 25th issue of *La Grande Revue* and a separate reprint of which was to be made the same year. Jacques Rouché was the manager of *La Grande Revue.*

artistick [*sic*]. . . . My wife writes me that you are working, and working well; I'm delighted.

I have not yet seen Nervi, or Genoa. Rather disappointed by the road between Chiavari and Rapallo, which I have just walked. Monotonous and spare foregrounds, no beautiful trees. But Santa Margherita [4] itself is charming. Au revoir, dear old Paul. Heaps of greetings to those around you.

Your
André Gide

194. Paul Valéry to André Gide

[Paris] Wednesday, the 15th [P. July 1908]
My dear André,

Degas returned the photos to me in these terms: "Thank Gide and Piot [5] for having passed on those photographs to me. Tell Piot I envy him. If I were younger, I would lose no time in putting myself in his hands. I would become his pupil. Ah! what an admirable craft, frescoes! They are what made the ancients so able, for they forbade *tampering,* which necessarily ruins us (seeing that it's obligatory with oils)."

And he congratulates you for having commissioned the work.

Such are, approximately, his words. Approximately, because I have a bad memory and in him the tone is three-quarters of the song.

I dined at his place several times recently, yet it was sometimes painful; he seemed to have aged quite a bit (less than this winter, however), and sometimes conversation is hard.

At one of the meals, we talked about literature. He knew nothing of Rimbaud. I amused myself by reciting him a few lines from *Le Bateau ivre.* The expression on his face was a comical (and intentional) mixture of despair and tongue-in-cheek.

But myself! Imagine, my old André, the more I went on with my *Bateau,* the sillier I found it all. And not me,—the boat! I hadn't looked at those lines or chewed them over for years and years. And there it was again, about to come into the harbor of the mind, and I found it . . . useless.

Could Mallarmé have been right? But there are still *Les Illuminations,* I think. Could it be a child's boat? Is it that, is it me? Tell me if it's you.

I have been feeling very poorly this summer. Sick as a dog, at my

---

[4] Italian seaside resort near Rapallo.

[5] René Piot (1869–1934) was a painter-decorator who specialized in frescoes. André Gide had intrusted him with decorating the entrance hall to his villa in Auteuil. The photographs in question were probably those of the frescoes, which had been passed on to Degas.

stomach. In one hell of a state. Somewhat better now but owing to tedious discipline, and probably not for long.

Read by chance Michelet's *La Révolution*. What a state of *literary* indignation that threw me into. All that is meant to be declaimed in some people's university, not one word worth *reflecting* on, not one sentence that could drop its shirt and fit in the mental bed of a gentleman. None of those contraptions have ever been *worked over* by the intellect (which would have dissolved and unstuck them), but sputtered out for the superficial public. . . .

What are you doing? I am sending this to Cuverville. Received a curious little letter from Azemmour,[6] from my friend Féline.[7] I infer from it that the government very naïvely lied in that affair, which was a *war operation*.

Your American pens are pure trash.

> Yours, without words,
> P. V.

195. *André Gide to Paul Valéry*

[July, 1908]

Poor dear townsman,

Are you still far from your family? When passing through Paris a week ago, on my way from Toulouse, I wanted to stop in at the rue de Villejust; but I had only twelve hours between trains, and my Aunt Ch. Gide took all the time I should have given to you. I brought with me Domi, who has about recovered from the measles, and the Drouins joined us here two days later.

Marcel stopped in to see you, in vain, a few days before he left.

I conveyed to Piot the part of your letter that interests him; but you probably know that Degas has since come to the villa. It was too late in the day, unfortunately, and with his bad eyesight to boot, he could hardly distinguish anything, it appears.

Your mention of Rimbaud made me think of the traveler on the P.L.M.* (See Jules Renard's travel notebook.) ". . . Lyons! second city of France. . . . How I've grown since then!" Au revoir, dear old Paul. Send news of you all, if writing doesn't annoy you as much as it does me.

> Very much your
> André Gide

---

[6] Moroccan city on the Atlantic.

[7] Pierre Féline, a childhood friend of Paul Valéry's, who introduced him to mathematics, and was to evoke their studious sessions together in two studies, one published by *Les Cahiers du Sud* in 1946 (*Paul Valéry vivant*) and the other by *Le Mercure de France* in the July 1, 1954, issue.

* *Translator's note:* The train route Paris-Lyon-Méditérranée.

— 1909 —

196. Paul Valéry to André Gide

Paris [P. June 22, 1909]

My dear André,

I was so tired Sunday I didn't write to you.

Our *six* doctors came at the appointed hour. I compressed them into the dining room that they might be farther away, more out of reach of eagerly cocked ears.[1]

One hour in there. We, among ourselves, each one eating himself up. What clocks [*sic*]!

They reappeared. Examination, auscultation, familiar questions, caged in again.

Result: another bacteriological test, more precise this time, as well as specimens taken by direct probing.

Feeding up, without too much meat; fresh air.

And then we'll see!

It means a breather of *x* weeks.

I got a very good impression of Chauffard. He is an alert celebrity, still young, especially in appearance, mustache, and manner—delightfully perfumed, intelligent looking, with pride in his big, rather prominent, curiously dull black, lackluster eyes—making the other consultant, a fat tall old surgeon from Beaujon, go through a "strait gate," as if he were saying: "Do go in first . . . since it is I who come first."

I'm full of pains and shattered through and through.

Yesterday Drouin came and must have found me exceedingly vague. We chatted, as well as I could.

In short, nothing has changed. We must continue to wait, stew in our own frightful juice, and just simmer abominably.

Give heaps of very affectionate greetings to your wife, and remain my . . .   P. V.

197. André Gide to Paul Valéry

[P. July 4, 1909][2]

Dear Paul,

I was unfortunately detained by my dedications[3] at *Le Mercure*, so sorry that I arrived much too late to see you; and your sister-in-law's letter makes

---

[1] Six doctors were consulted about a serious illness Mme Valéry had at the time. Among them were Dr. de Martel and Dr. Chauffard.

[2] Postcard, on the back of which are two photographs of Gide in his rue de Commaille flat in Paris.

[3] Gide was signing press copies of *La Porte étroite*, which had just been published by Les Editions du Mercure de France (1909).

me regret not having, on the off chance, arranged to meet you in the evening, which, as it happens, I spent alone.

I have some misgivings and am somewhat ashamed to send you my book at such a serious time; above all, may friendship not impel you to read it at once or to thank me for sending it; that would only embarrass me terribly for having sent it to you so inopportunely.

Faithfully, your
André G.

— 1910 —

198. Paul Valéry to André Gide

[Genoa] Wednesday, the 31st
[August, 1910]

No swimming, none at all, and in despair, for the ridiculous reason that I had whooping cough,[1] but without it, it's true, I should never have come *qui*.[2]

Besides, I am returning tomorrow. Jeannie is torturing herself over Paule, who is still suffering a great deal and mysteriously.

My eight or ten, or twelve, first days here were great. A memory stroke, as we say: a sunstroke. I had stuffed myself full of Genoa up til then. And each thing slipped back into a place all ready for it in my inner machine.

Then, I had the idiocy to go to Florence, which I cannot abide. That Arno, most particularly, is ridiculous: architecture without ideas. And everywhere, I saw, sniffed, sensed the hateful names of Ruskin, Bœklin [*sic*], all the Anglo-German artism, all the Cinquecentism and the Quattro. . . .

Nothing in Italy, up to now, has got the better of Genoa, in my opinion. And I am undertaking to impress this on the mind of a traveling companion.

One extraordinary, incredible thing is that I am returning to France with less pessimism than [I] should have predicted. Actually, we go outside to get an idea of what's inside. And the view was not as unfavorable as I had expected.

I returned dead-tired from that confounded Florence, where I endured unspeakable heat. (*N.B.* Florence is *north* of Montpellier.) The Tuscan speech makes me sick. Were it not for Jacques B.'s[3] delightful portrait at

---

[1] Valéry, having caught whooping cough from the Rouart children, went alone to Genoa to rest up.

[2] Here.

[3] Jacques-Emile Blanche.

the Uffizi and the group of antique busts, I should have been altogether robbed.

What I'm bringing back from there is boundless fatigue; I have been laid out as flat as can be for days and days. When I think of how this card will have to circulate in search of you, I sweat.

Your
P. V.

— 1911 —

199. Paul Valéry to André Gide

Wednesday. [Fall, 1911]

My dear A.,

I received your *Dostoïevski,*[1] I even read it. I found it exciting. That is to say, it would have excited me had I been all there. But with my wife ailing since her return from Burgundy, I am reduced yet again to that condition of seeing everything else as would a man who is attached to what's happening behind him. In this unnatural state, everything seems conditional. Each natural movement of the mind is brought back with a frightful twist.

The situation wouldn't be absolutely inappropriate to thinking about Dostoevski if my kind of anguish didn't happen to be exclusive of all literature. All literature of the painful kind seems to me invincibly unworthy of being cultivated; just as I consider or feel my own troubles to be. . . .

I shake your hand.

Your
P. V.

I shall try to visit you some day soon or when possible.

— 1912 —

200. André Gide to Paul Valéry

[P. May 31, 1912]

Dear friend,

I trust you're meaning to send Gaston Gallimard, at 79, rue Saint-Lazare, your poetry

---

[1] First separate commercial edition of *Dostoïevsky d'après sa Correspondance* (Eugène Figuière).

$+$ *La Soirée avec Teste*
$+$ *La Méthode de Léonard*
$+$ all the various fragments of that period; in short, everything that should go into this first volume of your works.[1]

It is up to you to decide whether it's necessary to include the article (December, '96) on *Une Victoire méthodique* (*La Conquête allemande*)[2] (and my opinion is: YES), the manuscript of which I've found among the first proofs and rough drafts of *Monsieur Teste*. As for the manuscript of your poems, I have stored it away so avariciously that in all the hustle of leaving for Cuverville, I am unable to lay hands on it again. But you have a copy, haven't you?

Sincerely, your
A. G.

201. André Gide to Paul Valéry

July 19 [1912]
Dear friend,

You know of the sad occasion that brought me to Paris the day before yesterday;[3] I had to return here yesterday, and was sorry not to have been able to see you before I left, but all my time was taken by Ghéon and attending to the review. Yet I should have liked to browbeat you a bit with regard to that book and convince you to make the right decision. Gallimard is afraid of bothering you with insistent demands for your texts. Are you hesitating? I want to be sure that your hesitation is not due to fatigue, sadness, a kind of renouncement. . . . This first volume I was thinking of (pending the next one, made up of unpublished material) does not seem to me that difficult to put together. As I had written or told you, it was a question of giving them:

Your poems,
La Soirée avec Teste,
La Méthode de Vinci,

Various articles from *Le Mercure* and fragments of *Sommeil d'Agathe* and something I no longer remember that took place in China. And this, in any order you like. Then what's wrong? Are you flinching?

How are you, poor dear friend? I'm writing to you with such apprehension! and perhaps these publishing matters, in the midst of your other concerns, will lead to a mere shrug of the shoulders. Don't even answer me,

[1] André Gide and Gaston Gallimard had asked Paul Valéry's permission to make a collection of his early works. A typescript of the whole was to be made and submitted to Valéry, who would then look over his poems before having them published and add some new texts. *La Jeune Parque* was to be one of them: he was to work on it for four years.

[2] Article published in the January, 1897, issue of *The New Review*, entitled *La Conquête allemande, essai sur l'expansion germanique.*

[3] Probably the death of a friend.

in that case. You know that, in view of certain kinds of grief, I should be ashamed to speak to you of all this. But when I left you, you yourself gave indication of some respite, a lull, if not a spell of fair weather. . . . Don't speak to me of the book if the subject irritates and tires you, but at least give me some news, that I may know whether I am right to be this sad when I think of you.

Au revoir, dear Paul; I think of you often, both of you. A letter from Paule a few days ago, but in which there was no mention of her sister. . . .

Your
André Gide

202. *Paul Valéry to André Gide*
[July, 1912 (in Gide's handwriting)]

Dear André,

I'm late. But *come fare?* [4] I have ten letters here "in abeyance," and some Havas matters; I won't mention work in progress, which is essentially interruptible. My worn-out brain is cracking.

And the worst of it is that as an obvious consequence of emotions, I have a pain in my chest, and a troublesome, rather alarming, continual shortness of breath.

No need to elaborate.

As for Motor [*sic*], I am still reluctant to have any part in it. I don't know whether the right to subscription is salable (I doubt it strongly): 1. probably for lack of interested parties, 2. it is not a question of social transformation or increase of capital but an outside venture. Note that this new venture calls for fifteen million!

Anyway, I don't know.

The military matter: F. is now publishing his helter-skelter book with a view to utilitarian ends; career, return to Morocco. I think that, meanwhile, he has botched the chapter I could see published in a review. And there is no way to come to any understanding through letters.

As for me, that is to say, the collection or herbarium of dried things, I'm considering it, scraping out the drawers, disgusting myself—and so much the better—for if I regretted my past, Lord! what an added burden. Up to now I don't see that volume: neither its form, nor its substance, nor its necessity.

Also, to come out within two minutes of the Mallarmé is, in three or four ways, terrifying. Must I climb onto a stage which, after all and in truth, is not mine? Seeing articles from *Le Mercure* or *Les Phalanges* [5] relive, and not wanting to, indorsing sonnets by an ex-me? Hasn't my domain since

---

[4] What can I do?
[5] A literary review founded and directed by Jean Royère.

then been this table, this kitchen table, on which I have suffered so much and not generally "for Art"?

Doesn't publishing what I've done mean sanctifying the very renunciation and catastrophe of that for which I renounced what I've done?

Often, in my mind, as an instantaneous escape from difficulties, I have handed you a bundle of all my papers, and have got the hell out, way out, and become alone again and released from everything.

You see (incidentally), people who speak of using their suffering are quite simply people who have not suffered enough. And the martyrs who didn't give in, the constancy of martyrs proves, above all, that their torturers lacked imagination.

One has a gift for suffering just as one has a gift for music. Everyone can hear, but only a small nucleus gets a pain in the guts from it.

"Be that as it may," I am numbering those confounded poems. All together, they come to very few—lines. I have another idea: break up the volume—prose and verse, somewhat mixed—like a very artificial working notebook, without classifying me more particularly as a poet than as anything else.

Then, if time permits, I would mess around with *Monsieur Teste* as follows: 1. *La Soirée;* 2. the ex-beginning of *Agathe,* which would make up the *inner essence* of M. Teste's night; 3. a little trip with *Monsieur Teste,* which I have already begun, and the core of which would be made up of fragments of my notes.

After all, a book of nothing but poems is very boring indeed. It seems to me that Nerval put out a successful miscellany of that kind, and for very small poets it's an advantageous miscellany.

My very best regards to your wife.

Your old gaunt
P. V.

203. Paul Valéry to André Gide

Sunday [P. Paris, July 21, 1912]

My dear André,

I was expecting to see you one of these days and specifically yesterday. I had nostalgidia, and through a letter from your wife, conveyed from Le Mesnil, I knew you were in the air.

Since you always do me good, I was expecting you. Well, too bad.

Now, tell me: I was truly sorry not to have been able to go to Orsay. I should have done it willingly if business had permitted, but Monday we have our general meeting,[6] and there have been nothing but discussions, telephoning, etc., morning and night. Moreover, I have the impression my

[6] Of the Agence Havas.

note to Ghéon was very short; and actually, I was then unaware of the accident referred to by your wife.

Anyhow, do you think he would agree to come to lunch with me, here, alone, in a few days? I don't dare suggest it to him without having your opinion. . . .

I, personally, am working off my worries and ambitions. Sleep and stomach or innards, still difficult. Fatigue, which I haven't been able to get rid of for so many months. A dazed brain, still full of stinking vapors, never really awake, never really asleep.

I drove my wife to Le Mesnil in the auto. She stood the rather bumpy ride quite well. I have no bad news or rather no news at all, for she never mentions her health to me.

As for the Book . . . I *am* hesitating. A very simple mixture of disinterest, pride, fatigue at the very thought of proofs, that innate scorn I have for my fundamental inability to finish anything, and finally, molecular demolition.

Some time ago, I set about living on the basis of a hundred thousand days a year. That couldn't work. Then came the Harpies and the Chinese tortures. Between yesterday, which laid me low, and the morrow, which in three or four ways makes me terribly anxious, I am.

If I haven't refused to go into print absolutely and upon receipt of your first letters, it is precisely by reason of the morrow. I could find myself in a great fix *tomorrow,* and I tell myself, in spite of everything, that in such a case a published book would be of some use to me. But what then? And here's another question. It seems to me that I would prefer my poems to come out in a nice edition, and I can see how it might be accomplished, at which printer's and in what form. I am prepared to bear the cost, using the N.R.F.'s imprint, if they're reluctant to have the book printed elsewhere.

That, then, would be the booklet of a beginner.

There would be enough left to make up a book of prose, with the ordinary format and looks, in your series.

I shall write to Gallimard, to talk all that over with him. I spoke to P. L.[7] about the plan, for I have been dedicating these poems to him for twenty years. He approved, and suggested a good title for the volume of prose and verse: *Mélanges.*[8] What do you say? But my other scheme eliminates this title.

Apropos of P. L., contributions are being collected for the Heredia monument. I'm obliged to put my name down for my humble twenty

[7] Pierre Louÿs.

[8] Valéry did not use that title until 1941—and in the singular. He gave it to a volume that contained, in addition to a group of articles, *Poésie brute, Colloques, Instants,* and *La Cantate de Narcisse.* As an epigraph, he wrote: "Mélange c'est l'Esprit," or "Miscellany is the Mind" (Gallimard).

francs. If you feel like it, when I stop in at Leclerc's [9] for me, I can pay out for you, but you're free (freer than I).

I am writing you on whatever I find at hand: in the midst of inextricable bits of paper among which I can't get my bearings. It's an analysis of surprise and expectation which I should like to have done with, and it's killing me and making me yawn.

Lots of greetings to the Drouins, if you have them with you. I've been absurd with Drouin. Ten times about to go and see him, ten times prevented.

Give your wife all the regards of a poor gentleman who went to her house, one evening, as others dash into a church.

Your

P. V.

204. Paul Valéry to André Gide

Sunday [October 14, 1912 (in Gide's handwriting)]

Dear fellow, since *Mélange* or *Harlequin* will not, in all probability, come out tomorrow, here is another idea due to circumstances, etc.

I have been urged for x months by young Gaspard-Michel,[10] a typography enthusiast, to let him make up a booklet of my verse for himself and a few of his friends, a booklet as sumptuous, strange, etc., as his imagination would have it.

I have objected to it up to now: 1. my disgusts, 2. my virtual involvement with *N.R.F.*

He spoke to me about it again today, and I can see the following combination:

I make up the booklet, nothing but verse. I print . . . copies, as chic as possible, fifty or a hundred of which would sell at a prohibitive price, the rest *ad amicos;* no press copies.

I ask the *N.R.F.* to put their name on the cover, in return for so much on each copy sold.

I myself will take care of the costs of the printer, a friend of my young friend's.

This very limited printing would not spoil the above-mentioned *Mélange.* And perhaps—if I'm not presumptuous—would prepare the way for it.

But what will you think of it? Gallimard? I should hate to offend that charming correspondent.

All the people are so friendly, it has become impossible to move. Tell me if I seem like a pig. . . . Consult your heart. . . .

If you think no, say so, it will be no.

[9] Probably the architect Charles-Alfred Leclerc, sculptor of numerous monuments; Prix de Rome, 1863.

[10] Author of *Divinités du Styx,* poems, 1931.

I am writing my paper for you on Saturday's market, disastrous, tempting. . . .

How amusing Italy is! How bewildered Germany seems! She looks with amazement upon the ass of Austria, who would seem to have forgotten her existence and, her nose in the Balkans, is inhaling the air of the South.

Some day there will be quite a fuss on that side.

Germany alone not expanding; that bitter remark would deserve some reflection. If the Turk, my neighbor across the way, weighs the situation properly, he'll be playing on velvet.

Good night, old André. I am going to bed. I'm thinking of those poor Bulggers who must be terribly cold by now in their dirty overcoats, on their black land.

Heaps of regards to your wife from your   P. V.

205. André Gide to Paul Valéry

Cuverville, October 15, 1912

My dear friend,

I have too great confidence in the good taste of A. Gaspard-Michel to be upset at what you suggest; on the contrary, it seems to me the best solution; for I should not want our plan to stand in the way of that rare edition for booklovers and friends of your poems; and the minute it bears the imprint of the *N.R.F.,* the *N.R.F.* can but subscribe to it. This at least is my opinion before having talked it over with Gallimard. Terms to be considered.

Can you be patient for two weeks? We'll talk about it again as soon as I get back to Paris; and with Gallimard, that it all may be settled, and with A. G.-M.[11]

Are the ladies at Le Mesnil in this fine weather? Both of us send all of you our regards and remembrances. See you soon.

Your
André Gide

— 1914 —

206. Paul Valéry to André Gide

Thursday [July 2, 1914 (in Gide's handwriting)]

My dear André,

In about two weeks, I think we're leaving for La Preste.[1]

The doctor from Montpellier sent me confirmation of his instructions.

[11] André Gaspard-Michel.

[1] Spa in the Pyrénées-Orientales, where Mme Valéry was to take a cure.

There's nothing for it but to go through my drawers very carefully. For it means ruination. I am taking the children. Paule is coming with us. A stopover in Montpellier, and then en route for that out-of-the-way spa which can't be reached by train; where there is nothing but the hotel-establishment, whose proprietor, at once nymph, doctor, and innkeeper, takes you for all he's been able to calculate since winter.

I received in due time your twofold *Caves.*[2]

The printing is good, very good, much better than Sainte-Catherine sometimes does.[3]

I very much like the type. As for the paper, it's strangely soft and almost too smooth. Better for certain poems and certain other genres than for a novel and the type used.

The portrait of the author is intimidating. (Holbein, Carlyle.) Nothing so curious as the remarks here and there about the book. I myself have no one opinion. I have lots of them, and sometimes I find fault with the *why* and approve the *how;* sometimes I feel just the opposite.

I really think that the rather general astonishment created is, this time, inherent in your work, an intrinsic property, so to speak. It is not due to a simple contrast with the expectation and habits of your fans.

Speaking in musical terms (according to my possibilities), I should say that you wrote this book, *finally,* by way of all the tonalities.

But since, for that same me, the greatest praise one can give a book is that it was an excellent exercise for its author, I am inclined to praise it.

Another thing. Tell me where Copeau [4] is. Exact address. I am *obliged* to approach him, as it were. I promised, I shall keep my word, and actually I don't know that I wasn't right to promise. It concerns a play by Bourgerel.[5] Give me the information quickly. My departure, my business affairs, and my budget schemes are overwhelming me. I should like to wind up this business as soon as possible.

All my remembrances to your wife, *et manibus.*

Your
P. V.

---

[2] The first two-volume edition of *Les Caves du Vatican,* without the author's name, which had as a frontispiece a portrait of André Gide by P.-A. Laurens (N.R.F., 1914).

[3] The N.R.F. were then having their books printed by the Sainte-Catherine Press, in Bruges.

[4] Jacques Copeau—who became one of the great stage directors of France—was, along with André Gide, Henri Ghéon, Marcel Drouin, André Ruyters, and Jean Schlumberger, one of the founders of *La Nouvelle Revue Française.* In 1913 he left the review to devote himself to the Théâtre du Vieux-Colombier.

[5] *L'Embarquement pour Cythère,* an elegy in five acts. Henri Bourgerel was also the author of *Les Suppliants. Les Pierres qui pleurent* (1898).

207. André Gide to Paul Valéry

Cuverville, July 4 [1914]

My dear Paul,

I wish I could think more joyously of your exodus to La Preste; my heart sinks a little. . . . Please drop me a line telling us about the effects of the long journey.

Interested by what you tell me about *Les Caves*. At the last minute, I eliminated the preface, or handrail, which would have probably forestalled certain . . . misapprehensions.

I really don't like to be grasped too quickly.

In general, it seems to me that the opinion which tends to prevail is that I am a "cold juggler." The proof that the book is not witty is that Anatole France would have written it differently.

Je hais la passion et l'esprit me fait mal.[6]

I shall put that line from Baudelaire as an epigraph on the cover of a new edition.

Read with most intense emotion the Bourgerel, which Copeau brought to Cuverville; I even wept, sobbed (actually); from the very beginning of Act II, I should have willingly said to the author, as a child might: "It's not fair!" The author would perhaps find that the "cold juggler" was talking. . . . Unfortunately, I fear that the director of the Vieux-Colombier talks in much the same way.

His address? The day before yesterday it was still: Cuverville. Now: Le Limon, near Ferté-sous-Jouarre, Seine-et-Oise.

But Copeau is already aware of your interest in the author, and I doubt that anything more one had to say could increase the keen interest he has in the play, or change his opinion of it. I believe, moreover, that he has already written to Bourgerel. Personally, it does not seem to me very desirable to see that at the Vieux-Colombier, whose audience, I fear, is the least apt to go for it. I nevertheless would have approved Copeau's accepting it, if only for a tryout; but I can't blame him for not accepting it.

One could quibble endlessly about the extra-literary qualities of the play and chiefly of the last acts, and according to one's temperament, congratulate or find fault with the author. The first act had given me some hope for a work that would have provoked the approval, even the admiration, of the *whole* house, as *Les Corbeaux*[7] did. Had I wept a little less, I should have admired more.

Au revoir, very dear friend. Affectionate remembrances to everyone

---

[6] "I hate passion and wit hurts me." *Sonnet d'Automne,* from *Les Fleurs du Mal.*

[7] A play in four acts by Henry Becque, performed for the first time at the Comédie-Française on September 14, 1882.

around you (Madeleine, I may add, is going to write), and happy prestations.

Your

André Gide

208. *Paul Valéry to André Gide*

La Preste, Wednesday [P. July 22, 1914]

My dear André,

Where to begin? You see where we are. It's a cul-de-sac of rocks, the bottom of the Tech River, that bottom being 1,100 meters high, the upper regions 1,500 to 1,600 high, green or greenish. Spain begins at the crests. The establishment is crammed between rocks, and under itself makes sulfur water.

A large terrace swarming with urinary cases, almost all old people from the Aude and Pyrénées-Orientales area.

Every night, a storm.

My wife took the journey fantastically well. Imagine, we left on the night of the 14th by train, in a car whose thermometer registered 100°. At Montpellier, Paule and Agathe were put up in the old Urbain-V ruin.[8] I saw that apartment again. The others were at my brother's. Montpellier gave me great pleasure, I should willingly have remained.

There, I had a long talk with Jeanbrau.[9] He has a curious mind, very political, calculating, I think. Anyhow, I have a feeling he's somebody. We considered, among other things, the actual death of Montpellier, with its university façade. In his case (and it's true), nothing can get done south of Bordeaux. With the winter weather too fine, and the summer too hot, result: he can't find students to help him, even with easy bibliographical work.

Palavas. I went swimming, old-style, twice, as I used to, but with children.

Sète, pitiful. Three boats, no absinthe-addicted crowds in the cafés along the canal. Still beautiful, and still more beautiful, the cemetery with its pink laurels and cypresses.

From Montpellier to here, an annihilating journey. Changed trains three or four times, with wife, kids, and packages; heat and dust.

The valley, from Arles-sur-Tech, of no interest. But Prats-de-Mollo charming, it was a holiday, dancing at night; huge trees and crowded little squares. The auto from La Preste carried off my people and others. After

---

[8] Valéry's family house, in the rue Urbain-V, Montpellier.

[9] A doctor, professor at the Montpellier Faculty of Medicine, who was treating Mme Valéry.

various scenes, I remained there, waiting for the car to return. Night came on. I spent an hour sitting on a bench.

Here, I am not very well. In fact, I feel very weary indeed. I'm letting myself go. Nothing appeals to me. I am deadly indifferent. The growing impression of surviving is unbearable. It seems to me that I *am* only on the surface. And no matter how much I might think or say the most profound things (which doesn't happen), I'd still have the feeling of dead limbs, sleeping words, things one stirs up without being there.

I have always been too present or too absent. But the scale is being weighed down and the statistics are changing.

As for my wife, she is sticking scrupulously to prescriptions. Jeanbraus' suggestion has made her do incredible things, for her. At Montpellier, she went up and down stairs. Here, she goes up and down between room, baths, and pump room. This morning she was rather tired from those gymnastics. Naturally, the doctor here claims the waters will do her an enormous lot of good.

The fact is that they have already singularly mobilized her. Going to Le Mesnil, coming back—what an affair just going to Mass was—and here she is, on the Spanish border!

All my regards to your wife and the Drouins. *Quid* of Domi? [10]

> Your
> P. V.

209. *Paul Valéry to André Gide*

La Preste, July 29, 1914

Dear André,

We are living here in anguish, without any fresh news. At two o'clock the fifty or so bathers fling themselves at the postman to get *La Dépêche*. And that's it for twenty-four hours.

I'm very worried, otherwise I would inquisitively observe this microcosm, this colony lost, as it were, at sea, trapped in the rocks. I worry—I don't know what to do—and besides, am not in very good health here: mist, cold mist, every day. I haven't seen the sun.

I left Paris without my military papers. In case of mobilization, I wouldn't know how to go about rejoining my regiment. I shall put myself in the hands of the military police, who will perhaps know where to send me. But the question that fills me with anguish, should everything fall apart, is the family. I don't see them all returning to Paris in a mass of concentration trains. Besides, I prefer that they not be in Paris, where anything can happen. But then how will they make out? I'll leave them the little money I have left. And then?

[10] Dominique Drouin.

These are my intellectual exercises. My wife isn't feeling too badly. Some days she's just fine. Up to now no *tangible* effects of the waters! Agathe is just fine. Claude, half. Paule, so-so. This weather is a pain. *Quid* of Domi?

Lots of greeting to your wife. And you, when will I see you? and who knows after what?

> Your
> P. V.

210. *André Gide to Paul Valéry*

Cuverville, October 4, 1914

Very dear Paul,

Finally, a letter from your wife this morning!

Finally, I know where you are and what has become of you all!

Probably the *concierge* at the rue de Villejust would have forwarded our letters to you (and I blame myself for not having written you sooner), but when Marcel stopped in again at the rue de Villejust, before joining us here, he had not yet managed to get news of you, and we were worried.

As far as I can remember, I must have written you when war was declared.* The alarming news at the end of July kept me, at the very last minute, from embarking for England, where Arnold Bennett was awaiting me,[11] and brought me back to Cuverville; I must have told you that already. Two days after mobilization was ordered, Marcel and I took the last train carrying civilians to Paris. In Paris, I got busy, or at least I tried to get busy, at the Red Cross. My task consisted in facing, behind a large table, streams of volunteers of all ages and all nationalities (there were even *"accidental* Austrians") who offered themselves as nurses, stretcher-bearers, interpreters, laborers, and handy men. After two weeks, we had written up two thousand cards, and chosen, classified, and trained teams that were ready to leave, at which point we were informed that "they" would not accept any of our men, so that all our work (there were eight of us working mornings and nights) was in vain. I then turned to the Office of Public Welfare, but all the serious jobs had already been filled, so that soon, after absurdly having taken no end of trouble, I had to resign myself to uselessness and inactive anguish.[12]

* *Translator's note:* In a note to Valéry, dated July 26, 1914, Gide wrote: ". . . news from 'the Outside' is so alarming that I am postponing [a trip to Newhaven]."

[11] The English writer Arnold Bennett (1867–1931) was a great friend of Valéry Larbaud's and André Gide's. He advised Gide what to read in English literature. In his *Journal* (July 7, 1932) Gide described him as follows: "I like his watchful generosity, his unflagging curiosity, his love of work."

[12] Subsequently, André Gide became vice-president of the administration of the Franco-Belgian Center, an organization that helped refugees from territories invaded by the Germans, both in Belgium and France. He worked there every day for eighteen months.

Cuverville, meanwhile, after my departure, became filled with my sisters-in-law, nephews and nieces, in addition to the Copeau family, *id est:* wife, mother-in-law (Danish), three children, and governess. The whole brood lived in such joyful intimacy that little Pascal Copeau, the youngest of the group (except for Odile), was heard to say: "I do hope the war lasts a long time!"

Meanwhile, events went from bad to worse, and on August 28, Copeau, whom I met at lunch at Arthur Fontaine's, read my mind, saying he considered that Cuverville was perhaps no longer the really safe place he wished for his family. I left first thing next morning, authorized to dispatch that family to the other side of the English Channel, where friends were ready to receive them. A few days before, mother-in-law and governess had already left for Denmark, which they planned to reach by way of the North Sea. Before the boat they managed to take, three Danish ships were blown up; two were blown up after. And it was not until three weeks later that we finally learned they were safe.

The journey I made from Paris to Le Havre, by way of Versailles and Dreux, added greatly to my anxiety; I was with families of emigrants from the Lorraine border who had just left their houses in flames, and had to flee any way they could, on foot, through fields. The tales we got out of them filled the imagination with horror. I knew Madeleine would never agree to leave Cuverville, or at any rate she would not go away until she was forced to evacuate the commune itself, where all the poor folk counted and relied on her. At any rate, I could send my sisters-in-law and their children, as well as the Copeaus, across the water. I was even thinking of dispatching along with them a number of urchins from the commune, and was already dreaming of nurseries that might be organized by Jean Schlumberger, across the Seine.[13] The conversation I had on that subject at Le Havre, where I spent the night, convinced me to give up my fanciful plan. It was at Le Havre, next morning, that I learned of the distressing communiqué which suddenly informed us that the Germans were at the Somme, when just the night before we had left them at the border. One of the Le Havre newspapers, refusing to understand, posted on their window: "front at the summit of the Vosges". . . but no, it was soon corrected: it should have read: "from the Somme to the Vosges."

The first effect of the communiqué's inaccuracy was to throw the department of the Seine-Inférieure into a panic. Le Havre was crawling with Englishmen; there was talk of new landings at any moment; along the whole line, from Montivilliers to the coast, trenches had been

[13] The family estate of Jean Schlumberger, "Val-Richer"—which Gide called "Blanc-Mesnil" in *Si le Grain ne meurt*—is situated not far from La Roque-Baignard, in Calvados. Jean Schlumberger was then living next to that large residence, in a smaller house, "Braffy," where Gide stayed rather frequently after the sale of La Roque.

dug. . . . Were *they* going to invade the area? Nothing was more probable. And even then I could see them advancing to Le Havre, then, pushed back, laying waste as they withdrew, according to their methods, which by that time I knew in detail. The Pays de Caux even offers excellent fields for skirmishes, if not pitched battles.

On September 2, the Copeaus and Valentine (the younger of my sisters-in-law) [14] left for Trouville, etc. Next day, Jeanne Drouin for Etretat. Domi stayed behind with us, since he could easily get on his bicycle at the last minute.

I thus remained with him, Madeleine, and three maids—one Alsatian who didn't speak a word of French, and two local girls, rapable at pleasure. The following ten days were days of abominable anguish, for, really, at the rate they were going, I was expecting them from one hour to the next, and, unable to read or keep busy in any way, spent my time imagining the worst. How I envied my brother-in-law in his town hall,[15] and all those who had a post, an occupation, a job . . . but that idle waiting. . . . Then one fine morning, we learned that the tide was definitely headed for the South, that it was turning away from Paris itself! Then the victory that finally allowed us to breathe.

And now that the Pays de Caux is reassured, nothing holds me here any more but my well-being. My sisters-in-law and their children have come back; we are awaiting the Copeaus from one day to the next. I think I shall return to Paris in a few days and seek some occupation or other in the Office of Public Welfare or the hospitals.

Ghéon, who was in charge of a small hospital at Nouvion-en-Thiérache, was swept up in the retreat of the rear, which he followed to Guise before returning to Paris, where he will now remain, staying at the Van Rysselberghes,[16] as is Copeau; and as I myself will be doing temporarily.

Marcel joined us here last Monday; he is attached to the defense of Paris (at the fort in Nogent), but has not been called. In a few days, he will start his courses again. Domi will accompany him to Paris, where he is to be a candidate for the *baccalauréat*. Ruyters is being kept at Evreux; he was found to have some kind of weakness of the heart which made him unfit for long marches; he's bored to death washing dirty laundry and supervising canteens.

Gallimard is at Vannes (but not in the army), where he has just had a very painful attack of appendicitis.

[14] Wife of Marcel Gilbert.

[15] Georges Rondeaux, mayor of Cuverville.

[16] The Belgian painter Théo Van Rysselberghe, a great friend of Verhaeren's and Gide's. Gide dedicated to him his lecture: *De L'Influence en Littérature*. Mme Van Rysselberghe, under the pen name of M. Saint-Clair, was the author of books of literary reminiscences. Her daughter Elisabeth was to marry Pierre Herbart.

Au revoir, dear friend. If by any chance you return to Paris, don't fail to let me know: at M. Van Rysselberghe's, villa Aublet, 44, rue Laugier, where you shall be welcome if you invite yourself for lunch or dinner.

May you at least rest up at Banyuls; even work . . . although it's not at all easy to think of *anything else!* Surely the good fresh air down there will overcome the upsets of Claude and Agathe; the important thing is that your wife is better.

We are absolutely delighted about it. Regards to your sister-in-law, and remembrances to Maillol, if you meet him.[17]

Your
André Gide

— 1917 —

211. *André Gide to Paul Valéry*

June 13, 1917

My dear Paul,

I am rapturously watching the progress of *La Jeune Parque*,[1] within myself first of all, for necessarily, and as I had predicted, such and such a line, which at first went unnoticed, today becomes my favorite. I know of no poem that is as much one's "daily bread" as yours. Going back to no more than a mouthful of it *each morning,* I deliciously magnify its nutritive value. . . . Dear friend! I may say that if I admired *La Jeune Parque* from the very first day, I admire it more each day, and differently each day. The following is a passage out of a letter from Valery Larbaud,* which Gallimard turned over to me:

"I received *La Jeune Parque!* an admirable poem, which I now know by heart and have circulated among the few Spaniards I see every day (in the vicinity of Alicante). I have translated and annotated passages of it: the lines about the shadow, the seascape at the end of the poem, etc. The other day, in the garden, a young girl began to quote the lines about the shadow. It was evening and she watched 'la souple momie' move down the path before her: 'Glisse, barque funèbre!' (*Deslizate, barco funebre!*) Unfortu-

---

[17] Aristide Maillol (1861–1944) was then living in Banyuls, where he had been born. After having left La Preste, Valéry and his family spent some time at Banyuls and met him there.

[1] *La Jeune Parque* had just been published by Gaston Gallimard (Ed. de la N.R.F.). It was dedicated to André Gide.

* *Translator's note:* French writer (1881–1957), author of *A.-O. Barnabooth* and *Fermina Marquez.*

nately, my translation is not in verse and is simply spoken, so that Valéry is being circulated here in the Homeric manner." [2]

Another: Suarès [3] is most enthusiastic. If by any chance you have a copy left for him, it seems to me that . . . For I can see that Gallimard doesn't want to divert any more from sales. I am awaiting Alibert's [4] exact address to send him one in Salonica. Ruyters? . . . I'll do it if you haven't already? Let me know . . .

I should have been very curious to chat with you about the lunch and what came after, but I was in a rush to disenrage Miomandre. [5] Lots of greetings to your women.

> Your
> André G.

212. Paul Valéry to André Gide

June 14, 1917

My dear André,

My moods are idiotically just about what I had predicted. You know them better than I, and have for a considerable time. And you know that one's being reacts to praise with gloom (a feeling that the praise is addressed to someone else who was, yesterday); reacts to silence or near-silence with irritation at being irritated about it. And reacts to the whole thing, alas! with an inevitable, growing nervousness.

I confess I have but one very pure diversion: the people who don't

---

[2] The passage referred to by Valery Larbaud is:

> . . . Mon ombre! la mobile et la souple momie,
> De mon absence peinte . . .
> Glisse, barque funèbre! . . .
>
> (. . . My shadow! mummy changeable and fleet,
> The color of my absence . . .
> Glide, O funeral bark! . . .
>
> [Translated by Jackson Mathews]

For Larbaud, Paul Valéry was a "great lyric interpreter of Mediterranean nature." See his booklet entitled *Paul Valéry et la Méditerranée* (Stols, 1926). In it he recalls this same event (p. 10).

[3] André Suarès (1866–1948) had a somewhat bumpy relationship with André Gide, but their admiration for one another was mutual. See Gide's *Journal* (*Feuillets*, 1911) for what he had to say about this "phenomenal writer."

[4] The poet François-Paul Alibert (1873–1953), author of *La Couronne de Romarin* (1927) and *Epigrammes* (1932). He also wrote a study of Gide: *En marge d'André Gide* (1930).

[5] André Gide is probably alluding to the disappointment of Francis de Miomandre, who was the first one approached to read *La Jeune Parque* at Arthur Fontaine's in April, 1917, and who had been replaced by Léon-Paul Fargue.

understand, and who let me know it so frankly that I feel like doing what one must not do: spill the beans.

... *Mens!* ...

Mais sache ... .[6]

Your letter did me a lot of good a while ago, and here are the facts: you couldn't believe to what degree my work was done with the precise, personal, and ever-present idea in mind of a few addressees. I used three or four imaginary auditors as *tools* for my work.

And you can imagine that I chose only the good and the best (as they say in Sète) for those essential roles.

(I am not saying that a few lines weren't intrusted to subordinate actors.)

Pierre did his part and you yours and I mine; and someone else.

That's a curious thing to confide. To clarify further, think of the vast duration that separates 1892 from 1913–17, *and what it took for me to build the bridge,* in matters of re-education and singular solutions. I might add (without much relation to that which I'm adding it to) that I found in the finished poem, once it was done, a vague impression of ... autobiography (intellectual, to be sure, and quite apart from the piece on Primavera, which was improvised in large part toward the end).[7]

I really feel that I lengthened and made disproportionate the speech to the serpent only out of the need to speak myself. ...

The technical story of that fragment is, as a matter of fact, most curious. It is also, in abridged form, the story of the entire poem, which can be summed up by this strange law: an artificial construction that came, as it were, to develop naturally.

This will lead me too far astray. These remarks, however, are my small profit. ...

I am also very touched by the fragment from Larbaud. Indirect testimony is the most precious. I'm sorry he didn't impart a bit more of the Spanish version—*Deslízate, barco fúnebre*—that's far more beautiful than in French.

I was expecting—we are still expecting—each day a word from you inviting one's self [*sic*] to lunch or to dinner. But even in your letter of today there is no mention of it. Look into the matter. We'll see each other Saturday at twelve-thirty at Georges-Ville's [*sic*].[8] You can then name your day.

... I'm beginning to find that street very close to mine indeed. The last luncheon! I dreaded it. Everything happened as it was fated to.

[6] ... *Lie!* ... But know ... Cf. *La Jeune Parque.*

[7] Cf. *La Jeune Parque.*

[8] At the salon of Mme Lucien Muhlfeld, who lived in the rue Georges-Ville, right next to the rue de Villejust.

I was invited to return Tuesday afternoon to meet Edm. J.[9] And this Tuesday *genuit* next Saturday, which *genuit* . . . Botheration.

I haven't sent to Ruyters [*sic*], for lack of an address.

As for Suarès, this is *gravissimo*. I'm holding my head. Before doing anything, I must absolutely consult with you.

H. de R.[10] wrote me the classic note: "Received. Thank you, I shall read with pleasure. . . ."

He's wrong, I fear. . . . But after all, it's perhaps . . . a return in kind. See you Saturday.

Your
P. V.

213. *Paul Valéry to André Gide*

Wednesday [P. June 17, 1917]

My dear André,

Mme Aurel [11] (whom I don't know otherwise) wants someone to recite fragments of *La J. P.* at a gathering at her home.[12]

(She has one every Thursday at five).

I don't know who suggested that she ask you for a *fifteen-minute* (it's the ritual time) talk on the author or the work.

She wrote me all that and asked me for your answer as soon as possible. You are to choose the Thursday (except for July 12 and tomorrow). *Answer me anything you like. Quickly.*

Were I in your place, I should be very annoyed at a piece of drudgery like that. . . . Therefore . . .

I have already alleged that you were very busy. (But if it appeals to you . . .)

Your
P. V.

214. *André Gide to Paul Valéry*

Thursday [P. June 28, 1917]

My dear Paul,

The idea of making an appearance, my own and yours, in Aurel's salon, terrifies me. True, I haven't the courage, despite my desire, and the delight

[9] The writer Edmond Jaloux.

[10] Henri de Régnier.

[11] Pseudonym of Mme Alfred Mortier (1882–1948), author of many novels, who then had a literary salon in Paris.

[12] In addition to the reading of *La Jeune Parque* by L.-P. Fargue at Arthur Fontaine's, another reading of the poem took place at the N.R.F., 35, rue Madame. It was read by Jacques Copeau, in the presence of André Gide, Gaston Gallimard, and Jean Schlumberger.

it would give me, to please you and give proof of my friendship.

Whom shall we not see there? with whom we hoped we had broken off relations . . . And what about Miomandre? And more especially because I should be afraid of speaking very badly.

Worked too much these past days; or at any rate, made every effort to. . . . Fatigue and yearning for green.

See you soon.

Your
André Gide

P. S. Did you see yesterday's Souday? [13]

215. Paul Valéry to André Gide

Thursday [end of June, 1917 (in Gide's handwriting)]

I. Received your letter, my dear André. I had just written that you must have left Paris!

So you see that the matter is settled. (I wrote you about it only for conscience' sake.) [14]

But I, who am going through the same ceremony for Lebey on Thursday! [15] Tell me, don't you pity me? *Durus est hic sermo,* as was said previously in the Holy Scripture.

II. *Ho visto il Souday.*[16] It's as good as it *could* be. Perfect! with a bit too much approximate biography.

What annoys me is that *waterproof* [17] of narcissism that sticks to my shoulders . . . since the Botanical Gardens. Yet have I ever looked that much at my navel?

Have I ever spoken of cultivating the Self?

M. Teste, if he's something—and I have reasons to doubt that he's something—is but a snapshot of an intellectual.

A Narcissus thinks he's just great, I believe, by definition. The whole thing is merely words that dispense both author and reader from any reflection whatever.

---

[13] A long article on *La Jeune Parque* by Paul Souday, in the June 28, 1917, issue of *Le Temps.* André Gide spoke of "yesterday's" Souday because *Le Temps* came out every evening, dated the following day.

[14] The reading of *La Jeune Parque* at Mme Aurel's never took place.

[15] Paul Valéry had agreed to read, at the home of some friends, a few pages of a collection of poems by his friend André Lebey, *Coffrets étoilés,* which was to come out in 1918 (Ed. de la Renaissance du Livre) with a preface by Valéry.

[16] *I saw the Souday.* The general tone of Paul Souday's article is given by the following excerpt: "Is it a masterpiece, which I believe is the opinion of Mr. Pierre Louÿs? One might hesitate in the face of that somewhat strong word. But a beautiful thing, undoubtedly."

[17] In English in the original.

But I personally am very satisfied. I can feel my umbilicus growing; it will soon become visible.

IV [*sic*]. I'm sorry that S. had nothing to say about the edition. Instead of speaking so much about *placandis manibus,*[18] he would have done better to praise the typography, in spite of a few broken italicized *f*'s.

V. My wife is writing to yours on the next table. It's about Cuverville. My sister-in-law Paule has a sprained ankle (my fault), which may change the traveling orders.

VI. P. L.'s eyes are bad, or rather his eye. I'm very grieved. This may end horribly.[19]

Your

P. V.

216. *Paul Valéry to André Gide*

Cuverville [P. July 27, 1917]

Dear André,

I have just gone barefoot to make my devotions to the Supreme Beech.[20]

That tree, which somewhat lessens the mystery of why Latin names are feminine, that tree would be worth my adding a few lines to the little ode. But the lines haven't come yet. I neither call them nor thrust them aside.

Besides, I am very convinced of the goodness of M. Ingres' advice: "Copy old engravings, and draw a great deal *from memory.*" Working from nature is a thing generally misunderstood. It is by this fact that realism got taken in. It confused two moments of the artistic act. Work *sub vivo* is necessary but not sufficient. It is perfectly incapable of compensating for personal mastery; and the latter, of inventing everything.

I therefore stand at the foot of the Beech merely looking at it, fingering it with my mind, yet not trying to make it speak.

It will speak by itself, far from here, once it has found, in my substance, a tract of land, some air, and a sun that are not present, less present, and more real.

I am not yet used to your departure, which took place before our reunion had matured.

I continue to be vague in a mind where nothing leads to anything. I don't even know if we would have chatted any *more?* I, at any rate. I am altogether lacking in strength these days. For example, I began this letter

---

[18] An allusion to the inscription in the Montpellier Botanical Gardens, *placandis Narcissae manibus,* which is the epigraph of Valéry's poem *Narcisse parle.*

[19] Pierre Louÿs died in 1925, almost blind.

[20] "Le Hêtre-Suprême," one of the most beautiful beeches on Gide's estate, Cuverville, was the inspiration for Valéry's poem *Pour Votre Hêtre "Suprême"* (see Valéry, *Œuvres complètes,* Vol. C), dedicated to Mme André Gide. Gide had the poem framed and hung it on the wall of the château at Cuverville.

with the intention of telling you a host of things . . . and I am in the process of producing a perfectly useless bit of writing. I had the feeling I should speak to you of what you read me.[21]

But it's strange, I am still unable to think about it clearly, out of your presence—I should even say, out of the place I heard it read by you.

Besides, it's a piece of writing whose genre is such that one's first impression (I gave you mine) is certainly the right one, since the very genre is to express those things which, either because of their delicate nature, or because of their relation to memory, *sunt ut sunt aut non sunt.*[22]

The portrait of another is all the more like the original as one is *struck* by the likeness *at first glance.* Seek as one may afterward, it's rather late to find the art.

Don't infer from this, at least not overmuch, that I am advising you to polish and rub down a bit more those passages I pointed out in which art is still noticeable. My very paradoxical opinion would be to keep them in an expurgated publication, and weaken them in a future and *complete* edition.

Note. The word *likeness* used above does not signify here yours to You (that would have no meaning for the unknown reader), but Your likeness and probability of likeness—to him—to Man.

One must not overlook the fact that the reader of any Heart Laid Bare (more Poe picked up by Baudelaire) [23] must be seriously brought to heel. He is one whose *idée fixe* is that something is still being hidden from him. Whatever one says, he finds the avowal incomplete.

That's why the virtuoso pieces are not really safe here. Being witty with one's confessor is serious: it's enough to make him forget to absolve you. He assumes that his penitent's composure is incompatible with sincerity: a purely idiotic idea, but an idea that people really get.

You see, I am speaking to you stupidly and theoretically of notebooks about which you doubtless wanted to be able to write: "This is my flesh, this is my blood."

But I *still* can't, I can't *today,* I can't *in writing,* profitably say anything more important about them.

With me—and it's singularly characteristic of me as an individual— "objective" comments easily precede the others.

[21] The first pages of what in 1920 was to be *Si le Grain ne meurt.* In his *Journal* of February 27, 1917, Gide wrote: "I advanced my *Memoirs* as far as the end of Chapter IV."

[22] This phrase, "are as they are or are not," refers to the words of the General of the Jesuits who, in the eighteenth century, answered those who wanted to reform the order: *Sint ut sint aut non sint,* "May things be as they are, or may they not be."

[23] Baudelaire took the title for his prose work *Mon Cœur mis à nu* from Poe's *Marginalia.*

I do feel that subsequent developments will evolve. You state a tremendous question: "Where does literature begin and where does it end?" I shan't go into it today. I can only tell that this work will inevitably be the key to all your works; people will look for that key, and they'll go on finding an explanation for everything you have and will have written. You mustn't lose sight of this point. In a certain sense, you are doing here everything you have already done and everything you will ever be able to do. It is a book that *will have* written your other books. . . .

But (I'm repeating myself), everything I say today is exhausted . . . . Marcel is sleeping, and I feel like imitating him.

The cannon is more formidable, unremitting, rolling out more ponderous waves at shorter intervals.

Jeannie, with Mme G.[24] and the children, is at Le Havre. The echoes of your recital are coming back to me. Claude, red in the face or pale, grasping what he can of paternal peculiarities. What does he think??

Jeannie has re-repeated to me how much you stirred your people, as the wondrous performer of my poems. I'm sorry to have missed my private audition but am not sorry to have stayed away from the show.[25]

I now should like to thank you for so many things. And yet, at a certain degree of intimacy, I don't like words. I find they lower that very degree. Not a word, then.

When will I see you? You have no idea. Rue de Villejust on your return, I suppose? Remembrances, regards to the V. R.'s.[26]

Your
P. V.

217. *André Gide to Paul Valéry*

Cuverville, November 1, 1917

Dear Paul,

Yes indeed! I did receive your letter, your two letters, your three letters.* Your impromptu on *Les Nourritures* I found most entertaining, and your sonnet on the fried fish in Genoa a delight. You should not allow yourself to be tired: I am more and more convinced that real youth begins around fifty.

Dear fellow, I don't know what to say about the conditions you mention, which Gallimard has proposed to you or wants to impose on you. I, of

[24] Mme André Gide.

[25] A "private" audition in the hall of the château at Cuverville. Gide, after having read Dickens, recited *Aurore*, one of Valéry's most recent poems.

[26] Van Rysselberghes.

* *Translator's note:* The only published letter from Valéry for this period was written in October, 1917, and consists of two poems, one inspired by a new edition of *Les Nourritures terrestres* and the other entitled *A Gênes*, describing "fried fish."

course, understand your point of view, and regret more than a little not having managed to provide a way out for myself in my agreements with *Le Mercure.* But I understand as well that Gallimard (and the N.R.F. in general) should make it a point of honor to have your name in his catalogue once and for all, and that he be anxious to feel you are part of the establishment. . . . I even understand (and it pleases me) that he should prove more obliging about all the other questions (make-up of the volume, royalties, etc.) than about that one. Up until now (with the one exception of *Hélène de Sparte,*[27] which should soon be brought back to *Le Mercure*) the N.R.F. has entered into permanent possession of all the books it has published.

But since Gallimard has left and consequently there's no hurry, we shall talk about it again the next time I pass through Paris (end of December). Let's not ruin our pens on that.

I am not writing to you properly; I am not writing to you. I am overwhelmed with work (in rather good form, fortunately), since—in addition to my translation of Shakespeare,[28] which I should like to be able to finish before 1918—I have to look over two translations of Conrad[29] and examine several English books that certain people have offered to translate for us. (Included in those "certain" is Guillaume Lerolle.)[30] Meanwhile, my personal work is awaiting, and it makes me wild.

Au revoir. I shall return to Egypt. Ah! I almost forgot. . . . Wouldn't you translate, in your *own* way, one or two pieces by Whitman?[31] I should be so happy to see your name among ours, in this edition of a selection of W.'s poems which we're going to produce, and which is already being set. Bazalgette's translation is of papier mâché.[32] You'll do it, won't you, and we'll talk about it again.

Here, we often speak of you, of you all. See you soon.

Your
André Gide

[27] By Emile Verhaeren.

[28] *Antony and Cleopatra,* the translation of which was to be published in the July 1, August 1, and September 1, 1924, issues of *La Nouvelle Revue Française.*

[29] Conrad's *Typhoon* was published in Gide's translation by Les Editions de la N.R.F. in 1918. The second translation must be that by Geneviève Seligmann-Lui of *Almayer's Folly* (N.R.F., 1919).

[30] Brother of Yvonne Lerolle, Eugène Rouart's wife.

[31] Gide was then in the process of preparing a collective translation of Walt Whitman's *Selected Works,* since he was not satisfied with Bazalgette's translation. This collective work was published in 1918 by Les Editions de la N.R.F., with, as co-translators, Jules Laforgue, Louis Fabulet, André Gide, Valery Larbaud, Jean Schlumberger, and Francis Vielé-Griffin. Valéry did not contribute to the volume.

[32] In 1909 Léon Bazalgette published a translation of Whitman's *Leaves of Grass,* and in 1914, that of another volume of his poems.

— 1918 —

218. André Gide to Paul Valéry

Cuverville, January 5, 1918

Dear old Paul,

Cannot find the address, or even the name, of the English critic to whom you had me send my *Nourritures*.[1] It would be exquisitely kind of you to fill out this envelope.

I should like to see your poems to the Witch of Georges-Ville.[2] . . . Absurd, that strangulated visit of last December! If you find a duplicate or a rough draft . . .

Au revoir. What cold weather!

Your
André Gide

219. Paul Valéry to André Gide
My dear André,

Saturday [March 2, 1918 (in Gide's handwriting)]

1. The Cipas: Carantec, Finistère.[3]

He spoke of coming to see Paris again, but I don't know whether he has.

2. I naturally had Ruyters marked down for a *Parque*. My notebook informs me that it must not have been sent, for lack of an address. If you can send him one, I should be pleased. Put in a dedication by proxy.   P. V. (For example: "To read in the Kong mines.")[4]

3. Received intense pound Méral (Swiss cheese).[5]

4. How was Murry's article on *Nourritures?* He wrote to me, two weeks ago, one evening he had reserved in his own notebook, in these terms: *"No articles. Must write to Valéry and Gide."*[6]

---

[1] John Middleton Murry, literary critic and essayist, well known for his studies on Keats and Shakespeare, and the husband of Katherine Mansfield.

[2] A nickname, not at all perjorative, given to Mme Muhlfeld, widow of the writer Lucien Muhlfeld, by friends whom she received daily in her home. Valéry sometimes referred to her also as "the Neighbor."

[3] Cipa Godebski, brother of Missia Godebska, who was the wife of Thadée Natanson. Among those who frequented his literary salon, rue d'Athénes, were Maurice Ravel and Jean Cocteau. [In a note dated February 27, 1918, Gide had asked Valéry for his address.]

[4] Norwegian mines in which Paul Valéry and Ruyters were shareholders.

[5] *Sic.* Probably an allusion to a package of that cheese.

[6] In English in the original.

I recommended to him Mardrus' book and Toulet's book.[7]

What do you think of him (Murry)?

5. Witcheries. Luncheon yesterday with J. E.,[8] Artus,[9] Le Grix,[10] Mauriac. We ate mussels.

Gossip, gossip, and gossip. Very boring for *my humble self,*[11] who did not know the people involved, and who is bored by gossip at the end of five minutes. *No matter.*[12] A lot of cock.

Great final fortissimo on the Gang of Swindlers.

I am discovering J. E. He's good as gold. And he seems so happy when he has put his finger on some evil or other that one could kiss him, were that idea ever to enter one's mind.

6. Fine, fine speech by Clemenceau, yesterday.

I am anxious to know the value of yesterday's attack in Champagne. I mean: the numbers the Krauts must have brought into play. The whole business haunted me all night.

7. You're worn out. Althought I am not, I'm completely inerm. Brain promoted to honorary membership. Can't possibly harness it to anything. I'm doing the children's homework. I say to myself: "Must I tackle the book on dreams?" and I draw back with fright, into inaction.

As for poetry, it's now antipodal to me. We no longer greet each other.

8. The cook is in bed. She burst a varicose vein the night of the false alarm, whereas Julie twisted her ankle.

That night we thought it was best to go to the cellar. There was tremendous confusion. The little one was bawling; Agathe, having awakened and dressed in a rush, her teeth clenched, worried me a lot. I was afraid the shock was harming her. She is still not well. We were tightly squeezed in that cellar, with a blessed candle stuck in a pile of coal!

9. It's terribly cold. Snow. Finger white.

10. Received Larbaud's *Enfantines.*[13]

At a Berthelot luncheon, M. Pierre Mille apologized to me for not yet having read the above-mentioned book. Nor did I, I told him.

[7] Dr. J.-C. Mardrus' *La Reine de Saba* and P.-J. Toulet's *Comme une Fantaisie,* both of which had recently been published.

[8] Jacques-Emile Blanche.

[9] The novelist Louis Artus, born in 1870, author of *Un Homme d'hier* and *La Maison du Fou,* among others.

[10] The writer and critic François Le Grix, managing editor of *La Revue hebdomadaire,* in which Gide was to publish, in the September 9, 1922, issue, a study entitled *Dostoïevsky, annonciateur du Bolchevisme.*

[11] In English in the original.

[12] In English in the original.

[13] Published in 1918 (Ed. de la N.R.F.). The novelist Pierre Mille mistook Paul Valéry for Valery Larbaud. The latter situated the action of one of his tales, *Portrait d'Eliane à quatorze ans,* in Montpellier, in the gardens of Le Peyrou.

Thereupon, he moved away. Q.E.D.

As a matter of fact, I had already read it. Something in it takes place in Montpellier.

Opinion too complex to be hastily written out. Questions of principle. Must not think I'm fixed.

11. Jeannie promises letter to your wife. Very busy at the moment. See No. 8 above *in principio.*

12. Received a *Publicidad* from Barcelona, in which an article on *J. P.*[14] Received with gratitude, devoured the entire issue with Spanish dictionary. Joy from that occupation. Spanish language very amusing, in its naïveté and the ease with which one can apply Grimm's law to it.

13. *Antony and Cleopatra,* by Gémier.[15]

J.-E. B.[16] runs it down, at top speed. I, who have not seen it, undervalue this mania—which is becoming mono—of actors mingling with the audience. It's more than a mistake, it's a piece of stupidity.

. . . I mention *yours.* J.-E. declares that, because of the Russians, a play with Bakst, Ida,[17] Stravinsky, etc., is impossible at present.

But, says the W.,[18] since they're Jews? . . .

14. Your P. V.

15. Must not conclusively forget answer to the two or three questions set forth in this "Notebook of an Artist."

212. *André Gide to Paul Valéry*

Cuverville, March 4, 1918

My dear Paul,

Your letters embarrass me terribly when I compare them to the *dulness*[19] of mine. I am still laughing at your description of the tragic night! But it probably wasn't much fun at the time. . . . As for your relations with J.-E. B., they absolutely delight me. We must try and organize a small luncheon at the Witch's, *with Drouin,* who seems to me to be stagnating a bit, and I've no idea how to whip him out of it. I should like to force him into collaborating regularly on some *Temps* or other. I think that appointment to Janson which he just missed getting has affected him a lot. (And it would have meant a 4,000 to 5,000 franc increase in salary, which would have come in awfully handy in the household!) We'll talk about it again.[20]

[14] *La Jeune Parque.*

[15] Firmin Gémier had just staged Shakespeare's play, translated by Népoty, at the Théâtre Antoine, Paris.

[16] Jacques-Emile Blanche.

[17] Ida Rubinstein.

[18] The Witch—that is, Mme Muhlfeld.

[19] In English in the original.

[20] Marcel Drouin had just missed being appointed professor of philosophy at the lycée Janson-de-Sailly. He was not appointed until 1932.

My *Typhoon* is coming out in *La Revue de Paris* with some rather unpleasant mistakes.[21] Well, it can't be helped.

I am writing to Godebski, and yesterday I sent Ruyters *La J. P.*

You ask me not to omit answering your questions. . . . I have looked through your letter for them, from beginning to end, but in vain. Is it with reference to Murry? His article was very nice; good, but inadequate, as he says. I answered him at length. Toulet's book? Do you really . . . ? I had had *Monsieur du Paur* and *Le Mariage de Don Q.*[22] sent here. I could have done without. We are awaiting Domi, his last leave before he's off to the front. He's going to arrive at the most tragic time.

If perhaps one day when you have nothing better to do (could that be possible?) you happen to pass a shop selling photos, you would give enormous pleasure to Joseph Labasque (*102° lourd, 5° groupe, 8° batterie, S. P. 206*)—and to me—if you would send him a few postcard-reproductions of Michelangelo's drawings (or fragments of the Sistine) or anything at all of the latter, and, if you find them, some Donatellos, which *of course*[23] I cannot find here. I shall explain to you the case of the aforesaid Labasque[24] (nothing to do with Lebasque).

But above all, don't do it if it's any trouble. Au revoir.

> Very much your
> André Gide

221. *Paul Valéry to André Gide*

Friday [P. March 8, 1918]

My dear A.,

Telephoned this morning to Nitrures.

Nitrures is a lady—why not a Ninevite Queen?—with a very clear voice.

The voice said that the Company is now buying shares in Kong. (Will it be a good speculation?)

I asked for the circular and the option form. Will give you my impression, if I have one.

*

Had seen your name in the Table of Contents of *La Revue de Paris*. Didn't know you were part of the establishment.

Even more surprised to see V.'s[25] name above yours. This calls for an explanation, which you will give me some day.

*

[21] Gide's translation of Joseph Conrad's *Typhoon* appeared in the March 1 and 18, 1918, issues of *La Revue de Paris*.

[22] P.-J. Toulet's *Monsieur du Paur, homme public* and *Le Mariage de Don Quichotte* were published in 1898 and 1902 respectively.

[23] In English in the original.

[24] A young poet of whom André Gide speaks in his *Journal* (October 2, 1915).

[25] Gilbert de Voisins.

Am bored. Writing nonsense on old subjects.

*

Am very sorry that Drouin failed to make Janson. I'm urging Julien[26] to kill his professor by doing certain of his "papers" in the style of the *Coup de Dés*.

*

Fort is a candidate for the Académie. I dream of founding a Society of Pure Letters. It would be indeed ridiculous. But suppose a Rockefeller or a Rothermere were persuaded to get that into his noddle, and would give thirty thousand francs a year to ten chaps, he'd manage it with ten million, and Richelieu and Goncourt would be the ridiculous ones.

I offer myself as a candidate for that Society.

*

Information.

The *Revue des Deux Mondes* prints 15,000 copies.

Le Correspondant prints 12,500.

I tell that to Vallette, whom I met yesterday: and I ask him: And you?— 6,000.[27]

These figures are all miserable. A French review should *now* print 90,000 or 100,000.

*

I was going to write you the names of the ten pensioned members of the Society—but I can only think of five—and I am disregarding my antipathies!

I'll tell Rockefeller to wait.

> Your
> P. V.

222. *André Gide to Paul Valéry*

Cuverville, May 5, 1918

My dear Paul,

I missed very much not seeing you when I came through Paris; I arrived at the rue de Villejust, at the only time I still had free, with a roll under my arm and a terrine of rillettes, hoping to share a lunch with you, but Charlotte[28] informed me that henceforth you were lunching at your employer's. . . .

[26] Julien Rouart, Paul Valéry's nephew, a student at the lycée Janson-de-Sailly.

[27] For *Le Mercure de France*.

[28] Charlotte Lecoq, daughter of a farmer in Samoreau, near Valvins, who had had friendly dealings with Mallarmé and was interested in literature. Mallarmé himself had found Charlotte a job with Julie Manet and the Gobillard girls in 1898, when she was twenty-four. She was to spend her entire life working for the Valéry family. In 1955, at the age of eighty-nine, she was still living at Mme Valéry's, rue Paul Valéry, in Paris.

I also came bearing lots of greetings from the Godebskis, with whom I had just spent some charming days in the company of the Allegret boy, a schoolmate of Claude's,[29] whom you met one day in the rue du Docteur-Blanche, and whose parents put him in my charge. I was supposed to take him to England shortly, where it had been decided he was to finish his studies; I was delighted at that excuse to travel, and he even more so, taking over the lines of your *L'Insinuant*[30] and applying them to me, but the long-range guns hurled the whole family out to Limoges, where he is being forced to go back to school to prepare in haste for the *baccalauréat* B.*

Here I am, stuck in Cuverville, where it's damp enough for a snail. We have been informed that there will soon be troops to put up. Rumor has it that they are colored troops, who will be billeted in the region. I can already imagine bamboulas in the beech groves. What news of your family? Just a note would give us great pleasure, especially if you tell me that you're working. Au revoir, dear old Paul. The great Beech remembers you and I am your friend.

André Gide

223. *Paul Valéry to André Gide*
Tuesday [early May, 1918 (in Gide's handwriting)]
My dear André,

Sorry to have missed your rillettes, which must have been terrific. . . . But since the departure of my entire household, at my insistence, I have been eating remarkably—much too remarkably—well in the avenue du Bois.[31]

In other words, around April 4, I sent the Rouarts and the Valérys *primo* to the château de Vassé, the home of one of Julie's relatives.[32] It's in the Sarthe: thick walls, moats, dampness. The older children were delighted at not doing a f. . . thing. The ladies fretting and overwhelming me with recriminations. The little doggy catching cold.

And then, what with concern about studies and not wanting to impose, they decided to look around for another place. Only Rennes (12 rue de Paris) seemed suitable. Pleasant house, it appears, and very high rent. Julien[33] is in a priest-ridden school. Claude, *patre imperante,* at the *lycée.* Both of them shedding tears over Janson and doing very little.

---

[29] Marc Allegret was at the lycée Janson-de-Sailly, in the same class as Claude Valéry. It was with him that Gide was to make his journey to the Congo in 1924.

[30] Published in *Charmes.*

* *Translator's note:* Here Gide inserted a variation on Valéry's poem *L'Insinuant,* describing the hard life of a student at the lycée preparing for the *baccalauréat.*

[31] At Edouard Lebey's.

[32] Mme Ernest Rouart.

[33] Ernest Rouart's son.

Any excuse will do: lack of books, idiotic professors, etc.

What bothers me is Claude's math., for his professor here pleased me and pleased him (which is far more important).

And I myself am doing nothing. Insomnia for the last three months. I've been getting gray hair over contemporary history and the questions it raises, this departure, etc. In short, a bad, a very bad trimester. Yet I'm at an age at which one should buckle down. But my music has stopped and my drawing has failed to come back.

I even took a complete holiday from the Witch. The day before yesterday I finally reappeared. And I didn't waste my time, since J.-E.[34] informed me of the astonishing news that you had taken in Doucet and that he was going to devote a hundred thousand francs to printing one copy of one of your things?[35] . . . (I thought of certain notebooks? . . .)

One proof of my having stopped is that I am writing to you at nine in the morning, a time never given to correspondence, but given to variously severe and reserved muses. What fatigue, this morning!

Disaster. The Degas exhibition. It's a betrayal. The family hung everything, everything. When you think that he had planned to intrust to Ernest[36] the job of sifting out his studio, of burning a lot, of . . . Then came senility, he made all the wills everyone wanted him to, and once dead, he suffered everything he had detested: his collection sold, the B.'s in charge of the sale; his rough sketches exhibited and put up for auction. That exhibition was painful for me, and yesterday's sale exasperating.[37]

I am told that Gallimard is back from America. Is it true?

Sometimes I vaguely toy with the idea of printing those little poems for myself, and also the *Narcisse,* a new text for which I have a kind of tenderness-weakness: but it's impossible.[38]

What a time! in which poems sell like hot cakes! True, the authors are not getting rich on them.

Au revoir, I am worn out, dull, and have a bitter taste in my mouth. Give lots of greetings to your wife, whom I can see with her gloves, on the threshold, awaiting *Le Journal de Rouen.* I kiss the Supreme Beech, which is not improper given its height. It reaches high . . .

Your

P. V.

[34] Jacques-Emile Blanche.

[35] Cf. Gide's answer, below, Letter 224. Jacques Doucet (1856–1929) was an art lover and a collector, and donated to the University of Paris its Library of Art and Archaeology and the literary library that bears his name.

[36] Ernest Rouart.

[37] The sale of Degas' works took place a few days later at the Galérie Petit, rue Decize, Paris.

[38] Valéry's poems were finally published in 1920 and entitled *Album de vers anciens* (Ed. d'Adrienne Monnier, then by the N.R.F.).

Royère recently manifested to me his wounded astonishment at not having received anything from you in reference to the death of John-Antoine Nau.[39]

224. *André Gide to Paul Valéry*

Cuverville, May 8, 1918

My dear Paul,

Terribly sad to hear that you're so flat out. Thank you for the news of your family; I am handing the pen over to my wife.

What you tell me about the Degas exhibition surprises me not at all. We sensed it. But it's no less painful for that. As it happens, Van Rysselberghe asked me for news of the sale; I shall pass it on. Also, why did Degas keep his rough sketches? Nothing more ticklish than what Ernest was commissioned to do. I'm happy for him, although grieved for Degas, that he did not have to take it on.

What is this news that J.-E. B. is going around spreading about my angel Doucet (you do say angel, don't you?)? * It's a pure fabrication, and I am furious. I shall have to make up my mind to poison the poisoner.

I cannot resign myself to the fact that the publication of your poems be delayed, or prevented, on account of the N.R.F.

In two weeks, upon my return to Paris, we'll talk about it again, and conclusively. Is Gallimard back? . . . Have not yet been notified.

Perhaps you know Royère's address; I wanted to write him—but where?

Your

André G.

I can imagine Doucet's face if that canard ever flies over to him. And it will fly!

225. *Paul Valéry to André Gide*

[May 11, 1918 (in Gide's handwriting)]

". . . Gentlemen, you would merit still more gratitude from our people were you to add to the Institute—created for those intellects that have remained in the fields without credit and ruthlessly drained by phynance [*sic*] companies—a chair of pure and applied gibberish, the appointee to which would talk to them day and night of the beauty and clarity of our dear French language, until their minds were brought to a maximum of fertile activity, thus producing—instead of postmen and tax collectors, who

---

[39] The poet and novelist John-Antoine Nau (1860–1918), who received the first Prix Goncourt in 1903 for his *Force ennemie,* was a good friend of the poet and critic Jean Royère, founder of the review *La Phalange.*

* *Translator's note:* The play on words in French is: "ma commandite (ou: comment dit-on?) par Doucet?"

are merely hirelings with no vitality, subjected to starvation wages—a kind of intensive flowering of the salt of humanity."

More applause. The Council, with no reference to the Phynance Committee, votes supplies of two hundred francs for the study of the ways and means entailed in the creation of that chair which has been so eloquently pleaded.

And since I've got you, here is a further plea (I don't know why people always come to me on such occasions)!

Mme. Fontainas writes me that Mr. Ph. Neel,[40] who is doing a translation of Conrad, has sent you several letters which are still unanswered. . . .

I'm going to advertise in the papers that Mr. P. V. does not answer silences *contracted* by Mr. A. G.

Gasp. . . . A letter arrived and has been brought to me. Mme. Georges-Ville [41] demands visit.

I feel better since noon yesterday. But Thursday was really altogether lacking in strength. Very downcast. The contrary of the Ascension.

What I should really like—let's ramble on—is that you find me a Doucet [42] like yours. I meet that creature, whom I used to know, twice a day and we look at one another without *douceur*. He lives at 46, avenue du Bois, next door to me.

If instead of renewing our memories, we re-knew one another,* I would inspire him to reprint *Narcisse* in a folio edition, with pictures.

The stupidity of such extravagance fascinates my weary mind.

What have I done this morning? Two pages of notes. The Spirit visited me during two cigarettes. Then came the news and the mail. *Spiritus exit.*

Last night reread . . . (a little . . .) *Das Kapital!* I am one of the rare men who has read it. It seems that even Jaurès ** himself . . .

While I was reading it, I worked up an article on the side.

Which makes the third in two weeks. An article in the mind—that is, a five-and-ten article.

One on the *Mémoire Lichnowski.*[43] The other on a masterpiece that I

---

[40] Philippe Neel translated into French Conrad's *Lord Jim, Nostromo, Gaspar Ruiz, Under Western Eyes,* and *Chance.*

[41] Mme Muhlfeld.

[42] Jacques Doucet.

* *Translator's note:* The play on words in French is: "Si au lieu de nous reconnaître, nous nous re-connaissions . . ."

** *Translator's note:* Jean Jaurès (1859–1914), head of the Socialist party in France from 1905 until his assassination in 1914.

[43] K. M. Lichnowsky (1860–1928), a German diplomat, had been ambassador to London in 1912. Working for closer relations between England and Germany, he was very disappointed by England's declaration of war, and, in his book *My London Mission,* pointed up the share of responsibility of the German statesmen.

once read a great deal, and the author of which has just been made a member of the Academy of Sciences. It's M. Koenigs.[44] I could see in it a method for *Le Mercure*. One day I'll talk to you about that little book, which I value tremendously—and have for the last ten years.

As for *Das Kapital,* that fat book contains very remarkable things. One has only to find them. It shows a rather heavy-handed pride. Is often very inadequate as far as rigor is concerned, or very pedantic for nothing, but certain analyses are terrific. I mean that the manner of grasping things is similar to the one I use rather often, and that I can translate rather often his language into mine. The objective is of no importance, and at bottom it's the same!

No explanation!

They let Degas' Duranty[45] be bought by Denmark (*nach* Berlin?), it's idiotic. It is one of the things we should have kept—completely French.

Well, see you soon?   P. V.

— 1919 —

226. *André Gide to Paul Valéry*

Cuverville, October 6, 1919

My dear Paul,

Really, I do hope to see you again soon. I think I may turn up in Paris around the 10th; will stop in at the rue de Villejust to see what's become of you. The annoying thing is not knowing on what perch to alight: the deserted villa is freezing and unfeasible without a cleaning woman; the Van R.'s have people visiting; the Allegrets are moving; I am told that the hotels are full. . . . *Vedremo.*[1]

Yes, I saw the Witch when I came through Paris, on my way back from Luxembourg; since I rang her up first, I found her "as it happens, writing to Valéry." I intrusted her and her letter with my greetings. . . .

After two almost full months, at Dudelange,[2] I found the house here still full, Madeleine not really too tired after a rather hard summer, in view of

---

[44] G. Koenigs (1858–1931), professor at the Sorbonne and at the Ecole des Arts et Métiers, and author of works on mechanics.

[45] Duranty, an art critic and novelist, was a friend of Degas, who did a portrait of him.

[1] We shall see.

[2] At the home of Mme Mayrisch Saint-Hubert, the wife of a wealthy industrialist from Luxembourg. A very cultured woman, who spoke perfect French, German, and English, Mme Mayrisch entertained French and German artists and writers in her château de Colbach, in Luxembourg. It was at her home that Gide was to meet Walter Rathenau and Ernst-Robert Curtius.

her troubles finding servants, food . . . , everything; Marcel in better shape than he has been in for a long time; I think my absence did him a lot of good. He even worked. . . .

As for me, I twisted my brain, during almost the entire summer, over some absurd work that I should have liked to talk over with you, if only we had been able to rub shoulders a bit, as we did two years ago. I'm persisting; but don't know whether I shall ever have done with it. In any case, I still have a long way to go.

"Gallimard Publishing Co.; capital 850,000 francs." Don't try to understand. It's a fact. I shan't have anything to explain to you; but a lot to tell you. And various problems to put to you, with refernece to *Le Mercure* and certain proposals from Plon? * All the above are *topics* [3] for tomorrow.

I can't for a moment believe that your mine is pumped out, or that your spring has run dry; the difficult thing is the bottling, but there's nothing surprising in the fact that you felt tired after the exertion of last winter. The idiotic thing is that you couldn't have any proper relaxation. If only the South Seas weren't so far off. . . . Au revoir. See you soon. Lots of affectionate greetings to your women.

André Gide

— 1920 —

227. Paul Valéry to André Gide

La Graulet, % Mme. Pozzi
near Bergerac (Dordogne) [1] [September, 1920]

Dear old André,

I am here. It's now a week since I left Paris in a worse state (and which for two months had been getting progressively more so) than I have ever known. A strange state, which only half yields to the extraordinary peace of a countryside that's so calm the wind is, as it were, unknown. I have not yet seen a leaf move; if some one of them happens to fall, it's after the manner of chestnuts, from the zenith to the . . . I have been marvelously welcomed, cared for, anticipated, driven about—but alas! here I *am*, here I

---

* *Translator's note:* A publishing house in Paris.

[3] In English in the original.

[1] Paul Valéry was then at the home of Mme Pozzi, whose daughter Catherine had married Edouard Bourdet [playwright, and administrator of the Comédie Française from 1936 to 1940] and become known as a poet. (Cf. the anthology following *L'Introduction à la Poésie française* by Thierry Maulnier, in collaboration with Dominique Aury. Gallimard, 1939.)

still *am!* I mean to say that those strange symptoms stay with me; they come on of a sudden—deep-rooted feelings of non-existence, *unbearable* burning *hands,* a quickening of the pulse, weakness. All that created, orchestrated, unleashed by a calamitous stomach and by a nervous system that's Dada. Really bad, bad. And, to finish me off, frightful summer homework, with dates that are drawing near, almost touching me, and almost *nothing* done! I could kick myself for having accepted such work, which I am unable, don't want, and don't know how to do, which sends my book of verse [2] *ad Kalendas,* and which out of a concern for Mammon I took on. And well, I'm really paying for those months of fatigue, dinner parties, prose, verse, notes, and conversation. I am turning white, like a piece of chocolate.

My family is still at Le Mesnil. Claude made a short stay in the vicinity of Dieppe; I don't know much about it, except that he saw a great deal of Sickert [3] and that they probably visited *many* [4] dance halls. . . .

I'm not sure whether you know Catherine Bourdet-Pozzi, who invited me to come here? Her insistence prevailed over the terror of railroads I had finally worked up. Her mother, who is the widow of the famous surgeon, makes me think ever so much of Madeleine, your wife. She has the same expression in her eyes, the same general air. Ten times a day I get the impression of being in Cuverville. But how is Madeleine? And you? I had thought of Luxembourg, but since you disappeared altogether, leaving no address, that vague plan vanished from my mind. Besides, it was the sea I was hoping for. But no one invited me in that direction, and I had neither the strength to choose a beach nor the desire to spend my time in some hotel. So I lingered in Paris until September, half-dead. Three-quarters.

I plan to propose to the Foundation: [5] 1. Breton, [6] 2. Aeschimann (whom I don't know, but he has no lack of talent, he's about as hard up as can be, he's Swiss, Foreign Legion, etc.). [7]

Do thank Mlle Mayrisch for her invitation. I couldn't come to her this year, and I prefer, truly, to present her with a less deteriorated individual. I should most willingly write her a note of thanks (which in truth I owe

[2] In 1920 Valéry was to publish his *Album des vers anciens,* a collection of his early verse, and *Odes.*

[3] Walter Sickert (1860–1942), the English painter and illustrator, a friend of Oscar Wilde's. Gide owned several of his works.

[4] In English in the original.

[5] The Blumenthal Foundation, which offered a grant of 5,000 francs to a young French writer. George Blumenthal was an American banker, a patron of the arts, and a Francophile.

[6] The surrealist poet André Breton. From 1913 to 1918, he had had regular dealings with Valéry.

[7] Paul Aeschimann, poet, author of *Feux d'Automne (1918–1944)* and *La Terre et l'Aigle* (1945).

her) directly, were it not that I had such trouble composing anything at all. You cannot imagine just how tired I am.

I see that Régnier has been put on the jury for the above-mentioned Foundation. That obviously means something, but I'm not yet sure what. I think he was absolutely nasty to you. I don't know what you've excogitated to pay him back; but in your place, I should consider things in the Corsican manner, and I'd look around my cellar for a small cask of Amontillado.[8]

Theoretically, at least, I profess that one must never forget a kindness or an insult. All would be well if that fair precept of recollection were generally practiced.

See you I don't know when, I don't know how.

Your
P. V.

228. *André Gide to Paul Valéry*

Saturday afternoon [October 2, 1920]

Dear old Paul,

Your letter dismays me. I should like to be with you. . . . But today I shall hold back my comments. I have but little time to write you, and you are doubtless expecting my account of the Blumenthal meeting.[9]

Present were Jaloux, Boylesve, Bergson, Régnier. Proust arrived forty-five minutes late, when the matter was already clinched. I had been warned by the Witch, the evening before, that Proust had taken in hand the candidacy of Rivière[10] (reasons of discretion, as a friend, and my relations with the N.R.F. kept me from proposing him, but I could only concur in that choice). It was Jaloux who first put up his name; Bergson immediately exclaimed that we couldn't make a better choice; the two others expressed similar opinions, and for a few minutes I had the pleasure of hearing a chorus of praise. We knew, on the other hand, that Mme de N.,[11] likewise, was voting for Rivière. He was therefore elected unanimously.

But we then learned that we had to award not one grant but *two*. As a matter of fact, not one of them had thought about a second candidate. I was awaiting the propitious moment to toss in Breton's name for consideration. But, to my great surprise, Jaloux made the first move and spoke of

---

[8] Probably an allusion to Poe's tale *The Cask of Amontillado.* Since 1900, when Gide had attacked Régnier's novel *La Double Maîtresse,* the relations between the two writers had been rather strained. In 1924 Gide sold all the books he had received from Régnier at the Salle Drouot. Régnier was to send him one of his later novels with the dedication: "For your next sale . . ."

[9] Valéry, who did not attend the meeting, had asked [the writer] Anna de Noailles to vote for him.

[10] Jacques Rivière (1886–1925) had then published: *Etudes* (1911) and *L'Allemand, Souvenirs et Réflexions d'un Prisonnier de Guerre* (1918).

[11] Anna de Noailles.

Breton before I did. So I brought out your letter, which I had carefully taken with me, and read the sentence in which you declared yourself in his favor, stating that I, too, would vote for him. But Jaloux, after having proposed Breton, of his own accord, then advanced the few objections (Dadaism), which, for that matter, were mine as well, with the result that after conferring (it was then that Proust made his entrance) we *postponed* Breton, deeming that what as a first choice might appear impudent and virtually disrespectful in the eyes of America, would no longer be so another year, or at any rate would be less censured. Moreover, we know that Breton, since he has been "reconciled" with his family, is no longer exactly in need; and also, he never went to war. . . . (Proust, likewise, proved to be very sympathetic to Breton; Régnier at first clearly hostile, but rather readily coming over to our opinion.) However, none of us had any other candidate to propose. Jaloux then proposed Thérive,[12] and we hesitated, when I got the idea of proposing André Salmon;[13] warm approval from Proust and Jaloux; the others visibly ready to fall into step. I therefore spent my day yesterday drawing up my memorandum on Salmon, which I am sending today to Mme B. and which will be passed on to you. I consider Salmon a very worthy fellow; he is currently crushed by journalistic chores, which he had to accept on *Le Matin,* for he is absolutely penniless; he behaved admirably during the war (volunteered) and had a very bad time of it; very decent, very honest—and what's more, extremely pleasing. I don't always like what he does; but he is certainly one of the young men who interests me most—if one can still call someone of 35 "young." In short, since they're postponing Breton, I shall vote for him, and with all my heart; and I urge you to give him your vote. We are supposed to meet again on the 18th at two-thirty. Will you be there?

Au revoir, dear old Paul. I received an exquisite little letter from Jenny [14] and am awaiting a short respite (I'm over my head in "business") to go and see her. I do hope she'll be able to give me somewhat better news of you. If you write me, address your letter to the *N.R.F.,* 35, rue Madame; for those addressed to the villa are directly whisked off to Cuverville, where I hope to go in a few days. Here (at the villa) I am all alone, with no cleaning woman, and leave in the morning, not to return until the curfew; which is EXHAUSTING!

Very much your
André Gide

[12] The critic and novelist André Thérive, born in 1891, who was to publish, in particular, *L'Expatrié* (1921), *Le Voyage de Renan* (1922), and *Les Portes de l'Enfer* (1925). It was he who finally received the grant.

[13] André Salmon, born in 1881, poet (*Les Féeries,* 1907; *Le Calumet,* 1910), novelist (*La Négresse du Sacré-Cœur,* 1920), and art critic, a good friend of Picasso's and Apollinaire's, and a defender of cubist painting.

[14] Mme Paul Valéry.

— 1921 —

229. André Gide to Paul Valéry

Monday morning [Spring, 1921]

My dear Paul,

Forgive me if the ear I lent you yesterday was so little concave and attentive; I was exhausted and worried. For two days, dizziness; less distressing than troublesome; the result of what? I don't know. Promising what? even less. Dear fellow, don't count on me for that Monnier evening: *id est:* get Adrienne not to *announce me,* and not to believe she has to use my name to attract an audience, which will come in just as large numbers for you alone. Quite simply, can't they indicate on the program that there will be readings by "a few friends" and if I am in a fit state to come and to read, Fargue will doubtless be kind enough to yield the cathedra to me for a few minutes. It is certain that if I am well, I should be more than pleased to read a fragment of *L'Architecte;* but I want to feel someone like Fargue nearby to take over.[1]

I am writing to Rilke.[2] But if you perhaps feel in the mood to write him yourself, which would give him great pleasure, here is the address:

[1] Adrienne Monnier, in her bookshop in the rue de l'Odéon, was then organizing poetry readings. There, she was to make known before publication *Charmes* and *Eupalinos ou l'Architecte.*

[2] Before the war, Gide had become friendly with Rilke, who had been living in Paris more or less continually since 1902. In 1910 Rilke sent a copy of his recently published *Notebook of Malte Laurids Brigge* to Gide, who then translated several fragments of it and published them in the July 1 issue of the *N.R.F.* Rilke, in turn, published his translation of *Le Retour de l'Enfant prodigue,* which helped make Gide known in Germany.

After having been away from Paris for many years because of the war, Rilke discovered Valéry, and wrote to Gide on April 21, 1921: "I can't tell you the deep emotion I felt upon reading *L'Architecte* and (here and there) a few other of Paul Valéry's writings. How is it possible that I didn't know of him for so many years? A few weeks ago, I translated fervidly those other "truly marine words"—the stanzas of *Le Cimetière marin* (June 1, 1920, issue of the *N.R.F.*), and it is now, I think, one of my best translations . . ."

To one of his friends, Monique Saint-Hélier, Rilke was subsequently to say: "I was alone, I was waiting, my whole heart was waiting. One day I read Valéry. I knew then that my waiting was over."

From that day on, Rilke never ceased to admire Valéry fervently, and expressed his admiration by translating Valéry into the German language. But he was to meet him only twice: on April 6, 1924, at Muzot, Switzerland, where he was living, and on September 13, 1926, at Julien-Pierre Monod's, in Anthy, near Thonon (cf. below, Letter 243). See *La Correspondance Rilke-Gide,* edited by Renée Lang (Corréa, 1952), and Renée Lang, *Rilke, Gide et Valéry* (Prétexte, 1953).

M. Rainer-Maria Rilke
Château de Berg-sur-Irchel
Canton de Zürich
Suisse

I am thinking about an article on you;[3] rash to speak of it already—and yet the fear of being unworthy, unskilled, incapable of carrying it through, is what still keeps me from it. . . .

Is it really possible that you feel so weary and disgusted, *knowing* how capable you are of illumination, such as that which you told me you experienced the other morning? You *owe* us this book, you owe yourself this book, which I can imagine only as the most important book of our time, and, I may add, dealing with literature only at one of its extremities. Despite the fact that I seemed distracted last night, don't for a minute believe that anything you said escaped me. If it is in my power to help you set about writing it . . . how my friendship would rejoice.

Au revoir.
André Gide

230. Paul Valéry to André Gide
Monday [May, 1921 (in Gide's handwriting)]
My dear André,

"Exhausted, worried"—I don't like those adjectives. Besides, they are singularly my own, and you are not going to extort them from me! But don't bother about that reading, if you think you'd find it tiring or merely boring. The Monnier program, which was submitted to me yesterday, bore the words: "Readings by Yonnel[4] and a few *amateurs*."

. . . .

Besides, I just—during that line of dots—phoned Adr. Monnier. Everything's settled.

Now, my dear old André, you have promised me something that is precious to me. You say that you feel inclined to do that article on me and that it seems to you difficult in certain respects. Well, but there is one very simple way for you to get round those difficulties.

You have known me for thirty years; you have only to do a kind of portrait . . . evolving. In other words, something corresponding to *Si le Grain ne meurt;* and the difficulties then are part of the resemblance. I see the work as almost easy and all the easier in that you will be more faithful, closer to observed "nature."

Don't forget to put in the shadows. Leonardo said that he who doesn't add them to his drawing will never be a good painter. . . .

---

[3] See below, Letter 231, n. 1.
[4] Jean Yonnel, who was to become a member of the Comédie-Française.

But all I ask you is not to speak (explicitly) of the "most important book of our time," as you so rightly say.

It is difficult for me to imagine, in the form of a book, the intellectual will power that went into my life, and my personal resistance to the influence of the dissipation, stupefaction, softening and insensatism brought to bear on modern man by the life he must lead, by the university, the newspaper, the fashions, the sham, the extremists, the opportunists, the various clergy, the artists, and generally by all those who make one believe, or by those who do believe.

I have tried to think what I thought, and I have done so with persistent naïveté. I am said to be *subtle,* and it's absurd. Rather, I am brutal, but I have, or did have, a mania for precision. An enormous portion of my work, —half-lost, half-useful,—was to make definitions for myself. To think by means of my own definitions was for me a kind of goal.

Etc.

I should like to see again the letter from that kind Rilke. Leave it in your pocket. If I meet you, you'll show it to me again.

Try to dispel your worries, and to do away with that dizziness, which is obviously caused by the stomach. Meredith was right when he lay the blame on the stomach for what we so often accuse an overworked brain.

Your old

P. V.

— 1922 —

231. Paul Valéry to André Gide

Tuesday [June, 1922]

Dear You,

You're so right. We never see each other. And indeed, I never see myself. I wrote *eighteen* letters today.

And I never even wrote you, or said, what your "essay" [1] *on my* humble *self* [2] wrenched out of me. I have the impression that I acted as if I were disgusted.

But how can I make you understand? Who will ever make himself understood? And who will ever gauge that extraordinary mixture of the fear of not being understood and the terror of being understood? Am I clear, now?

Friday, my old André, impossible. I am having a countess in to eat.

[1] An article published in *Le Divan,* in an issue of homage to Valéry (1922). Gide specified that he wanted to speak "of the man whom few know and whom his works carefully hide."

[2] In English in the original.

Saturday, then. At twelve-thirty, unless I hear to the contrary, I shall be at the Vieux-Colombier restaurant.   P. V.

232. *Paul Valéry to André Gide*

Monday [early August, 1922 (in Gide's handwriting)]

I am answering you directly (and also immediately), my dear André, for your letter, which just this minute arrived, does me good. . . .*

I assure you that I feel a kind of remorse regarding you. My answer to you was short and dry, I think, *nella mia ultima.*[3]

If you let me be hard, you shall see me be gentle.

And then, am being put off by a lot of turd. God's ten deturdments.**

Nothing new, nothing even old, in the way of a job,[4] and actually it would be as much of a bore to get one (which would surely be bad) as it is a worry not to.

(And you know that the franc is going down promptly, it appears, and all prices will triple.)

For a man who has a horror of worrying, and whom the slightest thing shatters and kills, I've really had it.

Well, hang it all. I don't care any more. The papers, vying with each other, are throwing Mallarmé and all the adjoining obscurity at my head.

I think I made a mistake with that printing of two thousand (five editions!) and, especially, in having sent copies to all those useless newspapers.[5]

And also, it came out three weeks too late.

I am with my mother, and myself. The rest are at Le Mesnil, where I shall go rather unwillingly. Perhaps I'll go for a short time to the Bassianos[6] near Trouville. And then?

Work: nil (since *La Danse,*[7] have done nothing).

Diligence: nil.

Sleep: 3 (out of 8).

Appetite: 4 (*idem*).

---

* *Translator's note:* The last published letter from Gide was dated July 22, 1922. In it Gide wrote that he had gone for a short holiday to the island of Porquerolles, as a guest of the Martin du Gards. Roger Martin du Gard had met Gide in 1913, in the offices of the N.R.F., after having published *Jean Barois.*

[3] In my last [letter].

** *Translator's note:* The French reads: "les emmerdements. Les dix emmerdements de Dieu."

[4] Paul Valéry lost his steady job when Edouard Lebey died, in February, 1922.

[5] *Charmes* had just been published by Les Editions de la N.R.F.

[6] The Prince and Princess Bassiano, friends of artists and writers. It was the Princess Bassiano who founded the review *Commerce,* on which Valéry was to work very actively, along with L.-P. Fargue and V. Larbaud.

[7] *L'Ame et la Danse,* preceded by *Eupalinos ou l'Architecte,* was published in 1922 by Gallimard.

Observations: is stupider than life.

To come back to *Charmes* (this time to the content). Those poems annoy me, for I don't understand how I could have written them. What strange considerations, as I remember, intervened in certain pieces! . . .

Yesterday, I suddenly wrote a 70-line ode, 10 × 8, improvised in one day, which has never happened to me. It is unpublishable and essentially *private*.* The audacity of it is great.[8] But upon rereading it, I saw it as a document for comparison. The work is naturally very inferior to that of *Charmes,* for time *does everything* in poems. But I saw what is rather difficult for me to see, *id est* the outcome of an improvisation by yours truly. When I improvise in that way, and the result's not very bad, it resembles *Le Cimetière Marin* in tone and movement. (But in lines of 8.)

The *Cimetière Marin* would therefore be typical of my true "poetry," especially the most abstract parts of that poem.[9] It's a kind of "lyricism" (*mi capisco*) [10]—clear and abstract, but the abstraction is propulsive far more than philosophical.

Understand if you can.

I understand why you gave up on *Hamlet*.[11] Pitoëff is Hamlet enough as it is. All the same, that Shakespeare was a blackguard. He had his people spout things exactly as one thinks them. . . . And unfortunately our classical theatre couldn't, didn't know how, or didn't want to do it. If it had, given its construction and admirable conventions, it would have been the "masterpiece of the human mind."

I clasp your hands. (I need to.)

Regards to your hosts or companions, male or female.

Scribe et me ame.   P. V.

233. André Gide to Paul Valéry

Cuverville, October 25, 1922

My dear Paul,

In spite of the great desire (and I was about to say: need) I had to see you again, it was impossible for me to wait for you. I now hope to meet you in the South. I am almost choking with supressed conversation. . . . I'm sorry for you, having to go to England in this cold weather,[12] but you can at least count on

cette pluie
où l'on se jette à genoux [13]

being worth a cold and the fatigue of the journey.

---

* *Translator's note:* In English in the original.

[8] The ode was never published.

[9] *Le Cimetière marin* was published in *Charmes* (1922).

[10] I know what I mean.

[11] Gide's translation of *Hamlet* was published in 1944 (New York, Schiffrin).

[12] Valéry was going to London to lecture in order to earn some money.

[13] [". . . that rain/In which we fall upon our knees."] From *Palme*, in *Charmes*.

And the lecture in Geneva? Will you have recovered enough from your grippe to bear all that? If Cuverville were espaliered, I would urge you to come and spend a few days; but even I have trouble bearing the frost. Will I be able to spend the winter here? Everything is still all right when only my wrist is paralyzed; but if my brain is, too . . . And no way to convince Madeleine to move. This will explain to you (in part) that sentence in my letter which caused you to be "lost in conjecture." * I shall clarify this further for you viva voce. Jeannie probably repeated to you what I told her about the . . . zeal of Desjardins [14] and . . . Fontaine,[15] with regard to you. Also spoke to the Witch, who enumerated to me the people who are "attending to you" and getting you a "job." They are overdoing it! overdoing it. . . . All the same, keep me informed, if something were to take shape. I don't consider that Desjardins' intervention is negligible, and I haven't resigned myself to the idea of Fontaine's being a quitter.

Meanwhile, *Charmes* is triumphing. This summer I met so many people who went into ecstasies over "the admirable edition" that I have come to wonder whether my criticism wasn't a bit too harsh (I'm, of course, speaking of the book's appearance).[16]

Don't judge me from my letters, dear friend. Yours are so full, so rich, so affectionate that in comparison I feel like a poor wretch. Yet I do have so much to tell you. . . .

"We must talk," indeed. Au revoir.

Your
A. G.

234. *Paul Valéry to André Gide*

14, Holland Park, London, W.11.
Monday (October, 1922)

My dear André,

I shall be here until Thursday, which will make ten days of England, where I would have been fine were it not for the great—obligatory—fatigue. I feel better here than in Paris.

---

* *Translator's note:* In a letter to Valéry of October, 1922, Gide wrote: "But the truth is that I no longer know how to arrange my life and don't dare to look ahead." On October 19, 1922, Valéry answered: "The last lines of your letter are so mysterious that they caused me to be 'lost in conjecture.' . . . We must talk."

[14] Paul Desjardins (1859-1940) founded *L'Union pour l'Action morale* and created in 1910, at Pontigny, in a secularized Cistercian abbey, *Les Entretiens de Pontigny,* international gatherings for the exchange of literary, social, aesthetic, political, and religious ideas and information. André Gide dedicated his *Nouveaux Prétextes* to Desjardins.

[15] Arthur Fontaine.

[16] *Charmes*, Editions de la N.R.F., 1922.

I spent yesterday, Sunday, at the home of Conrad,[17] who is terribly nice and almost affectionate. Spoke of you, necessarily. I told him that he ought to write his seafaring memoirs of Marseilles and Sète *in French*. He seemed rather attracted by the idea, which at the same time he rejected. . . . *Tibi.*

Saw Canterbury in passing. Glanced into the cathedral, where I should rather like to have seen an Anglican service. I would have done a column on it for Meyer.[18] . . .

At a luncheon at the home of Saint-Aulaire [19] (who is most amiable and equally well disposed toward literature), I sat next to M. Brunschvicq,[20] a round and simple man, to whom I said, upon leaving, that he must have felt very ill at ease sitting next to an enemy of Pascal's. He protested, declared that he was a Spinozist, etc. We parted satisfied.

Hardly had the time to rush about seeing again what I really like in London: the Embankment and the districts around St. Paul's. It irks me to return to Paris. Dinner parties, literature—damn! and that mess at home, with all the worries relating to it, and the letters, etc.

I feel like doing nothing but scribbling, and drawing nudes and heads. Ideas bore me. I'm fed up with them, and at bottom, I have never liked anything but the action—the intellectual action—they imply.

Within a week I have to do a kind of Eupalinesque thing for a budding art review. All that is peripheral. As for the sensual and cerebral novel, the mere thought of physically writing a volume makes me beastly and drives me wild.

And besides, there is still the question of my celebrated notes.[21] I end by deliberately imagining that I did nothing until the age of forty-five. And yet there is where my true self lies.

See you soon, perhaps. All my old-faithful regards to your wife.

Your old

P. V.

[17] Gide was to say of the writer Joseph Conrad (1857–1924): "What I liked about him most was a kind of innate nobility, harsh, disdainful, and somewhat despondent, the same that he attributed to Lord Jim (*La Nouvelle Revue Française,* December, 1924). See below, Letter 236, n. 5.

[18] Arthur Meyer, director of *Le Gaulois.*

[19] The French ambassador to London.

[20] Léon Brunschvicg (1869–1944), professor of philosophy at the Sorbonne, and to whom we owe, among numerous other works, an exhaustive edition of Pascal's *Pensées* and a book on *Spinoza.*

[21] In 1945 Valéry's unpublished notebooks numbered 257.

— 1923 —

235. *Paul Valéry to André Gide*

Monday, October 8, 1923

My old André,

I got back last night, and was so sorry to have missed you. I shall soon be off for London again the first chance I get, to give a lecture on . . . Hugo!

I will quote: "Hugo, alas!" The greatest remark of the century.[1]

Health very vague,—fluctuating between neuralgia, enteritis, and larynx-bronchial trouble.

Work continually postponed.

The pose [*sic*] is yours, yours with all my heart.

P. V.

236. *André Gide to Paul Valéry*

Cuverville, 9th [October, 1923]

My dear Paul,

Regret terribly having missed you, and by so few hours! it's absurd; but being obliged to return to Cuverville next day, couldn't wait for you. I still hope to see you again before you leave for England. When? If I were sure to find you unoccupied (or almost) and to be able to have a few good hours of talk with you, I'd come back just to see you. Dear old Paul, I am full of admiration for the last pages of yours that I read. I am not speaking of *Eupalinos*[2]—which I haven't yet finished exploring, and which is beyond all praise and makes me sometimes wonder whether I don't prefer your prose to your verse—but quite simply of those pages in *La Revue hebdomadaire*,[3] written to order, but as if you were playing.

So you have left [*sic*] for England. If I don't see you again between now and then, lots of greetings to Bennett[4] (an excellent letter from him) and perhaps to Conrad (he came to Cuverville, *dieci giorni fà*,[5] with wife and child and Aubry,[6] one day when the whole family was in Etretat). A lecture on Hugo! . . . yes, perhaps; but a novel by you, that's what I am

---

[1] André Gide's answer to the question: "Whom do you consider the greatest poet of the nineteenth century?" for a literary survey.

[2] *Eupalinos ou l'Architecte* was published by Les Editions de la N.R.F. in 1923.

[3] The July 14, 1923, issue of *La Revue Hebdomadaire*, entitled *"Pascal* issue," published an essay by Paul Valéry: *Variation sur une Pensée.* The issue also included articles by Mauriac, Barrès, and Maritain.

[4] See above, Letter 210, n. 11.

[5] Ten days ago.

[6] G. Jean-Aubry, essayist and critic, was also a friend and translator of Conrad's, and wrote a biography of him (Gallimard, 1947).

hoping and waiting for; you know it; I won't give up on it; we'll talk about it again. Distribute my regards to everyone around you.

Your
A. G.

— 1924 —

237. *André Gide to Paul Valéry*

Cuverville [P. October 25, 1924]

My dear Paul,

Since you have set the example, I shall type too. *Similia similibus.*[1] It's certainly very convenient, and I'm doing it more and more.

What happened is quite natural and is not even worth your questions.* The moment Gallimard spoke to me of the plan for a fund on your behalf, I had asked him to put me down for a contribution.[2] When I talked to him again, the other day, about the arrangements, I was surprised at not seeing my name among the very first on the list and beseeched him to rectify the oversight or omission as soon as possible. It was only natural; and Gallimard was not even to notify you of it. I am almost embarrassed that he did. You are not to thank me. As a matter of fact, I was counting on its being anonymous. It is extremely painful for me to feel that you are still so often plagued by worries that are unworthy of you, and it makes me suffer to the very depths of my friendship. I was overjoyed to seize this opportunity to intervene with something more than words. I will not let my name appear in this case, unless it can serve as an example.

I'm sorry I had to leave Paris without seeing you again. But you know, my trip to F.E.A. has been postponed.[3] Whence my hope of meetings in the near future. For the love of Apollo, don't let yourself be swallowed up by absurd obligations out of courtesy. Extricate yourself. Work freely; it's the best way to keep up your standing. Just a word of caution.

And take yourself down to the South as soon as you can. It's there that I should like to meet you. The air of Paris is poisoning us. That of

---

[1] The principle of homeopathy, as opposed to that of universally accepted medicine: *contraria contrariis curantur.* Paul Valéry's last letter was typewritten, as is this letter from André Gide.

* *Translator's note:* Valéry's letter in this connection is not published.

[2] Gaston Gallimard arranged for contributions to a fund for the publication of all Paul Valéry's works. [In a note of thanks to Gide, postmarked October 27, 1924, Valéry wrote that his idea was to "make it into a good business deal for those twenty believers."]

[3] André Gide was to leave for French Equatorial Africa on July 18, 1925. He returned in February, 1926.

Cuverville is hardly *bracing*.[4] How long will I manage to content myself with it? Meanwhile, I am holding fast to my work.

> Au revoir. Very faithfully yours.
>
> A. G.

238. *André Gide to Paul Valéry*

[Paris] December 26, 1924

My dear Paul,

I hear that you haven't been well. . . .

I am, alas, prevented from coming to see you, for although I'm in Paris, I am confined to a hospital on account of appendicitis, and am supposed to be operated on tomorrow.

I first spent over two weeks in my room suffering from the grippe; and just as I was starting to go out again and about to wend my way over to Villejust and Georges-Ville, all the nonsense began.

This short note *in order to let you know*[5] . . . and to assure you once again of my friendship.

My most affectionate greetings to your wife, your mother, your sister-in-law and the children.

> Your
> André G.

During the worst days of my grippe I turned to *Variété*[6] as a tonic and a febrifuge. What idiots say (thinking it's praise) "a poet's prose"? It's the prose of a prose writer, and I know none that is quite so beautiful. I admire it as much as your verse, if not more, that is to say, more than anything written up to now.

— 1925 —

239. *Paul Valéry to André Gide*

January 1, 1925

My dear old André,

I have had vague news of you by telephone. As soon as you can have visitors, I shall come and see you (for I've been starting to go out again the last two or three days). I send you all good wishes for this day and this century. And an unpublished definition of friendship as your New Year's gift.

When the mere chance that causes two men to meet, take stock of one another, gauge one another, etc., changes imperceptibly into a kind of

[4] In English in the original.

[5] In English in the original.

[6] Valéry's *Variété I* was published in 1924 by Les Editions de la N.R.F. The series was to be made up of five volumes.

necessity, an event that couldn't not have been, that *justification* (in the evangelical sense) of an accidental case is: friendship.

Friends are these two men who *saved* from chance and accident an occurrence that was commonplace and that would very likely have fallen, such as it was, into the statistics of the molecular shocks of mankind.

Any interest this conception of a definition of friendship may have, in its retroactive effect, will be given by you. It came to me as I thought of Us, of 1891, of 1925, and of etc.

Anyway, I am completely worn out this morning (like all the previous ones).

See you soon, my old André.

> Love.
> P. V.

240. André Gide to Paul Valéry

Sunday [P. January 11, 1925]

Dear Paul,

Perhaps you aren't acquainted with this article, published in a somewhat special review, in which there was also the first somewhat sensible article on *Corydon* (and that's why it was sent to me).[1]

Yesterday I returned to the villa,[2] a few days too soon, perhaps, judging from my weakness and fatigue.

Do tell the Witch that my first visit will be to her (I would say: to you, if I didn't dread all those steps of yours), but probably not before the end of the week.

> Very much your
> A. G.

241. Paul Valéry to André Gide

[P. November 26, 1925][3]

My dear André,

They *elected* me on *Thursday* (November 19).[4] This must make a strange impression where you are, in deepest Africa. I thought of many things when I learned of this almost unexpected accident. Your card from Bangui arrived this morning, the 26th. I have no idea what you're seeing and thinking. I am leaving on December 7 for Holland, summoned by

---

[1] The first edition of *Corydon*, without its author's name, dates from 1911. The first edition offered for sale appeared in 1924.

[2] The villa Montmorency, in Auteuil, Gide's Parisian residence. Roger Martin du Gard described it in his *Journal* as follows: "Strange, fabulous abode, where he doesn't seem much at home, and where, in fact, it would probably be impossible for anyone to feel at home" (*Notes sur André Gide, 1913–1951*, Gallimard, 1951).

[3] A postcard, with a view of Deauville, addressed to André Gide, % The French Bank of Africa, Brazzaville, French Congo, F.E.A., and forwarded to Fort-Archambault.

[4] That day there was a triple election at the Académie française: Louis Bertrand

many lectures. It will be so cold I'm terrified. When will we be able to exchange a bit of climate over the wire or wire-less? I only send you all our affection. Claude got married on *Saturday*.[5] What a week!

Your

P. V.

— 1926 —

242. *André Gide to Paul Valéry*

[Telegram]

Fort-Archambault, January 12, 1926

Applaud with all my heart.

Gide

243. *Paul Valéry to André Gide*

Paris [P. September 17, 1926]

Dear friend,

I received your letter from Dijon, *posted* * at Marseilles and announcing Gabès, in Anthy near Thonon, where I was delicately and nicely pampered by J. Monod.[1] Everything was perfect, minus the self who is becoming unbearable. I came back to see my mother, who caused great anxiety at Le Mesnil and whom I found better, after that alarm at ninety-five years old!

You are right to tell me that you no longer know who I am. There was a time when you yourself gave me that impression, which one should have without stop, both of others and of one's self. As for me, I never knew who I was,—and I always knew who I wasn't,—mistakenly or not. Now I am being wound up more and more by present circumstances. My life is a skein, the basic thread of which has got tangled up with so many strands of such different kinds that I make mistakes and get snarled up, even when I sleep.

(Barrès' seat), the Duc de la Force (Haussonville's seat), and Paul Valéry (Anatole France's seat). The candidates running against Valéry were Léon Bérard and Victor Bérard. His candidacy was supported by R. Boylesve, the Abbé Bremond, G. Hanotaux, and M. Prévost. He was elected on the fourth round, with seventeen votes for Valéry against fourteen for Léon Bérard, who was to be elected, in turn, a few months later.

[5] November 21, 1925, in Paris.

* *Translator's note:* In English in the original. The only published letter from Gide to Valéry in 1926 is an undated note in which Gide merely asks Valéry to recommend Mme Baladine Klossowska, a great friend of Rilke's, to a certain Heiblruth-Eos.

[1] It was there that Valéry received a visit from Rilke, who was then staying at Ouchy, near Lausanne. Rilke, who discovered Valéry in 1921, translated into German his *Poèmes* (1926) and was preparing a translation of *Eupalinos* (1927).

I don't know that lady called Durry of whom you speak. Or rather, I wonder whether I really don't know the name or whether it seems to me that I do, or whether I actually do, since I just read it? [2]

What the devil are you doing in Tunis? I was asked to go. But I already have my ration of lectures, and anyway, I've had enough of lectures. I am going to Vienna, Prague, and Berlin perhaps, Zürich, Berne, and Basle, in October-November. Not a word of German to my name. Well, we shall see. I get nothing out of it but the opportunity to go away. I don't know why one says: *f . . . le camp. Lever le camp* would be more exact. *F . . . le camp* is really to nail it down *et stare.**

I know that you had a hand in the conspiracy that caused my ribbon to be rounded.[3] If I didn't dread *Le Grain ne meurt,* I would say something exceedingly spicy. But ssh. I thank you without any positive profanities. I have for you a copy of *Analecta,*[4] which I had had set aside while you were in F.E.A. The text is just a hodgepodge. But the typography is a rather beautiful thing. Will give it to you on your return to these parts.

Au revoir, my old André, you're lucky to be able, and know how, to appear and disappear *ad nutum.* I am tired of being the prey of others, endless others of every shape, essence, and substance, *Amen!*

Your

P. V.

— 1927 —

244. *Paul Valéry to André Gide*

[Paris, February 27, 1927 (in Gide's handwriting)] [1]

My dear André,

I should like to leave—am dead—never worked so much or with such seasickness as I have the last *x* months. They're *murdering* me—and such troubles!

---

[2] The young writer and poet Marie-Jeanne Durry, who was to become professor of modern French literature at the Sorbonne, had just given a paper on Valéry at Pontigny. Gide was struck by it and wrote to Valéry suggesting that he meet Mme Durry. The meeting took place shortly after, in the rue de Villejust.

* *Translator's note: Foutre le camp* is a rather vulgar expression that might be translated as "get the hell out." But Valéry is here playing on the triple meaning of the word *foutre.*

[3] Paul Valéry had just received the rosette of the Legion of Honor. He had been named Chevalier of the Legion of Honor in 1923.

[4] A work that came out in 1926 (Stols, then Gallimard). Cf. *Tel Quel II.*

[1] It would seem that the exact date of the letter is, rather, February 25, 1927, to judge from Gide's *Journal:* "February 26, 1927. Paul Valéry has written me a heartbreaking letter. Will it be like this until death, and will we never again know leisure? 'O fruitful idleness?' People encroach frightfully on one another."

Trouble, too, about letters that have been sold; the F.'s, the L.'s, the M.'s are selling their P. V.'s hand over fist. The laws and men of law are powerless and absurd.

All this is poison.

I am writing five things at once, and the France speech is assumed to be finished and is not even begun—nor is the Costume![2]

And also, we had to get the Claudes settled, prepare the Agathine nuptials,[3] dine and lunch in town—preside yesterday at a Perrin banquet,[4] and Saturday at the Spinoza ceremony (!), and type, type on the Oliver,[5] type a *Stendhal*, type a *Mallarmé*, type a *Europe*, type a *La Fontaine*, type a *Paris*, type an *Alphabet*, type, type, type madly.

And go mad.*

And with all this—not to be paid! A slump in the de luxe editions on which I live. Received 5,000 instead of 48; zero instead of 25; zero again instead of 30.

I made rather specific terms with Lépine.[6]

I assure you that sometimes my head bursts with the number of things it kills itself trying to retain or omit; I sometimes think I'm going to have a fit,—of rage and rebellion.

All the best.

Your
P. V.

I realize that I am paying for everything with ideas—and those imbeciles who keep asking me for grandeur and length knock me out.

N.B.—Three weeks ago I heard Mr. Gillet[7] (Doumic's son-in-law) speak to me of you in words of most distinct praise. And he talked about *Le Grain*[8] extremely well. (But *I* don't have *Le Grain*.)

---

[2] Valéry did not officially take his seat in the Académie française until June 23, 1927 —that is, a year and a half after he was elected. In his speech he mentioned only once the name of Anatole France, whom he replaced, and only spoke of two of his works, refusing to forgive France for the contemptuous lack of understanding that caused him to exclude Mallarmé from the last issue of *Le Parnasse contemporain*.

[3] On July 5, 1927, Agathe Valéry married Paul Rouart, son of Alexis and grandson of Henri Rouart.

[4] A banquet in honor of the scientist Jean Perrin.

[5] The make of typewriter Valéry had been using since 1910. When he finally got a more modern one, he gave the Oliver to Professor Henri Mondor, who, in turn, made a present of it to Julien-P. Monod.

* *Translator's note:* The play on words in French is: "Taper, taper, taper. Et être tapé."

[6] A doctor, professor, and bibliophile from Lyons.

[7] The historian and critic Louis Gillet (1876–1943).

[8] *Si le Grain ne meurt.*

245. Paul Valéry to André Gide

Wednesday [P. May 19, 1927]

My dear André,

Mamma passed away this morning. I am leaving tomorrow for Montpellier. I had found her so feeble a month ago that I had little hope she would live for long. At ninety-six, each day is a bludgeon stroke.

I have the strange feeling of now being the only living person of a certain species.

She liked you very much.

Your
P. V.[9]

— 1928 —

246. André Gide to Paul Valéry

December 21, 1928

My dear Paul,

I found at the N.R.F. two little books by you [1] (for which, thanks) and am spending my evening with you. I read with keen interest and pleasure a preface to *Teste,* which I hadn't yet seen, [2] then went back to *La Soirée,* only to realize that I already knew many sentences by heart; then reread your letters of that period, which I have just had typewritten; and then was plunged into melancholy.

Oh! I know very well that both of us are harried to the point of crying for mercy. I always imagine you now as being worn out. I know you are not well. . . . Do you think that all this consoles me for not seeing you any more?

If only I knew when to find you alone; without too much upsetting your work or your attempts to get some rest. . . .

Call me, or come. I am as much as ever

your friend
André Gide

---

[9] Gide's answer was lost, but a letter of Valéry's alludes to it. This letter, which was never sent, was found among Valéry's papers. We have placed it at the end of the *Correspondence,* Letter 263.

[1] Probably *Monsieur Teste* (Gallimard) and *Note sur la Grandeur et la Décadence de l'Europe* (Champion).

[2] Preface to a new edition of *La Soirée avec Monsieur Teste,* 1927 (Gallimard), with the simplified title: *Monsieur Teste.*

— 1929 —

247. Paul Valéry to André Gide

January [1929] [1]

My dear André,

True, we hardly ever see each other. Theorem: if A no longer sees himself and P no longer sees himself, A and P no longer see one another.

As for me, I no longer see myself.

It's funny how when the business of writing (*sic effatus Ubu*) becomes professional it disgusts you and estranges you from yourself. My instinct thirty-six years ago didn't deceive me. Remember?

The basic substance hasn't changed. You know well that it's extremely simple. But things and other people have set up a coral ring between *Myself* and *myself*. I am an Atoll.

Built up between You and Myself is the fact that we are both public objects. If I speak to you or if I write to you, I don't know whether I am addressing you alone or *omnes gentes*. That tends to produce a kind of strabism, two points of view, or two accommodations.

When I think of us, I think of the time we were able to wander about on roads or beaches (Villerville, for example) and develop the feeling that we were altogether cut off from those vague others. That was a long time ago. Now we've so much of those other men and other women that they've become a pain in the—neck. In short, it is annoying to live as a third party with strangers, and to hear repeated over Some Loud Speaker what one had perhaps murmured in private, and to see things that were made to be forgotten changed into all sorts of external acts or events.

This makes me think—I can't remember what? Too tired. Last night was terribly hard, after a really black day during which I couldn't move a finger.

I shall ask you to come as soon as I can.

Au revoir, my old André.
P. V.

248. Paul Valéry to André Gide

Tuesday [P. February 5, 1929]

My dear André,

Since Jeannie gave me your letter from Algiers to read ten days ago,* it seemed to me that the subtlety of the debate and the exquisite knowledge it

---

[1] Letter written in pencil.

* *Translator's note:* There are no published letters from Gide in 1929.

has demanded from You and Me, from antiquity to today, justified my taking the letter from her. As I was going to write you, serious worries about health have arisen. All the young ones sick, including Claude, with complications due to his military status. Myself, still not really recovered, having to take a hand in it. Etc. All this is still going on; but well, I have to find fifteen minutes to straighten things out.

J. and I happen to agree with regard to the little anecdote you related in the *N.R.F.*[2] Each of us read it, and each one by chance. But we each had the same reaction, or almost.

Yet, for her—it was the *fact* that affected her; for me, it was the *principle.*

The *fact*—is the slight shock—which can be expressed or replaced by the following question: should one publish, remember, expose, emphasize a blunder made by a friend; argue publicly from an accident and make known a word that slipped out? This is fair in war. Doubtless. Is it therefore fair in peace? (When, besides, the friend in question is pretty well surrounded by spies and machine guns.)

That is what probably gave Jeannie an unpleasant surprise.

As for the *principle* . . . (I'm doing what everyone does: giving my temperament the importance of a principle. . . .)

My principle-temperament consists in a deep horror of the confusion between As-Regards-One's Self and As-Regards-Everyone.

This particular sensitivity became increasingly extreme as I got to be a public figure. Between my name and *myself,* I make an abysmal distinction. Between the public and myself—that is to say, between strangers en masse, the Unit of strangers, and the very special case which is One's Self—I find that one must interpose "form," the demonstration, the will to objectivity,—everything that sends the others back to themselves. The *others* have a right only to that part of us in which we are *others* to

---

[2] In the December 1, 1928, issue of *La Nouvelle Revue Française,* Gide published a few pages of notes entitled *Feuillets.* He recounted the following anecdote: " 'Excellent verse can be recognized by the fact that not one word can be changed or shifted,' wrote Paul Souday (*Le Temps,* November 28, 1927), quoting Paul Valéry, who spoke those words during a lecture at the Vieux-Colombier. I was there, and Valéry, anxious to give an example in the way of proof, chose the following two lines of Victor Hugo:

> *Oh! quel tragique bruit font dans le crépuscule*
> *Les chênes qu'on abat pour le bûcher d'Hercule,*

but made a false start, which caused me to sweat with anguish:

> *Oh! le tragique bruit . . .*

then wavered like an acrobat on a tightrope, but got his balance at once:

> *. . . que font au crépuscule . . .*

which allowed him to say as he left: 'Eh, my definition . . . what rot! and the audience was completely hoodwinked.' "

ourselves. They have that right, since we are in print,—and our duty is to give them that formulated substance—usable in its *generality*—just as it is to refuse them the rest.

But friendship is a very special thing. So that having two friends or three friends makes two or three *institutions incomparable* to one another. But which have one thing in common: the friend has a right to our foolishness, our slips, our weaknesses, etc.

(It's not that *this* is truer than *that*. The common mistake is to believe that a man who *gives way* is *truer* (or more sincere, as people say rather stupidly) than a man who *resists*. People believe that something fundamentally true comes out when a person lets himself go; that the creature in pajamas is truer than the "gentleman". . .)

It's just that the friend is *freedom*. A feeling of safety and delightful repose, or of exchanged vitality, etc.

And so—you can see what follows.

If you give away to strangers what I have confided to you who is not a stranger, you depart from your definition, you are no longer you, you are discomfort. I want to talk to you, but I see at once the hand of the writer, the page of your *Journal,* and the *nrf* with a pink wrapper.

I don't know whether all this will make you understand that even the magnificent things you have written about me on several occasions both delighted me and made me uncomfortable . . . to the strange point where I *saw* them rather than *read* them, and found myself incapable of going from word to word or from sentence to sentence. For beautiful as they were, I had the impression you were speaking to me in an external language. And doubtless you were writing for the public, but *I* could not put myself in the place of that P. V. *pro omnibus.* Impossible!

And this—which I don't maintain is singular—corresponds to an even more tiresome impossibility of mine. I am unable to praise my *intimate* friends except by that intimacy itself. Not very long ago I was asked to write about you. I made some attempts at it that disgusted me. I didn't have the time to force it, and also, my head at that moment was filled with preoccupations! . . . But even at leisure and with a free mind, I know that it is almost impossible for me to deal with you according to the public and in the face of it.

What can one do when one distinguishes, as fundamentally as I do, the person I know from the person suggested by his works?

Et cetera.

In short, I can only "reproach" you (to go back to the beginning) for not feeling what I feel—that is to say, for not judging as *private* * what I

---

* *Translator's note:* In English in the original.

consider as such. I don't at all believe that you committed a breach of friendship *in abstracto*. But in this particular case, you astonished *my* friendship.

Think what people might have made of your tale (and what they perhaps did make of it)! ("You can see what he takes you for . . ." etc.)

That's about it. And then again, after all, I don't really hate you, you know!

P. V.

— 1931 —

249. André Gide to Paul Valéry

Cuverville, January 23, 1931

My dear Paul,

Since I feel closer to you than the numerous people who yesterday were crowding under the Dome to see you,[1] I should like you to feel it as well. I just read your speech at one go and am no longer sorry about the torment and fatigue it caused you. It is admirable in scope and gravity, perfect in tone, written in *your* most beautiful style, that of our greatest men, and it pleases me to imagine our schoolboys of tomorrow learning long passages of it by heart, passages that stand up to those of Condé's funeral oration.[2] The end alone seemed to me a bit abrupt and the quotation from Balzac not worth what you yourself had just said, or would have said, on the subject.[3]

At any rate, you managed to remain perfectly the same while making yourself accessible to all, as was proper. It is at once an exemplary speech and Valéry at its best.

Here, I am trying to triumph over a wearisome bronchitis, which is hanging on as if this were trench warfare. Will I see you on my return to

[1] Marshal Pétain had been elected by the Académie française to the seat left vacant by the death of Marshal Foch; he had just taken his seat officially on Thursday, January 23, 1931. It was Paul Valéry who gave the address of welcome.

[2] In his *Journal*, on January 24, 1931, André Gide noted: "Remarkable speech by Valéry. Admirable in its gravity, scope, and solemnity, without any bombast whatever, and written in a most uncommon style, but noble and beautiful to the point of being, as it were, depersonalized. Rises far above everything that is being written today."

[3] Valéry ended his speech as follows: "Balzac, just thirty years ago, wrote: 'Has not Europe, without giving herself the time to wipe her feet, which are steeped in blood up to the ankles, has she not begun war over and again, without stop?' Would one not say that humanity, however lucid and reasoning it is, incapable of sacrificing its impulses to knowledge and its hates to its griefs, is behaving like a swarm of absurd and wretched insects irresistibly attracted by a flame?"

Paris? I should really like to; but you must have great need of rest, and I would prefer knowing that you were in the South, where, I may add, I shall soon go myself. From both of us many affectionate greetings to all of you.

Your old
André Gide

— 1932 —

250. Paul Valéry to André Gide

Tuesday, June 7, 1932

My dear André,

1. Thank you.

2. I telephoned, during Fez,[1] to tell you that at the house there was an *Idée fixe*,[2] a tall copy (no more beautiful for that), printed in your name, and awaiting you. It is still awaiting you.

3. *Goethe*.[3] I owe everything that's good and *accurate* in that memorial, —which killed me,—to Du Bos[4] and Gide, or you. Napoleon: external padding. Think of the audience I was speaking to. Whence the exclusion of everything I had cogitated, which was altogether different, and the inclusion of the facile, the relative.

The last week—from five in the morning to eight at night—without stopping! I reread that *Goethe* in Zürich, at the University! In point of fact, I had only read *Faust* and the Martens translation (1837, *excellent*) of the biological things. Skull and plant-life. *Pleased* me *greatly,* that book. Couldn't find the text on theories of light. You must be right with regard to the French details. I have never written so loosely, and at a gallop on the Remington.[5] Even disgusted on rereading it.

That's what it's like to have to play at being the Bossuets of the Third Republic! (with what remains of a subsiding ardor). But I do not want to write the kind of thing that at the same time made all I did—and that is

[1] Gide was then living at Fez, where he made frequent stays.

[2] *L'Idée fixe ou Deux Hommes à la Mer* had just been published by courtesy of the Martinet Laboratories.

[3] Valéry is alluding to the *Discours en l'honneur de Goethe* (Gallimard, 1933), which he gave at the Sorbonne on April 30, 1932, on the occasion of the commemoration of the hundreth anniversary of Goethe's death. Evoking the meeting of Goethe and Napoleon at Erfurt in 1808, Valéry compared the two men in their *extraordinary strength and freedom.* Just that year, Gide had brought out his *Goethe* (N.R.F., 1932).

[4] Charles du Bos (1882–1939) was the author of a monumental *Journal,* numerous critical essays, and *Le Dialogue avec André Gide.*

[5] Valéry's new typewriter.

still making all my time—something formed or acted upon *by bitterness,* and far more than bitterness.

I've been having convulsions for nearly a year now, and of the most secret kind. On the other hand, never had to produce so much. Between the Druggist[6] and the others, I have turned out so much against myself that I'm terrified, as it were. It was perhaps fortunate that out of economic or social necessity, I had to force myself that much to fabricate. But now I've really had it. *Et cetera.*

Paule left yesterday for Copenhagen.

I learned that your wife is feeling admirably well. Everyone here was charmed to see her in such a fine state. I myself was away. Vienna and Zürich . . . Give her my regards.

See you when?
P. Valéry

I should like to spend two or eight days *tecum* in some Ritz or other, with no mail, with no people.

I see that on the 9th you're working at the Polish L.[7] So am I, five days later.

251. André Gide to Paul Valéry

Cuverville, September 15, 1932

Dear friend,

Wasn't it Honegger,[8] whom I met the other evening on my arrival in Paris—where I had gone to spend three days—who told me that he was preparing a *Sémiramis* with you for Ida; and who also told me that you were prolonging your stay in Giens, where you can doubtless give yourself up to that "fruitful idleness," which delights me for you? But I should have liked to see you again and ask your advice: the German government has just bestowed upon us, both of us at the same time, a rare honor[9] which perplexes me greatly. Up until now, only the newspapers have informed me of it, and I don't know whom to thank or how to acknowledge it publicly. Most curious to know what you would have

---

[6] Publisher of *L'Idée fixe.*

[7] The Polish Library, or Bibliothèque polonaise, where Gide and Valéry each lectured in 1932.

[8] In collaboration with Arthur Honegger, Paul Valéry wrote *Amphion,* which was staged by Ida Rubinstein at the Paris Opera on June 23, 1931. He said apropos of Honegger: "I can't think of many living composers who would have understood and treated the problem as he did; and moreover, I don't believe that this ordeal will prove fruitless for his subsequent work." (Quoted by José Bruyr in his book: *Honegger et son œuvre,* Corréa, 1947.)

On May 11, 1934, the Paris Opera was to give a new opera by Valéry, with music by Honegger: *Sémiramis.*

[9] The "Goethe medal."

considered proper to do on this occasion. I remember your precious advice, in connection with a letter I had to write to Poincaré, and of which you kindly and most opportunely corrected certain improper phrasing.[10] Far more conversant than I am with protocol and customary procedures, you would be able to guide me. Perhaps just out of friendship you would be willing to dictate to me the phrases that are suitable to the occasion? Forgive me for troubling you with this, but you alone, in this case, can save me from making unfortunate blunders.

Marcel Drouin has brought to Cuverville a pamphlet from the *lycée* Janson-de-Sailly,[11] so that we could read your speech for the distribution of prizes,[12] which I find enchanting and excellent from every point of view. I don't know where to obtain this pamphlet, but perhaps you have a copy available for me? You would give me great pleasure.

Very much your
A. G.

252. *Paul Valéry to André Gide*

September 20, 1932[13]

My dear André,

I am at Grasse, after Giens and the beginning of a *viaje en España*[14] that came to nothing and stopped in San Sebastian.

The only good I got out of it all were twenty swims in the sea at Giens in August, fornications with water:

L'onde antique est tarie où l'on rajeunissait[15]

V. H. (*Alas! A. G.*)[16]

Impositions still going on.

As for the high honor, I know as much about it as you do: the newspapers, and that's all! It's not much.

And therefore I have thanked no one. If we get a confirmation, one of these days, we can put our heads together and work out suitable answers.

But these are rather embarrassing awards.

I don't even know how to get any information? I have just sent a card,

---

[10] See Gide's *Journal*, July 28, 1929.

[11] François Valéry, born in 1916, Paul Valéry's third child, was then a student at the lycée Janson-de-Sailly.

[12] That speech, given on July 13, 1932, was first published as a booklet by Les Editions des Presses Modernes in 1932, and then in *Variété IV* (Gallimard, 1938).

[13] Typewritten letter.

[14] Voyage in Spain.

[15] ["The antique water that used to restore our youth has dried up."] From Victor Hugo's poem *A Théophile Gautier* (1872) in *Toute la Lyre*.

[16] Another allusion to Gide's answer for a literary survey on Victor Hugo. See above, Letter 235, n. 1.

out of courtesy, to the ambassador, who is leaving Paris and whom I have met twice.

I never got the Janson pamphlet; perhaps it's awaiting me at Villejust. You shall have it if I have any, naturally.

I rented this foul typewriter from a grocer in Cannes: just look at all this!

I've found here, in a closet in my room, a pile of volumes consisting of excerpts from newspapers of 1870–1871–1872. The analogies with *us* are flabbergasting. In truth, *homo* makes me vomit. I feel like an *angel* (which Degas used to call me, I don't know why) and a *counter-angel*. Anything between the two makes me seasick. Man is *repetition,* and I am *constancy;* man is *surprises,* and I am . . . *deletions.* . . . *Understand* if you can. Can't be any clearer!

This grocer's typewriter is making me write a lot of . . .

Au revoir, my *old André*

P. V.

— 1934 —

253. André Gide to Paul Valéry

Cuverville, October 7, 1934

My dear Paul,

You have probably received a letter from Emmanuel Signoret, the younger, asking for your support. He insists that I intercede with you on his behalf. He must, on the other hand, have sent you a few of his poems.

I find it distinctly unpleasant to trouble you with this; but I have known E. Signoret since he was a child, for I have never lost interest in the family that the author of *Le Tombeau de Mallarmé,*[1] on his death, left altogether poverty-stricken. So see what you think you can and should do. Inclosed is the son's last letter, in which you will find full particulars with regard to his request.

Friendly greetings from both of us to all of you. See you soon, I hope.

Your

A. G.

---

[1] Included in Emmanuel Signoret's *Poésies complètes,* which Gide collected and had published by Le Mercure de France in 1938, was *Le Tombeau dressé à Stéphane Mallarmé.* In his preface Gide described it as "This dazzling *Tombeau de Mallarmé,* the second part of which, as a whole, constitutes a poem of such perfection that I doubt whether I know a more beautiful one in the French language."

― 1939 ―

254. Paul Valéry to André Gide

Le Mesnil, Juziers (S.-et-O.)
September 17, 1939

My dear André,

I told Herbart[1] by telephone that it would be useless for him to recommend you to the prefect of the Alpes Maritimes as of the 20th, the date on which the military authorities take power over all highway traffic.* I myself am very perplexed by this edict issued yesterday, for I wanted to go and fetch Agathe and her daughter in the vicinity of Dieppe—a coastal department—and don't know how to get permission to do it.

Yesterday, I saw François off for the barracks. I'm astonished myself at being affected by this (which had to happen) as drastically as I am. I'm sick inside about it and surprised to feel—especially the last few days—in a state of nervous demolition in depth.

And this more strongly pronounced owing to the atmosphere of the last week. Nadia[2] lives three hundred yards from here and until Thursday had put up Stravinsky, who is bound for America (if that is possible). We saw a lot of each other. S. read us the course he'll be giving on the *Poetics* (he, too) *of Music,*[3] which have analogies with mine (a rather curious thing).

F.,[4] who adores Nadia and music, was delighted by those discussions and exchanges, with occasional notes struck on the Pleyel. He seemed completely free entirely of the mind [*sic*], and put the idea of art, and especially of music, so *far and above everything else* that he amazed and moved me. Yesterday he played just a trifle of Bach on our Paris piano before bringing down his little suitcase and entering into that frightful

[1] Pierre Herbart, essayist and novelist, author of *Le Rôdeur, Contre-Ordre, Le Chancre du Niger* (preface by Gide), *Alcyon,* and *L'Age d'Or.* He accompanied Gide on his trip to Russia, and married Elisabeth Van Rysselberghe [the mother of Gide's daughter, Catherine].

* *Translator's note:* On September 3, 1939, France and England declared war on Germany.

[2] Nadia Boulanger, professor of accompaniment at the Conservatory of Music, sister of Lili Boulanger, the first woman to receive the Grand Prix de Rome for music, in 1913.

[3] Igor Stravinsky's *Poetics of Music* [published by the Harvard University Press in 1947] was not published in France until 1952, by the Librairie Plon (with a portrait of the author by Picasso). The book is a collection of Stravinsky's Charles Eliot Norton lectures at Harvard [given in 1942].

[4] François Valéry.

mixture of order and disorder into which he must enter. We have no way, at present, of corresponding with him. He is at Satory and probably can't leave the camp.

As for me, they want to put me to work doing a heap of useless things to which they have assigned people like us, who are no less useless. They had me give a so-called Message over the microphone, which won me compliments (30 per cent) and insults (the rest), via letters, signed and unsigned. Bravo for the insults!

But I am in no mood for anything. I'm fretting here and want to leave. I prefer Paris, in spite of the people. But I never do what I want, though I very rarely want anything.

I smoke, I smoke, I spend hours trying to work out calculations of no interest and with no results. The stupidity of men chokes me. And my own, I feel, sums up the whole of it, concentrating it into an essence, or an acid that would eat into itself.

I should like to be with you.

Paul

Yesterday, in Paris, I had just kissed François on the running board of the taxi; went into Potin's, on my way back, to buy some canned tuna. In came a long black shape who presented the palest of faces and a very antedated smile showing through locks of white-blond hair. It was Ida,[5] who, in a magnificent car, had also come to provide herself with canned food. We chatted a bit, about everything and nothing at all. That's all!

— 1940 —

255. Paul Valéry to André Gide
ACADÉMIE FRANÇAISE

Thursday [February, 1940]

My dear André,

I am writing between Maurras and Duhamel. A declaration in favor of Poland is being read. They are discussing whether or not to keep the words: *Polish government,* for which various members want to substitute: *Polish nation.* They are voting. I lift my finger, and I continue writing to you.

I was thinking of coming back to Nice, one of these days, to attend to the *Centre* situation,[1] which is getting back into shape, but there is no lack of

---

[5] Ida Rubinstein.

[1] Le Centre Universitaire Méditerranéen, located in Nice, founded in 1933, was organized by Valéry, who wrote up a *Projet d'Organisation du Centre universitaire méditerranéen à Nice* (printed by Gastaud, 1933). His post was to be taken away from him without warning in 1941 and given to Marcel Lucain.

annoyance, difficulty, and cupidity involved. I was supposed (I still am supposed) to make the journey with Monzie.[2] But he told me yesterday that he had to delay his departure, owing to circumstances . . .

Here, an atmosphere of waiting. I am very preoccupied with various general and private questions.

François, who was unable to stand the fatigue of the R.O.T.C. training and had lost over seventeen pounds in four weeks, was discharged, then asked to be detailed for auxiliary duty, and is, for the time being, an interpreter in Dieppe. Claude is a second lieutenant (it's called attaché) in the quartermaster corps and is in the east. He has suffered terribly from the cold. My son-in-law, too, is somewhere around there.

I was rather ill, this fall and winter. Fortunately, a last analysis showed a rather perceptible decrease of ureic nitrogen in my blood, and in that same blood, a little less sugar. . . . I was deprived of everything: meat, milk products, bread, sugar, spaghetti, starches—even dates! But I'm getting back to them a little.

I should really like us to meet, as you say. Nice is as pleasant in company as it is sad (in my opinion) for a lone being. I say *being,* for I have noticed that when one is alone, one is no more than a "being." And as one doesn't know where to go, when the street corner comes, one no longer has any right or left.

I haven't seen the Archambault article you mention. "Tenter de vivre!"[3] That, I think, is toward the end of *Le Cimetière marin*. But it's really of no account. Almost a cliché. At any rate: an utterance that was spontaneous, painless—therefore . . . *fatherless*. To my mind, *pater is est quem labor demonstrat.*

My inner self sends you all its regards, and I myself send you mine for the Bussys.[4]

---

[2] Anatole de Monzie (1875–1947), a politician who was several times Minister of Education. It was he who asked Valéry to organize and direct the Centre Méditerranéen.

[3] In the January 20, 1940, issue of *Etudes* there was an article by Paul Archambault (1883–1950): *Tenter de vivre,* or *Try to Live,* apropos of Gide's *Journal, 1889–1939,* which had just been published. [In a letter to Valéry dated February 5, 1940, Gide had commented: "An article (*about myself*) has just come out in the review *Etudes,* entitled *Tenter de vivre,* the words on which my *Journal* ends. Hoping not to have any reader who didn't know *Le Cimetière marin,* I thought it was enough to put those words in quotation marks; giving the reference, I thought, would insult the reader . . . True, the author of the article kept the quotation marks, but went about it in such a way as to give the impression that he attributed the words to me, or that I attribute them to myself, which is offensive to both of us. I have just written him rather sharply."]

[4] The painter Simon Bussy (some of whose paintings were owned by Gide and Valéry) and Dorothy Bussy, who translated into English several of Gide's works, more

I leave you now to go home and try to think a little of what I shall pronounce tomorrow morning at the College.[5] Last Friday, I let myself go and began elaborating a theory of State which suddenly frightened me, almost terrified even me, and I cut the circuit very abruptly.

Yours, my old André, *di cuore.*[6]

P. V.

— 1941 —

256. André Gide to Paul Valéry

[Interzonal or "family" card]

July 18, 1941

Dear fellow,

Received yesterday three books by you;[1] (in addition, some exquisite poems by the Reverend Father Cyprien).[2] Delighted. Overwhelmed. But of which I already know a number of pages.

As a note to *Mélange* (*Animalités*), p. 200: "Various kinds of tiger beetles, which the insect-hunter sees fly out in front of him on a sandy trail, outwit the latter by a sudden turn and immediately retrace their flight so as to swoop down backward." This in answer to your "?"[3] Ah! I should really like to see you again. I hope that you and yours are well. Here likewise!

André Gide

---

particularly, *L'Immoraliste, La Porte étroite, Les Caves du Vatican,* and *Les Faux-Monnayeurs.* She is also the author of the autobiographical novel *Olivia.*

[5] Since 1937 Paul Valéry had been professor of poetics at the Collège de France, a chair created especially for him.

[6] With all my heart.

[1] Probably *Les Pages immortelles de Descartes* (Corrêa), *Mon Faust* ("Les Cent-Une"), and *Mélange* (Gallimard), published in 1941.

[2] *Cántico espiritual et poésias* of Saint John of the Cross, translated into French verse by the Reverend Father Cyprien, with a preface by Valéry (Rouart, 1941).

[3] The corresponding passage in *Mélange* is as follows: "*Animalities:* if children play at catching each other, it happens that the one pursued takes it upon himself to reach an obstacle such as a large tree or a round and stationary table, and to turn around it at a speed opposite to that of his adversary—who will never reach him. Now never does a pursued animal get that idea (?)"

257. André Gide to Paul Valéry

Les Palmeraies, La Croix-Valmer (Var)
August 15, 1941

Dear Paul,

As you can see, I'm seizing the opportunity at once. Your excellent [letter] * has caught up with me here at the sea, for I left Cabris [4] for a month in the company of Mme Théo Van Rysselberghe, Elisabeth Herbart, and Catherine,[5] who, as I think I told you, is now called by my name. Great as my desire is to move closer to the rue de Villejust, I think I shall spend the winter in Nice. I dread the discomfort of Paris and the "moral problems!" that I've been given a glimpse of. Besides, there are very few people I wish to see again. You probably know that I have broken, not with Gallimard, but with the *N.R.F.* and its new editorship.[6] But the demon of curiosity might well entice me into being regrettably imprudent. It is better that I stay far from temptations and conversations. I should not be able, like you, dear Archimedes, to keep my nose in problems; I would constantly be lifting my head. . . .

Catherine suddenly set to work after having been discovered as a promising actress. I spend my time teaching her to speak alexandrines a little better than they're spoken on the stage today, and this winter she is going to try out for Molière.

I have almost no news of Cuverville.

Sent you a "family card" recently, to thank you for your two latest books (+ your *Descartes*), which gave me a way to live with you. Moreover, G. Taillefer [7] came to Cabris and played me her music for your *Narcisse*.

Convey, as soon as you can, my warm greetings to everyone in the rue de Villejust.

Your old faithful friend
André Gide

You have perhaps heard that, two months ago, the Legion kept me from giving the tamest of lectures, choosing to consider me as no more than an "apostle of pleasure," who henceforth should keep silent and hide.[8]

* *Translator's note:* There are no published letters from Valéry in 1941.

[4] In the Alpes-Maritimes, not far from Grasse. At Mme Mayrisch's estate, "La Messuguière."

[5] André Gide's daughter, who was to marry Jean Lambert.

[6] Pierre Drieu La Rochelle (1893–1945), in December, 1940, replaced Jean Paulhan as editor of the *N.R.F.* The last issue under the editorship of Paulhan came out in June, 1940.

[7] Germaine Taillefer, a composer (*Jeux de plein Air, Le Marchand d'Oiseaux, Pastorale*, etc.), who belonged to the "groupe des Six."

[8] On May 21, 1941, Gide was to lecture, in Nice, on the writer Henri Michaux. The lecture was banned by the Légion des Anciens Combattants [a veterans' organization]. The text was published two months later by Gallimard as a pamphlet entitled *Découvrons Henri Michaux.*

258. André Gide to Paul Valéry

Les Camélias,[9] Cap-d'Ail (A.-M.)
August 21, 1941

My dear Paul,

You yourself don't give a damn, I know, or at least so you say; but personally it pleases *me* to be able to love and admire you as a whole and not only in your works. I would suffer knowing that you were among the fortunate of this world and the profiteers. But I find the thought of your financial difficulties unbearable, and not only because you suffer from them, but because, in being injurious to you, they deprive us. The fact that toward the end of a life of effort and work, after all you have given to the world, to us all, you are "in need," that fact sickens me, shocks me, seems monstrous to me.[10]

That among all those men and women who admire you, there are none who are able to provide you with a full supply of coffee, sugar, and tobacco! it's unimaginable. Those who don't smoke could contribute and allow you to benefit from their abstinence. (I know well that, in spite of this, I'm still very far below what my vice demands, having, almost as much as you, got into the deadly habit of not being able to work without smoking.) (Fortunately, I don't have much trouble doing without coffee.) In spite of which, the question of money is still the most serious . . . Have you looked into the possibility of a few lectures in Switzerland? That, it seems to me, would be the least tiring for you and the most remunerative. Won't you publish your course at the C. de F.?

Catherine was altogether touched and blushingly delighted by your kindness. Your card will decorate her student's room in Nice. She told me of her desire to write and thank you; I fear she would do so very awkwardly, and almost hope that she confines herself to her desire. As for me, I'm thinking of settling down in a place of my own, in order to try and work a bit, needing to be alone, apart from the group formed by Mme Théo Van R., the Herbarts, and Catherine, who will put up at a "Scandinavian pension" at the end of the Quai des Etats-Unis.

Everything that is dear to us experiences "great difficulty in being," as Fontenelle put it; ourselves included. Thinking of you is a comfort to me.

Your
A. G.

[9] André Malraux's villa, where Gide had been invited to stay.

[10] Valéry, who had just been deprived of his office as director of the Centre Méditerranéen, feared that his course at the Collège de France would be discontinued. In fact, the course was continued from year to year until his death.

— 1942 —

259. André Gide to Paul Valéry

February 5, 1942

Dear Paul,

Faithful affection; constant good wishes, it goes without saying; but I disapprove of the warm water bath to remove the stiffness from your hand; it's a warm *sand* bath that's needed; preferable in every respect, the sandstone kind, you should be able to find it easily. As for orthedrine, I, too, resort to it from time to time; has an appreciable effect, it seems to me. Benzedrine was also recommended to me, haven't tried it yet. I am undergoing an autohemotherapy treatment in order to get the better of puritis, which has become intolerable again; whence insomnia; the "here we go again" kind, every night. Notwithstanding, rather good work. Weekly contribution to *Le Figaro*. See no one here but the Bussys and Roger Martin du G., who showed me your exquisite card. The Van Rys. family is well; but I live apart from them. To everyone around you, distribute our most friendly greetings.

Faithfully with you.
André Gide

260. Paul Valéry to André Gide

Tuesday. Lyons [P. April 28, 1942]

Dear André,

Will perhaps be in Marseilles tomorrow evening, at Mlle Fournier's, 140 rue Sainte.[1]

I shall be there for two days.

As for the N.R.F., I have come to an agreement with Claudel by telephone.

We're standing fast.

Either *us* and us alone or nothing. Us means you, me, him, Mauriac, and some Fargue or other. In short, possible people.

I have explained ten times that mixing these up with those means ruining everyone.

I should so much like to see you!

Yours.
P. V.

[1] It was at Mlle Fournier's, on September 19, 1941, that Valéry gave a talk on *Narcisse* (cf. above, Letter 9, n. 16).

261. *André Gide to Paul Valéry*

June 25 [1942]

Dear friend,

Osiris[2] gives me a good excuse for writing to you; happy that I can now hope you will be spared certain harassing anxieties.

I received an excellent card from M. Teste; and hope that his wife has received the one I addressed to her early in May, dated from Tunis, telling her of our meeting in Marseilles.

After three weeks of purgatory, in Tunis (heat, uproar, insomnia), I am relaxing, pouring out and refilling at Sidi Bou Saïd, alone in a charming villa put at my disposal by some new friends; but forced to go out quite a distance for meals. Work mediocre; somnolence, expectation, and hope, on a background of faithful friendship.

A. G.

Address: Sidi Bou Saïd is enough.[3]

262. *Paul Valéry to André Gide*

Saturday, July 4, 1942

Dear friend,

I received your card. Yes, that unexpected obelisk, fallen from an obscure triumph,* has come at a rather good time, just as my stage is vanishing. Imagine, I finished up with two lessons in . . . Law! to which I was led by an idea that's rather amusing in its ingenuity. The entire last lecture was meant for the occasion. . . .

Nothing new at the N.R.F. The death struggle from psychorrhaging continues. Claudel is here, for *Le Soulier de Satin,* at the Français, I think.[4] He has not got in touch with me. I imagine you're happy at Sidi Bou Saïd and eating and smoking your fill. I still smoke, but coffee hurts me. I have a mad amount of work on my hands, but of the useful type. And besides, I'm a bit mad myself, an old madman, with all the worries that implies. I have a most agreeable memory of Sidi Bou Saïd, which I caught a glimpse of and where I had a good lunch in the Arab-style district. It seems to me

[2] Valéry had just received the Osiris prize from the Institut National de France, a prize awarded every three years since 1899.

[3] Sidi Bou Saïd is situated next to Tunis. There, André Gide was to live through the exciting hours of the Tunisian liberation a few months later.

* *Translator's note:* "chu d'un triomphe obscur," an allusion to a line from Mallarmé's *Le Tombeau d'Edgar Poe:* "Calme bloc ici bas chu d'un désastre obscur" (*Steady block fallen here below from an obscure disaster*).

[4] *Le Soulier de Satin ou Le Pire n'est pas toujours sûr* was to be given for the first time at the Théâtre-Français on November 27, 1943, staged by Jean-Louis Barrault. Paul Claudel and Paul Valéry had met at Mallarmé's in 1891. After a meeting in the rue de Rome—one was then twenty-three years old, the other twenty—Paul Claudel, impressed by Paul Valéry's wit and style, told him: "You will be a great poet."

there were beautiful flowers. I envy you the swimming, which has now become an impossible luxury. Yours with all my heart, my old André.

P. V.

— Postscript —

[In May 1927, after the death of his mother, Paul Valéry began a letter to André Gide, who had just sent him his condolences. This letter was never completed and remained in a drawer, where it was found by Mme Valéry. We did not place it in the body of the *Correspondence,* since it was not part of the exchange, but we were of the opinion that it should appear in the volume.

Indeed, while Valéry never made up his mind to send it, probably out of reserve, neither did he make up his mind to destroy it, because it was a summing up that he valued. Such a summing up might have troubled him when he was alive. Not disclosing it would have troubled us.]

263. Paul Valéry to André Gide

Friday [May, 1927]

My good André,

Thirty or fifty times as many words have been written about me, favorably or unfavorably, as I myself have written in all my life. I get lost in all those "Selves" that have been created for me, and that resemble me as well as they can.

But you have portrayed—with the fidelity of an artist at the time of Van Eyck, and of a friend—what you saw and heard, being a witness to this strange and varied career. You are a witness to the fact that never have I done what I wanted (and, actually, I have always wanted very little; minimums are to my taste). Circumstances kept me for a long time in the dullest of states, the one most favorable to judging all things; then they exalted me; but *nothing,* unfortunately, *goes to my head;* and I get no feeling from those pleasures that might be thought to intoxicate me. You know me well enough to imagine how I feel at heart.

When I want to explain to myself all that to-do that's been made around me and the astonishing diffusion of my name (which has since given me the impression of being someone else's), I find three categories of reasons— the first and most effective of which is none other than the extreme poverty of our time as regards intellectual values. I have doubtless profited from the remarkable depletion that we have observed. When we were fifteen, what a lot of really great men were still living and breathing. Today, people have been reduced to erecting a statue to yours truly. . . . On the other hand, being away from Letters for a long time was of great use to me. During that period I saw from a good distance so many fashions and carnival floats file by, be acclaimed, disappear, and even reappear. . . . A disinterested observer was able to learn many of the reasons for which things don't endure.

And finally—of greatest importance and my true pride—*I owe to my friends almost everything I am*. They believed in me, who didn't believe in myself. They drew me, and shaped, in spite of me, a personage worthy of their friendship, their quality, their talents. And then again, they taught me so much, and about so many things.

My pride lies in the fact that I attracted that great and inestimable interest they have shown in me.

The next time you write about me, my old André, you must not forget this, nor forget yourself. Moreover, I still hope to make a little temple to my friendships. But when? I'm discouraged by all that separates me from my true work. You put your finger on the sore point at the end of your article.[1] In truth, I am being eaten alive—and I feel my ideas being crunched by the inevitable teeth of urgent things. I was a hundred times freer when I wasn't free at all. I used to cross the avenue, and discharge my duties; I then crossed it again, and found myself such as I was when I had left, between my notebook and my thoughts. . . . But at present,—you don't see me any more. It's because I don't see myself any more. I get up between five and six. I find a confused pile of obligatory things, a lot of foolishness that is promised, due, and I labor over these dreary works, written to order, without ever coming to the end of it. At eight o'clock the confounded postman. A prime minister's mail, but without the minister's offices and secretaries. Had I begun to get a bit excited about my tasks, this shock of letters stuns me and pulverizes my mind. At ten begin the visits. Until one o'clock I have to receive and talk, talk, talk. And by lunch time I'm dead. Then I have to rush around—for one must "live"—and I fly from one publisher, library, etc., to another. . . . At that point I'm *done for,* and it matters little whether I go out into "society." I'm no longer good for anything but that, toward evening.

Lectures help me to flee, to change fatigues. Since we're on the subject, I should have liked to see you on my return from the Germanys.[2] Strange impression . . . but I must leave you, time is pulling me by the arm.

Thank you, my old André. And that little note about my mother—how discreet, how perfect—two lines in depth that touch my soul.

[1] Probably an article Gide had planned to write about Valéry, but subsequently dropped. The articles Gide devoted to his friend are: *Paul Valéry,* in the Homage to Valéry issue of *Le Divan,* 1922; *Le Rayonnement de Paul Valéry,* in *Le Figaro,* July 25, 1945; and *Paul Valéry,* in *L'Arche,* October, 1945.

[2] In 1926 Valéry had made a lecture tour in Germany.

INDEX